AGRICULTURE, ECONOMY
AND SOCIETY IN
EARLY MODERN SCOTLAND

Boydell Studies in Rural History

Series Editor
Professor Richard W. Hoyle

This series aims to provide a forum for the best and most influential work in agricultural and rural history, and on the cultural history of the countryside. Whilst it is anchored in the rural history of Britain and Ireland, it also includes within its remit Europe and the colonial empires of European nations (both during and after colonisation). All approaches and methodologies are welcome, including the use of oral history.

Proposals or enquiries are welcomed. They may be sent directly to the editor or the publisher at the email addresses given below.

Richard.Hoyle@reading.ac.uk
Editorial@boydell.co.uk

Agriculture, Economy and Society in Early Modern Scotland

Edited by
Harriet Cornell, Julian Goodare and Alan R. MacDonald

THE BOYDELL PRESS

First published 2024
The Boydell Press, Woodbridge

ISBN 978 1 83765 048 4

The Boydell Press is an imprint of Boydell & Brewer Ltd
PO Box 9, Woodbridge, Suffolk IP12 3DF, UK
and of Boydell & Brewer Inc.
668 Mt Hope Avenue, Rochester, NY 14620-2731, USA
website: www.boydellandbrewer.com

A CIP catalogue record for this book is
available from the British Library

The publisher has no responsibility for the continued existence or accuracy of URLs for external or third-party internet websites referred to in this book, and does not guarantee that any content on such websites is, or will remain, accurate or appropriate

In memory of Ian Whyte (1948–2019)

CONTENTS

Contents

ILLUSTRATIONS

Full credit details are provided in the captions to the images in the text. The editors, contributors and publisher are grateful to all the institutions and individuals for permission to reproduce the materials in which they hold copyright. Every effort has been made to trace the copyright holders; apologies are offered for any omission, and the publisher will be pleased to add any necessary acknowledgement in subsequent editions.

CONTRIBUTORS

NORAH CARLIN taught history at Middlesex University and its predecessor institutions 1965–2002. Her books include *The Causes of the English Civil War* (Oxford, 1999) and *Regicide or Revolution? What Petitioners Wanted, September 1648–February 1649* (London, 2020). She is currently researching kirk and society in post-Reformation Midlothian.

HARRIET CORNELL is Peace and Conflict Resolution Evidence Platform (PeaceRep) Programme Manager, Edinburgh Law School, University of Edinburgh. She has been a Researcher on the project Agriculture and Teind Reform in Early Modern Scotland. She has published on social control in early modern Scotland.

JULIAN GOODARE is Emeritus Professor of History, University of Edinburgh. His books include *The Government of Scotland 1560–1625* (Oxford, 2004) and *The European Witch-Hunt* (London, 2016). He is Principal Investigator on the project Agriculture and Teind Reform in Early Modern Scotland.

KEVIN HALL is a PhD student in History, University of Edinburgh. His publications include 'Burgesses on the Edge', in Allan D. Kennedy (ed.), *Life at the Margins in Early Modern Scotland* (Woodbridge, forthcoming).

JOHN G. HARRISON has published extensively on the Stirling area. He has contributed to cross-disciplinary studies of historic landscapes, including Menstrie Glen, Flanders Moss, Ben Lawers and the setting of the Battle of Bannockburn in 1314. He is author of *Rebirth of a Palace: The Royal Court at Stirling* (Edinburgh, 2011).

R. A. HOUSTON is Professor Emeritus in History, University of St Andrews. He researches Scottish and English social history *c.*1450–1850, and has also published in many areas of European social history including literacy, urbanisation, law, medicine (psychiatry) and demography.

BRIONY KINCAID is a recent graduate in English Language and History, University of Edinburgh. Her chapter in this volume arose from an honours research project.

ALAN R. MACDONALD is Senior Lecturer in History, University of Dundee. His books include *A History of the Native Woodlands of Scotland 1500–1920* (Edinburgh, 2005), with T. C. Smout and Fiona Watson. He is Co-Investigator on the project Agriculture and Teind Reform in Early Modern Scotland.

GAINS MURDOCH completed his PhD at the University of Aberdeen in 2016. His thesis assessed Scottish attitudes to Empire during the eighteenth century and the prioritisation of the domestic economy. He is currently developing a research project on how a Scottish credit system emerged by the 1690s.

PHILIPP ROBINSON RÖSSNER is Professor of Early Modern History, University of Manchester. His books include *Scottish Trade in the Wake of Union 1700–1760: The Rise of a Warehouse Economy* (Stuttgart, 2008) and *Freedom and Capitalism in Early Modern Europe: Mercantilism and the Making of the Modern Economic Mind* (Cham, 2020).

BRIAN SMITH is Shetland Archivist. He is the author of *Toons and Tenants: Settlement and Society in Shetland 1299–1899* (Lerwick, 2000), and many articles about the history of Orkney and Shetland. He is co-editor (with John H. Ballantyne) of *Shetland Documents 1195–1579* (Lerwick, 1999) and *Shetland Documents 1580–1611* (Lerwick, 1994).

T. C. SMOUT is H.M. Historiographer Royal for Scotland. His many books include *A History of the Scottish People 1560–1830* (London, 1969) and *Nature Contested: Environmental History in Scotland and Northern England since 1600* (Edinburgh, 2000), a revised version of his Ford Lectures in the University of Oxford, 1998–99.

ACKNOWLEDGEMENTS

This volume is the first major output of a collaborative research project involving the Universities of Edinburgh and Dundee entitled 'Agriculture and Teind Reform in Early Modern Scotland'. The funding for the project came from the Carnegie Trust for the Universities of Scotland, so our primary thanks must go to them for providing the wherewithal to enable us to undertake the work, and to support a conference in Edinburgh in May 2017 at which early versions of several of the chapters in this book were presented. We also thank Shauna Thompson and Edinburgh Law School, for supporting the images and maps included in this volume. All three of us were involved in the research work for the project, alongside Dr Thomas Green, now at the University of Aberdeen, who worked as a research assistant. Special thanks must go to Professor Richard Hoyle, Visiting Professor of Economic History at the University of Reading, who contributed to the Edinburgh conference, and whose encouragement and support have been instrumental in the publication of this volume.

Harriet Cornell, Julian Goodare and Alan R. MacDonald
Dundee and Edinburgh
August 2023

NOTE ON CURRENCY AND MEASURES

The currency of Scotland before 1707 was the Scots pound. The pound was divided into 20 shillings, and each shilling was divided into 12 pence. Sums of money were sometimes expressed in 'merks'; a merk was two-thirds of a pound (13s. 4d.). After the 1707 Union, the pound sterling was introduced; £1 sterling was equal to £12 Scots.

Measurements of land area used a variety of terms, many of which related to the old Scots acre, which was about half a hectare. One oxgate or oxgang = 13 acres; one ploughgate = 8 oxgates, i.e. 104 acres.

Grain was measured by dry capacity measures. The basic measure was the firlot, which was an actual wooden barrel of a specified size, equivalent to about 36 litres. This related to other measures as follows: 4 lippies = 1 peck; 4 pecks = 1 firlot; 4 firlots = 1 boll; 16 bolls = 1 chalder. In Orkney and Shetland, grain was measured by weight, not capacity.

ABBREVIATIONS

AgHR	*Agricultural History Review*
BOS	Bank of Scotland Archives, Edinburgh
DOST	*Dictionary of the Older Scottish Tongue* (in the online Dictionaries of the Scots Language, at www.dsl.ac.uk)
EcHR	*Economic History Review*
JSHS	*Journal of Scottish Historical Studies*
NLS	National Library of Scotland, Edinburgh
NRAS	National Register of Archives for Scotland (in NRS)
NRS	National Records of Scotland, Edinburgh
OSA	Sir John Sinclair (ed.), *The Statistical Account of Scotland* (21 vols, Edinburgh, 1791–99). References to this work, often known as the 'Old Statistical Account', are initially given as volume and page numbers of the edition of Donald J. Withrington and Ian R. Grant (eds), *The Statistical Account of Scotland* (20 vols, Wakefield, 1972–78), with parish names and page numbers added in brackets to enable the use of the online edition (http://stataccscot.edina.ac.uk/)
PSAS	*Proceedings of the Society of Antiquaries of Scotland*
RBS	Royal Bank of Scotland Archives, Edinburgh
RCAHMS	Royal Commission on the Ancient and Historical Monuments of Scotland
RMS	*Register of the Great Seal of Scotland (Registrum Magni Sigilli Regum Scotorum)*
RPC	*Register of the Privy Council of Scotland*
RPS	Records of the Parliaments of Scotland, ed. Keith M. Brown *et al.* (St Andrews, 2007, online at www.rps.ac.uk)
SCA	Stirling Council Archives
SHR	*Scottish Historical Review*
SHS	Scottish History Society
SRS	Scottish Record Society
STS	Scottish Text Society

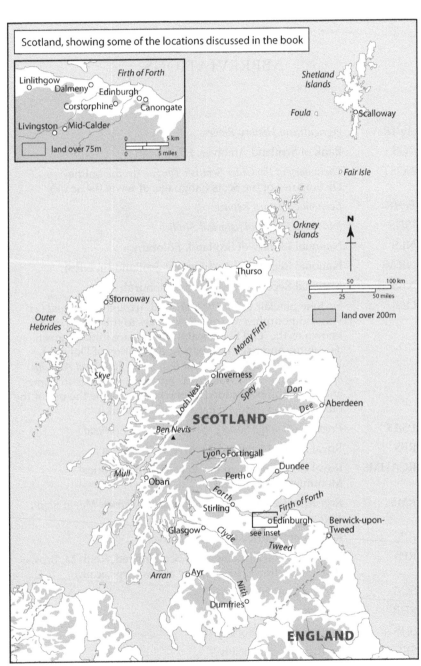

Scotland, showing some of the locations discussed in the book

Introduction: Exploring Scotland's Agricultural History

Harriet Cornell, Julian Goodare and Alan R. MacDonald

This book takes a fresh look at the rural economy of early modern Scotland. The primary focus is on the long period that preceded the rapid changes of the late eighteenth and early nineteenth centuries. It shows that this period, before the main era of agricultural 'improvement', was nevertheless far from static.

It is timely that this topic is being revisited now. Several classic studies of Scottish agriculture were published between the late 1970s and early 1990s, but, as we shall see, this productive period was followed by a gap in which scholarship moved into other areas. This book returns to the topic of agriculture with awareness of more recent scholarship.

Approaches to agriculture often begin with everyday farming practices. The book has much on this, and one chapter even looks at a farmer's own writing. By contrast, landlords and estate management are prominent in several chapters. Some of these chapters show landlords as innovators, while one chapter highlights small tenants' labour-intensive contributions to 'improvement'. Not all the chapters bring good news; there is a chapter on Scotland's most disastrous famine, that of 1622–23.

The book is about more than farming practices, though. Social, administrative and economic contexts of agriculture all receive attention. And the book opens with a cultural chapter, surveying the cultural context within which agriculture was 'imagined'. Some topics are best investigated at local level, and five chapters carry out detailed local studies. An ambitious conceptual chapter on models of capitalism in the 'mercantilist age' treats Scotland itself as a local study of a much broader phenomenon. The book concludes with a historiographical overview, contextualising the history of agriculture within the work done on other aspects of Scottish history since the 1990s.

More will be said later about the chapters that follow in the present book, but at this point we turn to a review of the state of research on the history of Scottish agriculture. This review falls into three sections. First there is a section on the early modern period. This is often concerned with eighteenth-century 'Improvement' and with the relationship of 'Improvement' to what came before it. How should agricultural change be periodised between about 1500 and 1850? Second there is a shorter section reviewing medieval studies, again focusing on questions of periodisation of agricultural change. A third section then reviews scholarship that has followed particular disciplinary and thematic perspectives.

* * *

Scholars studying Scottish agricultural change have always recognised the importance of changes that eighteenth-century writers called 'Improvement'. The term 'Improvement' appears frequently in historical writing, often as a general descriptor for a range of processes comparable to those that in England are sometimes grouped as an 'Agricultural Revolution'. But, while the term 'Agricultural Revolution' invites debate (as we shall see), the term 'Improvement' seems almost to *avoid* debate. It is a value-laden term that need not be taken literally, but serves us as a capacious but flexible container for all sorts of rural changes. Even the period covered by 'Improvement' is not always agreed. The eighteenth century, or some of it, is always included, but earlier or later periods are sometimes included as well.

Is 'Improvement' understood as a drastic, once-and-for-all change? A debate about this among historical geographers, mainly in the 1970s, raises issues that are still with us. The debate was started by James Caird in 1964. He pointed to the 'geometrical lines' in the modern farming landscape – lines drawn by surveyors enclosing earlier open fields to make compact individual farms – and argued, in a much-quoted phrase, that 'Scotland's rural landscape is in fact a landscape of "revolution" rather than one of slow evolution, a landscape deliberately created mainly in the 18th and early 19th centuries'.[1] Caird drew no explicit international comparisons, but the title of his paper, 'The Making of the Scottish Rural Landscape', echoed W. G. Hoskins's celebrated book of 1955, *The Making of the English Landscape*, which painted an evocative picture of slow, deep, evolutionary change over many centuries in rural England. Some previous studies of the Scottish landscape had seen it similarly. By contrast, Caird perceived a sharp and dramatic entry to agricultural modernity in Scotland.

Caird's arguments were vigorously attacked by Graeme Whittington in 1975. Whittington pointed to a number of seventeenth-century

---

1   J. B. Caird, 'The Making of the Scottish Rural Landscape', *Scottish Geographical Magazine*, 80:2 (1964), 72–80, quotations at p. 72.

developments, such as crop rotation and liming, occurring well before the period of Caird's 'revolution'. In a line of thought that was less directly relevant to the early modern period, Whittington also argued that, even in the nineteenth century and later, many north-eastern farms had survived with little change from an earlier era. Whittington also argued for change in the *sixteenth* century, linked to the end of the monasteries and to the balance between direct demesne farming and leasing to tenant farmers. He suggested that further research might prove that 'the death of the tradition of change and innovation, which is commonly believed to have taken place with the demise of "high farming" upon the dissolution of the monasteries may never have occurred'. He concluded that 'attitudes did survive from the monastic period which made continuous evolution, albeit often with a varied pace, possible and a revolution unnecessary'.[2] Whittington's sketch thus pointed towards continuous but slower changes from at least the late fifteenth century until the early twentieth century.

Subsequent contributions to the debate mostly sought middle positions between these extremes. Rather than reviewing the whole 1970s debate it is simplest to move to a landmark collection of essays edited by M. L. Parry and T. R. Slater in 1980, to which most of those who had been involved in the debate contributed. Although it did not resolve the debate, this book provided more detail and perhaps more clarity about the issues. Just a few of these issues can be noted here. Caird's own contribution laid more emphasis on the lengthy period of his 'revolution', from 1700 to 1850. The dramatic changes brought by enclosure still formed the basis of the argument, but enclosures occurred piecemeal in different regions.[3] Focusing on the seventeenth century, Ian Whyte also framed the discussion in the way that Caird did, seeking a transition from 'old' to 'new' within the broader early modern period, and seeing this in terms of top-down changes led by landlords. However, Whyte emphasised a different set of developments from Caird, notably a shift from multiple-tenant to single-tenant farms, a spread of written leases, and a growth in the marketing of agricultural produce.[4] A further collection of essays by historical geographers, edited by Whittington and Whyte in 1983, ranged more widely in theme and attempted a more synthetic view. Whittington's own contribution continued the debate with Caird, arguing that 'enclosure' was not a single process, that landlords' influence had

2   G. Whittington, 'Was There a Scottish Agricultural Revolution?', *Area*, 7 (1975), 204–6, quotations at p. 206.

3   J. B. Caird, 'The Reshaped Agricultural Landscape', in M. L. Parry and T. R. Slater (eds), *The Making of the Scottish Countryside* (London, 1980), pp. 202–22.

4   I. Whyte, 'The Emergence of the New Estate Structure', in Parry and Slater (eds), *Making of the Scottish Countryside*, pp. 117–35.

been overstated, and that more attention should be paid to gradual improvements by tenants.[5]

At this point we might pause to take note of how the debate was articulated. The geographers' focus was on what the landscape looked like – Caird's straight lines, for instance – and other spatial aspects of farming infrastructure, like undersoil drainage (a nineteenth-century innovation) or regional market centres. The straight lines were particularly important because they could readily be seen to represent a decisive and sudden break with the previous pattern of farming, in which peasants' arable landholdings had taken the form of intermingled strips of land in large, irregular common fields. These issues are vital, but the historian's interest can more readily extend into topics that do not articulate themselves spatially. One such topic is social structure. We may ask, for instance, whether 'farmers' were self-employed peasants, working the land mainly with family labour, or whether they were entrepreneurs, managing a large farm as a business in which the work of farming was carried out by waged farm servants. Not unexpectedly, these two models of social structure may have affected the appearance of the landscape – the peasants tended to have open, unenclosed fields, for instance – but social structure is nevertheless an issue in its own right.

Behind all this lie fundamental questions of how we explain changes in agriculture and rural society. Is change driven by technology, or by the exercise of power in society? All the scholars discussed so far were to some extent reacting against an older tradition of seeing agricultural change largely in terms of technology, in which 'innovations' caused agriculture to 'improve' from its former condition of 'backwardness'. We don't write history like that any more. We still study technological innovations, but we recognise that not everyone benefits from innovations, and that some people may even lose out. And we explain some social and economic changes, not in terms of innovations, but in terms of the exercise of power. Power itself is often contested, with different groups manoeuvring for advantage or even coming into open conflict.[6]

5 G. Whittington, 'Agriculture and Society in Lowland Scotland 1750–1870', in G. Whittington and I. D. Whyte (eds), *An Historical Geography of Scotland* (London, 1983), pp. 141–64. An earlier attempt at a synthesis of the work of historical geographers still has introductory value, though it predates the Caird-Whittington debate: R. N. Millman, *The Making of the Scottish Landscape* (London, 1975). In its geographical approach it can be contrasted with the most influential – indeed inspirational – work of social and economic history published in this period: T. C. Smout, *A History of the Scottish People 1560–1830* (London, 1969).
6 For a study of peasant-landlord negotiations in the four nations of the British Isles see R. A. Houston, *Peasant Petitions: Social and Economic Life on Landed Estates 1600–1850* (Basingstoke, 2014).

By the 1990s, when research on Scottish agriculture slowed, the general view seems to have settled somewhat nearer to Caird's than to Whittington's. Ian and Kathleen Whyte explicitly endorsed Caird in 1991. While noting that there were earlier 'improvements', they characterised these as slower and more evolutionary; there was a 'rapid acceleration of progress from the 1760s' which 'swept away' many of the landscape's earlier features.[7] More will be said about Ian Whyte's contribution to the debate shortly.

The most recent of the really important books focusing on early modern Scottish agriculture as a whole was published by Tom Devine in 1994. Devine argued strongly for a rapid transition – a 'revolution' indeed – taking place mainly in the period 1760–1815. He was aware that Ian Whyte and others had shown that seventeenth-century agriculture was far from static, and that some changes of the pre-1760 period, such as the shift to cash rents, fed into subsequent changes. Nevertheless the post-1760 changes deserved emphasis. Devine argued for a combination of technological change – enclosure, sown grasses – and social-structural changes – enlargement of farms, dispossession of subtenants and cottars. His ultimate criterion for establishing the revolution was 'a dramatic increase in crop yields'. His arguments were particularly striking because he perceived a contrast with England, where, he argued, historians had reached a consensus that no agricultural revolution had occurred; Scottish patterns were thus substantially different.[8]

Devine's argument for Scottish difference was modified from a perhaps unexpected quarter in 1996, when Mark Overton published a detailed restatement of the case for an English agricultural revolution. Overton's revolution had two main elements: dramatic increase in agricultural productivity (higher outputs relative to the inputs of land, labour and other things like fertiliser), and dramatic change in the rural social structure, with small subsistence farmers replaced by large farmers employing labour and producing for the market. He recognised that there were many relevant developments moving in this direction during the period 1500–1750, but located the 'revolution' firmly in the period 1750–1850 on the grounds that changes in the latter period were much more rapid and on a greater scale.[9]

---

7   Ian Whyte and Kathleen Whyte, *The Changing Scottish Landscape 1500–1800* (London, 1991), p. 54.

8   T. M. Devine, *The Transformation of Rural Scotland: Social Change and the Agrarian Economy 1660–1815* (Edinburgh, 1994), pp. 41–2, 165 and *passim*. Devine added that the previous debate among historical geographers had 'petered out' inconclusively (p. 19).

9   Mark Overton, *Agricultural Revolution in England: The Transformation of the Agrarian Economy 1500–1850* (Cambridge, 1996). See also Mark Overton, 'Re-Establishing the English Agricultural Revolution', *AgHR*, 44:1 (1996), 1–20.

Overton's 'revolutionary' arguments were widely accepted at the time, and continue to be influential.[10] From a Scottish perspective, moreover, Ian Whyte rapidly noted that Overton provided further reasons to see English and Scottish agriculture as developing in parallel.[11] Robert Allen has criticised Overton, however, arguing that increases in English productivity were slow and that they extended over a much longer period, beginning perhaps in the middle of the sixteenth century.[12] Although there seems to be no clear historiographical consensus on this debate, it can be observed that Allen's criticisms are focused on the issue of productivity, which may tacitly concede Overton's case for a revolution in rural social structure.[13]

The productivity debate relies on statistics that do not exist for Scotland, or at least have not yet been gathered. Future historians of Scottish agriculture will do well to pursue statistical approaches, even though statistics do not provide simple answers. (There is more on statistics below.) In the meantime, though, we can note that the case for a Scottish 'agricultural revolution', defined at least as a radical shift in social structure, is currently strong, and is strengthened by English comparisons. The displacement of small tenants and cottars, and the replacement of their holdings by larger, entrepreneurial farms worked by waged labour, particularly within the broad period 1750–1850, is surely a key aspect of how the development of Scottish agriculture should be understood.

Although no major overviews of early modern Scottish agriculture as a whole have been published since 1994, there have been important studies of some aspects. In particular, in 1998, the historical geographer Robert Dodgshon published a detailed study of the western Highlands over a long period, synthesising a large amount of data and producing a persuasive interpretation of the nature and periodisation of agricultural

10 See the favourable review by a senior agrarian historian, Joan Thirsk, in *EcHR*, 50:2 (1997), 378–9.
11 Ian Whyte, 'Is a British Socio-Economic History Possible?', in Glenn Burgess (ed.), *The New British History: Founding a Modern State 1603–1715* (London, 1999), pp. 174–97, at pp. 177–8. For an important earlier argument for Anglo-Scottish similarity see K. E. Wrightson, 'Kindred Adjoining Kingdoms: An English Perspective on the Social and Economic History of Early Modern Scotland', in R. A. Houston and I. D. Whyte (eds), *Scottish Society 1500–1800* (Cambridge, 1989), pp. 245–60.
12 Robert C. Allen, 'Tracking the Agricultural Revolution in England', *EcHR*, 52:2 (1999), 209–35; Robert C. Allen, 'The Nitrogen Hypothesis and the English Agricultural Revolution: A Biological Analysis', *Journal of Economic History*, 68:1 (2008), 182–210.
13 For a recent contribution to a related debate about agricultural productivity and population, also based on statistics, see Stephen Broadberry, Bruce M. S. Campbell, Alexander Klein, Mark Overton and Bas Van Leeuwen, 'Clark's Malthus Delusion: Response to "Farming in England 1200–1800"', *EcHR*, 71:2 (2018), 639–64.

change. Dodgshon argued for a gradual but fundamental transition from the economy of 'chiefs' – focused on retaining produce within the estate – to the economy of 'landlords' – focused on extracting produce that could be marketed for cash. Most of the change was in the eighteenth and early nineteenth centuries. As for the period before this, Dodgshon added that slow change could be perceived from 'at least the early seventeenth century onwards'.[14]

Some other works on the most 'revolutionary' period of agriculture may be mentioned here. Devine's conceptualisation and periodisation of Scottish agrarian transformation have been largely endorsed by Neil Davidson. Stressing issues of class relationships and power, Davidson brings Marxist clarity to the question of what is meant by 'capitalism' in a farming context. He follows Devine (perhaps with less nuance) in arguing that landlords were entirely responsible for carrying out the revolutionary transformation that he dates to the period 1747–1815.[15] There is more detail on 'improving' landlords, and others, in a paper by T. C. Smout that discusses what 'improvement' meant to contemporaries, and how knowledge of 'improving' techniques spread. Smout places the beginning of widespread improvement at about 1760, noting that some earlier improvers had lost money but that the upturn in agricultural prices now made investment more profitable. While continuing to acknowledge landlords' influence, Smout also pays attention to 'improving' tenant farmers.[16] Recently, Devine himself has returned to one important aspect of this revolutionary transformation: the 'clearances' of tenants and subtenants that were carried out, mainly through direct landlord initiative, in both Lowlands and Highlands during the late eighteenth and early nineteenth centuries.[17] The Lowland 'clearances' were undramatic

14 Robert A. Dodgshon, *From Chiefs to Landlords: Social and Economic Change in the Western Highlands and Islands c.1493–1820* (Edinburgh, 1998), p. 196 and *passim*. For commercialisation of seventeenth-century Highland agriculture see also Allan I. Macinnes, *Clanship, Commerce and the House of Stuart 1603–1788* (East Linton, 1996), pp. 69–71, 142–8.

15 Neil Davidson, 'The Scottish Path to Capitalist Agriculture 1: From the Crisis of Feudalism to the Origins of Agrarian Transformation (1688–1746)', *Journal of Agrarian Change*, 4:3 (2004), 227–68; Neil Davidson, 'The Scottish Path to Capitalist Agriculture 2: The Capitalist Offensive (1747–1815)', *Journal of Agrarian Change*, 4:4 (2004), 411–60; Neil Davidson, 'The Scottish Path to Capitalist Agriculture 3: The Enlightenment as the Theory and Practice of Improvement', *Journal of Agrarian Change*, 5:1 (2005), 1–72.

16 T. C. Smout, 'A New Look at the Scottish Improvers', *SHR*, 91:1 (2012), 125–49. Smout had also made the point about agricultural prices, suggesting a turning-point of c.1780, in *History of the Scottish People*, pp. 277–81.

17 T. M. Devine, *The Scottish Clearances: A History of the Dispossessed* (London, 2018). Mention may be made here of Andy Wightman, *The Poor Had No Lawyers: Who Owns Scotland (And How They Got It)* (Edinburgh, 2011). As its title indicates, this book focuses on present-day questions, but it contains

in that much of the population movement was readily absorbed by the growing towns, but the effect on agriculture was nevertheless profound and will require further study. As for the Highland clearances, all subsequent studies have been indebted to James Hunter's pioneering history of ordinary Highlanders' experience in the nineteenth century, *The Making of the Crofting Community*. In Hunter's original 1976 edition he began with only a brief chapter on the eighteenth century, arguing for the beginning then of commercial attitudes among landlords. However, in his extended preface to the revised edition in 2000, he stated that he would now date this change to the seventeenth century.[18]

How should the sixteenth century be understood in a review of the periodisation of agricultural change? The most important study of this period, a major book from 1982 by Margaret Sanderson, is hard to place in this review. Sanderson used a wide range of documentary sources to reconstruct the workings of the barony and the farm, but remained aloof from historiographical debates and comparative approaches. She was particularly interested in forms of peasant tenure and inheritance. Her most distinctive contribution concerned the sixteenth-century feuing of church land – a lengthy, complex process roughly comparable to the dissolution of the English monasteries. Most church land was transferred to medium or large lay proprietors, whose relationships with the sitting tenants await study. Sanderson herself gave detailed attention to those few ecclesiastical estates that were feued piecemeal to the tenants themselves, converting them into proprietors.[19] She followed this with a collection of essays of which about half addressed agricultural topics. Particularly noteworthy were an essay on rural labour, and an essay giving further detail on the small feuars – who, Sanderson acknowledged, mostly sold their holdings within a generation or two.[20]

Customs and tenurial practices are important in Sanderson's work, and three other scholars have also discussed this topic. Rab Houston has argued that customary law worked less effectively in Scotland than in England to protect tenants against their landlords, making Scottish

---

much historical information, with insights into the broader relevance of legal and conveyancing technicalities.

18 James Hunter, *The Making of the Crofting Community*, new edn (Edinburgh, 2000), pp. 23–4.

19 Margaret H. B. Sanderson, *Scottish Rural Society in the Sixteenth Century* (Edinburgh, 1982).

20 Margaret H. B. Sanderson, *A Kindly Place? Living in Sixteenth-Century Scotland* (Edinburgh, 2002). Sanderson summarised her views, and incorporated more historiographical discussion, in Margaret H. B. Sanderson, 'Rural Society and Economy', in Bob Harris and Alan R. MacDonald (eds), *Scotland: The Making and Unmaking of the Nation c.1100–1707*, vol. 2: *Early Modern Scotland c.1500–1707* (Dundee, 2007), pp. 166–82.

tenants unusually vulnerable when eighteenth-century landlords began to restructure their estates.[21] Julian Goodare has argued that sixteenth-century Scottish courts did sometimes uphold tenants' rights of inheritance that were recognised as being customary – but that the court of session turned against this during the early seventeenth century. Thereafter, no tenants were allowed more rights than were recognised in their written leases (always for fixed terms of years), and many were merely tenants at will.[22] Colin Shepherd has conducted a case study of landlord-tenant relationships in Aberdeenshire over a long period, perceiving a slow reduction of service obligations as relationships became more capitalist.[23]

The final scholar to discuss in this review of early modern rural scholarship is Ian Whyte, to whose memory this book is dedicated. Whyte's works have perhaps done more than any other's to inform our understanding of the periodisation of agricultural change. His major book of 1979, *Agriculture and Society in Seventeenth-Century Scotland*, hardly seems to have dated. It provides a detailed, all-round study of how agriculture was organised and of the systems of transport, communication and marketing within which it operated. Above all it provides a thoughtful and balanced account both of change and of continuity between the late sixteenth and the early eighteenth centuries.[24] Following this he conducted various regional studies, revealing regional details and complexities that the present review of periodisation can merely note.[25]

---

21 Rab Houston, 'Custom in Context: Medieval and Early Modern Scotland and England', *Past and Present*, 211 (May 2011), 35–76.

22 Julian Goodare, 'In Search of the Scottish Agrarian Problem', in Jane Whittle (ed.), *Landlords and Tenants in Britain 1440–1660: Tawney's 'Agrarian Problem' Revisited* (Woodbridge, 2013), pp. 100–16.

23 Colin Shepherd, 'Changing Tenurial Forms and Service Renders in the North East of Scotland between the Fifteenth and the Eighteenth Centuries: Evidence of Social Development, Capitalised Agrarianism and Ideological Change', *Rural History*, 26:1 (2015), 35–69.

24 Ian Whyte, *Agriculture and Society in Seventeenth-Century Scotland* (Edinburgh, 1979).

25 Not all of these can be listed here, but his studies of the Panmure estate in Forfarshire, with Kathleen Whyte, are a notable example: I. D. Whyte and K. A. Whyte, 'Continuity and Change in a Seventeenth-Century Scottish Farming Community', *AgHR*, 32:2 (1984), 159–69; I. D. Whyte and K. A. Whyte, 'Some Aspects of the Structure of Rural Society in Seventeenth-Century Lowland Scotland', in T. M. Devine and David Dickson (eds), *Ireland and Scotland 1600–1850* (Edinburgh, 1983), pp. 32–45; I. D. Whyte and K. A. Whyte, 'Debt and Credit, Poverty and Prosperity in a Seventeenth-Century Scottish Rural Community', in Rosalind Mitchison and Peter Roebuck (eds), *Economy and Society in Scotland and Ireland 1500–1939* (Edinburgh, 1988), pp. 70–80. Mention may also be made of Whyte's studies of the Dundas estate, which also features in Alan R. MacDonald's chapter in the present volume: Ian Whyte, 'Infield-Outfield Farming on a Seventeenth-Century

Whyte also published a major survey of the social and economic history of medieval and early modern Scotland, which remains the most comprehensive work on that topic.[26] He presented population changes as the main drivers of agricultural change before the eighteenth century: the growth of settlement in the central middle ages, the population collapse of the 1340s with the Black Death which prompted a proportional shift from arable to pastoral farming, and the expansion of population in the sixteenth century leading to a period of subsistence crises. More will be said about some of these themes in the next section of the present introduction.

Two of Whyte's papers from the 1990s are of particular interest in this review of periodisation, because they explicitly set out to review the periodisation of agricultural change. The first paper examined the late seventeenth and early eighteenth centuries.[27] Following on from Devine's account of landlord-directed change in the period after about 1750, Whyte argued that this was the correct approach to the question but that more weight should be given to the innovations of earlier landlords. Nor was the Union of 1707 as important as he had suggested in his 1979 book. Rather, attention should be given to innovations in the later seventeenth century, some of which responded to a remarkable series of improving statutes between 1660 and 1695. This was the period that saw the beginnings of significant enclosure, new crops (such as sown grasses) and new crop rotations. In the early eighteenth century there were signs of improved crop yields.

The second paper shifted back to examine the late sixteenth and early seventeenth centuries.[28] Whyte argued that this was a crucial, if ill-documented, period, in which Scotland's population began to increase considerably, and repeated famines occurred. Nevertheless, while growing poverty was all too apparent, Whyte noted signs of agricultural development or at least commercialisation. Despite growing pressure on the land, holdings seem not to have been subdivided, and there were even signs of reduction in multiple tenancy. Here, perhaps, were the roots of the changes that would create the larger capitalist farms of later centuries.[29]

Scottish Estate', *Journal of Historical Geography*, 5:4 (1979), 391–401; Ian D. Whyte, 'George Dundas of Dundas: The Context of an Early Eighteenth-Century Scottish Improving Landowner', *SHR*, 60:1 (1981), 1–13.

26 Ian D. Whyte, *Scotland before the Industrial Revolution: An Economic and Social History c.1050–c.1750* (London, 1995).

27 Ian D. Whyte, 'Before the Improvers: Agricultural and Landscape Change in Lowland Scotland c.1660–c.1750', *Scottish Archives*, 1 (1995), 31–42.

28 Ian Whyte, 'Poverty or Prosperity? Rural Society in Lowland Scotland in the Late Sixteenth and Early Seventeenth Centuries', *Scottish Economic and Social History*, 18:1 (1998), 19–32.

29 This overview of Whyte's contribution to the history of Scottish agriculture is

In the present book, we mainly follow Whyte in steering a middle course between the two extreme positions of 'revolution' and 'evolution', as they were articulated in the 1970s. More recent work has shown that the two positions are not irreconcilable. There can have been a revolution, but also a dynamic period before it. As we gain a more detailed picture, some of the sweeping generalisations of past scholars may no longer be necessary – and there will be scope for further generalisations, more securely grounded in the data.

If there was a 'revolution' in early modern Scottish agriculture, so far there seems to have been only *one* revolution. The studies in this book generally uphold the idea of a singular Agricultural Revolution, with the most dramatic changes taking place in the late eighteenth and early nineteenth centuries. Further agricultural 'revolutions' have been postulated for the twentieth century, both concerning social structure and concerning technology, but here we can merely note these arguments.[30] In the two centuries or so before *c*.1750, with which our book is mainly concerned, we see slow, evolutionary change, with important innovations from time to time, but these innovations do not come together in such a way as to constitute a 'revolution' in agriculture in any earlier period. Nevertheless, some understanding of medieval agricultural processes may help us to understand early modern processes also. Was agriculture in about 1550 a stable process that had been the same for a long time, or had there been significant changes – evolutionary or even revolutionary – in the medieval period?

* * *

There have been suggestions of dramatic agricultural change in the late middle ages at least. In the 1970s debate, Whittington pointed to a possible medieval-early modern transition, but Sanderson did not take up

indicative but not comprehensive. His most recent contributions to the topic have been Ian D. Whyte, 'Pre-Improvement Rural Communities: Lowland', and 'Landlord-Tenant Relationships in Scotland from the Sixteenth Century to Modern Times', both in John Beech, Owen Hand, Mark A. Mulhern and Jeremy Weston (eds), *The Individual and Community Life* (Scottish Life and Society: A Compendium of Scottish Ethnology, vol. 9; Edinburgh, 2005), pp. 329–42, 343–57. He also published extensively on population history, urbanisation and migration in Scotland, and on agriculture and other social and economic topics relating to Cumbria.

30 For a shift in the early twentieth century from landlord-managed estates to owner-occupied farms, see R. H. Campbell, 'The Agricultural Revolution of the Twentieth Century', *Scottish Archives*, 1 (1995), 55–62. Presumably Scotland also participated in many of the technological changes discussed in Paul Brassley, David Harvey, Matt Lobley and Michael Winter, *The Real Agricultural Revolution: The Transformation of English Farming 1939–1985* (Woodbridge, 2021).

his ideas. More recently, Whyte noted the monasteries' abandonment of direct demesne farming in the later middle ages, but rejected the idea that this represented 'decline'.[31] And there has been even less recent research on medieval agriculture than there has been on early modern agriculture. Still, some remarks about the periodisation of agricultural change in the middle ages may be made here.

Much medieval research has discussed the named units of land settlement, use and assessment. These units have various names, and these names are prominent in the sometimes scanty sources. However, their functions and relationships are not always clear. Ploughgates, oxgates, davachs and pennylands are often mentioned in agricultural contexts, and beyond them we find units like parishes and officiaries, valuations like old extent and new extent, and forms of cultivation like infield and outfield. What are the meanings of these terms that are used extensively over this period? How and when did they originate, how did they interact, and indeed how did they function?

Hypothetically at least, a given unit could represent a specified amount of various different things: an amount of land *surface area*; an amount of *work done* (thus an acre could be the amount of land ploughed in a day); an amount of *rent* or other fixed dues paid by the land unit (either a current amount, or a traditional valuation from the past; the dues themselves might be payable to the lord or the crown or the church); an amount of land needed to sustain a *farming community*; or an amount of land needed to sustain an *administrative structure* (such as a parish church and priest, or a lord's court or military following). A unit with a primary function would be likely to have further subsidiary functions, since rents, for instance, expressed a relationship between lord and community.

Many scholars have written on these topics, but it may be best to start with the work of Robert Dodgshon, who has reviewed a wide range of primary and secondary evidence for what he calls Scotland's 'patterns of territorial order'.[32] Probably the most important medieval debate so far has concerned the origin of the infield-outfield system and of the fermtouns or townships that operated this system. Dodgshon, who has studied this in most detail, argues for a mainly top-down process in which individual farms were forced to combine into fermtouns when assessments were imposed on them by lords, and that the arable land formed the key to the assessment. However, the details of this process remain obscure. The period over which the process occurred seems to have been long – from the eleventh century to the fourteenth or fifteenth.[33]

---

31 Whyte, *Scotland before the Industrial Revolution*, pp. 43–7.
32 Robert A. Dodgshon, *Land and Society in Early Scotland* (Oxford, 1981), pp. 58–89 and *passim*.
33 See most recently Robert A. Dodgshon, *No Stone Unturned: A History of*

Two perspectives on Dodgshon's work may be noted here. First, Joseph Donnelly has attacked Dodgshon's conclusions in a paper by turns combative and tentative. He focuses on the Berwickshire settlement of Auchencrow for which evidence survives over many centuries, though it is hard to interpret, and any study of a single small locality raises questions of typicality. Donnelly argues that pre-Improvement field systems in Scotland should be understood as fundamentally stable over a very long period, with their origins lost in prehistory.[34] Second, Ian Whyte has surveyed the period from about the twelfth to the fifteenth centuries, endorsing Dodgshon's arguments about infield-outfield, and concluding that although the later medieval period saw many changes, there was 'underlying continuity' in the late medieval period that continued until the 'landscape, economic and social revolutions that occurred from the 1760s'.[35]

There has been debate on the land unit known as the davach (Gaelic *dabhach*), found mainly in north-eastern Scotland. Again the contending theories can be regarded as top-down and bottom-up, indeed starkly so. Alasdair Ross assembled information about davachs from a wide range of medieval and early modern sources, traced their topography on the ground, and attempted to reconstruct their overall rationale and thus their origins. He concluded that davachs were likely to have been created by a king of the Picts in the late eighth or early ninth century in order to structure military service – an inescapably tentative argument when the only documentary sources are much later. While welcoming the detail of Ross's work, Alex Woolf has attacked his overall conclusions in an extended review, arguing that davachs were more likely to have been organised by communities themselves as they sought to establish a balance between arable and pasture land.[36]

Clearly there is scope for further medieval research to reconcile these widely-divergent arguments. Probably such research should be at least partly comparative. Dodgshon has studied the whole of Britain in some of his work, which should give his arguments additional weight. He has argued persuasively that regional diversity arose, not from completely different ecologies nor indeed completely different cultures, but from a single overall set of processes throughout Britain (and indeed beyond)

Farming, Landscape and Environment in the Scottish Highlands and Islands (Edinburgh, 2015), pp. 93–112.

34 J. Donnelly, 'In the Territory of Auchencrow: Long Continuity or Late Development in Early Scottish Field Systems?', *PSAS*, 130 (2000), 743–72.

35 Ian Whyte, 'Rural Society and Economy', in Bob Harris and Alan R. MacDonald (eds), *Scotland: The Making and Unmaking of the Nation c.1100–1707*, vol. 1: *The Scottish Nation: Origins to c.1500* (Dundee, 2006), pp. 158–73, quotations at p. 172. See also Whyte, 'Infield-Outfield Farming'.

36 Alasdair Ross, *Land Assessment and Lordship in Medieval Northern Scotland* (Turnhout, 2015); Alex Woolf, review in *SHR*, 96:1 (2017), 110–12.

in which local variations produced different outcomes.[37] The complexity of this set of processes makes Dodgshon's argument hard to summarise; indeed one recurring theme of his work is the inadequacy of any single simple model. Environment, technology and culture all affected field systems in complementary ways, with no single factor being dominant. He also argues that historical change can be found in any period, and that assumptions of stasis or long-term continuity across many centuries are likely to be misleading.

Returning to the question of infield and outfield, this can be framed within the broader European debate on the origin of what English and Continental scholars usually call open fields. The point about 'open' fields – which is also a key point about infield and outfield – is that they are large fields containing subdivisions. The question of open fields remains unresolved. A recent review of the European scholarship notes that some regular fields were planned from above, but regards these as exceptional. Nor can seigneurial demands for rent on assessed land be seen as an overall pattern. A more fundamental motivation for open fields, it has been argued, arose from peasants' need to cooperate on the first infields – the first areas of permanent rather than shifting arable culti-vation. Cooperation was particularly needed in ploughing and manuring. The medieval introduction of heavy ploughs in northern Europe was important here, but there was no single determining factor. Population growth probably motivated the creation of open fields, particularly when combined with the growth of towns and a market for grain. The chronology of these processes remains unclear, and varied from one region to another, but the period from the eighth to the thirteenth centuries may well have been transformative.[38]

*   *   *

This section of the introduction will review scholarship on Scottish agriculture and other related topics from a variety of disciplinary and thematic perspectives. Our review cannot be comprehensive, but it may bring out some relevant points. There are archaeological and ethno-logical studies, often focusing on agricultural technology. There are statistical studies, with a particular emphasis on demography – and, in the early modern period, on famine. Finally there are studies of

---

37 Robert A. Dodgshon, *The Origin of British Field Systems: An Interpretation* (London, 1980), p. 25 and *passim*.
38 Christopher Dyer, Erik Thoen and Tom Williamson, 'Conclusion: The Rationale of Open Fields', in Christopher Dyer, Erik Thoen and Tom Williamson (eds), *Peasants and Their Fields: The Rationale of Open-Field Agriculture c.700–1800* (Turnhout, 2018), pp. 256–75, at pp. 261–6.

particular approaches to land use – pastoral farming, woodland, and the broader environment.

Compared with early modernists, medievalists tend to use a wider range of evidence to supplement their often meagre documentary records: archaeology, placename studies, comparative historical models from better-studied medieval regions elsewhere, and comparative anthropological studies that shed light on patterns of behaviour in traditional societies. Early modern historians have more documentary evidence, but we too should be interdisciplinary and comparative whenever possible. Archaeologists, like historians, have tended to regard the medieval centuries – and the early modern centuries too – as relatively neglected by their discipline.[39] Archaeology tends to bring forward different questions about agriculture, being more interested in technology and in spatial patterning, and with less of a focus on change over time or on social structure.

One of the most important scholars of Scottish agriculture has been the ethnologist Alexander Fenton. He studied 'traditional' agricultural practices from earliest prehistory up to the early twentieth century. He had experience as a museum curator, which gave him a particular focus on material culture and physical processes, but he ranged widely, also taking in documentary, linguistic and other evidence.[40] His in-depth study of Orkney and Shetland is particularly noteworthy.[41] Fenton's overall arguments are hard to summarise for historians, partly because he did not take a historian's approach to periodisation. He can sometimes be read as arguing for continuity over very long periods, but he was well aware of changes wrought by 'Improvement' in the late eighteenth century, as well as medieval changes like the introduction of the heavy plough – on which he was, indeed, the leading expert.

39 For archaeological overviews see Piers Dixon, 'Rural Settlement Patterns on the Ground', in Keith J. Stringer and Angus J. L. Winchester (eds), *Northern England and Southern Scotland in the Central Middle Ages* (Woodbridge, 2017), pp. 237–71; and Stephen Rippon, Piers Dixon and Bob Silvester, 'Overview: The Form and Pattern of Medieval Settlement', in Christopher M. Gerrard and Alejandra Gutiérrez (eds), *The Oxford Handbook of Later Medieval Archaeology in Britain* (Oxford, 2018), pp. 171–92. For an earlier but more detailed collection of essays see Sarah Govan (ed.), *Medieval or Later Rural Settlement in Scotland: 10 Years On* (Edinburgh, 2003).

40 Among Fenton's many works, Alexander Fenton, *Scottish Country Life* (Edinburgh, 1976), is a comprehensive survey from about 1500 to 1900. Much of its material was revisited, extended and updated by Fenton's own and other contributions to Alexander Fenton and Kenneth Veitch (eds), *Farming and the Land* (Scottish Life and Society: A Compendium of Scottish Ethnology, vol. 2; Edinburgh, 2011). Also important is Alexander Fenton, *The Food of the Scots* (Scottish Life and Society: A Compendium of Scottish Ethnology, vol. 5; Edinburgh, 2007).

41 Alexander Fenton, *The Northern Isles: Orkney and Shetland* (Edinburgh, 1978).

The role of technology in shaping farming systems and settlement patterns is important to medieval debates. Proponents of bottom-up models sometimes emphasise the role of the plough in physically shaping the arable landscape. The heavy plough, or 'old Scotch plough' as it is sometimes known, was well adapted to Scotland's generally wet environment. It worked best when it made long, straight furrows, because of the length of the plough-team of six, eight, or even twelve oxen that were required to pull it. Even the slight curves at the ends of many furrows are explained technologically by the need to turn the plough-team. The heavy plough turned the soil to enable it to dry out, and a further drainage effect was produced by ploughing in strips, heaping the soil up towards the middle of the strip to produce long ridges or 'rigs'. All this is well enough known and uncontroversial, but the economic and social implications of the heavy plough sometimes need to be pondered. Farming and settlement practices may have been shaped by the need to maintain a system of sharing of ploughs themselves, or teams of plough-oxen. Strip farming, too, entailed systems for allocating strips throughout the settlement.

The heavy plough was a northern European development of the medieval period. Not only did it radically increase agricultural productivity, but it also changed the pattern of arable cultivation by enabling farmers to plough heavier and lower-lying soils. Fenton dated the introduction of the 'old Scotch plough' to the 'thirteenth or fourteenth centuries'.[42] This may well be relevant to the debate about infield and outfield, though Fenton himself did not contribute to that debate. Meanwhile, one archaeologist has even written of an 'agrarian revolution' that reshaped the farming landscape in the twelfth and thirteenth centuries.[43] This may pose difficulties for theories arguing for continuity back into the prehistoric period. Even in the early modern period and later, spade cultivation was practised in some areas of the western Highlands, but we can hardly assume that this provides us with an uninterrupted window on the prehistoric past.

Another approach to the history of agriculture is to look at statistics. Elizabeth Gemmill and Nicholas Mayhew have gathered medieval price and wage data from about 1260 to 1540, with the preponderance of the data falling in the second half of this period.[44] Then, from 1550 to 1780, we

42 Alexander Fenton, 'Cultivating Tools and Tillage: The Old Scotch Plough, the Improved Plough and Spades', in Fenton and Veitch (eds), *Farming and the Land*, pp. 655–78, quotation at p. 660.

43 Piers Dixon, *Puir Labourers and Busy Husbandmen: The Countryside of Lowland Scotland in the Middle Ages* (Edinburgh, 2002), p. 60.

44 Elizabeth Gemmill and Nicholas Mayhew, *Changing Values in Medieval Scotland: A Study of Prices, Money, and Weights and Measures* (Cambridge, 1995). See also Elizabeth Gemmill, 'Town and Region: The Corn Market in

have the price and wage data gathered by A. J. S. Gibson and T. C. Smout, which is cited by several contributors below.[45] An essential complement to these market-based studies is the detailed work of R. D. Connor and A. D. C. Simpson on weights and measures during the period from about 1350 to 1834, with a glance back to twelfth-century origins. The substance of their book deals with measures of length (for cloth and land), measures of weight (for coinage, wool, and other goods), and measures of capacity (both wet, for liquids, and dry, for grain).[46] As for price data, these tend to be recorded for goods traded internationally and for luxury goods; there are fewer data for goods that did not enter urban markets, or that were produced mainly for direct consumption. Still, there is much to be gathered from these statistics. Gibson and Smout themselves combined statistical and qualitative evidence to demonstrate a shift in the composition of the diet of the common folk, from a mixed diet of meat, dairy products and cereals to a lower-value (if still nutritious) diet dominated by oatmeal. This transition, which occurred mainly in the sixteenth century, remains one of the most important perspectives on the periodisation of the social and economic history of rural Scotland, and should be addressed in future research on the subject.[47]

There are also data, if less comprehensive, on population. The figure of 1,265,380 that Alexander Webster reported for the Scottish population in 1755 has always been recognised as a benchmark. Detailed investigation has shown that this figure is less precise than used to be thought, but Webster continues to be regarded highly.[48] The relationship of population and agriculture appears with particular intensity when there

---

Aberdeen *c.*1398–*c.*1468', in Ben Dodds and Richard Britnell (eds), *Agriculture and Rural Society after the Black Death: Common Themes and Regional Variations* (Hatfield, 2008), pp. 56–72.

45 A. J. S. Gibson and T. C. Smout, *Prices, Food and Wages in Scotland 1550–1780* (Cambridge, 1995).

46 R. D. Connor and A. D. C. Simpson, *Weights and Measures in Scotland: A European Perspective* (Edinburgh, 2004).

47 A. Gibson and T. C. Smout, 'Scottish Food and Scottish History 1500–1800', in Houston and Whyte (eds), *Scottish Society*, pp. 59–84.

48 The fundamental work remains Michael Flinn (ed.), *Scottish Population History from the 17th Century to the 1930s* (Cambridge, 1977). For the main subsequent studies see R. A. Houston, 'The Demographic Regime', in T. M. Devine and Rosalind Mitchison (eds), *People and Society in Scotland*, vol. 1: *1760–1830* (Edinburgh, 1988), pp. 9–26; Rosalind Mitchison, 'Webster Revisited: A Re-Examination of the 1755 "Census" of Scotland', in T. M. Devine (ed.), *Improvement and Enlightenment: Proceedings of the Scottish Historical Studies Seminar, University of Strathclyde 1987–88* (Edinburgh, 1989), pp. 62–77; Robert E. Tyson, 'Demographic Change', in T. M. Devine and John R. Young (eds), *Eighteenth-Century Scotland: New Perspectives* (East Linton, 1999), pp. 195–209; Michael Anderson, 'Guesses, Estimates and Adjustments: Webster's 1755 "Census" of Scotland Revisited Again', *JSHS*, 31:1 (2011), 26–45.

are famines, as there periodically were from the late sixteenth century up to 1700 at least. There is more on famine later in this introduction, but here we mention the pioneering overview by T. C. Smout, along with further studies of the famine of the 1690s.[49] The crisis of the 1690s was Europe-wide, as was the subsequent famine of 1738–41; this still affected Scotland, though not as much as some other countries.[50] The suggestion has been made of a fundamental transition in about 1620. Before then, Scotland was normally a net importer of grain, but from about 1620 onwards Scottish agriculture managed in normal years to produce a surplus for export.[51]

Although population statistics are almost entirely absent before 1755, it is still worthwhile to glance back at earlier periods. It can be assumed that the medieval population of Scotland, like that of other European countries, grew considerably in the period from about 1000 to 1350 and then plummeted with the Black Death, remaining low until the sixteenth century. Richard Oram, synthesising a wide range of fragmentary evidence, confirms this. He adds that there were earlier epidemics in the thirteenth century, that Scotland suffered in the Europe-wide famine of the 1310s, and that wind erosion destroyed some coastal farmland, particularly in the fifteenth century.[52] An overall pattern of population growth and contraction will surely have been reflected in patterns of settlement and land use, but a clear historiographical view of this has yet to emerge.

Pre-modern agriculture was not just about arable farming. Cattle and sheep formed an integral part of farming systems everywhere in Scotland. However, it helps initially to focus on upland regions where pastoralism predominated. Here a book by Angus Winchester about the hill country of the Scottish Borders and northern England is important.[53] Winchester

---

49　T. C. Smout, 'Famine and Famine-Relief in Scotland', in L. M. Cullen and T. C. Smout (eds), *Comparative Aspects of Scottish and Irish Economic and Social History 1600–1900* (Edinburgh, 1977), pp. 21–31; Karen J. Cullen, Christopher A. Whatley and Mary Young, 'King William's Ill Years: New Evidence on the Impact of Scarcity and Harvest Failure during the Crisis of the 1690s on Tayside', *SHR*, 85:2 (2006), 250–76; Karen J. Cullen, *Famine in Scotland: The 'Ill Years' of the 1690s* (Edinburgh, 2010).

50　Philipp Robinson Rössner, 'The 1738–41 Harvest Crisis in Scotland', *SHR*, 90:1 (2011), 27–63.

51　Julian Goodare, 'Reformation, Revolution and Union', in Edward J. Cowan (ed.), *Why Scottish History Still Matters* (Edinburgh, 2012), pp. 41–55, at pp. 45–6.

52　Richard Oram, '"The Worst Disaster Suffered by the People of Scotland in Recorded History": Climate Change, Dearth and Pathogens in the Long 14th Century', *PSAS*, 144 (2014), 223–44.

53　Angus J. L. Winchester, *The Harvest of the Hills: Rural Life in Northern England and the Scottish Borders 1400–1700* (Edinburgh, 2000). For a briefer survey see

brings out the distinctive seasonal patterns of stock management, as animals were moved by stages up into the hills in summer and down into the valley in winter. Pastoral farming was communal, with the community's animals herded together or roaming freely on the common upland pasture. Communal farming, however, required formal regulation in order to ensure, for instance, that all animals were moved away from the crop land before sowing, or to prevent individual farmers overstocking the common herd. Winchester takes a bottom-up view of local courts, emphasising their participatory character and the legitimacy that this gave them. But he also shows that pastoral agriculture changed considerably in his chosen period, 1400–1700. By the end of this period, communal farming was beginning to decline, with a growth of large landlord-managed flocks and herds.

As well as fields of grain, and fields of cattle and sheep pasture, early modern rural Scotland also had a third resource: woodland. Research on woodland history has been led by T. C. Smout and colleagues. Woodland was not just a source of wood for fuel and the manufacture of artefacts; all pre-modern woodland was also used for the grazing of animals and even sometimes for cultivation. The balance between these various uses, and between woodland and other uses for land, had to be managed actively. There are no sharp periodisations in woodland history before the twentieth century, but a slow decline in woodland cover during the medieval and early modern periods can be detected. There was also a trend, mainly from the eighteenth century onwards, towards more intensive management of woodland, with increasing demand for charcoal and tanbark. Intensive management could even lead to new planting.[54]

More broadly than any of these human uses for land, we find the land itself – the environment within which humans carry out numerous activities. Agriculture is only one such activity. Again, it has been T. C. Smout whose works have discussed the relationship between various different approaches to land. As well as farming there is hunting, and (in more recent times) a variety of leisure pursuits and scientific activity. The balance between what Smout calls 'use' and 'delight' is often contested.[55]

* * *

A. Fenton, 'The Traditional Pastoral Economy', in Parry and Slater (eds), *Making of the Scottish Countryside*, pp. 93–113.

54 T. C. Smout (ed.), *Scottish Woodland History* (Edinburgh, 1997); T. C. Smout (ed.), *People and Woods in Scotland: A History* (Edinburgh, 2003); T. C. Smout, Alan R. MacDonald and Fiona Watson, *A History of the Native Woodlands of Scotland 1500–1920* (Edinburgh, 2005).

55 T. C. Smout (ed.), *Scotland since Prehistory: Natural Change and Human Impact* (Aberdeen, 1993); T. C. Smout, *Nature Contested: Environmental History in Scotland and Northern England since 1600* (Edinburgh, 2000); T. C. Smout, *Exploring Environmental History: Selected Essays* (Edinburgh, 2009).

The contributions to this collection stretch from the fifteenth to the early twentieth century, although they focus mainly on the period between *c.*1550 and *c.*1750. They consist of a combination of case studies of agricultural practices in specific localities, examinations of specific incidents, infrastructure and ideas, and thematic discussions of longer-term processes.

In the opening chapter, Julian Goodare provides a conceptual background against which the chapters that follow can be set. He investigates the cultural meanings of agriculture for literate Scots *c.*1450–1700 through poetry, religious writings, proverbs, maps and paintings. He identifies six main 'discourses': moralising, metaphorical, mystical, Renaissance, humorous, and economic. Over time, the moralising discourse, in which agriculture provided the framework for discussing the morality of social and economic relationships, declined and was supplanted by an economic discourse, pointing the way towards the eighteenth-century Improvers.

Briony Kincaid examines dykes, which she defines as the walls (sometimes ditches) that delineated the spaces in which agriculture was carried out. While their primary purpose was stock management, dykes also enclosed kale-yards, barnyards and churchyards. They ranged from temporary 'fold dykes' of turf, serving seasonal purposes, to the 'head dyke', the permanent boundary at the upper limit of cultivation. Responsibility for their construction and upkeep is discussed, including how sanctions were imposed for damage or neglect, and they are set in the context of other artificial boundaries, such as hedges and legal boundaries delimited by symbolic march stones.

The catastrophic famine of the early 1620s is the subject of Kevin Hall's contribution. He investigates its causes, both actual and perceived, and assesses the responses of both central and local government. His central question is: What was the human cost? Ecclesiastical records are used to provide information about mortality, poverty, and the management of migration. An account of the famine's geographical extent is offered, and the Scottish experience of this disaster is discussed within a wider geographical context and in relation to the longer-term climatic phenomenon, the 'Little Ice Age'. Hall's stark conclusion is that this famine, although shorter than that of the 1690s, may have been even more intense.

Chapters 4 to 8 comprise local case studies, in the first of which Julian Goodare undertakes a micro-analysis of the 'Chronicle of Fortingall'. Written by an unbeneficed priest in Highland Perthshire who was also a peasant farmer, it provides a remarkably direct voice from the sixteenth century. There is detailed information on ploughing, sowing and harvesting, and a wealth of comments on the weather, markets and fairs, and prices. The source's discourse also shifts from these practical matters into moral and providential observations. Goodare disentangles these different threads, setting them in a broader comparative context and revealing something of how rural work was experienced by a real farmer.

The next two chapters focus on the immediate environs of Edinburgh, Scotland's biggest market for agricultural surpluses. Norah Carlin examines agriculture on the Midlothian estate of Corstorphine in the late sixteenth century using the testament of its laird, Sir James Forrester (d.1589). Consisting of lists of livestock and rents due, it reveals that rent was paid mostly in kind, both cereals and poultry, while money rents were present but less prominent. Forrester's estates are shown to have been actively managed, with contributions from wool production and clothmaking. The chapter reflects on the varying experiences of tenants in the different parts of the estate. In the next chapter, Alan MacDonald explores the organisation of agriculture on the Dundas estate, in West Lothian, in the early seventeenth century. The papers of Sir Walter Dundas reveal careful management of his lands and enable the reconstruction of the annual cycle of agricultural labour. Most significantly, they also record some early experiments in what would later be called 'improvement'. These included the extensive use of lime and the enclosure of arable land as the laird sought to maximise the opportunities for profiting from increased cereal production provided by demand from Edinburgh's growing population.

Brian Smith takes us to the opposite end of the country, with a vivid picture of the working life of Andro Smyth, an Orcadian lessee of Shetland, whose papers record his collection of rent, tax, customs duties and tolls, and his service as sheriff in c.1640. Historians have portrayed Shetland as a place where incomers from the Scottish mainland defrauded islanders and destroyed their culture, but Andro Smyth did none of these things. He was careful not to exceed his authority, and his papers provide a more nuanced view of seventeenth-century Shetland than has been achieved hitherto.

In a broader regional case study, John Harrison examines a large and varied area in central Scotland, drawing on a range of sources which bring smaller holdings as well as the big estates into the frame. With detailed discussions of liming, the introduction of new breeds of sheep, clearance of bogs and consolidation of holdings he shows that smaller tenants were open to innovation. Yet barriers remained before c.1750, including a lack of available capital and an aversion to risk. Small tenants, while adopting new approaches, remained reliant on shared resources from the wider landscape, precluding extensive enclosure and intensification.

The next three chapters are concerned with the relationship between agriculture and the wider economy. T. C. Smout considers the nature and use of 'fiars prices', a system that remained in use until 1925 but which remains only dimly understood. Set by local courts, they emerged in the sixteenth century as a uniquely Scottish way of assessing the market price of grain. Smout addresses the ostensibly simple question of what they were actually for. His answer is that they were a handy way of commuting a whole range of payments due in kind into a cash value, indicating that some payments recorded in kind were actually paid in cash. Adam Smith praised the fiars as a mirror of value, and they were consequently used to calculate fairer agricultural rents when prices were volatile, and to set the remuneration of schoolmasters and some clergy.

Gains Murdoch argues that the transformation of Scotland's rural economy could not have taken place without the establishment of a formal banking system, providing loans to landowners without easy access to liquid capital. Drawing on the records of the Bank of Scotland and the Royal Bank of Scotland, he considers the link between the development of Scottish banking and agricultural reform in the first half of the eighteenth century. He examines what proportion of loans went to landowners and whether there were regional biases in the allocation of such loans, placing these considerations within the context of contemporary economic thought, which prioritised the modernisation of the rural economy and felt that the emerging banking sector should be geared to serve its development.

Philipp Rössner offers a challenging interpretation of economic development, arguing that modern capitalism has much deeper roots than previously understood, and that it was not specific to Europe nor to any sector, but could be found in industry, commerce or agriculture. Much more than a purely economic phenomenon, it needs to be studied with reference to social, cultural, psychological, religious and institutional dimensions, and within a geographically broad comparative European framework. Moreover, the role of the state was crucial in the process of empowering capitalism. Rössner argues that the Scottish case provides an ideal example of capitalist dynamics, paying particular regard to agrarian improvement, commerce and the role of the mercantilist state in empowering Scotland's journey towards modern capitalism.

In the final chapter, Rab Houston rounds off the collection with a reflection on recent and potential future developments in early modern Scottish agricultural historiography. He sets agrarian history in a broader social and cultural context, drawing attention to a variety of methodologies from historical geography, archaeology, landscape history and legal history, concluding that scholars should focus on people rather than places, and reject the artificial separation of political history from social and economic history.

* * *

In conclusion, a call for scholars to synthesise is one that we editors endorse. A collection of essays like this one cannot achieve this directly, but it can provide materials for future syntheses. The chapters that follow take a wide range of approaches – from cultural to statistical, from local to international, and from closely empirical to broadly theoretical. They deal with everyday life, with administrative structures, with ecology, with technology, with 'improvement' (to return to that difficult but inescapable term), with wealth and poverty, and occasionally with disaster. We hope that these chapters will prove informative in themselves, and that they will stimulate further research, both empirically based and theoretically sophisticated. Some of this future research may integrate these various approaches, and offer fresh overall interpretations of the agricultural, economic and social history of early modern Scotland.

1

Imagining Scottish Agriculture
before the Improvers

Julian Goodare

Most of what we know about agriculture in early modern Scotland comes from written sources concerned directly to record its business aspects. Estate papers record landlords' dealings with their tenants. Testaments record farmers' possessions. Baron court minutes record the adjudication of disputes and the making of agricultural rules. All these records had to be written in order to keep track of people's property and to enforce property rights. Although they were written for the benefit of those with substantial landed property, they also give us glimpses of the farm work of the propertyless. Such sources have enabled historians – including those contributing to this book – to answer many questions about early modern agriculture.

But are there other questions that we can ask – questions that these businesslike records cannot answer? Here I have in mind questions about the cultural meanings of agriculture for educated and literate Scots. What did agriculture mean to these people, who were almost never farmers themselves? Even the literate elite lived in daily proximity to tilled fields in which they saw crops growing, pastures in which they saw cattle and sheep grazing, and farming settlements in which they saw poultry scratching. The peasants who worked those fields, herded those animals and inhabited those settlements were often their own tenants, some of whom they may have known personally. Everyday diets, even of members of the elite, contained many meat, dairy and grain products derived from those same fields, processed locally in recognisable ways by those same peasants. The elite also craved exotic luxuries, but these were paid for, as they well knew, by their tenants' rents. The seasonal round, even for the elite, was tangibly shaped by agriculture, with spring ploughing and autumn harvesting as intense periods in which landlords' attention would be drawn to their estates. Culturally speaking, how did members of the elite experience all this? What did agriculture mean to them?

This chapter will range beyond the familiar sources for agricultural history. It will examine, not what people *had* to write about agriculture, but what they *chose* to write about it when they didn't have to. One point should be stressed at the outset: the harvest of such voluntary writing is far from bountiful. The sources discussed in this chapter are all informative in some way, but also informative is the enormous silence maintained about agriculture by most literate Scots in this period. They must have noticed at least some of the farm work being done around them, but they didn't think it worthy of comment. It may be possible, in the conclusion, to make suggestions as to why this was so; but we must first examine the writings that *were* produced by people who noticed agriculture. These were often poets or preachers, whom we should not expect to analyse socio-economic conditions, or even to offer straightforward descriptions of rural scenes. But they can articulate cultural meanings with force and precision.

There were a number of different 'discourses' of agriculture – different ways in which people expressed their thoughts about it. These discourses sometimes overlapped, but it is useful to separate them for analytical purposes. In this chapter I analyse a '*moralising discourse*', denouncing sins against farmers; a '*metaphorical discourse*', using agricultural metaphors to speak about something else; a '*mystical discourse*', in which agriculture appeared during an emotional response to the broader environment; a '*Renaissance discourse*', responding to classical authors such as Virgil who had written about agriculture; a '*humorous discourse*', laughing at comical peasants; and an '*economic discourse*', in which, even before the Improvers, some writers commented on agriculture as an economic process, concerned with the production, distribution and consumption of goods.

* * *

Discussion of the moralising discourse may begin with Gilbert Hay, who declared in 1456 that farmers should be protected from damage during warfare. He defined farmers as 'plewmen, harow men, wyne men [i.e. wain men or carters], and all labouraris and delvaris of the erde'. This last phrase connected farmers closely to the earth which they were assumed to 'delve'. Hay gave an eloquent reason for protecting farmers:

> For thai travaile for all the warld, and for the commoun prouffit of every man. And sen thai ar commoun servandis till all men, all men suld have thame assurit in thair craft and laborage, bathe be law of nature, mannis law, and law writtin. For sen thair office is commoun,

and makis lifing and grathis, mete and clathe till all the warld, all maner of man suld defend thame as he wald defend his awin lyf, for thai mak na were.[1]

(For they labour for all the world, and for the common profit of every man. And since they are common servants to all men, all men should protect them in their craft and labouring, both by the law of nature, human law, and written [i.e. Roman] law. For since their duty is common, and makes materials, tools, food and clothing for all the world, each kind of man should defend them as he would defend his own life, for they make no war.)

Hay added that the same protection should be extended to farmers' plough animals and servants. This evidently did not protect the peaceable farmer from having his barn plundered or his cattle stolen, but he should be left enough oxen for a plough-team.

Robert Henryson, writing in the late fifteenth century, and William Dunbar, in the reign of James IV, both offered standard comments on oppressive lords. Henryson's lords falsely demanded a second gersum (a gersum was a periodic lump-sum payment in addition to the annual rent), and then excessive labour services.[2] Dunbar's had 'mailis and gersomes rasit ouir hie' (rents and gersums raised too high).[3] In both cases these were presented as perennial moral failings, not social and economic trends.

The poetic voice of the moralising commoner 'Jok Upaland' ('Rural Jock') is raised in King James V's minority (1513–28). Jock complains that lawless raiders have long caused 'our' land to lie untilled; they ride through our rye and trample our wheat. If the raiders could be suppressed, sheep and cattle would be undisturbed, and 'stakis' of harvested corn 'still mycht stand'.[4] Tony Milligan has treated Jock as a 'labourer stereotype', comparable to Piers Ploughman in England. Specifically, argues Milligan, Jock's possession of livestock marks him as a member of the 'upper peasantry'.[5] Such men are worthy of respect and protection.

---

1   Gilbert Haye, *Gilbert of the Haye's Prose Manuscript (AD 1456)*, vol. 1: *The Buke of the Law of Armys or Buke of Bataillis*, ed. J. H. Stevenson (Edinburgh: STS, 1901), pp. 239–41.

2   Robert Henryson, *Poems*, ed. G. Gregory Smith (3 vols, Edinburgh: STS, 1906–14), vol. 2, pp. 203–4 ('The Wolf and the Lamb').

3   William Dunbar, *Poems*, ed. John Small (3 vols, Edinburgh: STS, 1893), vol. 2, p. 90 ('Of Discretioun in Taking').

4   *The Bannatyne Manuscript*, ed. W. Tod Ritchie (4 vols, Edinburgh: STS, 1928–34), vol. 2, pp. 247–9 ('Now is the king in tendir age').

5   Tony Milligan, '"To ding thir mony kingis doun": Jock Upaland and the Scottish Labourer Stereotype', *Scottish Literary Journal*, 25 (1998), 26–36, at pp. 30–1 and *passim*.

The Complaynt of Scotland, an extravagant political tract of about 1550, probably by Robert Wedderburn, includes a complaint by 'Laubir', the personified third estate of labourers, of extortion and poverty. The specific agricultural issues are evictions of tack-holders, rent increases, extortionate teinding and excessive unpaid labour services. Dame Scotia rejects Laubir's complaints on the ground that the peasants' malice and inconstancy give them no right to complain, but the impression remains that extortion is really happening and that poverty is really the result.[6]

Sir David Lindsay's play 'Ane Satyre of the Thrie Estaitis' (1554) contains much reforming social comment. Rents are rising, and feuing of church lands over the tenants' heads is itself leading to increased rents. Some cannot pay these rents, and are being evicted.[7] Carol Edington has argued that this was more than a literary commonplace: 'In many ways extremely conventional in its approach, *Ane Satyre* does attempt to identify some of the specific causes of poverty in Scotland with a far greater degree of precision.'[8] Lindsay's remedy for these wrongs was partly moral and religious, but he also had a social programme, involving the feuing of lands to the tenants. However, he advocated feuing only for church lands. In principle, all tenants who suffered from the oppression of lords – secular as well as ecclesiastical – could have benefited from receiving feus. Perhaps Lindsay saw feuing to the occupants primarily as an alternative to feuing to outsiders, which was indeed occurring on church lands. Or perhaps his primary interest was in church 'reform', so that his attention was drawn only to church lands and their tenants.

Debates over the Reformation occasionally mentioned agriculture. The authors of the *First Book of Discipline* (1561) enjoined the lords of council 'that ye have respect to your poore brethren, the Labourers and Manurers of the ground, who by thir cruell beastes the Papists have before been opprest, that their life to them hath been dolorous and bitter'. They added that 'some Gentlemen are now as cruell over their tenants, as ever were the Papists, requiring of them whatsoever they afore payed to the Kirk, so that the Papistical tyrannie shal onely be changed into the tyrannie of the lord and laird'. In practice they mainly envisaged the discharging of mortuary dues, though they also objected to the secularisation of teinds.[9] From the Catholic side, Ninian Winzet castigated the Protestant

6 *The Complaynt of Scotland (c.1550)*, ed. A. M. Stewart (Edinburgh: STS, 1979), pp. 97–8, 108–13.

7 Sir David Lindsay, *Works*, ed. Douglas Hamer (4 vols, Edinburgh: STS, 1931–36), vol. 2, pp. 249, 255, 267.

8 Carol Edington, *Court and Culture in Renaissance Scotland: Sir David Lindsay of the Mount* (Amherst, 1994), p. 136.

9 *The First Book of Discipline*, ed. James K. Cameron (Edinburgh, 1972), pp. 156–7.

regime for 'rigour to the pure [i.e. poor] dune on your awin landis', and for evictions arising from the feuing of church land.[10] The moralising discourse was bipartisan.

The civil wars of the 1560s and 1570s gave rise to some sharply observed moralising commentary. Sir Richard Maitland of Lethington frequently expressed himself in verse on the shortcomings of these times. His poem 'Aganis Oppressioun of the Commounis' denounced oppressive landlords at length. This paraphrase brings out Maitland's substantive points:

> It is pitiful to see how poor tenants suffer from theft and oppression, which goes unpunished. Some suffer from extortionate rents, although they used to pay rent counted in pennies. Some are evicted. Some suffer from exorbitant demands for carriage service, being forced to leave their own work undone.
>
> Some tenants of church lands suffer because their teinds have been set in tack to laymen, and their lands have been feued over their heads to laymen. These laymen demand increased payments and evict those who cannot pay. Many tenants used to control their own teinds, but now their landlord has seized the teinds and makes the tenants bring them to his own yard. The tenants dare not move the stock [the other nine-tenths of the harvested corn] from the fields until this has been done, even though their children may starve.
>
> The present extortion and taxation of the common folk is unprecedented. Some land has been abandoned because people cannot afford to work it. Some who could previously afford horses and weapons can no longer afford them. To remedy this, landlords should let their lands to tenants at moderate rents that will enable them to live well and to have weapons with which they can serve their lord and country.[11]

Some of this is broad and vague – theft, extortion, taxation. But the critique of extortionate rents and labour services seems more specific. Even more sharply focused are the critiques of feuing of church lands and of tacks of teinds. This was direct social commentary on real social change.

In 1572, in an anonymous poem of wide-ranging social commentary, 'Lady Scotland' denounced the nobles in broadly similar terms, adding that impoverished peasants were having to 'ryve out the mures' (plough up the moors) and 'the bestialls gers intak' (convert the animals' grassland

---

10 Ninian Winzet, *Certain Tractates*, ed. J. K. Hewison (2 vols, Edinburgh: STS, 1888–90), vol. 1, p. 8.

11 *The Maitland Folio Manuscript*, ed. W. A. Craigie (2 vols, Edinburgh: STS, 1919–27), vol. 1, pp. 331–2. For Maitland as a moral and political poet see Alasdair A. MacDonald, 'The Poetry of Sir Richard Maitland of Lethington', *Transactions of the East Lothian Antiquarian and Field Naturalists' Society*, 13 (1972), 7–19.

to arable), thus bringing poor-quality land under the plough.[12] This point contradicts Maitland's account of land being abandoned, and may well be a more accurate observation at a time of population growth.[13]

One thread of moralising discourse, mainly in the fifteenth and sixteenth centuries, concerned the marketing of agricultural produce. The national and urban authorities sought to enforce open market trading, and to punish forestallers (those who bought goods before they came to market) and regraters (those who resold goods thus bought). Such trading was regarded as leading to immoral profiteering. The government in December 1551 condemned 'the malt men and uthiris regratouris of malt and bere that will nocht suffer the samin to cum to the mercat to be sauld indifferentlie [i.e. freely] to our soverane ladyis liegis', and complained that the lieges were 'hevile oppressit'.[14] Farmers themselves were never blamed for high prices, nor accused of profiteering.

There is little record of moralising preachers addressing farmers directly as farmers – with the exception of the radical covenanters of the Restoration period, who cultivated a popular audience. Michael Bruce (1635–93) reproved a West Calder congregation as follows:

> In the morning the barn calls for you; the plough calls for you; the harrows calls for you; various bargains call for you. The markets too say, make haste. Ye are deafened with the noise of these calls; so that ye never hear nor remember the calls that God's command hath given.[15]

But similar remarks from establishment ministers were vanishingly rare. Scottish Protestant ministers were clear on the religious importance of working in one's secular 'calling', but this was more often presented as commercial than as agricultural.[16]

* * *

12 James Cranstoun (ed.), *Satirical Poems of the Time of the Reformation* (2 vols, Edinburgh: STS, 1891–93), vol. 1, pp. 234–5 (The Lament of Lady Scotland, by 'P. R.', lines 243–74).

13 Ian D. Whyte, *Scotland before the Industrial Revolution: An Economic and Social History c.1050–c.1750* (Harlow, 1995), pp. 132–5.

14 *Acts of the Lords of Council in Public Affairs 1501–1554*, ed. Robert Kerr Hannay (Edinburgh, 1932), p. 612.

15 *A Collection of Lectures and Sermons: Preached upon Several Subjects, Mostly in the Time of the Persecution* (Kilmarnock, 1809), p. 233. I am grateful to Dr Michelle Brock for this reference and for a helpful discussion of the subject.

16 Gordon Marshall, *Presbyteries and Profits: Calvinism and the Development of Capitalism in Scotland 1560–1707* (Oxford, 1981), pp. 39–112. Late medieval English sermons seem to have used more farming metaphors: Philip Slavin, 'The Preacher in the Rye: Allegory and Reality of Rural Life in Middle English Sermons', in Tristan Sharp (ed.), *From Learning to Love: Schools, Law, and Pastoral Care in the Middle Ages* (Toronto, 2017), pp. 492–514.

Religious messages were particularly common in my next discourse of agriculture: the metaphorical discourse. Preachers and religious writers used a wide variety of metaphors and similes, and readily drew on agriculture as a source of them – though these did not necessarily derive from specifically Scottish agricultural practices. The Bible itself contained metaphorical threshing floors, winepresses and so on.

John Colville in 1602 drew on grain processing in an extended metaphor, from the harvested sheaves in the barn through to threshing, winnowing and the gathering of grain. The church, he wrote, seems 'bot as a barn or stak vharin doth appear no thing outvardly bot caf and stra' (chaff and straw), but 'being threschit, schakin and riddillit befor the vynd of treu tryall', it would produce 'a heap of Good corn'. Colville could find this metaphor in the Bible, however, without needing to observe Scottish farming. He continued with a metaphor from vines and grapes.[17]

One of the preacher's most important metaphorical uses of agriculture was to warn of God's wrath. This wrath was often expressed in the form of threatened or actual famine. William Adair, minister of Ayr in 1647, warned that 'for the wickednes of a people a fruitfull land is turned into barrennes, the heavens gloomes and utters by storms displeasure'.[18]

Fables are metaphorical. Robert Henryson's fables included a poetic description of spring farm work that viewed the key task of ploughing within a broader context of building of dykes, sowing seeds and harrowing:

> Mouing thus gait, grit mirth I tuik in mynd,
> Of lawboraris to se the besines,
> Sum makand dyke, and sum the pleuch can wynd,
> Sum sawand seidis fast frome place to place,
> The harrowis hoppand in the saweris trace:
> It wes grit joy to him that luifit corne,
> To se thame labour, baith at evin and morne.[19]

(As I walked in my path, I had great mirth in my mind / to see the busy work of labourers, / some making dykes and some ploughing, / some sowing seeds from place to place, / the harrows trundling after the sowers: / It was great joy to anyone who loved corn, / to see them labour both in the evening and in the morning.)

17 John Colville, *The Paraenese of Admonition of Io. Coluille* (Paris, 1602), pp. 28–9. The threshing metaphor is common in the Bible, e.g. Matthew 3:12.

18 NRS, Ayr Kirk Session minutes, 1646–53, CH2/751/3/1, fol. 41r. I am grateful to Dr Michelle Brock for this reference.

19 Henryson, *Poems*, vol. 2, p. 129 ('The Swallow and the other Birds', lines 1713–19).

The point of the fable was that the labourer was growing hemp and lint, which, the swallow correctly predicted, he would use to make nets to catch the birds.

John Stewart of Baldynneis (*c.*1545–*c.*1605) offered a simile from the mill-weir that turned a waterwheel:

> As from mylfa suift vater doune dois rout;
> To break it self And quhirle the quheill about.[20]

(As water rushes down from a mill-weir, / To break itself, and whirl the wheel around.)

John Welsh (1568/69–1622), minister of Ayr, cited the innovative practice of burning lime for fertiliser: 'Repentance is likened to an Iron-mill that breaks the Free-stones whereof the Lime is made, being burnt in the Kiln'.[21]

Seventeenth-century European poets began to associate the harvest with death and destruction.[22] We find this theme in Scotland. William Fowler (1560/61–1612) imagined that 'Dethe ... with his heuk' would 'draw on my fatal houer'.[23] William Birnie in 1606 saw death as 'the Lords harvest' which would be 'glaned in, by his angel with the sharpe sicle'.[24] This was arguably an inept metaphor, since real gleaners did not use sickles. Samuel Rutherford in 1631 imagined the Second Coming as a harvest: 'the Judge's feet are then before the door, and He must be in heaven giving order to the angels to make themselves ready, and prepare their hooks and sickles for that great harvest'.[25] The battle-field of Pitreavie, in 1651, was said to resemble 'a hairst field of stooks of corpses'.[26]

Proverbs are often metaphorical, and their choice of metaphor can be revealing. Although proverbs were popular and colloquial in form, the elite used them as well as the common folk.[27] The following study surveys

---

20 John Stewart of Baldynneis, *Poems*, ed. Thomas Crockett (Edinburgh: STS, 1913), p. 226 ('Ane schersing out of trew felicitie', lines 103–4).

21 John Welsh, *Forty Eight Select Sermons* (Edinburgh, 1744), p. 94.

22 Liana Vardi, 'Imagining the Harvest in Early Modern Europe', *American Historical Review*, 101 (1996), 1357–97, at pp. 1381–3.

23 William Fowler, *Works*, ed. Henry W. Meikle, James Craigie and J. Purves (3 vols, Edinburgh: STS, 1914–40), vol. 1, p. 225 ('Bright schyning sun and faire reflexing light', lines 10–12).

24 William Birnie, *The Blame of Kirk-Buriall* (Edinburgh, 1606), ch. 3 (unpaginated).

25 Samuel Rutherford, *Letters*, ed. Andrew A. Bonar (Edinburgh, 1891), p. 63.

26 Ebenezer Henderson, *The Annals of Dunfermline and Vicinity, AD 1069–1878* (Glasgow, 1879), p. 325.

27 Adam Fox, *Oral and Literate Culture in England 1500–1700* (Oxford, 2000), pp. 113–33.

the seventeenth-century Fergusson collection of proverbs.[28] A few were explicitly and solely metaphorical, such as 'When the tod preiches bewar of the hens' (when the fox preaches, watch out for the hens; no. 1445). Here the choice of metaphor illustrates people's understanding of the dangers posed to poultry by cunning predators. A few proverbs may also have encapsulated direct farming advice, such as 'Saw thinne and maw thinne' (sow thin and reap thin; no. 1183), though most proverbs were at least partly or even mainly metaphorical.

Overall, in the Fergusson collection, there are something over fifty proverbs alluding to agriculture (from a total of over 1,600). Taking arable farming first, there are six proverbs on ploughing (nos. 475, 510, 1119, 1130, 1480, 1615), one on sowing (1183), one on harrowing (1615), three on crops growing in the fields (1184, 1265, 1342), three on harvesting (37, 69, 1621), seven on grain processing (212, 241, 1026, 1033, 1120, 1231, 1519) and three on vegetables (608, 796, 1342). On pastoral farming, there are seven on cattle (71, 89, 231, 523, 1229, 1324, 1409), six on sheep (25, 62, 211, 788, 1435, 1595), one on goats (1436), five on pigs (48, 53, 75, 340, 345), seven on poultry (65, 72, 830, 1356, 1357, 1390, 1445), and three on herding and predators (821, 1435, 1445). There are two on dykes (796, 1176), one on mowing of meadows (1006) and, finally, two on the soil itself: 'Dirt pairts companie' (soil separates companions) (346) and 'Dirt bodds luck' (soil promises good luck) (367). The proverbial view of agriculture imagined a wider variety of activities than the more literary approaches to it.

* * *

I use the term 'mystical discourse' to categorise literary responses to the environment. This could be the cultivated landscape with its fields and farm animals, and I will focus on that in what follows. But the mystical discourse also embraced wild nature. T. C. Smout has pointed out that, although visitors to northern Britain hated mountains, the local inhabitants accepted and even enjoyed them.[29] And the mystical discourse could see the environment, not as the site of agricultural labour, but as God's creation.

Several fifteenth- and sixteenth-century chroniclers penned idealised literary descriptions of Scotland, and these usually mentioned agriculture. Andrew of Wyntoun's description of 'Bretayne' in the 1420s, in which he probably had Scotland mainly in mind, began with its many flowers and its wholesome air. There was agricultural productivity: plenteous

---

28 *Fergusson's Scottish Proverbs*, ed. Erskine Beveridge (Edinburgh: STS, 1924); the sample uses proverbs from the 'manuscript' version.

29 T. C. Smout, *Nature Contested: Environmental History in Scotland and Northern England since 1600* (Edinburgh, 2000), pp. 12–17.

peas, oats, bere (barley) and wheat, and fruit on trees. The cattle had so much grass in their pastures that they risked overeating. There were also fish in the 'flwde' (seas or rivers), and 'welth' in the wild wood; there were blackbirds and thrushes, and opportunities for hunting and hawking. There was 'habowndance' of fish (again), and of 'nedfulle thyng to mannys substance' (needful things for human subsistence).[30] Hector Boece's description of Scotland was similar, if more elaborate, in the 1520s. He fancifully mentioned a place in Atholl where the land was 'sa plentuus' (so fertile) that if it was well manured it would grow bere without any seeds. In another place in Atholl, however, when wheat was sown, it degenerated and turned into rye.[31] Agriculture was worth mentioning if it was anomalous.

Gavin Douglas's nature prologues to his *Eneados* translation (1513) blend Scottish and classical environments. Agricultural work appears most clearly in winter, when farmers have to care for their animals:

> Puyr lauboraris and bissy husband men
> Went wait and wery draglit in the fen.
> The silly scheip and thar litil hyrd gromys
> Lurkis undre le of bankis, woddis and bromys;
> And other dantit grettar bestiall,
> Within thair stabillis sesyt into stall,
> Sik as mulis, horssis, oxin and ky,
> Fed tuskyt barys and fat swyne in sty,
> Sustenyt war by mannys governance
> On hervest and on symmeris purvyance.[32]

(Poor labourers and busy husbandmen / went wet and weary, draggled in the fen. / The tender sheep and their little herdsmen / shelter under the lee of banks, woods and bushes; / and other tame, large animals, / settled into their stalls in the stable, / such as mules, horses, oxen and cows, / fed tusked boars and fat pigs in sty, / were sustained by human agency / on harvest and summer's advance provision.)

However, in May, Douglas attributes the growth of crops, not to farmers, but to 'Dame Ceres' (goddess of agriculture) and 'proud Pryapus' (god of gardens). He describes 'wyne grapis' which 'Endlang the treilyeis dyd

---

30 P. Hume Brown (ed.), *Scotland before 1700 from Contemporary Documents* (Edinburgh, 1893), pp. 16–17. This work conveniently collects several descriptions.
31 Hume Brown (ed.), *Scotland before 1700*, p. 82.
32 Gavin Douglas, *Virgil's Aeneid Translated into Scottish Verse*, ed. David F. C. Coldwell (4 vols, Edinburgh: STS, 1957–64), vol. 3, p. 63 (Prologue to book 7, lines 75–84).

on twystis hing' (all along the trellis hung on branches).[33] The classical theme also links Douglas to the 'Renaissance discourse', to be discussed in a moment.

Alexander Hume's poem 'Of the Day Estivall' (The Summer's Day) (1599) surveys the whole creation in one summer's day, full of 'naturalistic detail'.[34] 'The dew upon the tender crops' is visible, but there is little work to do among the growing crops at this season. The 'carefull husbandman' visits his crops, described as 'cornes, and vines'. The 'pastor' (herdsman) feeds his sheep and his 'rowtting kie' (bellowing cattle). In the midday heat, the sheep seek the shade of their sheepfold, and the cattle run to the river to cool down. At the end of the day the herdsmen drive the sheep and cattle home 'With pipe and lilting horne'. Hume's vision seems an idealised southern European one. Even on a summer's day, the three-hour siesta that his labourers are forced to take by the heat seems unusual. And his agricultural passages are set within a much broader view of the earth, with sky, air and encircling horizon, with wild animals and birds, bees, flowers and trees, and ships upon the sea.

The Bible provided models for a mystical discourse of agriculture. Psalm 104, a celebration of the natural world as God's creation, declared that 'He causeth the grass to grow for the cattle, and herb for the service of man: that he may bring forth food out of the earth', and 'Man goeth forth unto his work and to his labour until the evening'.[35] Several poets paraphrased this. However, for James VI in 1584, and Sir William Mure of Rowallan in 1639, the only 'work' to produce the crops was God's work; man's work was lost to sight.[36] Sir George Mackenzie of Rosehaugh did notice in the 1660s that 'Men take the Fields' and that 'Some plow the Ground'.[37] Archibald Pitcairne, in 1700, wrote: 'The eager Earth ... furnishes rich grain dedicated to the herd, rich grass, the reward of human labour.'[38] On the whole, though, writers mystically contemplating the bounty of the earth tend to focus on the land itself – the

33 Douglas, *Virgil's Aeneid*, vol. 4, p. 69 (Prologue to book 12, lines 74–81, 99–100).

34 Alexander Hume, *Poems*, ed. Alexander Lawson (Edinburgh: STS, 1902), pp. 25–33; cf. Gerard Carruthers, 'Form and Substance in the Poetry of the Castalian "Band"', *Scottish Literary Journal*, 26 (1999), 7–17, at p. 14.

35 Psalm 104, verses 14, 23 (Authorised Version).

36 James VI, *Poems*, ed. James Craigie (2 vols, Edinburgh: STS, 1955–58), vol. 1, pp. 86–7 (The ciiii psalme, lines 33–40); Sir William Mure of Rowallan, *Works*, ed. William Tough (2 vols, Edinburgh: STS, 1898), vol. 2, p. 153 (Psalm 104, stanzas 13–14).

37 Sir George Mackenzie of Rosehaugh, *Works* (2 vols, Edinburgh, 1716–22), vol. 1, pp. 16–20.

38 Archibald Pitcairne, *The Latin Poems*, ed. and trans. John and Winifred MacQueen (Assen, 2009), pp. 122–3 (poem no. 20).

environment – rather than on human activity. They do not show us farmers cultivating the land and gathering crops; rather, the land *itself* produces grain, cattle, sheep, cheese or whatever.

* * *

The Renaissance tended to value the city over the countryside. The city represented civilisation (literally so, indeed), while the countryside was boorish and unsophisticated.[39] The Renaissance also valued 'Arcadian' and 'pastoral' ideals, abstracted from the real countryside and standing in a complex relationship to it. There are Renaissance discourses of agriculture – and they are finely-wrought.

When Allan Ramsay published his celebrated edition of older Scottish poetry in 1724, he stressed the fidelity of 'these good old Bards' to local conditions, contrasting this with his contemporaries' preference for Greek and Italian models. 'Their Images are native, and their Landskips [i.e. landscapes] domestick, copied from those Fields and Meadows we every Day behold', Ramsay wrote.[40] However, this was almost wholly misleading. It is true that the first literary and poetic responses to specific places arise in the sixteenth century. Before then, imaginative literature tended to be set in imagined places.[41] But the 'good old Bards' of the fifteenth and sixteenth centuries were just as much influenced by Virgil and Horace as those of the eighteenth century. They created pleasant meads and fresh Auroras, connected only indirectly to the scenery of Scotland. Throughout our period, the imagined landscape of Greece and Italy merges with the real landscape of Scotland in cultural expression, with a resulting diffuseness in the focus on specific agricultural tasks.

In 1591, James VI's translation of Du Bartas' 'The Furies' included some lines on weeds in crops. The Earth, through hatred of Vulcan, repays us 'for the corne, that we do sow' with thistles and 'vaprous Darnell'. James then launches into a broad and inclusive list of weeds and hostile plants, not Scottish plants in particular, but evocative of direct experience of at least some of them.[42] The point, though, is the mythological setting and its story.

Sir George Mackenzie's prose romance *Aretina* (1660) was classical rather than pastoral in structure, but contained a few agricultural

---

39 Keith Thomas, *Man and the Natural World: Changing Attitudes in England 1500–1800* (Harmondsworth, 1983), p. 243.

40 Allan Ramsay (ed.), *The Ever Green, being a Collection of Scots Poems, Wrote by the Ingenious before 1600*, vol. 1 (1724; Edinburgh: Donaldson, 1761), pp. vii–viii.

41 A. A. MacDonald, 'The Sense of Place in Early Scottish Verse: Rhetoric and Reality', *English Studies*, 72 (1991), 12–27.

42 James VI, *Poems*, vol. 1, p. 128 (The Furies, lines 273–80).

comments.[43] There were neostoic platitudes, such as 'it were safer being a shepherd than a King'.[44] One of Mackenzie's inset tales encapsulated the pastoral debate between country and city. It began when 'A young Country Gentleman, accustomed at home to whistle following the plough, to domineere amongst a great many Countrey Clowns, and to feed a kennel of dogs, was by his friends brought into the City to court a young Citizen'. He told this woman of the pastoral delights of his father's house: 'what choice fields for hunting, and what excellent pasturages for herding, were there'. However, she replied that

> society is preferable to all these; for, when ye come to the City, ye acknowledge it is to better your spirits; and when we go to the Country, our end is only to refresh our bodies, So that the Country may be thought as justly to cede to the City, as the soul is preferable to the body.[45]

Thus Mackenzie presented the country's pursuits as mainly, but not entirely, agricultural: it had ploughing, herding and hunting. Strikingly, the young gentleman followed the plough himself. But the woman, representing the city, won the debate.

Another of Mackenzie's tales described the slaughter of a farm animal with unusual directness. A man was offered a job as a military officer, but his wife warned him 'that his complexion was so sweet, that he would not abide to stand where blood was shed. Notwithstanding whereof, he entreated her to let him see a calf killed'. She suggested that a chicken would be better –

> yet, to satisfie his desire, he behoved to see a calf killed: so the poor beast (I mean the calf) was brought to the utter court, where the Gentleman stood beholding it, and there seeing the knife in its throat, and hearing the poor beast bellow so sadly, the compassionate Gentleman, seemed to die for comradship with it.[46]

Here compassion is basically a virtue, though taken too far; the gentleman is weak but not entirely reprehensible. The 'poor beast' is genuinely seen to suffer.

The Renaissance made much use of animal symbolism. For instance, pigs symbolised cooperation and amiability, in contrast with dogs, which stood for disorder, individualism and competition.[47] An extensive

---

43 M. R. G. Spiller, 'The First Scots Novel: Sir George Mackenzie's *Aretina* (1660)', *Scottish Literary Journal Supplement*, 11 (1979), 1–20, at p. 8.
44 [George Mackenzie,] *Aretina; or, The Serious Romance* (Edinburgh, 1660), p. 202.
45 [Mackenzie,] *Aretina*, pp. 208–9, 212.
46 [Mackenzie,] *Aretina*, pp. 287–8.
47 Alasdair A. MacDonald, 'William Dunbar and *Colkelbie's Sow*: Dogs and Swine', *Notes and Queries*, 61 (2014), 481–2.

FIGURE 1.1. 'This idealised farming landscape shows open fields empty of workers.
Long, narrow cultivation ridges are prominent. Nothing is growing in the fields,
so perhaps the season is late autumn, after the harvest.
Source: 'The Prospect of the Town of Haddingtown', from John Slezer, *Theatrum Scotiae*
(1693). Image reproduced by the kind permission of the National Library of Scotland.

'bestiary' of about sixty animals was painted on the ceiling at Earlshall,
Fife, in 1620. It included a few farm animals like the cow, but mainly
depicted wild, exotic and mythological beasts.[48]

The painted panels in the Skelmorlie Aisle, Largs, executed in 1638,
include a partly agricultural 'Autumn' scene. There is a sunlit field of ripe
corn with a man who may be a harvester, while a team of four oxen may
be drawing a sledge to carry away the crop. In the centre, though, is a
winepress, copied from a Dutch engraving.[49]

John Slezer's engravings, published in the *Theatrum Scotiae* of 1693,
offer many views of the Scottish countryside as an audience may
have wished to see it. Their 'prospects' of towns or notable buildings
have a distant viewpoint that sets the central urban subject in a rural
context.[50] The cultivated land in Slezer's 'prospects' typically consists
of large fields of prominent rig-and-furrow.[51] The rigs curve gently. The
field itself is slightly convex, suggesting drainage channels round its edge
and producing an undulating effect that may have been partly stylised.
The rigs are usually bare, as they would be in late autumn and winter,
but the trees all have leaves and there is never snow. There are hardly any
actual workers in Slezer's fields. The few working people include carters,

48 Michael Bath, *Renaissance Decorative Painting in Scotland* (Edinburgh, 2003),
    pp. 147–67.
49 Bath, *Renaissance Decorative Painting*, p. 139.
50 The engravings and some of the supporting drawings are reproduced and
    discussed in Keith Cavers, *A Vision of Scotland: The Nation Observed by John
    Slezer, 1671 to 1717* (n.p.: HMSO and National Library of Scotland, 1993). The
    engravings have also been digitised at http://digital.nls.uk/slezer/.
51 Cavers, *A Vision of Scotland*, pp. 18–19 (Edinburgh from the Dean), 38
    (Haddington).

FIGURE 1.2. This picture shows pasture land. Five cows and a horse are attended by a herdsman with a staff. The thatched farmhouse in the foreground is of a prosperous type, with two chimneys and two windows. The building behind it also has a chimney, so it may be another farmhouse rather than an outbuilding. *Source*: 'The Prospect of Falkland from the East', from John Slezer, *Theatrum Scotiae* (1693). Image reproduced by the kind permission of the National Library of Scotland.

packmen or (in coastal and river scenes) boatmen; they thread their way between the fields rather than engaging directly in agricultural labour. The stooks of grain near Dunblane stand in a field empty of workers, like other seventeenth-century harvest scenes discussed by Liana Vardi.[52] Even more strikingly, Slezer depicts no scenes of ploughing, sowing or harrowing. These are farming landscapes, but they are not active, working landscapes.[53]

* * *

The literate elite gave most concentrated cultural attention to the lives and activities of the lower classes when they were mocking them. This leads us on to the 'humorous discourse' of agriculture. Peasants were mainly mocked when engaged in exuberant festivity or drunken brawls, but such mockery occasionally encompassed agricultural work. In 'Sym and his bruder' (*c.*1530), festivity leads the 'nolthird' (cattle herdsman) to neglect his duties, whereupon 'the nolt begowth till scatter' (the cattle began to scatter) and 'the ky ran startling to the corne' (the cows ran wildly to the corn).[54]

---

52 Cavers, *A Vision of Scotland*, p. 42; Vardi, 'Imagining the Harvest', pp. 1373–9.
53 The 'prospect' views of English fields in the early eighteenth century, similarly, were mostly static and empty of workers: Ian Waites, *Common Land in English Painting 1700–1850* (Cambridge, 2012), pp. 13–36.
54 Allan H. MacLaine (ed.), *The Christis Kirk Tradition: Scots Poems of Folk Festivity* (Glasgow: Association for Scottish Literary Studies, 1996), p. 27 ('Sym and his bruder', lines 122, 146–7).

A sixteenth-century 'Plough-Song' offers a humorous glimpse of attitudes to ploughing, including some striking practical details that Alexander Fenton has analysed. This is an art song, sung in three parts, not a folk song.[55] Its message is inconsequential enough. The singer, supposedly a ploughman, offers himself for hire to 'my Lord', whose plough has been idle because of a lazy ox. The ploughman urges the lord to assemble the servants, 'the hyndis all' – two dozen names are given. The ploughman promises to bring his own 'fair fresh ox' to replace the old one, the carcass of which he will receive as his fee. He also promises to bring 'all that belongs to the pleugh', launching into a detailed list of twenty-three components of the plough and accompanying equipment. He then starts ploughing, giving the calls with which the ploughman directed the oxen, and naming several of the oxen themselves. Finally he boasts that his plough-team of eight oxen is the finest in Scotland.

This tale, precisely because of its inconsequential message, can be taken as containing some credibly direct observations. Professor Fenton has shown that its list of plough components can be corroborated from other sources. The farm itself is evidently the lord's mains farm, worked directly with hired labour rather than being leased to a tenant. The list of 'hyndis all' includes a mower and a thresher. Most of the workers' names are humorous diminutives like 'Higgin and Habken', and few have surnames; these are not people worth taking seriously. Finally, the workers are said to have 'domination and pastorie of your common' – grazing rights on the common land.

There is less humorous material on harvesting than on ploughing, but there is an indication that harvesters eating meals in the open air were thought disorderly and irreverent. The Catholic controversialist John Hamilton, in 1581, likened 'Calvinian' worshippers to a harvesters' gathering: 'They behave thame selfis ressaving that pretended sacrament, as scheraris [shearers, i.e. harvesters] ressaving thair denner on the harvest feild.'[56]

We find a detailed account of rural women's work in 'The Wyf of Auchtirmwchty', a comic poem of gender trouble in the Bannatyne Manuscript (1568).[57] The husbandman finishes ploughing at the end of a

---

55   Alexander Fenton, 'The Plough-Song: A Scottish Source for Medieval Plough History', *Tools and Tillage*, 1:3 (1970), 175–91. This contains a parallel edition of the two extant texts.

56   John Hamilton, *Ane Catholik and Facile Traictise* (Paris, 1581), fol. 84r.

57   *The Bannatyne Manuscript*, vol. 2, pp. 320–4. For comparative discussion see A. A. MacDonald, 'The Wife of Auchtermuchty and Her Dutch Cousin', in Jan Frans van Dijkhuizen *et al.* (eds), *Living in Posterity: Essays in Honour of Bart Westerweel* (Hilversum, 2004), pp. 177–83 (I am grateful to Professor MacDonald for this reference and for helpful guidance). For a seventeenth-century English version see Christopher Marsh, '*The Woman to the Plow, and the Man to the Hen-Roost*: Wives, Husbands and Best-Selling Ballads in

windy, wet day, looses the plough 'at the landis end' (the end of a rig) and wearily drives his oxen home. Encountering his wife sitting comfortably by the fire 'with ane fat sowp' (mouthful), he proposes that tomorrow she will take over the ploughing and he will be 'hussy' (housewife). She agrees, instructing him on how to look after 'all the houss baith in and owt', and underlining the financial importance of this work in paying their rent: 'we haif ane deir ferme on our heid'. Next morning she takes a 'gadstaff' (goad) and 'disiuwne' (food for a midday meal), looses eight or nine oxen, and goes off to plough.

The husband now tries to follow his wife's instructions. He calls the seven goslings to feed, but the 'gredy gled' (a kite) takes five of them. While chasing the kite, he neglects the calves, which break loose and suck milk from their mothers. He sits down to spin, but leans too near the fire. He struggles with the butter churn, but a sow eats the contents. The clumsy blow that he aims at the sow kills the two remaining goslings. He puts kindling in the kiln, but it blazes up too quickly. Attending too late to the children, he finds that they have fouled their sheets; taking the sheets to wash, he lets them drift away down the burn. His wife meanwhile has 'stowtly steird the stottis about' (boldly driven the bullocks around), having had a much more successful day than her husband. He vows to return to his plough and to trouble his wife no more.

This tale is not entirely realistic, even discounting the comic role-reversal. We may wonder, for instance, whether there would have been goslings and weaned calves during the early spring ploughing season. Still, the poem contains some sharply-observed details of daily life. More broadly, it indicates the woman's own awareness of the financial value of a wide range of her tasks, notably dairying, poultry-keeping, grain processing and (beyond agriculture) spinning of thread.

Patrick Anderson's comic play *The Copie of a Barons Court*, probably written in the 1620s, offers a lively view of landlord–tenant relations. As a comedy it mocks everyone, but the rulers are mocked more than the tenants. The laird is an incompetent spendthrift; the lady's pride of pedigree prevents her son making a profitable marriage, and she borrows from a tenant behind the laird's back; the chamberlain is lazy and bickers with the bailie; the bailie is out of his depth in dealing with the tenants; the clerk is the only one who understands, but is not in a position to solve the problems. On the tenants' side, their worst fault is their low cunning in outwitting the frustrated bailie. They are seen to suffer genuine hardship and to face demands for high rents that they have difficulty affording.[58]

Seventeenth-Century England', *Transactions of the Royal Historical Society*, 6th ser., 28 (2018), 65–88, at pp. 83–5.

58 Patrick Anderson, *The Copie of a Barons Court: newly translated by whats-you-call-him, clerk to the same* ('Helicon' [Edinburgh?], 1680).

Before parting with the humorous discourse, it is worth returning briefly to proverbs. Some of the proverbs discussed earlier display a dry or grim humour, such as 'He that lippens to bone plews his land will ly ley' (He that trusts to borrow ploughs, his land will lie unploughed; no. 475) or 'Pryd & plew irones wold hav much uphold' (Pride and plough irons need much maintenance; no. 1130). Proverbs do not, however, mock the common people.

* * *

Economic discourse, the final discourse to be discussed here, is distinguished by the idea of economic choices affecting material prosperity. Many of the writers categorised here as 'economic' were also moral and perhaps Renaissance too, but they place the emphasis less on complaint and more on rationally pointing out the economic advantages of certain choices. Whether these choices were realistic is another matter.

There are economic threads woven into the sixteenth- and seventeenth-century genre of chorographical writing.[59] Chorography aimed to describe a region or nation in physical and human terms: its landscape, people, settlement patterns, culture, history and antiquities. This often entailed discussion of the rural economy and the work of agricultural production. In Donald Monro's meticulous catalogue of 251 western islands, written in about 1549, some of the most common phrases inform the reader whether a given island is 'fertile and fruitful', or 'inhabite and manurit'.[60] A description of the Orkney Islands from about 1592 often commented on agriculture, including a final note 'Of the Husbandrie used by the Orchadians', with sharply-observed detail on ploughing methods.[61]

John Leslie in 1578 envisaged possible agricultural improvement in Ayrshire, if the 'housbandmen' would choose to grow wheat:

> The ground almaist is alyke plentifulle in all thir places: the pastorall is plesand, as afor I spak, of quhilke we have cheis nane fyner, and buttir in gret quantitie; Bie skepis lykwyse nocht few. Thair is beir and aits meikle bettir and meikle mair copious, than with uthires

---

59 For a survey see Roger A. Mason, 'From Buchanan to Blaeu: The Politics of Scottish Chorography 1582–1654', in Caroline Erskine and Roger A. Mason (eds), *George Buchanan: Political Thought in Early Modern Britain and Europe* (Farnham, 2012), pp. 13–47.

60 Donald Monro, *A Description of the Occidental i.e. Western Islands of Scotland*, ed. R. W. Munro, appended to Martin Martin, *A Description of the Western Islands of Scotland, circa 1695*, ed. Charles W. J. Withers (Edinburgh, 1999), p. 295.

61 Margaret Hunter, 'Jo: Ben's Description of Orkney', and James M. Irvine, 'Jo: Ben Revisited', *New Orkney Antiquarian Journal*, 6 (2012), 34–47, 48–58; see particularly pp. 46–7.

natiouns; quheit lesse; It walde nochtwithstanding grow in mony places abundantlie, gif the housbandmen could persuade it to be to thair proffite.[62]

(The ground is almost equally plentiful in all these places: the pasture is pleasant, as I said before, from which we have cheese, none finer, and butter in great quantity; beehives likewise not a few. There is bere [i.e. barley] and oats, much better and in larger quantity than in other nations; wheat less; it would nevertheless grow in many places abundantly, if the farmers could be persuaded that it would profit them.)

Timothy Pont's famous maps were made in the 1580s and 1590s. Pont's primary interest was in human settlement rather than in physical geography. He showed some interest in agriculture, often depicting individual farming settlements, though he was more systematic in depicting towns and lairds' houses. He depicted some mills, placing them accurately.[63] He also recorded woodlands with care.[64] Arable and pasture land were not noted as such, but Pont's cartography had definite economic aspects.

The royalist writer Peter Hay, in 1627, offered a political and economic analysis of landlord–tenant relations, looking back to the sixteenth-century secularisation of church land. Despite the old abbots' misdeeds, they had been 'bountifull, and indulgent to their poore Tennantes'. The tenants were now oppressed by the heavy demands of the new secular landlords and their heritable courts. Lords commuted the teinds, previously valued in the fields, into fixed but higher payments. They demanded unreasonable carriage services. Hay's proposed solution, in line with current government policy, was to abolish heritable jurisdictions.[65]

The travel writer William Lithgow published a long poem of welcome to Charles I when the king visited Scotland in 1633. In it, a personified Scotland welcomed the king and commented extravagantly on various aspects of social and economic policy.[66] Lithgow, beginning with a

---

62 Hume Brown (ed.), *Scotland before 1700*, p. 118.

63 Kate Buchanan, 'Wheels and Creels: The Physical Representation of Right to Milling and Fishing in Sixteenth-Century Angus, Scotland', in Kate Buchanan and Lucinda H. S. Dean (eds), *Medieval and Early Modern Representations of Authority in Scotland and the British Isles* (Abingdon, 2016), pp. 55–67, at pp. 61–2.

64 T. C. Smout, 'Woodland in the Maps of Pont', in Ian C. Cunningham (ed.), *The Nation Survey'd: Essays on Late Sixteenth-Century Scotland as Depicted by Timothy Pont* (East Linton, 2001), pp. 77–92.

65 Peter Hay, *An Advertisement to the Subjects of Scotland* (Aberdeen, 1627), pp. 82–3.

66 William Lithgow, *Scotlands Welcome to her Native Sonne, and Soveraigne Lord, King Charles* (Edinburgh, 1633), sigs. B2–C2.

phrase that echoed Lindsay a century earlier, described the countryside in bleak terms:

> Ah! what makes now, my *Countrey* looke so bare?
> Thus voyd of planting, *Woods* and, *Forrests* fayre:
> *Hedges*, and *Ditches*, *Parks*, and closed grounds,
> *Trees*, *Strips*, and *Shaws* in many fertile bounds.

Thus 'planting' would create woods, enclosed fields with hedges, and 'parks' – the latter perhaps for hunting rather than agriculture. This was being hindered because landlords let their lands to tenants from year to year, and often changed the tenancies, granting the tenancy to the highest bidder, so that farmers had no security to make improvements –

> And so the *Peasants*, can not set nor plant
> *Woods*, *Trees*, and *Orchards*, which my *Valleyes* want.

Lithgow's solution was longer leases, either for a number of years or for a number of lives – 'leasses let at large, for yeares or lyves'. He imagined prosperous farmers working round the clock to bring in bountiful harvests:

> So may they sheare, and lead, and stakke their *Corne*,
> At Mid-night, Midday, afternoone, or Morne,
> Which shall bee their advantage and my gayne,
> When *Barnes*, and *Yards*, are fill'd with tymely grayne.

This may be fanciful, but the final line evokes one of the realities of harvest: there would initially be too many sheaves for the barn, and stacks would be constructed in the stack yard outside until some could be threshed.

Discussion of economic discourse may conclude with a few comments on how it merges with, or develops into, a discourse of 'Improvement'. Scotland produced little or no domestic literature of agrarian improvement in the sixteenth and early seventeenth centuries. England, by contrast, had a vogue for improvement, with Thomas Tusser, Gervase Markham and numerous other agrarian authors being widely read and frequently reprinted.[67] The Scots did at least notice this vogue; a Scottish edition of Tusser was issued in 1599.[68] Further research may indicate

---

67 Joan Thirsk, 'Making a Fresh Start: Sixteenth-Century Agriculture and the Classical Inspiration', and Andrew McRae, 'Husbandry Manuals and the Language of Agrarian Improvement', in Michael Leslie and Timothy Raylor (eds), *Culture and Cultivation in Early Modern England: Writing and the Land* (Leicester, 1992), pp. 15–34, 35–62.

68 Thomas Tusser, *Five Hundreth Pointes of Good Husbandrie* (Edinburgh: Robert Waldegrave, 1599; STC 24386). Tusser's twenty-three English editions made his book 'one of the fifteen most popular books in Elizabethan England': McRae, 'Husbandry Manuals', p. 45.

how far other English agricultural books, too, were read in Scotland. It should be noted that English manuals of agrarian improvement in the sixteenth and early seventeenth centuries usually assumed that the landlord was cultivating his demesne through direct management. They had little to say about dealings with tenants.[69]

Ideas of improvement became more prominent when Sir Robert Sibbald was appointed Geographer Royal in 1682. He circulated a questionnaire in that year, addressing numerous questions to members of local elites. Agriculture was only a subsidiary interest, though 'the chief products' of the locality were asked about. Nobles were asked 'What Forrests, Woods, Parks, Loughs, Rivers, Mines, and Quarries they have? What Fishing? &c.' – which seems almost deliberately to ignore the mainstream agricultural business of nobles' estates.[70] Sibbald's correspondents took a scientific view of the landscape, but it was a more static view than it would later become. Only later in the eighteenth century did commentators routinely appraise landscapes in terms of their potential for 'improvement'.[71] Even in England, a *literary* engagement with an economic attitude to agriculture began only in the 1720s with Defoe's *Tour of England and Wales*, according to Raymond Williams.[72]

* * *

A conclusion to this chapter may begin by glancing at some other possible discourses of agriculture. The six discourses discussed above encompass the main ways in which cultural meanings of agriculture were articulated, but they were not the only ones.

There could, for instance, be a *'legal discourse'*. Lawyers sometimes included in their treatises passages treating of legal rights to agriculture, its infrastructure and its products – of rights to mills, dykes, woods and moors, and to soums, teinds and multures. Legislators sometimes passed statutes on these things, and even commented, in the preambles to the statutes, on what they thought they were doing and why. All this would be worthy of further study. It is, however, connected to the businesslike compiling of rentals and tacks, and the minuting of decrees of baron courts – the routine records that I have set aside in order to focus on sources more expressive of cultural meaning.

A *'scientific discourse'* may be identifiable in some seventeenth-century intellectual writing. It is related to the economic discourse, but prioritises

---

69 McRae, 'Husbandry Manuals', p. 42.
70 Charles W. J. Withers, *Geography, Science and National Identity: Scotland since 1520* (Cambridge, 2001), pp. 78–9.
71 Smout, *Nature Contested*, pp. 18–21.
72 Raymond Williams, *The Country and the City* (London, 1973; repr. London, 1985), p. 62.

Figure 1.3. This bizarre picture, from 1627, may be the earliest illustration printed in any agricultural book in Scotland. Sir William Cockburn's book was about teinds or tithes ('*decimis*'), and had very little to do with ostriches, coconut palms or bananas. Where the printer, John Wreittoun, obtained the illustration is unknown. Perhaps he thought that readers would be flattered by being treated as knowledgeable about the products of distant lands.

© The British Library Board. *Source*: Sir William Cockburn of Langton, *Respublica de Decimis* (Edinburgh:. John Wreittoun, 1627), final unnumbered page.

knowledge for its own sake. Such knowledge was not usually about farming, but (for instance) discussion of plant species might mention species used in farming. Timothy Pont was partly scientific. Edward Lhuyd in 1699–1700 studied popular beliefs in a scientific way, and compiled information about management of domestic animals. Thus Highlanders were in the habit of tying withies to heifers' ears in springtime, 'because they are unruly'.[73]

A *'humanitarian discourse'* emerged at times of famine or threatened famine. This was related to the moralising discourse, but was distinct from it in expressing a direct wish to help the needy, or a direct sympathy with the suffering of the needy, rather than castigating the sins of those held to have caused the suffering of the needy. Examples are readily found.[74] Gilbert Hay was humanitarian, at least in part, in his approach to warfare.

There is even an occasional *'ecological discourse'*. In 1570, the Regent Lennox's men were criticised for having slaughtered the distinctive 'quhyt ky and bullis' (white cows and bulls) that lived in the forest of Cumbernauld,

> to the gryt distructioun of polecie and hinder of the commoun weill; for that kynd of kye and bullis hes bein keipit thir mony yeiris in the said forest, and the lyke was not mantenit in ony uther pairtis of this Ile of Albion.

> (to the great destruction of infrastructure and harm to the public interest; for that kind of cows and bulls has been kept these many years in the said forest, and the like was not maintained in any other parts of this island of Britain.)[75]

These animals were evidently the breed now known as White Park cattle. The 'Cadzow' herd at Lennoxlove today seems to be descended from those at Cumbernauld.[76] It is unusual to find a sixteenth-century writer seeking to protect a species.[77]

73 J. L. Campbell and Derick Thomson, *Edward Lhuyd in the Scottish Highlands 1699–1700* (Oxford, 1963), pp. 57–61.

74 Karen J. Cullen, *Famine in Scotland: The 'Ill Years' of the 1690s* (Edinburgh, 2010), p. 123.

75 Richard Bannatyne, *Memorials of Transactions in Scotland 1569–1573*, ed. Robert Pitcairn (Edinburgh: Bannatyne Club, 1836), p. 348. Boece and Leslie also mentioned these cattle: Hume Brown (ed.), *Scotland before 1700*, pp. 81, 131.

76 Janet V. Dohner, *The Encyclopedia of Historic and Endangered Livestock and Poultry Breeds* (New Haven, 2001), pp. 236–8.

77 Early modern writing on sustainability tended to focus on arable or woodland: Paul Warde, *The Invention of Sustainability: Nature and Destiny c.1500–1870* (Cambridge, 2018), pp. 17–144.

Do any of these writers look directly at agricultural work and simply describe what they see, without any moralising or other agenda? Direct observation for its own sake is rare, but there is one example. The 'Buke of the Chess', a late medieval allegory, describes a 'teilman', a tiller of the soil or farmer, who feeds the whole elite – he 'mon [i.e. must] sustene the quene knycht roke and king'. We see him harvesting, and herding cattle:

> This teileman has a huke to cut his corne
> A wand or quhipe in to his handis borne
> To call his cattell to thair pastur richt
> And bringis thaim quhair thai suld rest all nycht.

(This farmer has a sickle to cut his corn, / a staff or whip carried in his hands, / to call his cattle to their proper pasture, / and brings them where they should rest all night.)

The author then mentions Abel as the first farmer, and Noah's 'wyne treis'.[78] But this almost artlessly-observed 'teilman' brings us within sight of a positive and direct vision of Scottish farm work, and of agricultural produce as sustaining both the elite and the common folk. A final proverb also highlights the importance of the ordinary workers in the fields: 'More then Master mawes the meadow' (It takes more than a master to mow the meadow).[79]

So why didn't people write more about agriculture? Ignorance may have been one reason. We occasionally find writers getting their seasons disordered, for instance. People witnessed agriculture, but they found it uninteresting and could not be bothered to understand it. A lack of interest in agriculture may also have been a more studied posture. Writers wanted to show that they, or their readers, weren't rustic or unsophisticated. Explanations for absence are always difficult, however. It is surprising, for instance, that writings about the countryside say little about hunting, an aristocratic rural pursuit.

One reason for reticence about agriculture may have been fear of the common people. Liana Vardi has noted that, after the German Peasants' War of 1525, Continental artists gradually ceased to depict peasants with worrying edged tools like scythes.[80] Slezer's deliberately empty Scottish countryside fits this pattern. Members of the elite did not want to be reminded of the mass of the people.

---

78 *The Asloan Manuscript*, ed. W. A. Craigie (2 vols, Edinburgh: STS, 1923–25), vol. 1, p. 125 ('The buke of the chess', lines 1347–59).
79 James Fraser, *Chronicles of the Frasers 916–1674*, ed. William Mackay (Edinburgh: SHS, 1905), p. 135. This proverb is not in Fergusson.
80 Vardi, 'Imagining the Harvest', pp. 1373–86.

Which aspects of agricultural work are most prominent in the sources? There is little on rural housing or farming infrastructure – kale yard, barn, byre, malt kiln, mill, shieling. On arable farming, there is a fair amount on the central tasks of ploughing and harvesting. Grain processing is seen to involve threshing, which was biblical, but not drying of grain and malt, which was not. Animal herding comes up in connection with shepherds, though these are sometimes artificial Renaissance characters. Stock management also involved the construction and repair of dykes, but these are rarely noticed. Dairying is almost completely ignored, even though classical pastoral literature had had milkmaids. Women's work in general is obscured. Indeed the emphasis on a few agricultural highlights, like ploughing, obscures a wide range of tasks – carting, peat-cutting, tending of poultry, cultivating kale yards and so on.[81] Finally, real agriculture was much affected by landlord–tenant relations. These are discussed vaguely in the fifteenth and sixteenth centuries, but disappear during the seventeenth. Imagining agriculture was a selective process.

The six discourses of agriculture showed considerable continuities throughout the period 1450–1700. However, there were also changes over time – particularly with the moralising discourse. There were far fewer denunciations of sinful, grasping landlords in the seventeenth century. Such denunciations were familiar in late medieval *'contemptus mundi'* (against worldliness) discourse, and in sixteenth-century 'reforming' discourse. But, after about 1596, the leadership of the church increasingly accommodated itself to the political order, and radical critiques of the *status quo* began to run in new channels that offered no discomfort to landlords.

There were fewer chronological developments in the metaphorical, mystical, Renaissance and humorous discourses. Sermons and proverbs used agricultural metaphors throughout our period. The mystical discourse, too, was a constant in poetry and religious literature. Renaissance discourse was diverse, but the pastoral theme occurred throughout the sixteenth and seventeenth centuries, and was still going strong in the early eighteenth century when Ramsay complained about it. Humorous discourses of agriculture continued, but became less coarse with the rise of eighteenth-century politeness.

The main development here concerns the literary descriptions of Scotland and Scottish regions. They initially sat within the mystical discourse, but shifted during the sixteenth and seventeenth centuries, assimilating themselves to the emerging economic discourse. The

---

81 Cf. James Turner, *The Politics of Landscape: Rural Scenery and Society in English Poetry 1630–1660* (Oxford, 1979), pp. 165–73.

productivity of the soil was no longer a natural or divine wonder, and became instead a factor in rational calculation.

Finally, then, the economic discourse was the main growth area during this period. It became notably more prominent during the seventeenth century. By the early eighteenth century, members of the elite who looked at agricultural work being carried out would be well aware, from within their own imagined culture, that workers, farmers, landlords and estate managers were making economic choices. Their culture had also begun to tell them that it might be possible to make more profitable 'improving' choices in future.

2

The Use of Dykes in Scottish Farming 1500–1700

Briony Kincaid

Seldome lyes the divel dead by ane dycksyd.
— Scottish proverb[1]

A seventeenth-century proverb, pointing out the Devil's busy activity every day in Scotland, also reminds us that Scottish folk encountered dykes every day in the course of their busy activity in farming. Dykes were everyday aspects of the infrastructure of farming, vital but often overlooked. This chapter aims to bring these dykes to life.

* * *

The ability to separate areas of land was crucial to prevent livestock damaging crops; this role was often fulfilled by dykes within the fermtoun communities. These fermtouns were collections of families who lived close together and farmed partly together, partly as individuals. Their dykes were upright freestanding structures used to separate families' crop areas from communal land, animals from oats, or a lord's private property from the fermtoun's domain. Other means of dividing land included ditches, and indeed during the enclosing movement both ditches and dykes were often used in combination.[2]

Whilst the study of farming in early modern Scotland has covered a wide range of topics, little research has been done into how farming people used the dykes and what these dykes were like. Fenton and Leitch have offered a broad overview, covering mainly the period since

1 *Fergusson's Scottish Proverbs*, ed. Erskine Beveridge (Edinburgh: STS, 1924), no. 1176.
2 RPS, 1669/10/54.

agricultural 'Improvement' but with some attention to the earlier period.[3] Dodgshon has investigated the division of land among tenants in addition to field systems and other agricultural matters, but he has not considered the variation in dykes or the people involved with the life of a dyke.[4] Fenton's studies of Scottish farming in this period also touch on dykes; however, he does not explore this topic in depth for mainland Scotland, limiting his main investigation to Orkney and Shetland.[5] Robertson has researched head dykes and their placement in the landscape.[6] Shepherd has mentioned briefly that there was 'an extensive array of pre-"Improvement" boundaries' in north-eastern Scotland.[7] This chapter sets out to analyse dykes both in their physical nature and in people's relationships with them.

Some of the sources are from the first half of the eighteenth century and thus from the end of early modern farming, although it must be remembered that it was only after about 1750 that agrarian change spread quickly.[8] These sources were not disregarded in the present study as they contain valuable information about dykes which is still relevant to earlier in the period because the shift from the infield-outfield farming system to greater enclosure of fields and larger-scale livestock rearing was gradual.[9] While this shift began in some areas in the seventeenth century, it did not reach everywhere until well into the eighteenth century.

The principal sources used were baron court books and rental books. Note was taken of all mention of dykes and matters where dykes would have been involved. These were then separated by the aspect of dykes they related to, thus enabling comparison of differing practices relating to similar circumstances. This produced a surprising volume of material which proves that dykes were important to farming people. Some court books contained more than others about dykes, perhaps because some baron courts left issues about dykes to birlaw courts.[10] Maps and estate

---

3 Alexander Fenton and Roger Leitch, 'Dykes and Enclosures', in Alexander Fenton and Kenneth Veitch (eds), *Farming and the Land* (Scottish Life and Society: A Compendium of Scottish Ethnology, vol. 2; Edinburgh, 2011), pp. 773–90.

4 Robert A. Dodgshon, *The Origin of British Field Systems* (London, 1980).

5 Alexander Fenton, *Scottish Country Life* (Edinburgh, 1976); Alexander Fenton, *The Northern Isles: Orkney and Shetland* (Edinburgh, 1978), pp. 89–100.

6 Isobel M. L. Robertson, 'The Head-Dyke: A Fundamental Line in Scottish Geography', *Scottish Geographical Magazine*, 65:1 (1949), 6–19.

7 Colin Shepherd, 'Agrarian and Settlement Characterisation in Post-Medieval Strathbogie, Aberdeenshire 1600–1760', *Rural History*, 22:1 (2011), 1–30, at p. 6.

8 T. M. Devine, *The Transformation of Rural Scotland: Social Change and the Agrarian Economy 1660–1815* (Edinburgh, 1994), pp. 35–59 and *passim*.

9 Fenton, *Scottish Country Life*, p. 14.

10 T. C. Smout, *A History of the Scottish People 1560–1830* (London, 1969), p. 126.

plans from the seventeenth and eighteenth centuries have been consulted as well as an expenditure book and a labour journal.[11] The parliamentary statutes provide some material, showing that dykes were important enough to concern parliament.[12]

This chapter focuses on the physical structure of dykes, the penalties for failing to look after a dyke or for damaging a dyke, the role of dykes in farming, and their seasonality or permanence. Other issues such as who paid for the dykes, and who decided where to build them, are also addressed briefly. First, the function of the dykes will be investigated to provide a background to the rest of the findings.

Yard dykes were used to mark out one family's patch of continuously cultivated land from another's or their area for storing crops. These were walls built around the kale yard where various types of brassica were grown for food and the stack yard where crops could be kept away from animals once harvested.[13] This practice was most common in the Lowlands but later in the early modern period, this was spreading into the Highlands.[14] Kale yards were either attached to the family's house or were separate structures nearby.[15] Baron courts frequently attest to the importance of kale yards – and to the importance of their being enclosed by adequate dykes.[16]

Lairds used dykes to exclude tenants and livestock from their gardens and parks. Additionally, dykes were used to enclose areas of land for purposes of containing. The head dyke enclosed all the land which was used for growing crops from that which was only ever used for grazing.[17] Fold dykes could contain livestock to prevent them destroying crops or to fertilise the ground with manure as in the tathe folds.[18] Using folds to contain the animals was compulsory in areas such as Kintyre where, during the summer and harvest, an animal owner would be fined if their animal was found outwith a fold.[19] Pound-folds were also important;

---

11 *Life and Labour on an Aberdeenshire Estate 1735–1750*, ed. Henry Hamilton (Aberdeen: Third Spalding Club, 1946), pp. 63–79.

12 RPS, 1607/3/17; 1621/6/33; 1641/8/223; 1669/10/54.

13 Fenton, *Scottish Country Life*, pp. 171–3, 178.

14 Smout, *A History of the Scottish People*, p. 153.

15 Robert A. Dodgshon, *No Stone Unturned: A History of Farming, Landscape and Environment in the Scottish Highlands and Islands* (Edinburgh, 2015), p. 165.

16 Ian Whyte, *Agriculture and Society in Seventeenth-Century Scotland* (Edinburgh, 1979), p. 59.

17 Smout, *A History of the Scottish People*, p. 120.

18 R. A. Dodgshon, 'The Origins of Traditional Field Systems', in M. L. Parry and T. R. Slater (eds), *The Making of the Scottish Countryside* (London, 1980), pp. 69–92, at p. 103.

19 'Regulation of Agriculture in Seventeenth Century Kintyre', ed. A. I. B. Stewart, *Stair Society Miscellany*, vol. 3 (Edinburgh: Stair Society, 1992), pp. 218–19.

in Kintyre each toun had one.[20] These contained any livestock found in forbidden areas, until their owners claimed them and paid a fine.

* * *

There is a good deal of information about the building of dykes by paid specialists. However, for tenants, herds and labourers, the dykes which they used to control their farmed lands were usually built by themselves, choosing where to erect them and using local materials. Mentions of building such dykes are rare in the sources; it was a part of life which did not need recording and would usually not have been discussed in the baron courts. Building these dykes would not have involved a monetary cost but simply an outlay of time and energy.

Some tenant farmers, such as in Stitchill, hired workers to build fold dykes.[21] This is surprising as the work was of a temporary nature and less labour-intensive than building dry-stone dykes so it could be expected that tenants would build these themselves. Landowners, whether individuals or ecclesiastical, hired labourers or special dyke builders to construct dykes when they were needed, as in Melrose and Monymusk.[22] Alternatively, they may have had agreements with their tenants whereby the tenants paid for some of their rent in days of labour for the landlord. This is unlikely to have been recorded often, as such agreements were probably mostly just spoken. Dyke construction may have become more common with the rise of the enclosing movement, as there are few refer-ences to payments for it in sources from before 1700. However, this may simply be because most estates did not record this type of regular labour.

There were enough opportunities for dyke building to be a livelihood for some men. The Edinburgh justices of the peace laid down rates of pay for dry-stone dykers, masons and fold-dyke builders in 1656. Building fold dykes was paid by quantity of work completed, not the time spent working: 'A Bigger of Fold Dyks, is to have Twenty Pennies Scots, for each Rood of his Work, being sufficiently done'.[23] A 'rood of work' was a measurement of area used by masons and other construction workers: one square 'rod', equal to 36 square ells or 342¼ square feet.[24] In other areas payments varied from 6s. 8d. Scots for a masonry dyke of unspecified

20 'Seventeenth Century Kintyre', p. 220.
21 *Records of the Baron Court of Stitchill 1655–1807*, ed. George Gunn and Clement B. Gunn (Edinburgh: SHS, 1905), p. 158.
22 *Selections from the Records of the Regality of Melrose 1662–1676*, vol. 2, ed. C. S. Romanes (Edinburgh: SHS, 1915), p. 123; *Life and Labour*, pp. 64, 85.
23 'An Assessment of Wages Made by the Justices of the Peace for the Shire of Edinburgh', *Scotland and the Protectorate*, ed. C. H. Firth (Edinburgh: SHS, 1899), pp. 405–9.
24 R. D. Connor and A. D. C. Simpson, *Weights and Measures in Scotland: A European Perspective* (Edinburgh, 2004), p. 87.

size, to 41s. for a paddock dyke.[25] On the Monymusk estate the landlord paid his workers 4d. sterling (4s. Scots) per day for constructing stone dykes in 1747.[26] Such 'cowans' – the contemporary term for builders of stone dykes – were paid by the day around Edinburgh in 1656, at a rate of 8s. per day.[27] This suggests that building dry-stone dykes was a more arduous and slower task than constructing fold dykes of turf.

Generally, it was tenants who decided where to build the dykes which they needed, as this did not concern other people. However, sometimes baron courts were involved: an inquest for three neighbourhoods in Lanarkshire decreed that dykes must be built around both corn and meadow areas.[28] These dykes were presumably to exclude livestock from the crops and the growing hay. In an assedation (lease) by the abbey of Glenluce, the leaseholder was responsible for 12 roods of dyke-making per year; this seems to indicate that the landlord would direct the work.[29] In an Orkney parish in 1688, Arthur Baikie of Tankerness obtained the labour of all the parishioners: 'Tankernes s[e]rvands in St Androis parochine, with the parochiners th[ai]rof, entered the building of the dyks of the quoy appoynttit for a park'.[30]

Parliament was not usually interested in the control of grazing animals as part of everyday farming, but it did want to keep animals out of other parts of the infrastructure of rural areas. After the Reformation, dykes around churchyards came to be of concern, and an act was passed in 1597 laying down the parishioners' responsibilities.[31] In the later seventeenth century, the improvement of roads came to interest both local and central agencies of government.[32] This led to acts such as that of 1669 ordaining 'that where laboured land lies upon the sides of highways that the said laboured land shall be fenced with dyke and ditch or hedge'.[33] A 1661 act launched a broader programme of improvement, requiring heritors to 'plant, ditch and inclose' in order to plant trees.[34] Some heritors seem to

---

25 *Diary and General Expenditure Book of William Cunningham of Craigends*, ed. James Dodds (Edinburgh: SHS, 1887), p. 112; *Rentale Dunkeldense 1505–1517*, ed. Robert K. Hannay (Edinburgh: SHS, 1915), p. 296.

26 *Life and Labour*, p. 70.

27 'An Assessment of Wages', p. 408.

28 *Court Book of the Barony of Carnwath 1523–1542*, ed. William C. Dickinson (Edinburgh: SHS, 1937), p. 54.

29 R. C. Reid (ed.), *Wigtownshire Charters* (Edinburgh: SHS, 1960), no. 60.

30 *Diary of Thomas Brown, Writer in Kirkwall 1675–1693*, ed. A. Francis Steuart (Kirkwall, 1898), p. 52. A quoy was an enclosure, often taken in from common land.

31 RPS, 1597/11/10.

32 John G. Harrison, 'Improving the Roads and Bridges of the Stirling Area c.1660–1706', *PSAS*, 135 (2005), 287–308.

33 RPS, 1669/10/53.

34 RPS, 1661/1/348. For the context of enclosure at this time see Whyte,

have done so, since the act was amended in 1669 to deal with the problem of patches of ground on estate borders that were 'unfit or incapable of bearing a dyk or receaveing a ditch' (presumably boggy or rocky areas); these patches were to be allocated to one proprietor, with compensation to the other, so that a march dyke could be constructed between the estates.[35]

In Fintray, tenants paid instalments for building the churchyard dykes in the early eighteenth century; this came to £1 4s. 8d. sterling (£14 16s. Scots).[36] Kale yards, however, were rarely addressed in baron courts. There is only one mention of location, found in Kintyre records, which simply states that 'at everie dwelling house ther sall be a kaillyaird'.[37] Elsewhere, this decision was seemingly left to the tenants, either as an individual family or perhaps in consultation with their neighbours.

* * *

The question of ownership of dykes is complex. Permanent dykes will have been considered immoveable rather than moveable property, and thus pertained heritably to the landlord. As Lord Stair expressed the distinction in 1681,

> Any thing is called moveable, which by its nature and use is capable of motion, as things immoveable are the earth, sea, and things fixed to the earth, not to be removed therefrom, as trees, houses, &c. which though they may possibly be moved, yet it is not their use so to be.[38]

Stair did not mention dykes, but permanent dykes clearly came into the same category as houses – they were immoveable because it was 'not their use' to be moved. The above-mentioned 1661 and 1669 statutes regarded march dykes as pertaining to landlords. But some dykes were temporary – and we shall see that some court books regarded some dykes as pertaining to tenants.

Dykes could be communal, if in the infield or outfield, and around folds. Kale yards were used by individual families and therefore the dykes surrounding these would likely have belonged to the respective family although it could be that some families' yards shared a dyke.[39]

Agriculture and Society, pp. 126–30.

35 RPS, 1669/10/54. This and the previous 1661 act, known as the March Dykes Acts, are still partially in force.

36 'Court Book of the Barony of Fintray 1711–1726', ed. James Cruickshank, *Miscellany of the Third Spalding Club*, vol. 1 (Aberdeen: Third Spalding Club, 1935), pp. 39, 42.

37 'Seventeenth Century Kintyre', p. 218.

38 James, Viscount of Stair, *Institutions of the Law of Scotland*, ed. David M. Walker (Edinburgh, 1981), p. 291 (title II.i.2).

39 Fenton, *Scottish Country Life*, p. 178.

Rules regarding not breaking down neighbours' dykes reinforce the hypothesis that these dykes were privately owned.[40] However, this reference of ownership could simply refer to use; the neighbour's dyke was so called because it protected an area of land which the neighbour was cultivating at that particular time.

For the barony of Forbes, this sense of ownership or personal use is not found as all tenants are to help each other 'in speciall for bigging of keill zaird dykis' in cases where these are communal or possessed jointly.[41] This suggests that ideas of ownership of these local dykes varied across the country such that in some places kale-yard dykes could be owned privately and in other areas they were shared. Other private dykes were those belonging to a lord such as his park and yard dykes.

The Glenorchy court book in 1621 demanded that the head and fold dykes be repaired 'be the awnaris and possessouris thairof'.[42] This may suggest that even the head dyke had individual 'owners', who on this reading would be the tenants whose lands adjoined each section of the dyke. Albert Bil has queried whether a system of individual responsibility for sections could really have ensured that the head dyke was consistently and effectively maintained, and has suggested that the dyke was really maintained communally.[43] This may be compatible with the Glenorchy evidence if we posit that the 'awnaris and possessouris' were to act collectively. However, there is also much evidence (some of it cited elsewhere in this chapter) of individuals being prosecuted for failing to maintain their dykes, so the question may remain open.

* * *

Dykes had different forms depending on their different functions. The 'head dyke' was a key permanent boundary, often following a contour line at the upper limit of arable cultivation. Angus Winchester has shown that the entire farming year pivoted around the head dyke, with an 'open' autumn–winter period in which animals were allowed below the head dyke and a 'closed' spring–summer period in which they were held above it to protect growing crops.[44] The head dyke was the most important division in the pre-Improvement landscape, and a few head

---

40 *Baron Court of Stitchill*, p. 50.
41 'Forbes Baron Court Book 1659–1678', ed. J. Maitland Thomson, *Miscellany of the Scottish History Society*, vol. 3 (Edinburgh: SHS, 1919), p. 297.
42 'Portions of Rentals, Court Books, Household Books, and Inventories of Breadalbane', *The Black Book of Taymouth*, ed. Cosmo Innes (Edinburgh: Bannatyne Club, 1855), p. 353.
43 Albert Bil, *The Shieling 1600–1840: The Case of the Central Scottish Highlands* (Edinburgh, 1990), p. 117.
44 Angus J. L. Winchester, *The Harvest of the Hills: Rural Life in Northern England and the Scottish Borders 1400–1700* (Edinburgh, 2000), pp. 52–68.

dykes survive to this day.[45] The head dyke could be moved if the fermtoun grew, but this was uncommon.[46] Often it was a single boundary, but a detailed study of Highland Perthshire has revealed two roughly parallel dykes, the 'head dyke' and the 'over head dyke', at the upper limits of the infield and outfield respectively. The two dykes enabled farmers to manage their grazing animals in a more sophisticated way, moving them to different pastures at different seasons.[47]

The many other dykes used to separate land and to mark boundaries or property could be seasonal or semi-permanent.[48] The tathe fold was used to contain animals during the night on an area of land which would be used for growing crops later in the agricultural year; by keeping the animals there each night, the land was fertilised. After this, the dykes would be pulled down, as at Inver in Aberdeenshire, where six men spent a third of a February day 'casting down at the Toath fold'.[49] These dykes were generally earthen dykes which were then composted and used as fertiliser, as at Cluny.[50] Sheep folds were also temporary and were moved around.[51] Seasonal dykes such as the tathe fold needed to be substantial structures despite being in use for only a few months.

Other temporary dykes were not to contain animals but to exclude them, such as the one built around a haystack in Dunkeld diocese. Once the hay had been used or moved, the dyke would be dismantled.[52] Lastly, the demand in the Breadalbane records that the head and fold dykes be 'yeirly beittit bigit and upholdin' (amended, built and maintained each year) suggests that not all fold dykes were seasonal; they might remain in some form throughout the year, even though, like the head dyke, they required maintenance.[53] Similarly, the dykes around kale yards remained in place for many years.[54]

Dykes were used as boundary markers, taking their place among several ways of marking property boundaries. A boundary in the parishes of Alyth and Blair, Perthshire, was described in detail in 1595. It partly followed 'ane auld dyk', presumably broken but still useful as a boundary marker. At one point the boundary followed 'the waster dyk of the eistmest corne fald of the saides landis of Ardomie', indicating that fold

45   Robertson, 'The Head-Dyke'.
46   A. Fenton, 'The Traditional Pastoral Economy', in Parry and Slater (eds), *Making of the Scottish Countryside*, pp. 93–113, at p. 98.
47   Bil, *The Shieling*, pp. 116–17.
48   Shepherd, 'Agrarian and Settlement Characterisation', p. 7.
49   *Life and Labour*, p. 124.
50   Dodgshon, *No Stone Unturned*, p. 134; *Rentale Dunkeldense*, p. 186.
51   *Rentale Dunkeldense*, p. 186.
52   Ibid., p. 293.
53   'Rentals, Court Books, Household Books, and Inventories of Breadalbane', p. 353.
54   Ibid.

dykes could be treated as permanent structures. However, much of the boundary used only occasional boundary stones, as when the boundary went 'linalie vast [i.e. west] to ane gray stane callit the Manstein, quhilk stone salbe carnit [i.e. cairned] about with stones'.[55] This was a legal and conceptual line on the ground, not a physical boundary.

Even when dykes could keep animals' movements in check, humans were more agile. In 1663 the laird at Forbes repeatedly ordered that no one was to cross his garden or orchard dykes. Those doing so would be fined for trespassing, or if they were a servant their master would be liable.[56] There seems to have been little expectation that the dyke itself would keep people out. Indeed, temporary fold dykes were not always expected to keep animals out by themselves. Some Galloway farmers were reported to 'watch their cattell and sheep in the folds at night ... constantly from the beginning of May, till the corne be taken off the ground, for fear they should breake the fold-dikes in the night time'.[57] These dykes clearly had some effectiveness, but they needed constant supervision.

The materials commonly used in dykes were stone and turf. These could either be used in combination or separately although stone walls only became common with the advent of land enclosure and agricultural improvement.[58] Seasonal dykes usually did not involve stone. The traveller Thomas Kirke in 1679 saw dykes as normally being of turf – 'every small house having a few sodds thrown into a little bank about it'.[59] One construction material that was never used was wood, which was not abundant in early modern Scotland.

A common method of constructing dykes, as for dwellings, was the cutting of turf or sods from the ground in blocks which were then arranged for building.[60] These sods were called 'fale' in the Fintray records and 'divot earth' in Breadalbane. In Forbes such a dyke was an 'earth dyke'. The *Dictionary of the Older Scottish Tongue* distinguishes between fale and divot, defining fale as being 'of greater thickness than divot'.[61] It could be that in Fintray the dykes were made of larger blocks of sod than in Breadalbane. Or perhaps it was just the terminology

55 *Bamff Charters, AD 1232–1703*, ed. James H. Ramsay (London, 1915), p. 141.
56 'Forbes Baron Court Book', pp. 243, 246, 299.
57 Andrew Symson, 'Answers to Queries concerning Galloway', in his *A Large Description of Galloway 1684* (Edinburgh, 1823), pp. 70–108, at p. 97.
58 Fenton, *Scottish Country Life*, p. 16. For a detailed discussion of early 'improved' dykes in connection with eighteenth-century woodland management, see T. C. Smout, Alan R. MacDonald and Fiona Watson, *A History of the Native Woodlands of Scotland 1500–1920* (Edinburgh, 2005), pp. 164–72.
59 P. Hume Brown (ed.), *Early Travellers in Scotland* (Edinburgh, 1891), p. 254.
60 'Court Book of the Barony of Fintray', p. 29.
61 *DOST*, s.v. faill n. (2).

that varied. In Perthshire, fold dykes used both stone and 'divot earth', although this was probably only for the semi-permanent folds.[62]

Various references to earth dykes can be found in parliamentary statutes and in baron court books.[63] Additionally, the map *A General survey of Inverness & the country adjacent to the foot of Loch-Ness* seems to depict dykes as wavy lines, suggesting that these were earthen dykes. However, these lines may represent hedges or possibly stone walls, and unfortunately the map has no legend. It also post-dates the early modern period so increasing the likelihood that the lines represent hedges.[64]

Where stones were used in dykes this may have been to provide a foundation or binding element – either internally to give structural support, or as coping on the top of the dyke, as in Urie.[65] There were also some dykes made mostly of stone, such as the head dykes. Churchyard dykes, indeed, were built with stone and mortar.[66] Yet other dykes, built by cowans, were of dry stone without mortar.[67] Stone dykes were often topped off with turf to give extra height.[68] Fenton has investigated the dykes in common use in Orkney and Shetland. These vary in structure but are built to suit the landscape, some having large gaps to allow the wind to pass through.[69] In mainland Scotland, dykes would have also been constructed with the weather conditions and local materials in mind, but these may have differed in a number of ways from those in the Northern Isles.

The size of a dyke was key to its functionality. There was even a specific term, found in the Stitchill records, to describe a dyke capable of keeping cattle in or out: 'hirdwell' or 'hirdwill'.[70] Many disputes between tenants over the size of their dykes were recorded by the baron courts; this was clearly of great importance to the farming people.[71] There are references to 'the right proportions', although what these measurements were was not

---

62 'Rentals, Court Books, Household Books, and Inventories of Breadalbane', p. 353.
63 RPS, 1681/7/132; 'Forbes Baron Court Book', p. 246.
64 *A General survey of Inverness & the country adjacent to the foot of Loch-Ness*, Board of Ordnance. Register of Plans 1700–1800, 3rd. Division, North Britain, [1800], fol. 14 (Public Record Office: WO 55/2281), http://images-teaching. is.ed.ac.uk/luna/servlet, work record ID: 0043182 (accessed 4 April 2017).
65 *The Court Book of the Barony of Urie in Kincardineshire 1604–1747*, ed. Douglas Barron (Edinburgh: SHS, 1892), p. 111.
66 RPS, 1597/11/10.
67 *Baron Court of Stitchill*, p. 168.
68 Fenton, *Scottish Country Life*, p. 16.
69 Fenton, *The Northern Isles*, pp. 96–7.
70 *Baron Court of Stitchill*, p. 50. Cf. *DOST*, s.v. hirdwill.
71 *Baron Court of Stitchill*, p. 95; 'Forbes Baron Court Book', pp. 243, 297; *Court Book of the Barony of Carnwath*, pp. 5, 68, 102, 159; 'Corshill Baron Court Book', ed. John Sheddon-Dobbie, *Archaeological and Historical Collections relating to the Counties of Ayr and Wigton*, vol. 4 (1884), pp. 168, 185.

usually stated.[72] This lack of detail suggests that dyke size was common knowledge. In the Monymusk work agreements, some dimensions are given. William Glenning was requested to build a dyke '42 inches thick at bottom and 30 at top',[73] and Peter Craigmyle and James Adam were to build half dykes, one yard tall.[74] From this it can be surmised that 'half' likely refers to the height and thus a standard dyke would have been taller. 'Half' may have been meant literally, where a normal dyke was double the height, about two yards tall; or 'half' may have simply meant 'not full-sized' and thus a full-sized dyke could be anything that is a good bit more than one yard high. However, these entries date from 1741 and 1738 respectively, a time when enclosing land was becoming more common, so we cannot be certain that the dykes of this period were the same as those of earlier periods, despite Fenton's evidence of a similarly sized pre-enclosure turf dyke in Caithness which had a height of six feet.[75] There is also the possibility that a 'half' dyke could be a *thinner* dyke. Evidence from Orkney and Shetland in a more recent period shows the existence of 'single' and 'double' dykes, the former being constructed of a single width of stones.[76]

Dykes needed wide bases to support their height. Each dyke would have required large quantities of materials to build. Using turf cut from nearby would have been easier than gathering stones to build the dyke, although when the land needed to be cleared of stones, the dykes generally had more stones.[77]

The hill dyke on Fair Isle, Shetland, divided the whole island between the southern cultivated land and the northern sheep pasture. It is shown on a map of 1752, and is probably much older. It ran for over 400 metres, archaeological investigation showing it to have been about 8 metres wide and 2 metres high.[78] It took full advantage of landscape irregularities, meandering from one rocky outcrop to the next and providing shelter in its angles. The old dyke has been replaced by a more recent, straighter one, still in use for its original purpose of stock management.[79]

There could be 'yetts' (gates) in dykes, or stiles to enable people to climb over them. A charter of lands in the lordship of Urquhart, Inverness-shire, in 1509, called for the repair of roads and bridges, including their

---

72 'Corshill Baron Court Book', p. 168.
73 *Life and Labour*, pp. 66–7.
74 *Life and Labour*, p. 64.
75 Fenton, *Scottish Country Life*, p. 179.
76 Fenton, *The Northern Isles*, pp. 96–7.
77 Fenton, *Scottish Country Life*, p. 15.
78 Canmore (National Record of the Historic Environment), at http://canmore.org.uk/event/647665; J. R. Hunter, *Fair Isle: The Archaeology of an Island Community* (Edinburgh, 1996), pp. 2, 41–3.
79 Fenton, *The Northern Isles*, p. 89.

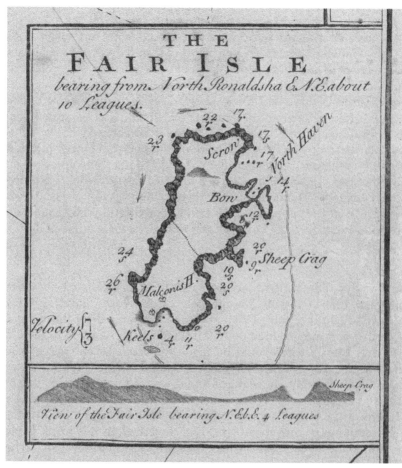

FIGURE 2.1. This map of Fair Isle in Shetland shows the island's hill dyke, as the largest human feature in the landscape, bisecting the island. The farming settlements were (and still are) located to the south of the dyke, with pasture land to the north. Murdoch Mackenzie's survey of Fair Isle was carried out in the 1740s. The dyke's earlier history is undocumented, but it was a key part of the island's well-established agricultural system and is likely to date further back for several centuries, perhaps many centuries. Hardly any upstanding dykes today can be shown to date back to the pre-Improvement period – even the Fair Isle dyke, which is still in use, has shifted its position – but this map shows the importance of dykes in the early modern landscape.
Source: Murdoch Mackenzie, *Orcades, or a Geographic and Hydrographic Survey of Orkney and Lewis Islands* (Edinburgh, 1750). From the third edition (London, 1776), Fair Isle inset on Map 4. Image reproduced by the kind permission of the Bibliothèque nationale de France (BnF).

'fald-yettis' and 'stilis'.[80] Although charters were in Latin, these terms were given in the vernacular, presumably because they were demotic terms for which the clerk knew no Latin equivalent.

An occasional access gap in a dyke, closed with turf when not in use, was known as a 'slap'. A witchcraft case in Bute in 1662 provides a vivid picture of a dispute about who controlled a 'slap' in a fold dyke. John McFie and his father and brother 'flitted [i.e. moved house] out of Kerecreoch to Lochly', which would entail bringing three loaded horses through a fold belonging to Margaret NcWilliam. However, NcWilliam was determined to stop them. McFie's family, 'comeing to the slap which they had casten downe before, they found the said slap bigged [i.e. built] up and NcWilliam lyeing thairupon'. McFie's father attempted to pull down the slap, but NcWilliam 'bigged up as he caste downe', whereupon a brawl ensued.[81] The image of the owner lying on top of her dyke to protect it from being broken, and then scrambling to rebuild it, underlines both the importance of dykes and their occasional vulnerability.

* * *

Could a 'dyke' be a ditch? According to the *Oxford English Dictionary*, from early times onwards, the meaning of the word dike/dyke 'varies between "ditch, dug out place", and "mound formed by throwing up the earth", and may include both'.[82] It would make sense to expect that earth dug from a ditch could be made into an adjacent raised bank. When the sources from early modern Scotland are clear on the subject, they overwhelmingly show that a dyke was a raised barrier; there is very little explicit mention of sunken barriers, whether called dykes or not. Some areas of Scotland may also have lacked the deep soil in which ditches could most conveniently be dug. Nevertheless, it is worth paying attention to the few occasions where the sources seem to speak of ditches.

The *Dictionary of the Older Scottish Tongue* also recognises the ambiguity of the word 'dyke', giving two definitions: '1. A ditch or fosse', and '2. A wall (of earth, turf, or stone) made for enclosure or defence or as a dividing line. Very common after 1530.'[83] Most of *DOST*'s quotations for sense 1 are early, and few or none of them are found in clearly agricultural contexts; most of them are military.

The accounts of the bishopric of Dunkeld provide some relevant evidence. In 1509 there was a payment to John Robertson for 'digging

---

80 *RMS*, vol. 2, no. 3390 (8 December 1509).
81 'Papers Relating to Witchcraft 1662–1677', *Highland Papers*, ed. J. R. N. Macphail (4 vols, Edinburgh: SHS, 1914–34), vol. 3, pp. 14–15.
82 *OED*, s.v. dike/dyke.
83 *DOST*, s.v. dyke n.

dykes in Ardblair'.[84] These records, in Latin, referred to dykes as '*fossarum*', which might suggest ditches. However, in 1513 there was a payment for bringing 'faill' (turf) for the dyke at Clony, which surely indicates a raised barrier.[85]

An act of parliament 'in favours of planters and inclosers of ground', encouraging tree-planting, ordered that 'no person shall break doun or fill up any ditch, hedge or dyke whereby ground is inclosed and shall not leap or suffer their horse, nolt or sheep to goe over any ditch, hedge or dyke'.[86] The order not to 'break doun or fill up' indicates clearly that parliament thought that a barrier could be either sunken or raised. However, the phrase 'ditch, hedge or dyke' seems to indicate that a 'dyke' was not a ditch. Moreover, the statute was framed in hypothetical terms, making provision for what should happen *if* ditches existed. It does not prove conclusively that people in early modern Scotland actually did use ditches as barriers.

We find something similar in a local record, the Kintyre acts of bailiary of 1672. In order to prevent boundary disputes, one of these acts ordered 'that march dykes be digged in all touns quhair it may be done and that march stones sheuchs and ditches be made'. A 'sheuch' was a trench, so these 'dykes' were clearly ditches. They also seem to have been intended to form a physical barrier to animals rather than just to mark a property division, since the court's next order was that all persons should keep their animals off their neighbours' grass 'untill the march dyks be digged'.[87] This may be an unusual case, and it should be noted that this source states an *intention* to have dykes 'digged', rather than necessarily showing that this was a regular practice.

What about hedges? Hedges are mentioned occasionally, but seem to have been much rarer than dykes. Parliament in 1458 legislated to encourage 'plantacione of woddis and heggis and sawing of browme', indicating that a hedge was seen as a source of brushwood rather than as a boundary.[88] The traveller Thomas Morer in 1689, noting that there were few enclosures in Scotland, suggested that people objected to hedges because they sheltered birds that damaged crops.[89] A specialised use of hedges in monastic gardens is suggested by a lease of abbey yards in

84   *Rentale Dunkeldense*, pp. 103–4.
85   *Rentale Dunkeldense*, p. 184.
86   RPS, 1685/4/73.
87   'Seventeenth Century Kintyre', p. 220.
88   RPS, 1458/3/28.
89   Hume Brown (ed.), *Early Travellers*, p. 267. Morer also suggested that leases were too short to encourage improvement, or that tenants simply had 'want of industry'.

Coupar Angus in 1541, specifying that the tenant 'sall wphald the heggis, dykis, and alais'.[90]

* * *

Once a dyke had been built, it needed regular maintenance. Damage could be caused by animals jumping or knocking against the dyke, by people climbing over, by general weathering, or, occasionally, by wilful destruction.[91] As with the construction of dykes, landlords had agreements with people to maintain them. This was again also the case on church lands.[92] Tenants were expected to keep their dykes maintained well enough to be a barrier to animals and could be fined for failing to do so.[93]

The seventeenth-century interest in 'planting' led to a view that planting trees could reinforce dykes. Corshill baron court, in 1678, attributed the 'decaying of the yaird dyckes' to the tenants' 'sloath of negligence of not planting of trees about the yaird dyckes'. Tenants of each merkland should plant six trees each year, and 'uphold thair owne respective dyckes sufficiently'.[94] Tree planting indicates that these were permanent dykes, likely to be kale-yard dykes. In Kintyre, the Act of Neighbourhood ordering that 'the kaillyard dyike sall be planted with trees round about at an equall distance' looks as though the aim was to reinforce or protect the dykes.[95]

Similarly, the Forbes court book records the expectation of individual tenants to maintain their dykes; again, this probably refers to kale-yard dykes.[96] In Cluny the shepherd's role included looking after the sheepfold dyke.[97] The laird of Glenorchy entered a lifetime contract with 'Adame Hadden dyker' whereby Hadden would repair the laird's 'park dykes'.[98] Other records give details of the numbers of workers, and their payments, either in money or in kind, but lack details of who the workers were.[99] In Kincardineshire there was an expectation placed on the tenants of one fermtoun, Montequheiche, regarding the laird's yard dyke; in 1621 tenants were told to repair the dyke or each be fined 40s. 'to be peyit be ilk

---

90 *Rental Book of the Cistercian Abbey of Cupar-Angus*, ed. Charles Rogers (2 vols, London: Grampian Club, 1879–80), vol. 2, p. 208.

91 RPS, 1607/3/17.

92 *Rentale St Andree: Being the Chamberlain and Granitar Accounts of the Archbishopric in the Time of Cardinal Betoun 1538–1546*, ed. Robert K. Hannay (Edinburgh: SHS, 1913), p. 82.

93 *Baron Court of Stitchill*, p. 95.

94 'Corshill Baron Court Book', p. 147.

95 'Seventeenth Century Kintyre', p. 218.

96 'Forbes Baron Court Book', p. 243.

97 *Rentale Dunkeldense*, p. 186.

98 *Black Book of Taymouth*, pp. 421–2.

99 *Life and Labour*, pp. 100, 108.

dissobedient'.[100] However, as this is the only such occurrence found in the sources it can be assumed that landlords generally hired men to maintain their own dykes, either directly or through labour rent agreements, whilst the tenants concerned themselves with the dykes they used.

Where land was let out on a lease or tack, the leaseholder could be made responsible for caring for the dykes and ensuring they were left in the same condition as when the lease started.[101] Most tenants were careful in these tasks as dykes were essential and there were also penalties for those who failed in their duty.

Some lairds made tenants pay for damage caused by poor upkeep. Baron court books contain reminders that tenants are to maintain their dykes at a certain standard.[102] In Corshill, tenants would be fined 40s. if they did not maintain their dykes well enough.[103] The laird of Glenorchy was stricter in imposing a £10 fine for dykes which did not meet requirements, and for kale-yard dykes which failed to keep animals out.[104] Other lairds were more lenient, issuing warnings before fines, as in Carnwath in 1534.[105] The Forbes baron court book states that tenants must pay for damage to their dykes if it is deemed these are not well constructed; they must pay 'the skaith that they sall sustein in defalt of sufficient dykis'.[106] It is unclear whether this refers to all dykes or to the communal dykes mentioned earlier in that court's business. If it refers to the communal dykes it does not specify whether every tenant would contribute a part or if an individual would be fully accountable.

Landlords could appoint an officer to ensure that dyke standards were met by all their tenants. In 1711, George Young's role was to enforce Fintray dyke standards by measuring them.[107] Dykes were crucial to keeping order within the farming community, therefore anyone who violated upkeep regulations faced consequences. This importance is evident from the number of disputes between neighbours over damage done to dykes necessitating an order that tenants 'keip guid nighbour heid' in the Forbes barony.[108]

Rental books recorded payments made to various people for mending dykes whilst other sources reveal who these hired labourers were. In the St Andrews archbishopric rentals, both granitar and chamberlain accounts

100 *Court Book of the Barony of Urie*, p. 37.
101 'Court Book of the Barony of Fintray', p. 46.
102 'Seventeenth Century Kintyre', p. 216.
103 'Corshill Baron Court Book', p. 147.
104 'Rentals, Court Books, Household Books, and Inventories of Breadalbane', p. 353.
105 *Court Book of the Barony of Carnwath*, p. 159.
106 'Forbes Baron Court Book', p. 297.
107 'Court Book of the Barony of Fintray', p. 20.
108 'Forbes Baron Court Book', p. 297.

contain payments to individuals for repairing dykes.[109] The granitar of Lothian financed dyke maintenance early in the sixteenth century.[110] It is unusual to find records of tenants looking after their own dykes, as this was a routine task. However, the Stitchill court book includes one case where a dispute had arisen over whose duty it was to repair a particular dyke. It was decided that the responsibility fell to the tenant whose land was nearest the dyke.[111] When a landlord paid for dykes to be maintained, these were usually his own. Work agreements of the Monymusk estate record many payments made to individuals and groups of labourers for time spent repairing dykes.[112] These are eighteenth-century records, but although the wages may have changed, the type of work and the labourers probably had not changed drastically.

* * *

Various offences could be committed in connection with dykes. Dyke-breaking was one of the most common offences in baron courts.[113] Intentionally damaging a dyke was a serious offence. In Corshill in 1680, relating to new park dykes, the fine was £4.[114] It seems that this heavy fine was because breaking a dyke was also an act of trespass. Indeed parliament ruled in 1607 that a fine of up to £40 could be levied.[115] For other dykes the approach was less severe; in Kintyre in 1653, and in Fintray in 1720, the fine for breaking dykes was 40s. Scots.[116] Similarly, in the barony of Forbes in 1675, anyone who broke the dykes and the planting around them was fined 40s.; for a repeat offence the fine would double to £4.[117] It appears that these fines did not increase over time, although for a second offence the punishment was greater. However, given the lack of evidence from the sixteenth century, fines of earlier in the period could have varied. Accidental damage of a dyke, whether by a person or an animal, was also frowned upon, and the perpetrator, or animal's owner, was usually fined. In Stitchill in 1722, the fine was 1s. sterling (12s. Scots).[118]

In cases where a dyke had not been maintained to the required standard, so that animals had been able to get in, there were repercussions for the

---

109 *Rentale St Andree*, pp. 82, 91, 106, 121, 137, 167, 175, 208.
110 *Rentale Dunkeldense*, p. 249.
111 *Baron Court of Stitchill*, p. 140.
112 *Life and Labour*, pp. 86, 87.
113 Whyte, *Agriculture and Society*, p. 45.
114 'Corshill Baron Court Book', p. 152.
115 RPS, 1607/3/17.
116 'Court Book of the Barony of Fintray', p. 39; 'Seventeenth Century Kintyre', p. 222.
117 'Forbes Baron Court Book', p. 299.
118 *Baron Court of Stitchill*, p. 184.

person responsible for the dyke. As in Corshill, sometimes a birlawman would judge whose fault it was.[119] In Carnwath, a dispute arose between two tenants, each of whom accused the other 'for the wrangws distrucione of his corne in defalt of the uphalding of his dik'. The inquest ruled that both dykes were insufficient, so each would need to compensate the other's damage. Both tenants were also fined.[120]

Animals sometimes got into the crops even if dykes were well kept, and this was treated differently. In Fintray, any sheep that was found in a fold where it was not meant to be could be thrown out of the fold, but if doing so injured it then the person who had thrown it out would be liable.[121] This was in 1714 when sheep farming for profit rather than just for subsistence was increasing. However, in Kintyre, a person could legally kill pigs found on their land.[122] As an extra precaution, the baron court of Leys ordered tenants to appoint a lookout to watch the fold nightly and ensure that no animals broke down the dykes.[123] A harvest could easily be devastated by stray livestock, as farming near subsistence level allowed no room for losses.[124]

Baron courts sometimes forbade people to cross dykes by 'climbing' or 'leaping'.[125] If dykes were low enough to jump over, a common dyke height of two yards would perhaps be too high. On the other hand, to 'leap' a dyke may not have meant jumping straight over it but could have meant an action whereby a person pushed themselves up and over in one movement. Therefore, a height of about two yards could be correct.

The baron court of Godscroft in 1629 ordered that no person was to 'goe ovir dykis to break doun' in order to get into the wood; the penalty was 6s. 8d. Scots.[126] It has been suggested, though, that woods and forests were usually too large and remote to be enclosed by dykes before the eighteenth century at least.[127]

The most dramatic episode of destruction of dykes involved the 'Galloway Levellers' in 1724. They demolished the dry-stone dykes that

---

119 'Corshill Baron Court Book', p. 185.
120 *Court Book of the Barony of Carnwath*, p. 102.
121 'Court Book of the Barony of Fintray', p. 28.
122 'Seventeenth Century Kintyre', p. 217.
123 'Extracts from the Court Books of the Baronies of Skene, Leys, and Whitehaugh 1613–1687', ed. John Stuart, *Miscellany of the Spalding Club*, vol. 5 (Aberdeen: Spalding Club, 1852), p. 232.
124 Fenton, *Scottish Country Life*, p. 3; Smout, *A History of the Scottish People*, p. 132.
125 'Court Book of the Barony of Fintray', p. 31; 'Forbes Baron Court Book', p. 243; *Court Book of the Barony of Urie*, pp. 18, 26; 'Corshill Baron Court Book', p. 152.
126 Historical Manuscripts Commission, *Report on the Manuscripts of Colonel David Milne-Home of Wedderburn Castle*, ed. Henry Paton (London: HMSO, 1902), p. 85.
127 Bil, *The Shieling*, pp. 99–100.

landlords had had built to replace arable land with cattle parks. The Levellers operated in large groups of hundreds or even thousands. Their main demolition tool was a 'kent', a long iron-shod pole, which they used as a lever. There is a report of seven miles of dykes being levelled in three hours.[128]

Offences concerning dykes were familiar enough to become metaphorical. The poet Sir David Lindsay, in 1530, used the phrase 'dyke lowparis' (leapers) to condemn priests who had entered into their church benefices improperly.[129] And a popular proverb went, 'If thow steil no my kaill brik no my dyk'.[130] Both of these related ideas – the leaping over dykes, and the breaking of dykes – thus attracted cultural recognition.

Finally, dykes even had magical significance. Stephen Maltman, in Leckie, Stirlingshire, in 1628, confessed that he had healed Patrick Wright's son by a nocturnal ritual at a march dyke. He made Wright stand on one side of the dyke with the child in his arms, while he himself stood on the other side. Wright then had to pass the child across the dyke to Maltman, who recited a magical prayer before passing the child back to his father again.[131]

* * *

Dykes were at the heart of the spatial articulation of early modern farming. They both linked, and separated, arable and pasture land. Dykes also framed many other features of the inhabited landscape: parks, kale yards, stack yards, sheepfolds, pound-folds, roads, churchyards. The head dyke framed the whole of Scotland, often following a contour line, to divide the cultivated land from the rough upland pasture.

Sources from early modern Scotland reveal information about many aspects of dykes, particularly regarding the cost of them but also about the responsibilities of tenants, the materials and dimensions, the function and the ownership of dykes. Within the scope of the present research it has not been possible to study specific areas in depth, so change over time has been difficult to detect. The sources in general give the impression that changes over time were not extensive; this was before the period in which enclosure programmes would render dykes innovative. Similarly, the present study has not attempted to chart regional variations. Further research could be done to identify variations over both time and space, including looking in greater detail at drawn sources such as maps, and

128 John W. Leopold, 'The Levellers' Revolt in Galloway in 1724', *Journal of the Scottish Labour History Society*, 14 (1980), 4–29, at p. 6.

129 Sir David Lindsay, *Works*, ed. Douglas Hamer (4 vols, Edinburgh: STS, 1931–36), vol. 1, p. 85 ('The Testament of the Papyngo', line 992).

130 *Fergusson's Scottish Proverbs*, no. 796.

131 Alaric Hall, 'Folk-Healing, Fairies and Witchcraft: The Trial of Stein Maltman, Stirling 1628', *Studia Celtica Fennica*, 3 (2006), 10–25, at pp. 17–18.

making more use of archaeological reports. Scottish records could be compared with those from neighbouring countries. Even the court books that have been at the heart of the present study could yield more information about seasonal maintenance and other cyclical patterns. In the meantime, this chapter has presented a broad picture of dykes in farming life in Scotland.

3

The Famine of 1622–23 in Scotland

Kevin Hall

It is altogether possible it is the worst example of a subsistence crisis in the entire seventeenth century.[1]

Michael Flinn identified the famine of 1622–23 as a severe demographic crisis. Flinn's assertion that the 1622–23 famine was a national catastrophe is backed by Karen Cullen, in her benchmark study of the better-documented 1690s famine.[2] Yet there is still no nationwide study of the 1622–23 famine's impact, its human cost to Scotland. This chapter sets out to increase our understanding of a disaster which, even in academic circles, has often been overlooked.

The primary task is to quantify the severity of the famine and its death toll. Few burial registers of the time have survived, but a greater number of baptismal registers exist, and these are crucial to the analysis that follows. The kirk session minutes of several parishes provide qualitative data, and occasionally further quantitative data. The importance of qualitative data in distinguishing periods of 'dearth' and scarcity from true famine cannot be overestimated.[3] While price statistics highlight a period of dearth, as we shall see, the kirk session minutes provide individual human details – such as a poor family seeing three of their children die in little more than a month.[4]

An examination of the attempts made by local and central authorities to alleviate the disaster will ask: were enough measures taken in time to

---

1   Michael Flinn (ed.), *Scottish Population History from the 17th Century to the 1930s* (Cambridge, 1977), p. 117.
2   Karen J. Cullen, *Famine in Scotland: The 'Ill Years' of the 1690s* (Edinburgh, 2010), p. 10.
3   R. W. Hoyle, 'Britain', in Guido Alfani and Cormac Ó Gráda (eds), *Famine in European History* (Cambridge, 2017), pp. 141–65, at p. 142.
4   This case, in Yester, is discussed below.

minimise loss of life? And I will briefly look at the causes of famine, both actual and perceived. What exactly did happen, and what did those living through the disaster assign as the cause?

* * *

In September 1621, John Lauder, minister of the small rural parish of Tyninghame in East Lothian, warned his congregation that 'the present [time was] threatening great dearth and famyne'.[5] Lauder was a local man, his father had been a bailie of Tyninghame, so he knew the area, the topography, the people and the regional climate.[6] He knew that harvest failure was imminent and famine would soon be upon his congregation. It was a famine which Lauder attributed partly to the sins of his congregation: 'God had punished the pepill' for their sin and absenteeism from the kirk on the Sabbath day.[7] A month before, Lauder had called his parish to fast and seek God's forgiveness. Henry Charteris, minister of North Leith, had also called for a regional period of fasting.[8] The week-long fast was held in North Leith for the following reasons:

> That it wald pleis the Lord of his mercie to send and continew goode wedder to the wining and ingathering of the same and that he plague us not with famein as justlie he may do according to our sins.[9]

Fasting in the hope that it would appease God and atone for the collective sins of the people was a common event in early modern Protestant Scotland, more common than for England.[10] But in Scotland the origin of the call to fast could be seen in some quarters as incendiary to God, thereby exacerbating the crisis. The presbyterian chroniclers David Calderwood and John Row both objected to a nationwide call to fast in the summer of 1623, for it had come from a synod of bishops. They both mentioned a storm following this period of fasting, and Calderwood went so far as to say that 'the hearers and beholders thought verilie that the day of judgement was come'.[11]

---

5 NRS, Tyninghame Kirk Session Minutes, 1615–50, CH2/359/1, p. 43.
6 Hew Scott (ed.), *Fasti Ecclesiae Scoticanae: The Succession of Ministers in the Church of Scotland from the Reformation* (7 vols, 2nd edn, Edinburgh, 1915–28), vol. 1, p. 424.
7 NRS, Tyninghame Kirk Session Minutes, CH2/359/1, pp. 44–5.
8 Scott (ed.), *Fasti*, I, p. 154.
9 NRS, North Leith Kirk Session Minutes, 1605–42, CH2/621/1, p. 428.
10 Natalie Mears *et al.* (eds), *National Prayers: Special Worship since the Reformation*, vol. 1: *Special Prayers, Fasts and Thanksgivings in the British Isles 1533–1688* (Woodbridge, 2013). Scotland observed twenty-six national fasts from 1560 to 1621, in comparison to England's six from 1533 to 1621.
11 John Row, *History of the Kirk of Scotland 1558–1637*, ed. David Laing (Edinburgh: Wodrow Society, 1842), p. 332; David Calderwood, *History of the*

In the early 1620s Scotland experienced prolonged periods of stormy and wet weather, as Alan MacDonald and John McCallum have demonstrated through a study of church court records. Ministers were always expected to attend presbytery meetings, and those absent without good cause were fined. That tumultuous weather was frequently accepted as cause for non-attendance bears witness to the high levels of precipitation and storm-force winds which battered Scotland between 1619 and 1623.[12] On the Isle of Skye at Easter 1623, a ferocious storm deposited 'thick banks of beach shingle' almost half a mile inland, and 'huge numbers of boulders were deposited by storm waves' on the east side of the island.[13] Storm-force winds and persistent rain wreaked havoc on crops during the early 1620s, but unfortunately no quantitative data for rainfall exists for Britain prior to 1677.[14] Apart from the analysis of official records by MacDonald and McCallum, our best impression of seventeenth-century weather comes from qualitative sources, the personal accounts of diarists and chroniclers.

In an age of less sophisticated agricultural production, and when there were protectionist tariffs on most forms of victual, it is no great surprise that at least two years of devastating famine followed on from four years of frequently wet and stormy weather. The really bad harvests were those of 1621 and 1622. The former failed through flooding in the autumn, while the latter was catastrophic, with crops failing to ripen as a result of bad weather throughout the year, and cattle dying from disease. Fortunately, the harvests of 1623 and 1624 were good, but the failure of the 1622 harvest led to severe food shortages in 1623 that did not entirely abate until early 1624.[15] Most of the surviving price series for grain and grain products show 1623 as a peak year.[16]

Kirk of Scotland, ed. Thomas Thomson (8 vols, Edinburgh: Wodrow Society, 1842–49), vol. 7, p. 577.

12 Alan R. MacDonald and John McCallum, 'The Evidence for Early Seventeenth-Century Climate from Scottish Ecclesiastical Records', *Environment and History*, 19:4 (2013), 487–509, at pp. 499–500.

13 Alastair Dawson, *So Foul and Fair a Day: A History of Scotland's Weather and Climate* (Edinburgh, 2009), p. 111.

14 Joyce Macadam, 'English Weather: The Seventeenth-Century Diary of Ralph Josselin', *Journal of Interdisciplinary History*, 43:2 (2012), 221–46, at p. 230.

15 Flinn (ed.), *Scottish Population History*, pp. 120–3; T. C. Smout, 'Famine and Famine-Relief in Scotland', in L. M. Cullen and T. C. Smout (eds), *Comparative Aspects of Scottish and Irish Economic and Social History 1600–1900* (Edinburgh, 1977), pp. 21–31, at pp. 22–3.

16 A. J. S. Gibson and T. C. Smout, *Prices, Food and Wages in Scotland 1550–1780* (Cambridge, 1995), tables 2.1, 2.2, 2.3, 2.4, 2.6, 2.11, 3.1 (pp. 51, 54, 55, 56, 58, 64, 84). These prices mostly come from burghs, and are patchy overall. The famine's effect on animals is particularly poorly documented. Gibson and Smout gathered hardly any prices relating to animals for 1623; the main

In pastoral areas such as the Highlands, meat, milk and cheese may have formed a larger proportion of the staple diet, and animals may not have been fed on cereals or their by-products. These areas may have been less affected by the famine, but they probably experienced some of its effects. Richard Hoyle's study of a similar upland pastoral area of Lancashire concludes that 'there was a catastrophe in the animal as well as the human population'.[17] Furthermore, in Karen Cullen's study of the 1690s famine in Scotland, there is evidence of livestock deaths attributable to prolonged periods of stormy weather.[18] Cullen also notes that in the event of Highlanders slaughtering their cattle for food to survive the 1690s famine – as opposed to exchanging at least some of them for a more balanced diet – they would then have faced a problem of stock depletion after the first year of famine; a second year could have been devastating.[19] The famine of the 1620s, although not so prolonged as the better-documented 1690s famine, did last over two years.

* * *

A nationwide famine was a considerable test of the nascent poor law of Scotland, which had first been enacted in 1575. Almost mirroring the English poor law (except that in England each parish had to provide work for the able-bodied poor), the 'Old Scots Poor Law' as it is now known would govern the way in which Scottish parishes provided for the poor until 1845.[20] The system was operated in practice by kirk sessions and funded by voluntary collections, though the law also contained a provision that a stent – a local tax – could be imposed if necessary. One of the questions raised by the famine would be: was a stent necessary?

A recent book by John McCallum contains a detailed and valuable study of the operation of the poor law during the 1623 crisis. McCallum finds that kirk sessions continued to support the regular indigent poor but were unwilling to do much beyond this. They made little attempt to help the migrant poor except to offer them payments to move on. Sometimes they even employed officers to force migrants out. If this failed and the migrants perished in the parish, the parish paid for their burial. McCallum concludes that 'Kirk session relief kept going during some of the most difficult times', whilst acknowledging that during the most extreme stress, 'the relief system showed its limitations and …

exception, the table of burgh prices for tallow and candle, shows no significant change for that year (table 6.18, p. 220).

17 R. W. Hoyle, 'Famine as Agricultural Catastrophe: The Crisis of 1622–4 in East Lancashire', *EcHR*, 63 (2010), 974–1002, at p. 999.

18 Cullen, *Famine in Scotland*, p. 42.

19 Ibid., p. 47.

20 Rosalind Mitchison, *The Old Poor Law in Scotland: The Experience of Poverty 1574–1875* (Edinburgh, 2000).

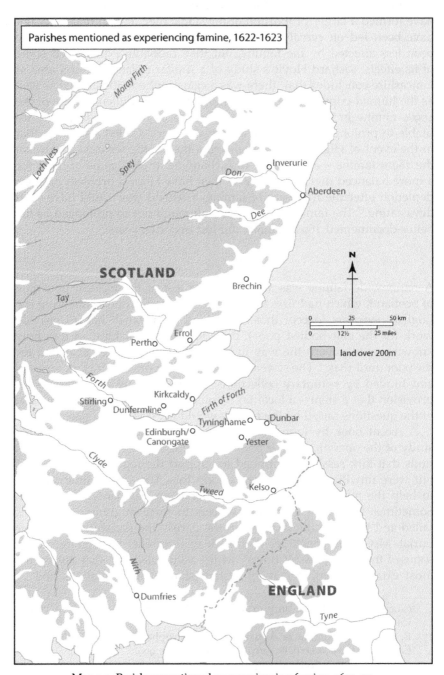

MAP 3.1. Parishes mentioned as experiencing famine, 1622–23.

seriously struggled to cope'.[21] My focus is different from McCallum's, since I am interested principally in famine and the experience of famine, while he focuses more on the activities of kirk sessions. The two topics are nevertheless linked. If my interpretation differs at all from McCallum's, it may be due to the influence of viewing several years of baptism and burial registers within some of the same parishes where we have both read the kirk session records.[22]

In Edinburgh, a stent had been in place since 1591, and the town was better prepared than most.[23] In the capital's conjoined burgh of Canongate, monthly collections were taken by the elders and deacons and backed up by the bailies. The elders and deacons of the parish would 'pas throw the streit on Monday befoir noone and the bell to ring at twa houris in the efter noone' to summon the people to convene at the burgh's tolbooth when the bell rang and pay their contributions. Those found not to have paid would be reported to the bailies, who would require them to double their contribution.[24] Aberdeen too was well organised; in the parish of St Nicholas the poor were allocated financial assistance based upon their age, disability and gender. The younger recipients of alms – mostly women with children – received their money weekly, whilst the elderly and disabled received a quarterly pension.[25]

Many seeking refuge and assistance at the time of the crisis would flock to the towns – where many of them would sadly perish. The larger burghs were nevertheless reasonably well equipped to deal with dearth. Numerous rural parishes also regularly had a surplus of funds for poor relief in non-crisis years.[26] However, the 1622–23 famine was a national crisis, requiring higher levels of funding to provide for greater numbers of people. Understandably then, several parishes showed signs of great strain. This will be discussed more fully below but the broader operations of the poor relief system can be illustrated from the following examples.

In Mid-Calder in Linlithgowshire, the kirk session records have survived from 1623 onwards. Although fragmentary, they provide inval-uable qualitative data. On 19 January 1623, the weekly collection for the poor amounted to 15s. 7d., of which 12s. 8d. was spent on a winding sheet to bury John Gray.[27] This left merely 2s. 11d. for distribution to the poor. Mid-Calder's weekly collections during the famine typically amounted to

21 John McCallum, *Poor Relief and the Church in Scotland 1560–1650* (Edinburgh, 2018), pp. 103–32 (quotation at p. 131).
22 A later section of this chapter will discuss the value of the baptism records.
23 Laura A. M. Stewart, 'Poor Relief in Edinburgh and the Famine of 1621–24', *International Review of Scottish Studies*, 30 (2007), 5–40.
24 NRS, Canongate Kirk Session Minutes, 1619–29, CH2/122/2, p. 271.
25 NRS, Aberdeen St Nicholas Kirk Session Minutes, 1620–60, CH2/448/4, p. 163.
26 McCallum, *Poor Relief*, p. 86 and table 3.2.
27 NRS, Mid-Calder Kirk Session Minutes, 1604–73, CH2/266/1, p. 58.

between 10s. and 15s., and there is no evidence to suggest that the session had a separate fund for poor burials.[28] At the time, there were eighteen individuals on the Mid-Calder poor roll.

Most alms recipients in 1620s Scotland were women. The poor roll for the parish of Dunbarney in Perthshire was almost exclusively female (94 per cent during the famine) and the numbers seeking poor relief dropped dramatically in the years immediately following the famine.[29] Unfortunately, no pre-1623 records for the parish have survived, but the fact that the numbers seeking poor relief were 157 per cent higher during the crisis than they were six years later indicates severe hardship in the parish. The collection of poor relief in rural parishes during the famine carried on much the same as it had prior to the crisis, but rural parishes could not match the resources available to the burghs. For example, in September 1623 in urban Canongate, the sum of £10 was taken from the 'marriage box ... for the suppliement of the puir'. Canongate session also had a separate fund in 1623 collected by the bailies of the burgh purely for poor burials.[30]

In the parishes of Menmuir and Mid-Calder, the entire weekly collection was often given to a single individual or was split between two or three recipients.[31] In Yester, the collection was taken weekly but distributed monthly, and boosted by fines imposed on any transgressors within the congregation, an important component of the poor relief funds.[32] Although this system was well-intentioned and -maintained, it was inadequate in time of crisis. In Mid-Calder, of the eighteen women on the 'ordinar' poor list of 1621, only thirteen were listed in the session minutes of 1624. The other five must either have perished, or along with thousands of others taken to the road in search of better help elsewhere. The session records of Mid-Calder hint at high mortality, as the elders bought a new bier 'for carrying off the deid to the kirk yaird'.[33] Several other parishes, including North Leith, Kirkcaldy and Burntisland, also acquired new biers in 1623.[34]

The strain on parochial poor relief was exemplified by a proclamation made by the presbytery of Dunbar. Licensed begging was usually

---

28 McCallum, *Poor Relief*, p. 90. Canongate had a separate fund for this purpose, as will be seen below.
29 NRS, Dunbarney Kirk Session, Collections and Testimonials, 1602–31, CH2/100/1.
30 NRS, Canongate Kirk Session Minutes, 1619–29, CH2/122/2, pp. 177, 187.
31 NRS, Menmuir Kirk Session Minutes, 1622–1701, CH2/264/1; Mid-Calder Kirk Session Minutes, CH2/266/1.
32 McCallum, *Poor Relief*, p. 87.
33 NRS, Mid-Calder Kirk Session Minutes, CH2/266/1, p. 60.
34 NRS, North Leith Kirk Session Minutes, 1605–42, CH2/621/1, p. 452; Kirkcaldy Kirk Session Minutes and Accounts, 1614–45, CH2/636/34, p. 96; Burntisland Kirk Session Minutes, 1602–67, CH2/523/1, p. 204.

restricted to the pauper's own parish, but, realising that few parishes could cope, the presbytery licensed each parish to send their beggars to seek assistance from wherever they could find it. In Tyninghame it was noted that 'gif any parosche within this Presbyterie wer not abill to sustaine thair awin puir then they sould have licence to seik utherways [outside] the bounds of this Presbyterie'.[35] The seriousness of the situation in East Lothian can further be seen from the accounts of the tiny parish of Yester. In 1621, the poor box contained £26 5s. at the annual reckoning of accounts. By 1622 the surplus had dropped to £21, and by 1623 it was reduced to under £4, despite being bolstered by one-off payments by wealthy locals such as Lord Yester.[36]

* * *

Thus, despite the best efforts of the kirk in providing for the poor, the system simply could not cope with demand. More funds were needed as food prices were rising, and many would not have been able to contribute as they had done before. The system carried on under great strain, but many – especially migrants – were beyond its scope. Their experience was one of catastrophe.

In many of the parishes for which records of the famine period have survived, a clear narrative of unsustainable pressure emerges. Several saw their funds seriously depleted – or worse. The entry in the records of Burntisland for 29 June 1623 is worth quoting in full, as the admission that the poor box was empty also comments on the famine's economic and human cost to the community:

> Public intimatioun is maid of a collection for the puir Seeing as the puir box is emptied. And consideddering the puir aboundantly increis comeing frome all places And the famine continews quhairby many puir folkis deis and ar found deid in the streitis.
> Item, payit for twa wynding scheitis to puir folkis 27s.[37]

Poor folks being found dead in the streets would have been almost as alarming for early modern Scots as it would be for us today. Calderwood mentions bodies lying in the streets of Edinburgh.[38] The old parish registers for neighbouring Canongate contain one entry for 'four puir bodyis found partlie deid in the streitis and partlie in houssis' and another lamentable one for 'ane puir body that deid upon the middin', both of

35 NRS, Tyninghame Kirk Session Minutes, CH2/359/1, p. 48.
36 NRS, Yester Kirk Session Minutes, 1613–43, CH2/377/1, pp. 81–93; cf. McCallum, *Poor Relief*, p. 108.
37 NRS, Burntisland Kirk Session Minutes, 1602–67, CH2/523/1, p. 203.
38 Calderwood, *History*, vol. 7, p. 577.

these in May 1623.[39] A few incidents of poor strangers dying on the streets of Edinburgh and Canongate do not truly convey the full horror of this famine, as one might reasonably ask how the numbers could be so small in the capital. An answer to that can be found in the records of a parish on the periphery of the burgh, as we shall see.

The only other surviving parish burial records which regularly listed the place of death were those of Kelso. As in Canongate, locals provided informal poor relief, sheltering the migratory poor – contrary to the kirk's instructions. On 6 February 1623, a poor child was noted to have died in John Lawless's house, on the 11th a 'puir woman' died in John Brown's house, on the 13th a 'puir child' died in Alexander Fortingall's stable, and on the 16th another 'puir child' died in Margaret Pringle's house.[40] Almost all of the unnamed poor women and children who died in Kelso during the famine had been offered shelter, but the records list the place of death for only one poor man, who perished in the kirkyard.[41] In the small Aberdeenshire parish of Inverurie, further evidence exists of the hospitality and charity offered to the poor. On 28 December 1623, the parish register records that 'Bessie Chalmer begger dyed in Thomas Jonstouns hous'. Bessie was one of eight people to perish in Inverurie that month, and one of fifty-one to die in the parish that year.[42] Such high mortality figures were commonplace all over Scotland, particularly on the east coast.

We have seen then that many of the localities were under heavy stress during the crisis. The burden of poor relief essentially fell on the shoulders of parishioners, either by way of contributing to organised collections, payment of fines for moral transgressions, or simply offering a poor stranger a roof over their heads for what proved to be their final few days or hours of life.

* * *

What was the central government doing? To set the answer to this question in context, it is necessary to go back to 1619. The privy council in October 1619, citing the 'plentie' of the recent harvest, imposed import duties of 10s. per boll on wheat, malt and barley, and 6s. 8d. per boll on all other victuals.[43] Despite the protests of the royal burghs, the tariff stood.[44] The council reasoned that Scotland was at the time a net exporter

---

39 NRS, Canongate Old Parish Registers – Burials, OPR 685/3/200, p. 23.
40 NRS, Kelso Old Parish Registers – Burials, OPR 793/50, p. 287.
41 Ibid., p. 336.
42 NRS, Inverurie Old Parish Registers – Burials, OPR 204/10, p. 143. The other seven were Helen Maky, John Jackson, Elspet Steward, Antone Scot (poor boy), Janet Weir, Robert Fergus and Issobel Salbie.
43 *RPC*, vol. 12, pp. 94–5.
44 *Records of the Convention of Royal Burghs of Scotland 1615–1676*, ed. J. D.

of grain and they feared a capital drain on the economy, claiming that 'a grit penuritie and scarstie of moneyis' would occur without protectionist tariffs.[45] The tariffs on victuals were revised and increased, and were still in place when the realisation of a forthcoming poor harvest occurred in autumn 1621. In November of that year, facing 'grit scairstie and penurie of victual within this year to come', the privy council banned exports of grain – but the tariffs on imports remained.[46] They were finally repealed on 1 April 1622, thereby encouraging Scottish merchants to import grain, which came mainly from established trading routes to the Baltic.[47] Before then, the fear of a dearth of gold had been greater than the fear of a dearth of food. The abolition of the tariffs meant that imports would not be officially recorded, so the question of how much grain was imported during the famine may unfortunately be unanswerable.

In June 1623, with the famine becoming more serious, the privy council attempted to organise a nationwide implementation of the poor law stent or taxation.[48] Five of Scotland's thirty-three sheriffdoms – Selkirk, Berwick, Roxburgh, Perth and Aberdeen – implemented the poor law to the extent of placing a stent on parishioners. Mixed responses trickled in over the following months with as many questions being thrown back at the privy council as there were instructions in the latter's June proclamation. For instance, Berwickshire's justices wanted to know whether the taxation would be applicable 'upoun infeftments only, or annual rentis dew by bandis, both or aither of thame'.[49] How could a tax be implemented when the local authorities did not know exactly whom to tax and to what extent? The justices of Renfrewshire agreed to implement a weekly tax, parish by parish, and further declared that badges would be issued to the indigent poor to license them to beg. A team of men would be appointed to remove vagrant beggars, and anyone found helping migrant poor would face penalties ranging from 20s. to £5.[50]

The Perthshire justices informed the privy council that they intended to employ constables to keep out the vagrant beggars, paying them 13s. 4d. per week 'if they cannot be conducit [i.e. hired] for less'.[51] This was a very low rate of pay; unskilled day labourers in this period usually received 5s. or 6s. per day.[52] At a second meeting of the justices of

---

Marwick (Edinburgh, 1878), pp. 74–7.
45 *RPC*, vol. 11, p. 455.
46 *RPC*, vol. 12, p. 598.
47 Hoyle, 'Britain', p. 160.
48 *RPC*, vol. 13, pp. 257–60. There is an analysis of this programme, and the local response, in Julian Goodare, 'Parliament and Society in Scotland 1560–1603' (PhD thesis, University of Edinburgh, 1989), pp. 442–4.
49 *RPC*, vol. 13, p. 822.
50 *RPC*, vol. 13, pp. 805–6.
51 *RPC*, vol. 13, p. 816.
52 Gibson and Smout, *Prices, Food and Wages*, pp. 267–8, 278.

Perthshire, on 2 September, it was decided that the 'proper pure of every parochione' would be sustained by the 'heretours, wadsett havearis, lyverenteris and thair tenentis' on whose land they resided. If a parish was overburdened with poor, then a supplication could be made to two adjoining parishes for further assistance.[53] This innovative approach would have seen the propertied classes directly providing for those on their land, but with an added guarantee that they could seek assistance in the event of a shortfall in funds.

The responses from Perthshire and Stirlingshire were equally concerned with the suppression of migrant vagrants, with Stirling justices stating that 'thay war all willing' to comply with the instruction for implementation of the stent 'providing thay war frie of extraneane pure, and speciallie the Heiland pure', which they asked the privy council to arrange.[54] This exiguous mention of migrating Highland poor is one of the very few pieces of evidence indicating that the famine's impact north of the Mounth was equally, if not more, severe than it was elsewhere in Scotland. The Stirling justices probably knew well that they could not relocate the Highland poor and so would never fully implement the poor law.

By contrast, the justices of East Lothian bluntly refused to implement the stent, saying that it 'keipis no proportioun according to the diversity of mens rankis' – essentially saying that this was a greater burden on the middling sorts than on the nobility. They threatened that they were all 'willing to discharge our selffis' and quit their positions rather than implement the stent.[55] The privy council may have been furious at such a response, which seems worthy of 'a special prize for meanness';[56] however, the threat of mass resignations rendered central authorities impotent. East Lothian would carry on as before and the privy council could do nothing about it.

Attempted implementation was thus inadequate and hastily arranged. Nothing better exemplifies this than the response of the sheriffdom of Edinburgh (Midlothian):

> The said Act of Parliament can not gudlie be put in execution this present yeir in respect of these difficulties and reasonabill caus evidentlie sene and perceavit in the contrair, Viz: because the haill pure ar impotent, opprest, and overcum with seikness and famyn, sua miserable and weik that they can hardlie transport tham selffis fra ane parochin to ane other, and that the tyme of the making of this Act of Parliament it is thoght that thair wes nather sick greit famyn, sick greit number of pure, nor sa greit a visitatioun of seikness. Quhairfor the Justices of the

53 *RPC*, vol. 13, pp. 819–20.
54 *RPC*, vol. 13, pp. 807–8, 815–17, 819–21; quotation at p. 808.
55 *RPC*, vol. 13, pp. 836–8.
56 Goodare, 'Parliament and Society', p. 443.

Piece thinkis verie expedient that the execution of this Act be dispensit this present yeir.[57]

Edinburgh's response to the privy council may have been tinged with parsimony, as the landed elite surrounding the capital sought to avoid another tax. But the response was also a brutally honest assessment of the scale of the crisis and an acknowledgement that thousands were certain to die in the summer and autumn of 1623.

*   *   *

Mortality is at the heart of how a famine should be understood and even defined. The excess mortality, beyond the normal death rate, will include deaths from famine-related diseases as well as those from starvation itself. Famines have other demographic effects, such as migration, that need to be accounted for separately.[58]

So how many Scots perished, over what extent of the country, and what type of background did they come from? To gather material to answer these questions, I re-examined the Old Parish Registers, the records of baptisms and burials, viewed by Flinn and his team in the 1970s. As well as compiling aggregate data as Flinn did, I have noted details of the socio-economic status and exact location of the dead at time of death wherever possible. In doing this, I was able to identify groups most at risk during times of dearth and establish levels of support offered by locals to incomers seeking respite and shelter. In addition to the records used by Flinn, the burial records for the parishes of Canongate, Inverurie and Errol have been examined. Although not all complete, they are an invaluable source of information. My examination of baptismal records is more extensive than Flinn's, coming from twenty-one parishes. All burial and baptismal records were examined over a minimum period of ten years (1618–27) and the following methodology was applied to determine mortality increase and fertility decrease. For mortality, the peak years of famine (1622 and 1623) were excluded, and the average over the other years was taken as the baseline mortality rate. For fertility, the process was similar; the years immediately following the peak mortality years were excluded, and the average over the remaining years was taken as the baseline fertility rate. Lastly, the kirk session records were also examined. Flinn did not use these extensively, as they do not provide standardised demographic data, but they can offer both quantitative and qualitative information on the famine's impact.

---

57 *RPC*, vol. 13, p. 817.
58 Tim Dyson and Cormac Ó Gráda, 'Introduction', in Tim Dyson and Cormac Ó Gráda (eds), *Famine Demography: Perspectives from the Past and Present* (Oxford, 2002), pp. 1–18.

I will start by returning to the north-eastern parish of Inverurie. The town lay to the north-west of Aberdeen in the valley of the River Don. The baptismal registers are incomplete and often cover only a few months of the year, but the complete years suggest that the annual birth rate in the parish was around 23 to 26. Based on 35 births per 1,000 head of population per year, the population would therefore have been somewhere between 650 and 700.[59] The normal annual mortality rate would have been 25–30, but in 1622–23, over 100 deaths were recorded in the parish, equating to a near 14 per cent population loss over just two years.

It is possible to discount one of the Inverurie deaths from our reckoning, as on 28 May 1623, the parish register records the murder of John Jonstoune by his friend John Lesley, after an argument blew out of proportion when the two had been drinking ale together.[60] Thus, ale was still being consumed by some people in quantities, as can be seen in other burghs too. For example, in Ayr, during the height of the famine in the summer of 1623, the kirk session thought it necessary to issue a lengthy act against drinking after ten o'clock in the evening.[61] In England, the central government ordered the suppression of the production of strong ale in October 1622, to divert barley and malt to food supplies.[62]

The devastating impact of famine upon a small semi-urban parish like Inverurie can be gauged both from the alarming decline in baptisms in the years immediately following the famine, and from an examination of the names listed for burial. The parish register for late October and November 1622 records eight deaths, and at least three of the deceased were probably connected. The first was a servant boy, John Clerk, employed by Thomas Fergus. John may well have been related to Elspeth Clerk who passed away twenty-three days later, and the Thomas Fergus who died just five days after Elspeth may have been John's master.[63] In the two years immediately following the famine, the register records only 24 baptisms: 11 in 1623 and 13 in 1624. Both these years have complete records, so it is evident that the birth rate in the parish fell dramatically because of famine.[64] This is an issue to which I will return.

59 'In early modern Europe, the birth rate remained fairly constant at about 35 per 1000 people, which is about the natural maximum': Mark Konnert, *Early Modern Europe: The Age of Religious War 1559–1715* (Calgary, 2007), p. 22.
60 NRS, Inverurie Old Parish Registers – Burials, OPR 204/10, p. 135.
61 NRS, Ayr Kirk Session Minutes, 1621–46, CH2/751/2, pp. 36–7.
62 *Calendar of State Papers, Domestic Series 1619–1623*, ed. Mary A. E. Green (London, 1858), p. 455. Weaker ale was a staple drink, but *strong* ale, which required more malt per unit volume, could be dispensed with in a crisis.
63 NRS, Inverurie Old Parish Registers – Burials, OPR 204/10, p. 133.
64 Ibid.

The baptismal and burial records for Canongate suggest that the burgh had a population of around 3,500–4,000.[65] When examining the burial records from 1618 to 1638 there are four years of unusually high mortality which stand out, and 1623 is one such year (the others being 1626, 1629 and 1630). It is only in 1623, moreover, that the burial records list unnamed poor strangers who had died in the streets. Baptisms saw a noticeable decline in 1623 and 1624, before numbers returned to near normal by 1625. The number of births per year in Canongate had reached a new high in 1621, and this mini baby boom can be seen in the records of many other places across Scotland in 1621. In fact, in 14 of the 21 parishes in which baptismal records from 1618 to 1627 were examined, 1621 had either the highest or second-highest birth rate.[66] This baby boom was no doubt connected to Scotland's economy having been stable, if not robust, in the years leading up to the famine, with one historian describing the period as the 'doing-nicely-thank-you years from about 1603 to 1620'.[67] But a baby boom occurring just two years before a devastating famine would have tragic consequences in many Scottish communities. In an age where familiarity with the Scriptures was commonplace, it is altogether possible that to many of the young families in Scotland seeing their firstborn children perish, another Passover was taking place – only this time it was in Scotland, not Egypt, that God's wrath was striking the country for the sins of the people.[68] The year of 1623 could, with some justification, be called Scotland's Passover.

In Kelso, where baptism rates were 28 per cent higher than average in 1621, child and infant mortality accounted for just over 50 per cent of the dead in 1623, but it is not clear how many of those deaths were infants under the age of three. The clerk keeping Kelso's burial register simply listed all child mortality as 'bairne' or 'ane puir bairne'.[69] These records have a high number of incomer infant and child deaths, with the months of July, August and September being particularly bad for the migrating children. In July 1623, 10 of the 40 children to die in Kelso were unnamed poor children from outside the town.[70] In Dunfermline in 1622, child and infant mortality accounted for 45 per cent of the dead, with 23 of the children being described as 'infant' or at an age before they could speak. In 1623, child and infant mortality in Dunfermline

65 NRS, Canongate Old Parish Registers – Baptisms, OPR 685/3.
66 They are Abercorn, Anstruther, Canongate, Dunfermline, Dysart, Duns, Edinburgh, Errol, Falkirk, Glasgow, Inveresk and Musselburgh, Kelso, Kirkcaldy, Lasswade, Linlithgow, Leith (North), Mid-Calder, Monikie, Montrose, Newbattle and Perth.
67 Julian Goodare, *State and Society in Early Modern Scotland* (Oxford, 1999), p. 130.
68 Exodus 12.
69 NRS, Kelso Old Parish Registers – Burials, OPR 793/50, pp. 328–48.
70 Ibid., pp. 331–7.

accounted for 34 per cent of the dead, with almost half that number being infants.[71] In both 1622 and 1623, infant mortality in Dunfermline peaked in the third quarter of the year, with 26 infants dying during August 1623, or an infant dying every 29 hours. This period was the 'hungry gap', with the previous year's harvest having been used up but the current year's harvest not yet in.

The only other parish for which the burial register of 1623 has survived is Errol, located 9 miles east of Perth. Flinn's team did not use this as it is only partial and thus unsuitable for gathering quantitative data, but it still offers qualitative material – especially when compared with the complete baptismal register. The latter suggests that the population was around 2,000 at the time of the crisis, with an average birth rate of 72 per year. With a population of this size one would expect to see an annual burial rate of 60 to 65 persons, or five to six burials per month. It would most definitely be an unexpected event to see five burials in one day – but that is what happened on 12 October, when Patrick Daw, Robert Duncan, Gilbert Gardner, Thomas Jackson and Gilbert Monorgun were all laid to rest.[72] Errol's burial records have survived only for the months of February, October and December 1623, but these records still show deaths equal to half a year's expected mortality for a parish of this population. One can only guess at the famine's impact in Errol during the peak mortality period of August and September. But the parish records do show that the annual birth rate fell by over 30 per cent immediately after the famine.[73]

As stated earlier, I looked at the records for 21 parishes, with each parish providing full baptismal records for at least the period 1618–27. Accepting the formula of 35 births per year per thousand population, then these records cover an area with an estimated population in excess of 85,000. Can this be related to Scotland's population as a whole? As Flinn acknowledged, 'before 1755 there is no source from which it is possible to estimate a total of Scottish population'.[74] However, a consensus exists among Scottish historians that the early seventeenth-century population would not have exceeded 1 million people.[75] The sample size used here of almost 10 per cent of the population can thus be taken as being broadly representative of the nation's experience of the 1622–23 famine.

*   *   *

71 NRS, Dunfermline Old Parish Registers – Burials, OPR 424/110, pp. 24–39.
72 NRS, Errol Old Parish Registers – Burials, OPR 351/40, p. 158.
73 NRS, Errol Old Parish Registers – Baptisms, OPR 351/10.
74 Flinn (ed.), *Scottish Population History*, p. 4.
75 Maureen M. Meikle, *The Scottish People 1490–1625* (n.p., 2013), pp. 3–4; Ian D. Whyte, *Scotland before the Industrial Revolution: An Economic and Social History c.1050–c.1750* (London, 1995), p. 113.

Crisis mortality can be identified, not just from the burial records, but also from the baptism records. Famine often leads to a subsequent decline in births. The French social historian Jean Meuvret was among the first to recognise that a direct correlation exists between the high mortality of crisis years and subsequent decline in the number of births. Describing the connection as 'an indisputable and symptomatic fact' in his study of mortality crises in late sixteenth- and early seventeenth-century France, Meuvret observed that 'an abrupt upsurge in deaths coincides with an equally abrupt decrease in conceptions'.[76] In their benchmark *Population History of England*, Wrigley and Schofield argue that 'A doubling of mortality in one year would lead to the long-run loss of about 31 per cent of the normal annual number of births.'[77] A definite connection exists then between famine mortality and a decline in birth rate immediately following the crisis.[78] It should be possible then to turn this around and say that, in the absence of burial statistics *during* a famine, a sharp decline in the number of baptisms immediately *after* a known crisis may be taken as evidence of high mortality in that parish, because one inevitably follows the other.

With this in mind, what can be learned of the Scottish experience of famine in 1623 from the baptism records prior to and immediately following the famine? In 1621, every one of the registers recorded a higher than average number of births, with a total of 3,431 baptisms, 16 per cent higher overall than the combined annual average of 2,950. In Dumfries, where the records end in 1624, the average number of baptisms before the crisis was 118 per year, with a record high of 143 in 1621. In 1622 there were 115 births and in 1623 and 1624 just 71 and 57 respectively.[79] The birth rate in Dumfries dropped by 39 per cent from average following the famine, and in 12 of our 21 parishes the birth rate dropped by at least 30 per cent from average for the years 1623 and 1624.

The birth rate fell by 35 per cent in Dunfermline and by 33 per cent in Kelso.[80] Two further parishes, Perth and Kirkcaldy, recorded a drop in the

76 Jean Meuvret, 'Subsistence Crises and the Demography of France under the Ancien Regime', *Population*, 71 (2016), 547–54, at p. 549. This article was first published in 1946. See also Emmanuel Le Roy Ladurie, 'Famine Amenorrhea (Seventeenth-Twentieth Centuries)', in Robert Foster and Orest Ranum (eds), *Biology of Man in History: Selections from the Annales, Economies, Societies, Civilisations* (London, 1975), pp. 163–78.

77 E. A. Wrigley and R. S. Schofield, *The Population History of England 1541–1871*, 2nd edn (Cambridge, 1989), p. 364.

78 See also Karen J. Cullen, Christopher A. Whatley and Mary Young, 'King William's Ill Years: New Evidence on the Impact of Scarcity and Harvest Failure during the Crisis of the 1690s on Tayside', *SHR*, 85:2 (2006), 250–76, at pp. 265–7; Flinn (ed.), *Scottish Population History*, pp. 180–5.

79 NRS, Dumfries Old Parish Registers – Baptisms, OPR 821/10, pp. 103–12.

80 NRS, Dunfermline Old Parish Registers – Baptisms, OPR 424/20; Kelso Old

birth rate of almost 30 per cent over the years 1623 and 1624.[81] Given the excessive mortality in Dumfries, Dunfermline and Kelso, as highlighted by Flinn and his team, one can safely assume that a 30 per cent (or greater) fall in birth rate from average is indicative of high mortality during the famine.

In Kinghorn, the kirk session announced an extraordinary collection to take place in July 1623. Stating that the aim was to alleviate 'the grit necessitie of the puir within this congregatioune', the intimation came with a demand that everyone was 'expectit to schew thair Christian charitie in gevin liberalie'.[82] The parish was under considerable strain; the birth rate dropped by 52 per cent in the years 1623 and 1624.[83] This figure is far in excess of the benchmark 30 per cent figure as an indicator of high mortality, and, given the proximity to Kirkcaldy and Burntisland, two parishes known to have suffered very high mortality, it seems certain that Kinghorn suffered similarly. Records from Burntisland, Dunfermline, Dysart, Kinghorn and Kirkcaldy confirm that the famine's impact along the Fife coastline was severe.

Records from other burghs and rural parishes demonstrate that the entire east coast of Scotland was affected. The baptismal registers for Brechin begin only in 1624, but in that year there were only 48 baptisms. In every year after that there were over 100, so something was clearly awry in Brechin through 1623–24.[84] In the nearby parish of Menmuir, the poor roll in 1623 was more than twice the size it was in the years following the famine, and in the parish of Monikie, 18 miles south of Brechin, the birth rate dropped by almost 40 per cent in 1623–24.[85] The birth rate in Monikie did not recover until almost five years after the famine. In Mid-Calder, where the average annual birth rate was around 58, there were only 16 baptisms in 1623 and 19 in 1624.[86]

Returning to the East Lothian parish of Tyninghame, 3 parishioners were buried in March 1623, with Alexander Davidson being the last on 20 March. There then follows a lengthy gap in the records before a further 9 burials are listed between 19 October and 1 December.[87] Nothing may seem unusual there, until one considers that the complete

---

Parish Registers – Baptisms, OPR 793/10.

81 NRS, Perth Old Parish Registers – Baptisms, OPR 387/20; Kirkcaldy Old Parish Registers – Baptisms, OPR 442/10.

82 NRS, Kinghorn Kirk Session Minutes, 1581–1632, CH2/472/1, p. 129.

83 NRS, Kinghorn Old Parish Registers – Baptisms, OPR 439/10, pp. 75–118.

84 NRS, Brechin Old Parish Registers – Baptisms, OPR 275/10, pp. 17–45.

85 NRS, Menmuir Kirk Session Minutes, CH2/264/1; Mid-Calder Kirk Session Minutes, CH2/266/1.

86 NRS, Mid-Calder Old Parish Registers – Baptisms, OPR 694/10.

87 NRS, Tyninghame Kirk Session Minutes, CH2/359/1, p. 48.

session records for 1619, 1620 and 1621 list burials of only 29 parish-ioners, suggesting that the tiny parish had an average mortality rate of 10 deaths per year. The 12 deaths listed in the fragmentary records of 1623 surpass the annual expected mortality figure, and there were no doubt further burials during the peak mortality months of July, August and September.

* * *

Some of the parish records tell us, not just about mortality statistics, but about measures taken to deal with the crisis, and the overall experience of famine. Beginning with the capital, Edinburgh had implemented a monthly collection, or stent, to provide funds for the local poor, in 1591, so was better prepared than most burghs to cope with the crisis.[88] This raised around £2,500 annually during the 1620s, almost ten times the amount raised by the stent in Alloa, where the 147 contributors paid an average of 3s. each per month.[89] The capital's preparedness has been clearly demon-strated by Laura Stewart who also highlights the capital's intense efforts to stem the influx of beggars, with 'streetkeepers' being hired in 1623 and 1624 to expel beggars and a five-man guard posted at the port of Leith to prevent any illicit cargoes of the destitute disembarking.[90] Yet some of the migrant poor undoubtedly made it into Leith, as can be seen from increased expenditure on winding sheets. Between 1620 and 1622, the session of North Leith purchased just one winding sheet for an unnamed poor man, whereas in 1623 the session made 14 such purchases.[91]

What was the incomer mortality in Edinburgh itself? As mentioned earlier, David Calderwood wrote of corpses being found on the streets, and the parish register for the adjoining burgh of Canongate records several poor folks lying dead in the streets. A further clue to the fate of many of the destitute is found in the kirk session records of St Cuthbert's, a parish in the shadow of Edinburgh Castle. Throughout June, July and August of 1623, its session was occupied with providing for the parish poor or expelling 'all beggeris that is strangeris … within aucht dayis'. However, on 24 August, the kirk officer was to have 2s. apiece for making 'strangeris graves', because of 'the great number departing this lyf for the present'.[92] Whether the 'great number' was 30, 50, or even in hundreds is beyond recovery, and nothing further may ever be known of the destitute migrants who perished in and around St Cuthbert's.

88   Stewart, 'Poor Relief in Edinburgh', p. 8.
89   Stewart, 'Poor Relief in Edinburgh'; NRS, Alloa Kirk Session Minutes, 1609–57, CH2/942/5, pp. 107–9.
90   Stewart, 'Poor Relief in Edinburgh', p. 16.
91   NRS, North Leith Kirk Session Minutes, 1605–42, CH2/621/1, pp. 400–57.
92   NRS, Edinburgh St Cuthbert's Kirk Session Minutes, 1618–29, CH2/718/4, pp. 288, 296.

The high levels of mortality in Kirkcaldy have already been examined, but there is more information about how the town coped with the crisis. The session conducted a macabre census of the unknown dead, as the kirk owed 'ane grit sowme' of money to the treasurer who had purchased their winding sheets.[93] The gruesome task of preparing Kirkcaldy's poor incomer dead was given to the parish's own poor, as a condition for receiving alms. On 15 July 1623, the session ordained that 'when any poore body that is a stranger dies the nixt that getts the kirks weeklie almes sall wynd them under the paine of loseing thair weeklie duetie'.[94] By the end of October, the census shows that the parish poor had prepared 151 migrant dead for burial. In February 1624, with the crisis abating, the treasurer of Kirkcaldy submitted his accounts of expenditure for the parish poor, whose number had been reduced by one-third to 30 people.[95] Being paid for washing, winding and preparing the incomer dead for burial had contributed to the survival of the local poor in Kirkcaldy.

In nearby Burntisland, mortality levels were high.[96] From the spring of 1623 to November of that year, the kirk session bought 35 winding sheets and paid the grave-maker for digging 329 graves.[97] Most of the winding sheets were purchased in July and August. The session paid rates varying from 9s. to 12s. for winding sheets, suggesting a difference in either size or quality. The 9s. sheets may well have been smaller ones for children or infants. In early July, when the death toll accelerated, the session commissioned the construction of 'a littil beir for the young puir anes' for which they paid £2 8s. Throughout July and August, the cost for winding sheets and grave digging was increasing, but the costs listed for 'going with the bier' to collect the dead were not increasing proportionately.[98] It seems likely that the outlay for the children's bier was a pragmatic decision and that the grave-maker received a lower rate for collecting the corpses of children. The kirk session was still purchasing winding sheets at a rate of up to 7 per week as late as February 1624.[99]

Seven paupers dying each week – one per day – is a truly awful death toll to contemplate, but this mortality rate was exceeded in the summer and autumn of 1623 in several parishes. The Chronicle of Perth claimed that 'X or XIJ deit ordinarlie everie day, from midsomer to mychaelmas,

---

93 NRS, Kirkcaldy Kirk Session Minutes, CH2/636/34, p. 103. There were also payments to the treasurer 'for wynding scheitts furneist be him to sundrie poore folkis depairtit' in October 1622: p. 85.
94 Ibid., p. 99.
95 Ibid., p. 111.
96 Flinn (ed.), *Scottish Population History*, p. 119.
97 NRS, Burntisland Kirk Session Minutes, 1602–67, CH2/523/1, pp. 203–7.
98 Ibid.
99 Ibid., p. 211.

within this burgh'.[100] This would come to over 1,000 deaths, and may well have been exaggerated; the highest *daily* death toll in any burial register was 7, recorded in Dunfermline on 11 September and in Kelso on 2 August.[101] In Kirkcaldy too, the death toll was high, as the kirk session register records that a poor person died on average every 35 hours in the town during the summer of 1623.[102] In Kelso, the average daily death toll in August 1623 was 3, with the highest figure, 7, matching that of Dunfermline above. On 2 August, 'Johne Broun a puir auld man' was laid to rest along with 'ane puir bairne in James Boswells' (house), 'ane puir woman' and 4 others. On 3 and 5 August, 4 of the 6 dead were listed as 'bairne' with one of them being an unnamed 'puir bairne' who died in John Cochrane's house. By December, Kelso's death toll had slowed to an average of one every other day, but still included many unknown children and infants, such as the 'puir boy' in James Pringle's house who passed away on 10 December.[103]

The parish of Yester, like Kirkcaldy, employed its own poor to prepare the dead for burial. One stranger who was found dead in the summer of 1623 was prepared for burial by an unnamed 'puir woman' from nearby Danskine, who was paid 3s.[104] The session paid for several winding sheets – both adult and child – for the poor throughout 1623. They were mostly for unnamed people, as for instance on 12 October when three sheets were purchased 'for the puir in Yester' at a cost of 37s., whilst others were for named parishioners, such as Margaret Hay or 'a sone of Thomas Dickson'.[105] But perhaps nothing highlights the famine's impact on East Lothian more than the accounts relating to the Ordingtoun family in Yester. The family were regular recipients of alms in 1623, usually receiving around 10s. per week. On 29 June, the session paid 16s. 'to by ane winding scheit to ane of Sandie Ordingtouns bairnes' and on 3 August two more winding sheets were purchased at a cost of 31s., both for Ordingtoun's children.[106] A poor family lost three of their children within 35 days, tragic in any era. Neither the burial nor baptismal registers for Yester have survived, so the session records are all that we have. However, the high infant mortality that they record makes it likely that the parish had experienced the mini baby boom seen elsewhere in Scotland in 1621.

100 *The Chronicle of Perth 1210–1668*, ed. James Maidment and John Mercer (Edinburgh: Maitland Club, 1831), p. 24.
101 NRS, Dunfermline Old Parish Registers – Burials, OPR 424/110, p. 32.
102 NRS, Kirkcaldy Kirk Session Minutes, CH2/636/34, p. 101.
103 NRS, Kelso Old Parish Registers – Burials, OPR 793/50.
104 NRS, Yester Kirk Session Minutes, CH2/377/1, p. 87.
105 Ibid., p. 95.
106 Ibid., p. 93.

The burial registers of Dumfries also point to another socio-economic group suffering disproportionately: those involved in textiles, clothes and shoe manufacture, and their wives and children, were listed prominently among the dead. During September 1623, the register records the deaths of two cordiners, two weavers, one tailor, and several wives and children of men engaged in these trades.[107] This high mortality rate can also be seen in Dunfermline, suggesting that textile trades were particularly vulnerable in times of dearth. Perhaps people stopped buying clothing when they had to focus on buying food for survival, but further research would be needed to confirm this.

Citing the lower levels of infant mortality recorded in the burial registers, Flinn argued that the disproportionately high adult mortality in Dumfries was indicative of typhus, the 'famine fever'.[108] A small further piece of evidence supports this suggestion. As Flinn noted, over a fifth of the dead in Dumfries were 'extranier', not from the parish.[109] Now, a few of these 'extranier' dead were also listed as prisoners – and they all died within a very short time, on 26 September, 2 and 3 October. The first to die was unnamed, but the last two were 'James Rae prisoner pauper' and 'John Marchtoun prisoner pauper'.[110] These rapid deaths are striking – and in the confines of a tolbooth, typhus would wreak havoc quickly.

In Stirling, the kirk session records for 1623 read much like St Cuthbert's in Edinburgh, with the session's priorities being sustaining their own poor and dealing with the many migrant incomer poor. On no fewer than four occasions from June to August 1623 the session made intimation to help their own 'indigent puir' and to exclude the incomer poor.[111] Stirling's session also released large sums for purchasing winding sheets for the poor dead, with one sum paid out in August being as much as North Leith's total annual expenditure for winding sheets.[112] Further evidence of high mortality in Stirling can be seen from earlier in August when the session employed a gravedigger's assistant. Thomas Thomson was paid 12s. to 'help Finlay Liddal in the burreals and bearin of the beir'.[113] In Stirling, as in Edinburgh, we can only guess at the number of migrants who died, but the kirk did ensure Christian burials for them.

* * *

Scotland did not suffer alone in 1622–23, and the Scottish experience of this famine merely represents one thread of a broader pan-European

---

107 NRS, Dumfries Old Parish Registers – Burials, OPR 821/60, p. 16.
108 Flinn (ed.), *Scottish Population History*, p. 123.
109 Ibid., p. 119.
110 NRS, Dumfries Old Parish Registers – Burials, OPR 821/60, p. 16.
111 NRS, Stirling Kirk Session Minutes, 1614–27, CH2/1026/2.
112 Ibid., p. 248.
113 Ibid.

narrative. In England – where this famine was to be the last seen there – its impact was felt in south-western England and in Lancashire.[114] Fears of impending famine prompted the mayor of London to report to the privy council on a survey of corn, and to buy in supplies from France, as early as February 1623.[115] Richard Hoyle and Jonathan Healey have recently researched the famine's human cost in Lancashire and found evidence of high mortality. The famine probably affected Wales too, although no nationwide study has been undertaken there.[116] Famine was also recorded in Italy at this time, where 'the food problems of the Italian states intensified especially during the 1620s, with famines both at the beginning and end of the decade'.[117]

Finally, then, I attempt to answer the macabre question of just how many people died. Qualitative evidence clearly shows that the famine had a significant impact in terms of mortality. From Inverurie in the North East, right down the coastline to Fife, the Lothians, and the Borders, the human cost was nothing short of catastrophic. In the South West in Dumfries there was appalling loss of life, especially among the migrating poor, and in the gateway to the Highlands in Stirling, the kirk expenditure on poor burials was exceptional, whilst on the periphery of the capital, mass graves were dug for the unknown poor. Moreover, the population may have taken several years to recover. The Orkney sheriff court lamented in February 1628 that 'many lands are laid lay and weast [i.e. untenanted] by the frequent death of the labourers of the ground, these years bygone, thro' the great scarcity, famine, and death of the land'.[118]

Statistical evidence, though fragmentary, supports the picture drawn from the qualitative sources. In 12 out of the 21 parishes for which baptismal records survive, baptisms decreased by 30 per cent or more in the years 1623 and 1624.[119] A decrease of this magnitude and

---

114 Todd Gray, *Harvest Failure in Cornwall and Devon: The Book of Orders and the Corn Surveys of 1623 and 1630–1* (Exeter, 1992); Hoyle, 'Famine as Agricultural Catastrophe'; Jonathan Healey, 'Famine and the Female Mortality Advantage: Sex, Gender and Mortality in North West England, *c*.1590–1630', *Continuity and Change*, 30:2 (2015), 153–92; Colin D. Rogers, *The Lancashire Population Crisis of 1623* (Manchester, 1975); Susan Scott and C. J. Duncan, 'The Mortality Crisis of 1623 in North-West England', *Local Population Studies*, 58 (1997), 14–25.

115 *Calendar of State Papers, Domestic 1619–1623*, pp. 487–8.

116 Hoyle, 'Britain', p. 145.

117 Guido Alfani, 'Famines in Late Medieval and Early Modern Italy: A Test for an Advanced Economy', *Dondena Working Papers*, 82 (2015), p. 6.

118 Quoted in George Barry, *The History of the Orkney Islands*, rev. edn (London, 1808), pp. 475–6.

119 Baptisms decrease by 30 per cent or more (figures in brackets are NRS OPR references): Abercorn (661/10), Anstruther (403/20), Dunfermline

suddenness is a strong indicator of famine-related mortality. Thus, famine-related mortality can be said to have occurred in 57 per cent of those areas with surviving records. This may well be an underestimate; all 21 of the parishes showed *some* decrease in baptisms (at least 12 per cent). And more than half of the less-affected parishes (those with decreases below 30 per cent) were towns, which may not be representative of the rural majority. On the other hand, we have no statistics from the Highlands. At any rate, if we apply the figure of 57 per cent to a cautious estimate of the total population (900,000), we find that areas in which about 513,000 people lived were affected. And the effect was directly on *mortality* – not on other causes of population decrease, such as emigration.

Now, what was the scale of the famine's effect on these people? In the areas where it is possible to make a reasonable estimate of population loss percentage with some accuracy, Dunfermline, Kelso and Dumfries, the population loss varies from 20 per cent (Dunfermline) to 11 per cent (Dumfries). As it could be expected that at least 3 per cent of the population would die annually anyway, these figures indicate excess mortality – directly attributable to famine or associated disease – of 17 per cent and 8 per cent respectively. The mid-point between these two figures, 12.5 per cent, seems to be the best figure that can be suggested for the scale of famine-related mortality in the affected areas of Scotland. Applying that to the affected 57 per cent of the country's parishes and assuming (conservatively) that these were the *only* parishes affected, then a figure of just over 7 per cent overall mortality for Scotland emerges.[120] In numerical terms this is just over 64,000 deaths from starvation and famine-related diseases. And many of them, as we have seen, were children and infants – victims of Scotland's Passover.

(424/20), Dysart (426/10), Errol (351/10), Falkirk (479/20), Inveresk (689/10), Kelso (793/10), Lasswade (691/10), Mid-Calder (694/10), Monikie (311/20), Newbattle (695/10). Baptisms decrease by under 30 per cent: Canongate (685/3), Edinburgh (685/1), Glasgow (644/1), Kirkcaldy (442/10), Linlithgow (668/10), Montrose (312/10), North Leith (692/1), Pencaitland (716/10), Perth (387/20).

120 This figure of over 7 per cent is comparable with mortality in Ulster during the 'Great Famine' of Ireland. See Liam Kennedy, Kerby A. Miller and Brian Gurrin, 'People and Population Change 1600–1914', in Liam Kennedy and Philip Ollerenshaw (eds), *Ulster since 1600: Politics, Economy, and Society* (Oxford, 2012), pp. 58–73, at p. 66.

4

Weather and Farming through the Eyes of a Sixteenth-Century Highland Peasant

Julian Goodare

The Chronicle of Fortingall can be read as the diary of a sixteenth-century Scottish peasant.[1] It was written by the unbeneficed parish priest of Fortingall, in Highland Perthshire. He carried out his own farming, almost certainly for subsistence, and wrote about his experience of farming in his chronicle. It is extremely rare in this period to encounter words written by someone whose hands have held not only a pen but also farming tools. These words deserve close attention.

The chronicle is not primarily a personal diary; it is a semi-public and largely anonymous document, unlike (for instance) the personal account-book kept by the fifteenth-century Tuscan peasant Benedetto del Massarizia.[2] The focus is on the community and its relationship with God, rather than the author as an individual; the chronicler does not even

---

1   'The Chronicle of Fortirgall', in *The Black Book of Taymouth*, ed. Cosmo Innes (Edinburgh: Bannatyne Club, 1855), pp. 107–48. ('Fortirgall' is an older spelling.) Innes's edition is a reliable transcription, but I have also used the original manuscript at NLS, MS 50300. Digital images of the manuscript are online at: https://digital.nls.uk/229918123. Innes's edition reorganised the text, gathering its annalistic material together and presenting it more fully in chronological order than it appears in the manuscript. Future study of the manuscript may reveal more about how it was compiled. Other writers may have contributed to its non-annalistic material.

     The Chronicle's material on weather and farming is reproduced in an appendix to this chapter. In what follows, citations of this material are given, in brackets in the text, using the season and date listed in the appendix, thus (S1566, W1576–77). Other citations of the Chronicle are to page numbers of Innes's edition, thus (p. 137). Citations of the court records also printed in the *Black Book of Taymouth* are given similarly.

2   Duccio Balestracci, *The Renaissance in the Fields: Family Memoirs of a*

name himself.[3] Most of his text is local obituaries and other such events. However, there are twenty-eight entries about the weather and farming, dated between 1554 and 1577, totalling something over a thousand words. Here the chronicler adopts a perspective of direct observation and first-person commentary, pushing at the traditional boundaries of the genre.[4]

The chronicle's discourse moves between what we might regard as *meteorological data* (actual weather), *economic data* (prices, meagre harvests, or deaths of livestock), *moral commentary* (sufferings of poor men, or landlords' extortion) and *providential commentary* (God's grace, for instance in keeping prices low). As a priest, the chronicler probably saw his comments on weather and farming as a meditation on the relationship between the temporal and the eternal. His sympathies were with 'poor men' like himself (p. 141).

* * *

The settlement of Fortingall, with the tract of farming land around it, was in the lower valley of the River Lyon, about 130m above sea level. Around it the land rose rapidly to over 400m in almost every direction, and in some places higher still. These heights were well beyond the reach of arable farming. In the comparable settlement of Lix, above Loch Tay, not far from Fortingall, the head dyke was usually at 750 feet (230m), with shielings above it at much higher altitudes.[5] The head dyke marked the upper limit of arable land, and served to manage grazing animals by keeping them off the crops during the growing season.[6] However, as we shall see, not all of the land below the head dyke was used for crops.

Fifteenth-Century Tuscan Peasant, trans. Paolo Squatriti and Betsy Merideth, intro. Edward Muir (University Park, PA, 1999).

3 The chronicler's identity and ecclesiastical and social status are discussed further in Julian Goodare, 'The Chronicler of Fortingall', unpublished paper. He may well have been Dougall MacGregor, one of the sons of James MacGregor (*c.*1480–1551), dean of Lismore, compiler of the Book of the Dean of Lismore. For the chronicle in the Gaelic cultural context of the Book of the Dean, see Martin MacGregor, 'The View from Fortingall: The Worlds of the Book of the Dean of Lismore', *Scottish Gaelic Studies*, 22 (2006), 35–85. I am grateful to Dr Martin MacGregor for discussions of the chronicle in this context.

4 For the local chronicle as an evolving genre see Alexandra Walsham, 'Chronicles, Memory and Autobiography in Reformation England', *Memory Studies*, 11:1 (2018), 36–50.

5 Horace Fairhurst, 'The Deserted Settlement at Lix, West Perthshire', *PSAS*, 101 (1969), 160–99.

6 Briony Kincaid, 'The Use of Dykes in Scottish Farming 1500–1700', Chapter 2 above in the present volume.

FIGURE 4.1. Fortingall today, looking across the plain from the north.
The River Lyon flows across the middle of the picture. The landscape
is more heavily wooded than it was in the early modern period.
Source: Photograph by Julian Goodare.

The antiquary and naturalist Thomas Pennant visited what he called the 'little plain of Fortingal' in 1769 and 1772. He noted antiquities that he thought were Roman, as well as the 'wonderful yew tree' in the churchyard.[7] Glen Lyon itself, he wrote, was 'narrow, but fertile'; this seems to have been higher up the valley, but the remark about fertility surely applies also to the 'little plain'.[8] The Fortingall Yew has become celebrated in modern times, and is now thought to be 5,000 years old, the oldest living thing in Europe. The chronicler will have seen the yew tree every day, but he did not mention it – it did not make news, after all. The early Christians who chose to site their church next to it must have felt that it was special, but its cultural role in the sixteenth-century landscape remains obscure.[9]

7   Thomas Pennant, *A Tour in Scotland and Voyage to the Hebrides 1772*, ed. Andrew Simmons, intro. Charles W. J. Withers (Edinburgh, 1998), pp. 397–8.
8   Thomas Pennant, *A Tour in Scotland, 1769*, 4th edn (London, 1776), p. 102.
9   For cultural understandings of trees see T. C. Smout, 'Trees as Historic Landscapes: From Wallace's Oak to Reforesting Scotland', in his *Exploring Environmental History: Selected Essays* (Edinburgh, 2009), 153–67.

FIGURE 4.2. Fortingall in about 1750, from William Roy's military survey. Tiny farming settlements, each shown as a handful of dots, are scattered all along the River Lyon. The map also shows arable fields with their cultivation ridges. The chronicler lived next to the church, on the same site as the present-day church, shown on the map as 'New Kirk of Fortingaul'.
Source: National Library of Scotland, Roy Military Survey of Scotland, 1747–55.

William Roy's military survey of 1747–55 included Fortingall in its detailed mapping.[10] The Roy map appears to show two farming townships in the immediate vicinity of Fortingall: one adjacent to the church itself, and one to the west, around what the map calls 'Glen Lyons house' (the building, probably built in the early eighteenth century, that preceded the present Glenlyon House).[11] The houses of the church's township seem to be a little to the west of the church, between the church itself and the burn, the Allt Odhar, that flows southwards into the River Lyon.

The Roy map also depicts the arable land of each of these townships. In general its representations of farming land and settlements are not precise, but they may be indicative.[12] The Glenlyon House township has

10 The Roy map is online via the NLS website. For discussion of it see Christopher Fleet, Margaret Wilkes and Charles W. J. Withers, *Scotland: Mapping the Nation* (Edinburgh, 2011), pp. 88–9. This book reproduces the map of the Fortingall area at a large scale: fig. 4.13, pp. 90–1.

11 Alexander Stewart, *A Highland Parish, or the History of Fortingall* (Glasgow, 1928), pp. 119–20.

12 The published 'Fair Copy' of the map may exaggerate the extent of arable land, but there may also be a (perhaps countervailing) problem of failure

about four fields, each depicted as a block of parallel strips, to the west of the settlement. The church's township has perhaps six or seven such fields, stretching from the church itself down to the River Lyon. It seems quite possible that such pre-Improvement fields had existed continuously since the sixteenth century and even before. Probably some were infield and others outfield. The Roy map shows arable land covering most of the low-lying land in the 'little plain', but not all of it. To the south-west of the two settlements, a large triangle of land in the bend of the river is bare; we shall return to this.

Fortingall's 'little plain' was thus more fertile than other parts of Highland Perthshire, though in a broader context its farmland was hardly bountiful. In the modern terms of the British Geological Survey, the whole of the plain is 'alluvium' or 'river terrace deposits' of mixed gravel, sand, silt and clay. The soil is a 'mineral podzol' according to Scottish government soil maps.[13] The British Land Utilisation Survey in the 1930s found a 'much higher proportion of arable land' than the higher valleys of the Lyon and the Tay, while noting that the plain was liable to flood. The slopes were cultivated up to 650 feet (200m), beyond which was nothing but heath and moorland.[14]

* * *

In calling the chronicler a 'peasant' I am making a broad, general and (I hope) unsurprising statement about him. He was a family farmer of the kind that has existed in many societies in many historical periods and continues to exist in many parts of the world today. His brief and allusive statements about his status offer neither certainty nor precision – but most farmers in sixteenth-century Scotland were peasants, and the chronicler does not seem to have been unusual *as a farmer*. His literacy and his elite connections were unusual, of course, and he was probably a richer peasant rather than a poorer peasant; but his literacy and his elite connections did not make him unusual in the way that he went about his farming.

We can thus consider the chronicler in the context of further generalisations that can be made about peasants, past and present. Peasants are self-employed family farmers who carry out farming at least partly for their own direct subsistence, and who have some traditional or hereditary connection to the land that they cultivate. The external inputs to their farms are small, and their involvement in markets is partial.

---

to represent outfield land as arable: G. Whittington and A. J. S. Gibson, *The Military Survey of Scotland 1747–1755: A Critique* (Lancaster, 1986), pp. 37–8, 60.
13 https://map.environment.gov.scot/Soil_maps/.
14 L. Dudley Stamp (ed.), *The Land of Britain: The Report of the Land Utilisation Survey of Britain, Parts 9–12, The Highlands of Scotland* (London, 1944), pp. 569–70.

Their individual holdings of land are embedded in broader communities, giving their farming a collective element. Peasant farming is rooted in the local environment – including the weather that is prominent in the present investigation.

In modern studies of peasants, they are understood as active agents in which their traditional practices have economic rationality. 'Subsistence' is not just about survival, but about maintenance of future productive capacity. Peasants' emphasis on tradition gives them stability over long periods of time, but they are not archaic, not exotic, and not outdated. Modern history has seen peasants decline in Europe, but peasant farming has spread in other parts of the world.[15]

Such a broad definition is not very helpful for detailed analysis, and indeed I am not proposing that it should be used for detailed analysis. But it should be stressed that the chronicler made it clear that he worked personally on his farm. His most direct statements to this effect were: 'On 23 March that year, I began to sow in the Borllin of Fortingall' (W1575–76) and 'On 22 March I began to sow oats' (W1576–77). One cannot rule out the possibility that such statements were shorthand for 'I commanded my workers to sow oats', and indeed the chronicler may have had others working for him from time to time, as many peasants did. But he would almost certainly have worked alongside them. Many of his other statements about farming have a similar flavour of hands-on experience rather than detached observation. He thus cannot have been a full member of the clan elite; clan elites, like any other sixteenth-century elites, had an aristocratic disdain for manual labour. We shall return to this later.

A scholar like Alexander Chayanov, the Russian agrarian economist whose work continues to inspire peasant studies, would ask various questions about the chronicler:

- What did his family consist of, and, related to this, what were his family's processes of household reproduction – how was land inherited?
- What proportion of his farm's produce was marketed, and what proportion was consumed directly?
- How much hired labour did he use, and was his use of hired labour seasonal or permanent?
- What were the key constraints on his efforts to maximise production?

---

15 See, for example, Henry Bernstein, Harriet Friedmann, Jan Douwe van der Ploeg, Teodor Shanin and Ben White, 'Forum: Fifty Years of Debate on Peasantries 1966–2016', *Journal of Peasant Studies*, 45:4 (2018), 689–714; Eric Vanhaute, *Peasants in World History* (London, 2021).

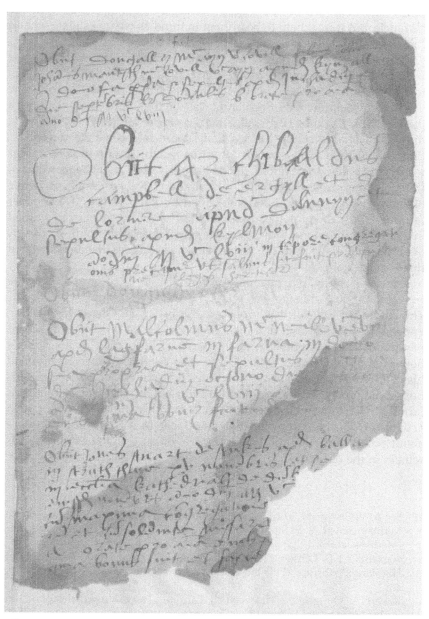

Figure 4.3. A page from the Chronicle of Fortingall, showing the way in which the text has been compiled piecemeal. The entry in outsize handwriting, an obituary for the fourth earl of Argyll in 1558, is unusual.
Source: NLS MS 50300, folio 1r. Image reproduced by the kind permission of the National Library of Scotland. https://creativecommons.org/publicdomain/mark/1.0/.

These questions, as we shall see, are largely unanswerable from the chronicle, but it may help to bear them in mind as we investigate what it can and cannot tell us.[16]

The chronicler gave hardly any details of his own farm. The closest we get to it is this remark, which I have already quoted: 'On 23 March that year, I began to sow in the Borllin of Fortingall' (W1575–76). The 'Borllin', also known as Bordland, was in the immediate vicinity of the modern village of Fortingall.[17] By specifying a location in this way, the chronicler indicated that his fields were in more than one place. Presumably there was a pattern of strips in which individual holdings were distributed throughout the township rather than being concentrated in one area. Some such distributions were permanent, while other townships practised periodic redistribution of strips.[18] The broader farming landscape may have been similar to one that has been studied in nearby Strathbraan.[19] The chronicler's own farm – his holding of strips of land – may have been the 'glebe' attached to the parish benefice, but this is not certain.[20]

Peasant farming was a family affair. Priests were supposed to be celibate, but concubinage was widely, even conventionally, practised.[21] The chronicler himself was probably a priest's son. One of his fleeting appearances in his own chronicle seems to be its third-person record of the death of Gregor, son of the vicar of Fortingall, in his father's house, on 16 November 1571 (p. 137). The chronicler never mentioned his children's mother, but we may infer that there was a woman in his household, and that she took the lead in carrying out female-gendered farming and household activities. We learn little, however, about such activities from the chronicle. Women appear in it from time to time – about one-fifth of the obituaries are of women – but their daily lives remain in the background.

16 See A. V. Chayanov, *The Theory of Peasant Economy*, ed. Daniel Thorner, Basile Kerblay and R. E. F. Smith, with a foreword by Teodor Shanin, 2nd edn (Madison, 1986).

17 Alexander J. S. Gibson, 'Territorial Organization and Land Assessment in Highland Perthshire' (PhD thesis, University of Lancaster, 1988), pp. 276, 277, 281.

18 Robert A. Dodgshon, 'The Scottish Farming Township as Metaphor', in Leah Leneman (ed.), *Perspectives in Scottish Social History* (Aberdeen, 1989), pp. 69–82.

19 David C. Cowley, 'Archaeological Landscapes in Strathbraan, Perthshire', *Tayside and Fife Archaeological Journal*, 3 (1997), 161–75.

20 The fragmentary evidence on the nature of the glebe, and on who held title to it, is discussed in Goodare, 'The Chronicler of Fortingall'.

21 Margaret H. B. Sanderson, *Scottish Curates and Parochial Chaplains 1429–1560* (Edinburgh: SRS, 2016), pp. xxv–xxvi.

Peasant farming was also a community affair. The chronicler was interested in the farming of the whole community, not just his own farm. In one year there was 'good corn in all places' (S1566), and there were various other mentions of weather and farming events in 'all places' (W1561–62, W1562–63, S1564, S1564, S1577) and 'many places' (S1563, W1570–71). These 'places' were apparently farmland and farming settlements in the immediate vicinity. The chronicler named one such settlement, Balnacraig (S1576).

*   *   *

Anyone who writes about the seasons must begin with an awareness of a regular pattern. The seasons come round with familiar regularity, indeed inexorable regularity. This in itself may be worthy of comment. But, beyond that regular pattern, there are variations. What was different about *this* season? In the chronicle, we encounter both the basic, regular pattern, and the variations presented by individual seasons. To some extent we discern the former behind the latter.

The single most striking point about seasons in the chronicle is that only two seasons were mentioned by name: winter and summer. These seasons, though, were prominent in the text. Many of the entries referred explicitly to 'winter' or 'summer', and every entry can broadly be assigned to one of these specific seasons. Overall there were about 13 named mentions of 'winter', and 17 of 'summer'. When periods that we might think of as spring or autumn were discussed, the discussion tended to run on from the season before. Thus, the account of winter 1560–61 ran continuously as far as May, while several accounts of summer continued until September or even October, like this account of the summer of 1576:

> All June, July and August there was really harsh weather, with much rain and wet until September; then there was really fine weather until 16 September. After that, really harsh weather. No oats had been harvested in Fortingall by 23 September, except for a really small quantity, mainly in Balnacraig. All October, harsh weather; much corn not harvested nor carted away. (S1576)

Why this was so, and why spring and autumn were not named, we shall see in a moment.

As well as mentioning seasons by name, the chronicler also mentioned months by name – and the pattern with which he did so is revealing. Instead of focusing on the heart of winter and the heart of summer, he revealed particular interest in what we would call early spring, and in what we would call autumn, as the following tables demonstrate:

TABLE 4.1. Frequency of mentions of months in the Chronicle of Fortingall

January	4	May	2	September	6
February	5	June	1	October	5
March	12	July	1	November	0
April	3	August	4	December	2
				Total	45

This picture is filled out a little, but not substantially changed, by the smaller number of mentions of dated religious festivals:

TABLE 4.2. Religious festivals mentioned in farming context in the Chronicle of Fortingall

St Patrick, 17 March (two mentions)

St Columba, 9 June

Nine Virgin Saints, 15 July

All Saints, 1 November

St Andrew, 30 November

Yule, 25 December

winter quarter (Martinmas, 11 November, to Candlemas, 2 February)

Lent quarter (Candlemas, 2 February, to Whitsun, 15 May)

Thus we find two intersecting patterns. In the first pattern, there are two named seasons, but they do not flow directly into each other. Instead, in the gaps between them, the second pattern focuses on shorter periods, typically a month at a time. Time seems to slow down and then speed up again. Why?

The weather in summer was crucial to the future success of the harvest in autumn, but there were fewer pressing farming tasks in summer itself. So the chronicler could write about 'the summer' as a broad entity. August, September and October, by contrast, pressed individually on his consciousness, with the urgent need to gather in the harvest. One such entry mentions 'Poor harvest, particularly in October and part of September' (S1567). More will be said about the harvest below.

Farming work slowed down again in the winter, so 'the winter' appears as another broad entity. But March pressed more keenly on the chronicler's consciousness than any other month. It was vital to get the ploughing and sowing completed as early as possible. Several of the mentions of March related to these tasks; again this will be discussed further below. The other mentions of March concerned frost and snow, and occasionally storms. The chronicler gave the impression that these forms of bad weather were unusual in March.

There were also 22 mentions of specific dates in a farming context, 7 of which were religious festivals. As with the mentions of months, these were also concentrated in March (8 mentions), with half of the rest (6) being in January and February, and hardly any in the summer (only 2 dates for the months of April to August inclusive). Some of the weather-related events were assigned to specific days, especially the beginning or ending of snow, frost or storms. Most of the mentions of specific days, however, related to discussions of farming or markets.

* * *

Much has already been said about the weather in the preceding discussion of the seasons, but more can be learned by focusing specifically on weather. About half of the entries concerning weather and farming used the actual word 'weather', sometimes several times (22 mentions, occurring in 13 entries out of 28). And many of these entries expressed a farmer's needs and hopes.

We may perceive broad weather patterns by returning to the seasons, and dividing the chronicler's comments on the season's weather into those that he characterised as good or bad overall. In total, he had 2 good winters and 10 bad ones, 7 good summers and 6 bad ones. There were also 23 seasons on which he either wrote nothing or else his comments did not address the weather. We can perhaps infer that those seasons were neither especially bad nor especially good, though the inference must remain tentative.

This tells us something about what a farmer expected from each of these seasons. Let us take winter first. The two good winters were 1562–63, when it was fine, with no frost and snow, and 1569–70, when it was fine. That was the best the chronicler could say about any winter. He thus hoped for *absence* of *harmful* weather during the winter. In a good winter, it would not snow – because snow might kill his livestock – and it would not freeze in February and March – because frozen ground might delay his ploughing and in turn his sowing. With summer, however, he hoped not only for absence of harm, but also, more positively, for specific *good* weather. In a good summer, there would not be too much wind – which might flatten his grain crops – or rain – which might cause them to rot. Also, positively, there would be plenty of sunshine and warmth – which would ripen his grain crops and promote the growth of grass for his livestock. Thus his experience of winter tended to be that things were either bad, or else all right and thus unremarkable. His experience of summer could also be a bad one – but, if it was not bad, he could also notice, and remark on, sunshine and warmth that were positively good.

This analysis could be extended by suggesting that winter was about *survival*, while summer – or at least the ensuing harvest – was about *fruitfulness*. Survival is important, but it may be easier to celebrate fruitfulness. There is probably something in this suggestion, but two cautionary remarks should be made. First, in this analysis of the chronicler's comments I have focused exclusively on the weather, setting aside his comments about farming for separate discussion in a moment. So we are not explicitly analysing fruitfulness here. Second, fruitfulness was not just about the grain harvest; spring calves and lambs were surely important, and even cheeses from summer dairying may have had their own significance.

The chronicler's good and bad seasons were unevenly distributed across his 23 years. The central period – broadly the 1560s – was much the best. Of the 9 good seasons that he reported, 8 fell into the period from the summer of 1561 to the summer of 1570 (19 seasons in total). Within that period, moreover, there were only 3 bad seasons. Earlier and later, things were much worse. From the winter of 1554–55 to the winter of 1560–61 (15 seasons in total), he reported 6 bad seasons and only 1 good one. From the winter of 1570–71 to the summer of 1577 (14 seasons in total), he reported 7 bad seasons and no good ones at all.

This impression of favourable weather in the 1560s may be strengthened by considering that Scottish farmers would generally like the weather to be warmer and drier. One of the three bad seasons of the 1560s was the summer of 1567, which was bad because it was too hot and dry. That season was clearly problematic, but it does at least look as though Scotland in the 1560s was not experiencing the worst effects of the Little Ice Age.

There are no systematic data on sixteenth-century Scottish weather patterns – or, at least, no data more systematic than the chronicle itself.[22] However, the intensity of winters in the western Baltic can be reconstructed from data including Danish Øresund tolls and the dates of freezing of Baltic ports. A detailed analysis of this data has identified a period of severe 'ice winters' in 1554–76, in between two periods of 'decreased severity' in 1501–53 and 1577–92.[23] Weather patterns in one region cannot be extrapolated automatically to other regions, but there are

22 The mostly fragmentary qualitative data for the period *c.*1300–1600 are placed in broader context by Alastair Dawson, *So Foul and Fair a Day: A History of Scotland's Weather and Climate* (Edinburgh, 2009), pp. 101–9.

23 Gerhard Koslowski and Rüdiger Glaser, 'Variations in Reconstructed Ice Winter Severity in the Western Baltic from 1501 to 1995, and Their Implications for the North Atlantic Oscillation', *Climatic Change*, 41:2 (1999), 175–91.

grounds for seeing this data as relevant to Scotland. Baltic ice formation is affected by the incidence of westerly winds (strong westerlies mean less ice), so Scottish and western Baltic weather patterns could have been connected. The western Baltic data also show correlations with seventeenth-century Swiss data, indicating that broader European patterns were at work. There are further complexities, such as the possibility of an inverse relationship between freezing conditions and *stormy* conditions (winds inhibit the formation of ice). Still, the chronicler in his Highland valley does seem to have been experiencing, and recording, weather patterns that could have been found much more widely.

The chronicler's weather data can be compared with the data gathered by Alan R. MacDonald and John McCallum from presbytery records during the 11-year period 1615–25.[24] Presbyteries tended to record extreme weather, mainly storms and snow – two of the main weather phenomena that also interested our chronicler. They could also pinpoint weather events month by month, and even day by day, in a way that the chronicler also did. The chronicler, though, made further longer-term comments on the weather, season by season, whereas presbyteries tended to be interested in short-term weather events.

One question prompted by MacDonald and McCallum is: does 'storm' mean snow or high wind? They argue that either was possible, and that the meaning needs to be sought in the word's context.[25] In the chronicle, too, the word 'storm' carried both meanings on occasion, but the connection with snow seems to predominate:

Storms in the chronicle
- The greatest snow and storm (W1554–55)
- Snow or storms (W1556–57)
- Much snow at the beginning of March … Frost and storms until 25 March (W1560–61)
- A great storm, with snow, hail and wind (W1571–72)

The last of these winters was harsh elsewhere in Scotland too; from Soutra we hear of the death of John Carnoch, carter, 'in the great storme of snaw' in November 1571.[26] The chronicler mentioned snow as having fallen in six winters (W1554–55, W1556–57, W1560–61, W1561–62, W1571–72, W1575–76). There was also a much earlier winter of 'great snow', which evidently attracted the chronicler's attention when drawing material from

24   Alan R. MacDonald and John McCallum, 'The Evidence for Early Seventeenth-Century Climate from Scottish Ecclesiastical Records', *Environment and History*, 19:4 (2013), 487–509.
25   MacDonald and McCallum, 'Early Seventeenth-Century Climate', p. 495.
26   Margaret H. B. Sanderson, *A Kindly Place? Living in Sixteenth-Century Scotland* (East Linton, 2002), p. 66.

a fifteenth-century source (W1404–05). This does not mean that snow fell only in these years, however. Rather, these mentions indicated *heavy* snow, with the assumption being that snow would fall every winter. This assumption becomes clear when we find comments about *little* snow (W1558–59) and *no* snow (W1562–63). Fortingall was close to the Cairngorm area which in recent times has received by far the most snow in Britain;[27] a winter with no snow would indeed have been exceptional.

The question of 'wind' can be expanded by looking at the use of that word specifically. Two of the four mentions of 'wind' were connected with 'storm'; snow was also mentioned. The other two mentions of 'wind' were connected with rain:

Wind in the chronicle
- At the beginning of April, harsh frost, snow, strong winds (W1560–61)
- A great storm, with snow, hail and wind (W1571–72)
- Harsh August, wind and rain (S1574)
- May, much wet and rain and wind (S1577)

A meteorological view of 'storms' treats them as being entirely about strong wind. Here it is worth briefly placing the Fortingall data in context of broader historical studies. Most storms are localised, and the chronicler's storms do not match up with the two storms that are recorded as having been widespread in north-western Europe – those of January 1553 and November 1570.[28] The broader records also show a period of greater storminess from 1570 to the 1620s.[29] The Fortingall data do fit this pattern, with three of the four mentions of high wind coming in the chronicle's short final period between 1570 and 1577. The linking of wind and rain probably has its own significance, since the two of these together would be more likely to damage standing crops than either one of them on its own.

One may also ask what the chronicler meant by 'fine' weather ('fayr' in the original). This evidently denoted sunny, bright weather, but had no necessary connotations of warmth. The term could be applied to the winter (e.g. W1556–57). A warm summer could be described as 'hot' (S1557). Still, when a summer is described as 'really fine, good weather' (S1570), the implication may well be that it was warm as well as sunny.

27 Alison L. Kay, 'A Review of Snow in Britain: The Historical Picture and Future Projections', *Progress in Physical Geography*, 40:5 (2016), 676–98, at p. 680.

28 Hubert Lamb, with Knud Frydendahl, *Historic Storms of the North Sea, British Isles and Northwest Europe* (Cambridge, 1991), p. 38.

29 Lamb, *Historic Storms*, p. 33.

A further implication may be more important: whether in winter or summer, 'fine' weather was almost certainly dry.

The chronicle's weather data are hardly extensive, but they are more than anecdotal. In the chronicle we do not merely have an isolated record of a single event. There are enough data, and of a sufficiently varied nature, to offer a sense of the chronicler's overall attitudes. He was mainly troubled by bad weather, and mainly in winter, but he could also welcome positively good weather. He clearly thought of weather with farming in mind; and it is to his explicit remarks about farming that we now turn.

* * *

Most of the chronicler's statements about farming were attached to, and even subordinated to, his statements about weather. However, they have their own importance, and require separate discussion here. First the various crops and livestock will be inventoried, following which something will be said about farming processes.

The grain crops mentioned were bere and oats (W1576–77; S1577); there were also generic mentions of 'corn' (S1566, S1567). These are the crops that one would expect in the Highlands. Grain prices – to be discussed in a moment – were quoted as prices of bere, oatmeal and occasionally malt. The peasants almost certainly had kale yards (small plots for cabbage or borecole, known as kale), but the chronicler did not mention kale. Eighteenth-century estate surveys, too, tended to limit themselves to field crops and to ignore the kale that was universally grown.[30]

Pastoral farming was important throughout the Highlands. The precise balance between livestock and arable varied, and a distinction has been drawn between the highly pastoral 'cheeselands' in upper Glen Lyon, and the 'mixed farms' in the Fortingall area at the foot of the glen.[31] Cattle were directly mentioned only once in the chronicle, when they were among the animals that died in a harsh winter (W1554–55). Plough-oxen may be implied in the various mentions of ploughing, to be discussed in a moment – though some Highland ploughs were drawn by horses.[32] Sheep and goats were also mentioned, as victims of two harsh winters (W1554–55, W1570–71). In one of these winters 'wild horses and mares' also died (W1554–55); probably these 'wild' horses were farmed in a semi-feral manner, as a breeding herd that was allowed to roam the

---

30 Robert A. Dodgshon, *From Chiefs to Landlords: Social and Economic Change in the Western Highlands and Islands c.1493–1820* (Edinburgh, 1998), p. 222. Kale yards were mentioned in the early seventeenth-century court books (p. 353).

31 Albert Bil, *The Shieling 1600–1840: The Case of the Central Scottish Highlands* (Edinburgh, 1990), pp. 112–13.

32 It was said in 1794 that horses had 'ever' been the draught animals in the region, and that oxen had 'never' been used: [William] Marshall, *General View of the Agriculture of the Central Highlands of Scotland* (London, 1794), p. 34.

hills for much of the year.[33] There were probably shielings in the higher ground for summer grazing – Fortingall was in a region where shielings were common – but the chronicler did not mention these.[34]

Winter fodder was crucial for livestock. The chronicler mentioned 'grass', no doubt for hay (S1567). Hay was common in the Highlands but not universal.[35] There was also mention of 'fodder', probably straw, as being 'scant' in a harsh winter (W1570–71). All the chronicler's brief mentions of livestock, in fact, concern losses of stock in winter. Limited capacity to overwinter livestock was a crucial constraint on traditional agriculture, as he seems to have recognised.[36]

As well as pastoral farming as such, there seem to be allusions to hunting. The chronicler mentioned 'deer and roes' (W1561–62) – the 'deer' probably being red deer. Deer hunting was a prerogative of chiefs; herds of deer might be trespassed upon by rival clans, but were not routinely exploited by peasants.[37] There was also river fishing, but the chronicler did not mention this.[38]

Most of the chronicler's mentions of farming were placed in the context of his discussions of the seasons – either the harshness of the winter, or the success or otherwise of the grain harvest that followed the summer. In his view, farming news consisted simply of good news and bad news.

The good news all concerned the harvest. The chronicler made 13 fairly explicit mentions of harvests, 6 of which he said were good – all in the 1560s. The usual term he used was 'good' (S1563, S1564, S1565, S1566), or occasionally 'fine' (S1569) or 'good and fine' (S1561). These characterisations were all made with attention to the weather as well as the harvest, most explicitly as 'a good summer and harvest' (S1565). Of these 6, 5 used the actual word 'harvest', while 1 said 'good corn' (S1566). No doubt this was all welcome news, but these phrases were all brief.

Bad news about harvests, expressed at more length, can reveal more about how the chronicler saw the difference between a bad harvest and a good one. What he said about individual bad harvests can be summarised as follows:

- poor harvest; weak growth on higher ground (S1557)
- poor harvest (S1559)
- poorest harvest ever seen; much hunger and dearth (S1560)

33 Bil, *The Shieling*, pp. 164–7.
34 Bil, *The Shieling*, fig. 12 (p. 149) and *passim*.
35 Dodgshon, *From Chiefs to Landlords*, p. 204.
36 Dodgshon, *From Chiefs to Landlords*, pp. 223–5.
37 Dodgshon, *From Chiefs to Landlords*, p. 86.
38 River fishing was mentioned in the early seventeenth-century court books (pp. 352, 389). For a broader tendency to under-record river fishing see Susan Kilby, *Peasant Perspectives on the Medieval Landscape: A Study of Three Communities* (Hatfield, 2020), pp. 156–62.

- dry, hot summer; corn shrivelled in the kiln; poor harvest, particularly in October and part of September (S1567)
- worst ever weather at harvest; continual rain (S1574)
- no oats harvested in most of Fortingall in September; much not harvested nor carted in October (S1576)
- harsh weather April to June; bere seed weak until after 9 June (S1577)

The last of these statements is not directly about the harvest, but slow crop growth seems to imply that a poor harvest followed. The hot, dry summer of 1567 also impeded crop growth. Weather was explicitly and differently linked to the harvest in 1574, with rain at harvest-time itself; presumably this made it difficult to cut the crop and let it dry before carting it to the stack yard. Both in 1567 and in 1576, the chronicler commented on harvesting taking place in September and October, which he evidently considered unusually late. A delayed harvest could be a bad harvest, either because of slow summer growth or because the delay was forced by bad weather in August and September.

Ploughing and sowing interested the chronicler repeatedly. His comments on it, all consisting of bad news, can be summarised as follows:

- not much ploughing until 26 February, and only in low-lying places (W1554–55)
- little ploughing in the winter (W1556–57)
- no ploughs worked until late March (W1571–72)
- harsh March; on 23 March, I began to sow in the Borllin of Fortingall (W1575–76)
- no oats sown in March; on 22 March I began to sow oats (W1576–77)

Thus there were two issues here. Frost could delay the start of ploughing, while rain could delay the sowing of seed. Either of these problems would shorten the growing season and increase the risk that the crop would not ripen fully. Three of the harvests that followed these problematic springs were themselves noted as poor (S1557, S1576, S1577).

Finally, we learn a little about grain processing after the harvest. Kilns for drying grain were mentioned (S1567). The mentions of malt prices (to be discussed in a moment) also implied kiln-drying. Mills were discussed in connection with a freezing winter: 'All kinds of victuals were really dear, because no mills could grind because of the frost. All corn, from Perth to Dunkeld and other places around, far and near, came to the mill of Dunkeld' (W1571–72). This indicates that grain was normally ground in mills, rather than hand querns. Dunkeld's urban mill was presumably a large vertical-wheel mill, but local mills may have been smaller and have had horizontal wheels; the chronicler's implication that local mills were numerous would support this. If there were numerous mills, this would in turn imply that tenants were not 'thirled' to the landlord's mill but were free to use mills of their choice.[39]

* * *

Although the chronicle contains little systematic farming data, it offers more on prices and markets. There is specific information about grain prices for 14 seasons. Much of the information is qualitative, either simply stating that prices were high or low, or sometimes making a further comment about the relationship with the harvest, or about hunger. There are also quite a few actual prices quoted – perhaps not enough to justify calling them a statistical series, but still worth examining.

TABLE 4.3. Prices in the Chronicle of Fortingall

Date	Grain prices per boll	Commentary
Summer 1557		shortages and high prices, Nov. 1556 to May 1557; high prices in summer
Winter 1557–58		
Summer 1558		
Winter 1558–59		cheap foodstuffs
Summer 1559		
Winter 1559–60		
Summer 1560	fiar of oatmeal £2.00 (40s.) fiar of bere £2.00 (40s.)	really high prices; hunger
Winter 1560–61		really high prices
Summer 1561		really high prices of all things
Winter 1561–62		
Summer 1562		
Winter 1562–63		really high prices in all places, Nov. 1562 to May 1563

---

39 For Highland mills see Dodgshon, *From Chiefs to Landlords*, pp. 116–17. Multure was mentioned, probably implying thirlage, in the early seventeenth-century court books (p. 363).

Date	Grain prices per boll	Commentary
Summer 1563	oatmeal £3.33 (5 merks) fiar of oatmeal £2.66 (4 merks)	really high prices in summer; the lady of Strathord took £3.33 (5 merks) for the fiar of oatmeal
Winter 1563–64		
Summer 1564	oatmeal £0.90 (18s.) malt £1.40 (28s.)	cheap foodstuffs
—	—	—
Summer 1569	fiar of bere £3.00 fiar of oatmeal £2.66 (4 merks)	high prices in summer; cheap food after harvest
Winter 1569–70		
Summer 1570		foodstuffs really cheap
Winter 1570–71		
Summer 1571		
Winter 1571–72	oatmeal £2.20 (44s.) in Perth malt £1.70 (34s.) in Perth oatmeal £1.28 (25s. 8d.) by 17 March malt £1.50 (30s.) by 17 March	high prices for foodstuffs
—	—	—
Summer 1574	malt £3.66 (5½ merks) oatmeal £2.89 (4⅓ merks)	
Winter 1574–75		
Summer 1575	fiar of bere £3.33 (5 merks) fiar of malt £3.33 (5 merks) fiar of oatmeal £3.00	fixing of prices at Kenmore, 15 July
Winter 1575–76		high prices for foodstuffs in winter and Lent

Commentary on prices encompassed both of the chronicler's two seasons, about equally. In summer, there were seven instances of high prices (S1557, S1560, S1561, S1563, S1569, S1574, S1575), and two instances of low prices (S1564, S1570). In winter, there were four instances of high prices (W1560–61, W1562–63, W1571–72, W1575–76), and one instance of low prices (W1558–59), to which may be added two mentions of high prices in the winter and Lent quarters, November to May (S1557, W1562–63).

The pattern was a little different when the chronicler quoted actual figures for prices. He did so in 7 seasons, 6 of which were summers (S1560, S1563, S1564, S1569, W1571–72, S1574, S1575). The only detailed discussion of winter prices concerned the freezing winter of 1571–72, when prices were high because the only mill that could operate was in Dunkeld. The chronicler explicitly quoted prices charged in Perth: £2.20 for oatmeal and £1.70 for malt. These prices reduced considerably by 17 March, to £1.28 and £1.50 respectively, presumably because the ice melted and other mills resumed their operations. This seems to have been an unusual episode.

The impression, then, is that the summer prices were *peak* prices. When the chronicler commented on high winter prices, he seems to have been saying that prices were *already* high. Prices may have remained high, or even increased further, in the following summer, but he did not comment on that. The idea that prices were lowest immediately after the harvest and that they climbed steadily over the twelve months that followed has recently been questioned for England, but there is little reason to expect that prices would routinely *fall* in the summer from a winter peak.[40]

Four sets of quoted prices were fiars prices. These were publicly-stated official prices rather than market prices. In later centuries at least, fiars prices were set ('struck') in each county in February each year.[41] This may have been the practice in sixteenth-century Perthshire too, though information is scanty. The chronicle implied that fiars prices were still current in the summer (S1569). The fiars prices in the chronicle can be compared with those for Fife, the only fiars price series that survives for this period.[42] The results illustrate the local nature of prices, and the wide range of variation. Indeed, even though the chronicler's intention seems to have been to record extreme prices, the fluctuations seem to have been more severe in Fife.

TABLE 4.4. Fiars prices in Fortingall and Fife

Date	Fortingall	Fife
Summer 1560	fiar of oatmeal £2.00 fiar of bere £2.00	fiar of oatmeal £0.90 fiar of bere £1.33
Summer 1563	fiar of oatmeal £2.66	fiar of oatmeal £2.60

40 Richard W. Hoyle, 'Prices and Seasons in Late Seventeenth-Century England', in Wouter Ronsijn, Niccolò Mignemi and Laurent Herment (eds), *Stocks, Seasons and Sales: Food Supply, Storage and Markets in Europe and the New World c.1600–2000* (Turnhout, 2019), pp. 37–60.
41 For the system of fiars prices, see T. C. Smout, 'What Were the Fiars Prices Used For?', Chapter 9 below in the present volume.
42 A. J. S. Gibson and T. C. Smout, *Prices, Food and Wages in Scotland 1550–1780* (Cambridge, 1995), table 3.1 (p. 84).

Date	Fortingall	Fife
Summer 1569	fiar of bere £3.00 fiar of oatmeal £2.66	fiar of bere £3.58 fiar of oatmeal £3.00
Summer 1575	fiar of bere £3.33 fiar of oatmeal £3.00 fiar of malt £3.33	fiar of bere £4.16 fiar of oatmeal £4.00

The chronicler, like other contemporary commentators, welcomed low prices and deplored high prices. We might have expected farmers to prefer high prices, but high prices were connected with *shortages*. A farmer with a large farm could sell his surplus at a higher price, but even he would have a smaller surplus. And a smaller farmer – a peasant, in fact – might well be buying grain, rather than selling it, when there were shortages. In these terms, nobody really benefited from high prices.

The chronicler saw a relationship between the amount harvested and the subsequent price level, but he thought of this at least partly in moral and providential terms. The one named person who benefited from high prices was Janet Ruthven, Lady Strathord: 'Summer 1563 was really dear. The boll of oatmeal was 5 merks. The fiar price of oatmeal in many places was 4 merks. The lady of Strathord took 5 merks for the boll of oatmeal for the fiar' (S1563). The chronicler made no further comment, but his most likely reason for including this information at all was that he thought that Lady Strathord was profiteering immorally. As for providence, the chronicler invoked this in the following year. The 1563 harvest was a good one, and oatmeal prices in 1564 dropped by more than two-thirds. 'There you may see the grace of God', he remarked (S1564).

The question of who actually bought and sold grain at these prices remains as opaque in the chronicle as it tends to be in other sources, but the remark about Lady Strathord is suggestive. It was landlords rather than tenants who marketed grain surpluses, presumably from the produce rents that they collected.

The chronicler was terse, but vivid, when he discussed the effects of grain shortages. Actual 'shortages' were mentioned only once (S1557), but shortages seem to be implied in numerous other mentions of poor harvests or high prices. And actual 'hunger' was mentioned only once (S1560), but was probably more common. Still, there were no mentions of deaths from famine. The chronicler himself, related as he was to an aristocratic family, was probably not at personal risk of starvation, but he might well have mentioned deaths from starvation if these had occurred; he did mention people dying from exposure in winter storms (W1571–72).

Worse and death-dealing famines would hit Scotland in the late 1580s and late 1590s, shortly after the chronicle was written.[43]

Finally, the chronicle yields a fragment of information about marketing systems:

> On the feast of the Nine Virgin Saints [15 July] 1575, the fixing of prices and the market were held and begun at Kenmore at the end of Loch Tay, and there was no market nor fair held at Inchadney where it had habitually been held. (S1575)

The chronicler seems to have disapproved of the moving of this annual fair, either because the new location was about 2km further from Fortingall, or else because Inchadney was a pilgrimage church. The 'fixing of prices' is intriguing; perhaps the Campbells of Glenorchy, the lords under whose authority the fair was held, exercised authority over the prices. What specific goods were bought and sold annually remains obscure. One might speculate about a connection with cattle droving, but this merely underlines the absence of information in the chronicle about prices and markets for livestock.[44]

* * *

Farming was undertaken in an intimate relationship with the broader environment, and it is worth glancing at what the chronicler said about his environment. He mentioned three different kinds of land in a farming context: 'the mountains' (W1554–55), 'higher ground' (S1557) and 'low-lying places' (W1554–55). Mountains were places for upland grazing – and not just in summer, since livestock were in the mountains in winter. The 'higher ground' and 'low-lying places' were both mentioned in connection with grain farming.

There were also peat bogs. Although the chronicler did not mention bogs in connection with farming, he was aware of them: three men were killed by a rival clan 'in the pet mos in mekill Culdyr' in 1576 (p. 141). Peat bogs had farming relevance: peat was used for fuel, while 'bog-hay', consisting of spring plants including bog cotton, could furnish spring grazing.[45] As well as peat, farmers used turf for fuel, and for construction

43 S. G. E. Lythe, *The Economy of Scotland in Its European Setting 1550–1625* (Edinburgh, 1960), pp. 16–23. See also Kevin Hall, 'The Famine of 1622–23 in Scotland', Chapter 3 above in the present volume.

44 In later centuries at least, Kenmore and Fortingall were close to a junction between two droving routes, one from Skye along Glen Lyon, and one from the north via the Drumochter Pass: A. R. B. Haldane, *The Drove Roads of Scotland* (London, 1952), pp. 80, 112.

45 T. C. Smout, 'Bogs and People in Scotland since 1600', in his *Exploring Environmental History*, pp. 99–111. Peat-cutting was mentioned in the early seventeenth-century court books (p. 353).

of dykes and buildings, but the chronicler did not mention turf.[46] Perhaps he was not short of fuel.

The wide River Lyon, unbridged at this date, must have shaped people's interaction with the land every day. The chronicler's mention of 'the Ford of Lyon' seems to indicate that there was only one important ford (p. 136).[47] The river appeared in the chronicle when it froze: 'men and women could well cross on the ice of the River Lyon in several places' (W1554–55, W1571–72). The importance of fords also emerges indirectly when we hear of people drowning in rivers (pp. 137, 141). There may have been floods – the River Tay seems to be unstable and prone to flooding in this area[48] – but the chronicler did not mention floods. In the Roy map, the ploughed land in the Fortingall plain appears to draw back from the low-lying area by the river. This could well have been related to flooding – either a proneness to periodic flooding, or gravel deposits from previous floods rendering the land unsuitable for grain crops, or both.[49] The Glenorchy baron court in 1621 ordered farmers not to plough too close to rivers (pp. 359–60). Flood risks may have been greater when the river froze – something that has been less studied because it hardly ever happens in modern British rivers.[50] Once a river freezes, the breakup of the ice in the spring can cause violent floods.[51]

There seems to be nothing about woodland in the chronicle – probably because it was less affected by the seasonal fluctuations that attracted the chronicler's attention. The parish of Fortingall had 'many large woods' of

46 Cf. Alexander Fenton and Angus Martin, 'Peat and Turf', in Alexander Fenton and Kenneth Veitch (eds), *Farming and the Land* (Scottish Life and Society: A Compendium of Scottish Ethnology, vol. 2; Edinburgh, 2011), 751–72.

47 The ford's location is unknown. Cf. Duncan Campbell, *The Book of Garth and Fortingall: Historical Sketches Relating to the Districts of Garth, Fortingall, Athole, and Breadalbane* (Inverness, 1888), p. 5.

48 D. J. Gilvear and S. J. Winterbottom, 'Channel Change and Flood Events since 1783 on the Regulated River Tay, Scotland: Implications for Flood Hazard Management', *Regulated Rivers: Research and Management*, 7:3 (1992), 247–60, at pp. 257–8.

49 The minister of Fortingall in 1792 reported: 'It is a fertile beautiful bottom. The soil is dry, light, and rather gravellish': *OSA*, XII, p. 426 (Fortingal [*sic*], p. 450). He did not mention floods; there had been a disastrous flood in the area in 1791, but perhaps the report was submitted before that. For this flood, and for flood damage in general, see Robert A. Dodgshon, *No Stone Unturned: A History of Farming, Landscape and Environment in the Scottish Highlands and Islands* (Edinburgh, 2015), pp. 86–8.

50 In England, the Thames was recorded as freezing four times in the sixteenth century: Ian Currie, *Frosts, Freezes and Fairs: Chronicles of the Frozen Thames and Harsh Winters in Britain since 1000 AD* (Coulsdon, 2001), pp. 3–4.

51 Spyros Beltaos and Terry Prowse, 'River-Ice Hydrology in a Shrinking Cryosphere', *Hydrological Processes*, 23:1 (2009), 122–44.

birch and fir, growing naturally, in 1792;[52] these may well have existed also in the sixteenth century. Wood itself had many uses in a farming community, and the open woodland that may have been found in this area was also used as pasture for livestock.[53] Finally, there is nothing about pests or predators – even wolves, which sometimes attracted attention in the Highlands.[54]

* * *

Before concluding, it may help to remind ourselves briefly that the chronicler's language about weather and farming is direct and hands-on – and that this is unusual. In particular, it contrasts sharply with the indirect, detached and often metaphorical language used by the poems in the Book of the Dean of Lismore – the chronicler's cultural milieu.[55] The following instances collect many and probably most of the references to farming in these poems. A satire against a disliked chief calls him 'meagre rye' rather than 'wheat', and a 'balk of straws' (uncultivated rig) rather than a 'tall and stately cornyard', among a much larger vocabulary of non-agricultural abuse (pp. 49, 57). A long list of sins and transgressions mentions that it is 'not good to plough by night' (p. 243). A comical diatribe against a person alleged to be a beggar includes a few agricultural or at least domestic items in a long list of things for which he might beg: 'a butter-crock and meal … gleanings of rye … a hen with her eggs … rennet that has lost its strength' (pp. 17–19). More positively, a successful hunter is rewarded with 'the picked ox of the team of six' (p. 29), while a celebrated chief rules over wheat fields, cows in milking folds, and rich pastures (p. 37). Mentions of seasons (e.g. pp. 71, 145) and weather (e.g. pp. 23, 141, 169, 179) rarely if ever occur in farming contexts. And such passages are not only indirect, but rare. The aristocratic world of Gaelic poetry, like contemporary poetry elsewhere in Scotland, has little time for agriculture.[56]

* * *

52 *OSA*, XII, p. 427 (Fortingal [*sic*], p. 451).
53 T. C. Smout, Alan R. MacDonald and Fiona Watson, *A History of the Native Woodlands of Scotland 1500–1920* (Edinburgh, 2005), pp. 77–123. Heather, briars, thorn and broom were mentioned in the early seventeenth-century court books (pp. 352–4).
54 Wolves, rooks, hooded crows and magpies were mentioned in the early seventeenth-century court books (p. 356).
55 The chronicler, as we have seen, was probably the Dean's son. The remainder of this paragraph gives page references from W. J. Watson (ed.), *Scottish Verse from the Book of the Dean of Lismore* (Edinburgh: Scottish Gaelic Texts Society, 1937).
56 Cf. Julian Goodare, 'Imagining Scottish Agriculture before the Improvers', Chapter 1 above in the present volume.

We may well 'know' about pre-industrial farming, in an intellectual way. As part of this knowledge, we may well note that pre-industrial folk experienced the weather and the seasons more forcefully than we do ourselves. We probably remember that farmers' success or failure, season by season, mattered to them. But this knowledge often reaches us through a filter of statistics or a framework of abstract concepts. We treat past records of human experience of weather and farming as topics for coolly detached analysis. This is not wrong, but it is not the only way in which we should approach the evidence.

A coolly detached view of the Fortingall chronicle would observe that, in themselves, many of its remarks about farming do not really add to our knowledge. We already knew, from many other sources, that the main arable crops in the Highlands were oats and bere. We already knew that some farms in Highland Perthshire raised semi-feral horses. And so on. We may also be frustrated at the large range of farming topics on which the chronicle is entirely silent.

There is slightly more hard information when it comes to the weather, and the weather's effects on farming. We did not know from other sources that the 1560s were better for farmers in this area than the 1550s or 1570s. And the handfuls of mentions of prices are small but genuine additions to the fragmentary data for this period.

Overall, though, the Chronicle of Fortingall is a document about direct, individual experience, not statistics. It is important for the way in which it brings home to us what weather and farming *meant* to a farmer at this time. We see through his eyes. This enables us, not merely to know, but to *apprehend*.

Thus, when we read the chronicler's terse but direct words, we find ourselves sharing his experiences. We shiver with him in the cold winters. We feel his astonishment when the mighty River Lyon freezes over. We share his sympathy for the farm livestock, and even the wild animals, struggling in the snowdrifts. He even mentions the animal deaths before the human deaths that ensue:

> On the afternoon of 22 February, there was a great storm, with snow, hail and wind, so that no man nor beast could raise their heads, nor travel nor ride. Many animals perished out in that storm, and many men and women perished in several places. (W1571–72)

Then, as winter shows signs of opening out into warmer weather, we hope that the frozen ground will thaw, and that the rain will lift, so that the chronicler can get on with his ploughing and sowing. Once the crops begin to sprout, we watch the seedlings anxiously with him in a doubtful growing season. We share his indignation when a local aristocrat resorts to profiteering during a summer food shortage. And we share his relief when the next harvest is a plentiful one after all, and prices are halved.

A full appreciation of the Chronicle of Fortingall should recognise, therefore, that most people's daily concerns in pre-industrial Scotland were those that the chronicler expressed. Other primary sources for the period may be more informative in a coolly detached way – but, in the directness of his experience, the Fortingall chronicler can show us things that really mattered in history. Indeed, perhaps no other single historical source from this period can show us so much.

Appendix

Entries on Weather and Farming in the Chronicle of Fortingall

This appendix presents the textual evidence on which this chapter is based, in tabular form, season by season. Altogether the chronicler wrote about 1,100 words about weather and farming, constituting about one-seventh of the whole text of his chronicle.

The main farming-related entries are spread across 23 years, from the winter of 1554–55 up to the summer of 1577. The table below presents this period as 46 seasons. Within these 46, the chronicle has farming-related entries for 28 seasons, fairly evenly distributed. The periods of most frequent commentary are winter 1558–59 to summer 1563 (9 entries out of a possible 10), summer 1569 to winter 1571–72 (6 out of 6), and summer 1574 to summer 1577 (6 out of 7). The largest gap is summer 1572 to winter 1573–74 (4 seasons with no relevant entries, and fewer entries on other topics). In addition, there is a much earlier entry for winter 1404–05, taken over from a previous chronicle.

A few entries discuss more than 1 season. Two in particular (winter 1559–60 and winter 1569–70) begin with a given winter and then comment retrospectively on the previous summer. This has been dealt with in the table by repeating small portions of text, as noted in square brackets within the translation.

The translation is intended as an aid to comprehension of the text. 'Evill' is translated sometimes as 'poor' (a poor harvest), sometimes as 'harsh' (harsh frost), and sometimes as 'heavy' (heavy rain). 'Ran' and 'weyth' are both translated as 'rain' except when they occur together. 'Fayr' is usually translated as 'fine', but 'fayr frost' has been rendered as 'dry frost', and one 'fayr' winter has been rendered as 'mild'. Editorial comments are given in square brackets (if brief) or in footnotes. In the quoted text, ellipses thus … denote lacunae in the original (the MS is damaged in places), while ellipses in square brackets thus […] denote text about non-farming matters omitted by me as editor.

Date	Text
Winter 1404–05 (p. 112; fol. 7r.)	Anno Domini M° quadringentissimo quarto magna nix cessidit supra terram generaliter in festo omnium sanctorum et semper in addendo ...[57] usque ad festum sancti Patricii.
Winter 1554–55 (pp. 124–5; fol. 12r.)	...[58] and afoyr Andermes frost snaw quhylis. Item the xiij da of December in the yer of God ane thousand fyv hundyr liiij yer the frost began and the great snaw began on Yowl da at ewyn and ilk da fra that furth mayr and mayr snaw without ony thoyfft quhyl the xvij da of Januar. It was the grettast snaw and storm that was sein in memorie of man lewand that tym. Mony wyld hors and meris ky sceyp gayt peryst and deyth for falt of fud in the montanis and in al udyr partis and thowch part of thowff com the xvij da of Januar fra that furth it began agayn tyl snaw and frosst quhyl the xxij da of Februar on the quhylk day men and wemen myth weyll pas on the ies of Lyon in syndri placis and lytil thylt in few placis quhyll the xxvj da of Februar and[59] bot in layth placis.
Summer 1555	
Winter 1555–56	
Summer 1556	
Winter 1556–57 (p. 126; fol. 20r.)	Item the wyntyr in the yer of God ane [M][60] v^c lvj yer it wes rycht fayr vodyr and ...[61] snaw of [sic] or stormis and part of fayr frost variabil vodyr lityl tylt in that wontyr [...] Item the Lentren quartyr the yer abone vryttyn mekill[62] and lestand lytyl snaw Merche dry Apryill.[63]
Summer 1557 (p. 127; fols 20r., 20v.)	Yer lvij fayr wodyr all the yer bayth wontyr and Lentren quartyr skant of ...[64] and bayr and deyr the symmyr lvij ...[65] quhill mydsymmyr and then gud w...[66] ...bundance. Symmyr the yer of God ane M v^c lvij dry and het [...] This symmyr vas deyr ewyl haryst and layth in the heland.[67]

57 A word is missing here.
58 The scribe has left a blank space of about five words at the start of the line.
59 A short word may be missing here.
60 Conjectural restoration of damaged text.
61 A word is missing here.
62 The text is worn at the end of a line, but there does not seem to be room for the words 'snow' or 'frost' that the chronicler may have had in mind.
63 In the MS (fol. 20r.), but not in the printed edition, the text about summer 1557 follows immediately at this point.
64 A word seems to be missing here (possibly 'victuals').
65 About two words are missing here.
66 About three words are missing here, presumably beginning 'weather'.
67 The phrase 'layth in the heland' is difficult. 'Layth' could be a noun or an

Date	Translation
Winter 1404–05	In 1404, the great snow fell upon the whole land from the feast of All Saints [1 November], and more was continually added … until the feast of St Patrick [17 March].
Winter 1554–55	… and before St Andrew's day [30 November], frost and snow from time to time. On 13 December 1554 the frost began, and the great snow began on the evening of Yule day [25 December]. Every day after that, more and more snow, without any thaw, until 17 January. It was the greatest snow and storm that any man living at that time could remember having seen. Many wild horses and mares, and cows, sheep and goats, perished and died for lack of food in the mountains and in all other places. Although a partial thaw came on 17 January, from thenceforth it began again to snow and freeze until 22 February. On that day, men and women could well cross on the ice of the River Lyon in several places. There was not much ploughing, and not in many places, until 26 February, and only in low-lying places.
Summer 1555	
Winter 1555–56	
Summer 1556	
Winter 1556–57	In winter 1556 the weather was really fine and … snow or storms and partly dry frost … variable weather, little ploughing in that winter […] In the Lent quarter of that year,[80] much [snow? frost?] and a small amount of snow lasting until March; dry April.
Summer 1557	In 1557, fine weather all year in both winter and Lent quarters,[81] shortage of [foodstuffs?] and desolate.[82] Prices were high in the summer of 1557 … until midsummer and then good [weather?] … abundance.[83] Summer 1557 dry and hot […] This summer was dear, with a poor harvest, and weak growth on higher ground.

80 This 'quarter' probably ran from Candlemas (2 February) to Whit Sunday (15 May). Lent itself in 1557 ran from 3 March to 16 April.

81 These 'quarters' are probably the periods between Martinmas (11 November) and Candlemas (2 February), and from then until Whit Sunday (15 May). The chronicler here is returning to the winter of 1556–57, about which he has already written in a previous entry.

82 It is conceivable that 'bayr' here is a noun, 'bere', but the adjective 'bare' (desolate) seems more likely.

83 This word, isolated at the end of a damaged paragraph, might be taken to indicate an 'abundant' harvest, except that in his next entry, still explicitly on the summer of 1557, the chronicler states that the harvest was poor. Perhaps this is about 'abundance' of something other than grain, such as young

Date	Text
Winter 1557–58	
Summer 1558	
Winter 1558–59 (p. 128; fol. 20v.)	The vyntyr eftyr that vas rycht fayr and gud and lytil snaw bot mekil frost and gud scheyp of vittellis.
Summer 1559 (p. 129; fol. 1v.)	lix yeris […] Evill symmyr harist.
Winter 1559–60 (p. 129; fol. 1v.)	vyntyr the yer lix ane fayr Merche[68] and frosty quhill the xvj da [of] Merche.
Summer 1560 (p. 129; fol. 1v.)	Item the symmyr lx yeris rych[t] deyr evyll haryst that evyr [wa]s seyn. […] mekill hungyr and darth …[69] ther the feyr of maill and bayr xls.
Winter 1560–61 (p. 129; fols 1v., 21r.)	A fayr vyntyr evyl Februar …[70] snaw. Item the begynnyn of that Merche mekill snaw frost and stormis quhill the xxv dayis of Merche fra that furth fayr vodyr rych[t] deyr. Item the begynnin of Apriill [*sic*] evill frost snaw gret vindis and fra that furth gud veddyr. Item the May rych[t] dry and het and frost[71] and vynd.
Summer 1561 (p. 130; fol. 21r.)	Item the symmyr the yer ane M v^c lxj yer rych[t] der all stwff fayr gud vodyr that haryst rych[t] gud and fayr […] that samyn haryst so ves […][72] and gud w…[73]
Winter 1561–62 (p. 130; fol. 21v.)	Meklle snaw in all partis mony deyr and rays slain[74] that yer.

adjective, while 'the heland' could mean 'higher ground' or 'the Highlands'. The latter meaning is unlikely, since the chronicler was located well within the Highlands, and elsewhere in his text shows no interest in treating the Highlands as distinct. As for 'layth', the word occurs twice more in the chronicle, both times as an adjective (pp. 125, 142). In the first of these it appears to be a variant spelling of 'laich' (low-lying), while in the second it clearly means 'weak' (of growth). I have preferred the latter meaning here, as the only adjective that makes sense in context. There remains a small possibility that 'layth' is a noun, in which case it might mean 'harm', and 'the heland' might mean 'the Highlands' after all.

68 The text here runs directly on from the summer of 1559: 'Evill symmyr harist vyntyr the yer lix ane fayr Merche'. I have read 'vyntyr the yer lix' as beginning a new clause, but the text could instead be read as meaning 'a poor summer, harvest and winter; in 1560, March was fine'.

69 About four words are missing here.

70 About four words are missing here.

71 The 'st' of 'frost' seems to have been altered or deleted.

72 Several words are missing here, some of which seem to have been about non-farming matters.

73 Several words are missing here.

74 'Slain' may imply that hunters killed them, but this seems a less likely meaning in context.

Date	Translation
Winter 1557–58	
Summer 1558	
Winter 1558–59	The winter after that was really fine and good, with little snow but much frost. Foodstuffs were really cheap.
Summer 1559	In 1559, a poor summer and harvest.
Winter 1559–60	In winter 1560, March was fine, and frosty until 16 March.
Summer 1560	In the summer of 1560, prices were really dear, with [the most?] poor harvest that ever was seen […] much hunger and dearth … the fiar price of oatmeal and bere was 40s.
Winter 1560–61	A fine winter, [but] harsh February … snow. Much snow at the beginning of March. Frost and storms until 25 March; from then, fine weather, [but] really dear. At the beginning of April, harsh frost, snow, strong winds. From then on, good weather. In May, really dry and hot, and frost and wind.[84]
Summer 1561	In summer 1561, all things were really dear. Fine, good weather. That harvest was really good and fine … that harvest was … and good [weather?].
Winter 1561–62	Much snow in all places. Many deer and roes died that year.

---

livestock. Or, perhaps more likely, it could be about an unfulfilled *hope* or *prospect* of abundance.

84 'Frost and wind' seem incongruous after what the chronicler has just written about heat. However, high pressure could lead to cold nights, and frost in May is not inconceivable.

Date	Text
Summer 1562	
Winter 1562–63 (p. 131; fols 21v., 22r.)	Item the vyntyr sexte tua yer rych[t] fayr nodyr snaw nor frost. The nyxt Lentren quartyr rych[t] dry and deyr in all partis. Jeius [*sic*] Maria sit semper. [...] That samyn vyntyr rych[t] fayr and guid vodyr rych[t] deyr in al partis.
Summer 1563 (pp. 131–2; fol. 21v.)	Item the symmyr the yer of God ane M v^c sexte tre yeris rych[t] deyr viz. the boll of maill v merk and the feyr of meill in mony partis iiij merk and the lady of Straythort tuk v merk for the boll of maill for the feyr. Ane gud symmyr and gud harist.
Winter 1563–64	
Summer 1564 (p. 132; fol. 21v.)	That symmyr meklle rayn contynele gud sayp of vittellis in al partis. The yer afor that the boll of mail gef in part v merk and this symmyr it vas for xviij s. and the malt for xxviij. Ther ye ma se the grace of God. ... haryst[75] sexte four yeris ane gud harist. September rych[t] ...
Winter 1564–65	
Summer 1565 (p. 134; fol. 23v.)	Item ane gud symmer and harist viz. sexte and fyv yeris.
Winter 1565–66	
Summer 1566 (p. 134; fol. 23v.)	Item anno Domini ane M v^c sexte sex yeris ane gud symmyr evyl August veyth in September gud corne in al partis evil October.
Winter 1566–67	
Summer 1567 (p. 135; fol. 23v.)	The symmyr sexte sevin yeris rycht dry and het that brynt[76] kill corne[77] and gyrs in mony partis of Scotland ...[78] evyl haryst and naymly October and part of Septembar.
Winter 1567–68	
Summer 1568	
Winter 1568–69	
Summer 1569 (p. 136; fol. 25v.)	haryst rycht fayr vodyr and gud sayp of vyttellis thoch the symmyr afoyr that vas rych[t] deyr the fayr of bayr tre [*sic*] pund ilk boll and the boll of mail iiij merk.

75 A word seems to be missing here. The reading 'haryst' is uncertain.
76 A word may be missing here.
77 The translation of 'kill corne' is not certain.
78 One or two words are missing here.

Date	Translation
Summer 1562	
Winter 1562–63	The winter of 1562, really mild, neither snow nor frost. The next Lent quarter really dry, and dear in all places. Jesus, Mary, let it always be so. […] That winter really fine and good weather. Really dear in all places.
Summer 1563	Summer 1563 was really dear. The boll of oatmeal was 5 merks. The fiar price of oatmeal in many places was 4 merks. The lady of Strathord took 5 merks for the boll of oatmeal for the fiar.[85] A good summer and good harvest.
Winter 1563–64	
Summer 1564	Much rain that summer. Continued good cheap prices of foodstuffs in all parts. The year before that [i.e. 1563], the boll of oatmeal sold for 5 merks; this summer it was sold for 18s., and malt for 28s. There you may see the grace of God. In 1564 there was a good harvest. September was really …
Winter 1564–65	
Summer 1565	A good summer and harvest in 1565.
Winter 1565–66	
Summer 1566	A good summer in 1566. Harsh August. Rain in September. Good corn in all places. Harsh October.
Winter 1566–67	
Summer 1567	The summer of 1567 was really dry and hot; it shrivelled corn in the kiln, and grass in many parts of Scotland. Poor harvest, particularly in October and part of September.
Winter 1567–68	
Summer 1568	
Winter 1568–69	
Summer 1569	That harvest, really fine weather, and foodstuffs very cheap.[86] The summer was really dear; the fiar price of bere was £3 per boll, and of oatmeal 4 merks per boll [see also below].

85   The lady of Strathord was Janet Ruthven, daughter of William, 2nd Lord Ruthven, and wife of John Crichton of Strathord. The couple are mentioned in 1544 and 1573: *RMS*, III, no. 3013; *RMS*, IV, no. 2259. Strathord seems to have been near the Ordie Burn south of present-day Bankfoot, on the road from Dunkeld to Perth.

86   This harvest is that of 1569. Chronologically, this passage is recorded between two major political events: the assassination of Regent Moray (23 January 1569/70) and the execution of Gregor MacGregor of Glenstrae (7 April 1570). The immediately preceding entry, however, is an obituary dated 12 October

Date	Text
Winter 1569–70 (p. 136; fol. 25v.)	that wyntyr and haryst rycht fayr vodyr and gud sayp of vyttellis thoch the symmyr afoyr that vas rych[t] deyr the fayr of bayr tre pund ilk boll and the boll of mail iiij merk.
Summer 1570 (p. 136; fols 25r., 25v.)	The symmyr sexte ten yeris rycht gud and all vittellis gud sayp the ['haryst rycht fayr vodr' *crossed out*] Awgust rych[t] fayr and gud vodyr [...] September ewyll vodyr and Octobar quhill the xv day and than guid vodyr and fayr.
Winter 1570–71 (p. 137; fol. 25v.)	The wyntyr and Lentren quartyr ewyll wodyr mony seip and gayth ded skant of fodyr in mony plassis.
Summer 1571 (p. 137; fol. 25v.)	It vas rych[t] ewyl wodyr in September and October.
Winter 1571–72 (pp. 137–8; fols 25v., 26r.)	Item that wynthyr rych[t] fayr wodyr quhyl the fyftein day of Januar and fra that furth quhyl the xxij day of Merche gret frost that na plwis ȝyd quhil aucht dayis eftyr that and men mycht weill pas and repas on the ies of Lyon the tryd day of Merche [...] the xxij day of Februar ther com eftyr nown ane gret stroym and snaw and hayll and wynd that na man nor best mycht tak wp ther heddis nor gayng nor ryd and mony bestis war pareist furth in that storm and mony men and vemen war pareist in syndry partis and al kynd of vyttellis rych[t] deyr and that becaus na millis mycht gryn for the frost. All cornis com til the mill of Dunkell out of Sanc Jonisthown betuyxt that and Dunkell and all vydr bundis about far and neyr. The maill gef that tym in Sanc Jonisthown xliiij s. the malt xxxiiij s. and or Sanc Patrykis day the maill vas for xxv s. viij d. and the malt for xxx s.
Summer 1572	
Winter 1572–73	
Summer 1573	
Winter 1573–74	
Summer 1574 (p. 140; fol. 29r.)	Item the symmyr in the yer of God ane M v^c lxxiiij yeris rych[t] ewil vodyr and deyr the bol of malt five merk and half merk and the bol of mail iiij merk and 3[79] merk. Evil August wynd and ran. [...] That samyn harist ewil vodyr that evyr was sein continual weyth.
Winter 1574–75	

---

79 This '3' probably means 'one-third', as also proposed by Cosmo Innes.

Date	Translation
Winter 1569–70	That winter … really fine weather, and foodstuffs very cheap [see also above].
Summer 1570	The summer of 1570, really good, and all foodstuffs very cheap. In August, really fine, good weather. […] In September and October, harsh weather until 15 October, then good, fine weather.
Winter 1570–71	The winter and Lent quarter, harsh weather. Many sheep and goats died for shortage of fodder in many places.
Summer 1571	It was really harsh weather in September and October.
Winter 1571–72	That winter, really fine weather until 15 January, and from then on until 22 March, great frost, so that no ploughs operated until a week after that. Men could well cross and return on the ice of the River Lyon on 3 March. […] On the afternoon of 22 February, there was a great storm, with snow, hail and wind, so that no man nor beast could raise their heads, nor travel nor ride. Many animals perished out in that storm, and many men and women perished in several places. All kinds of foodstuffs were really dear, because no mills could grind because of the frost. All corn, from Perth to Dunkeld and other places around, far and near, came to the mill of Dunkeld. Oatmeal cost 44s. in Perth, and malt 34s. By St Patrick's day [17 March], oatmeal cost 25s. 8d., and malt 30s.
Summer 1572	
Winter 1572–73	
Summer 1573	
Winter 1573–74	
Summer 1574	In the summer of 1574, really harsh weather, and dear. The boll of malt, 5½ merks; the boll of oatmeal, 4⅓ merks. Harsh August, wind and rain. […] That harvest, the worst weather that ever was seen; continual rain.
Winter 1574–75	

1568. The chronicler has set out, perhaps in early 1570, to write an account of the winter of 1569–70, but is also trying to catch up with 1569. The remark about 'really fine weather, and foodstuffs very cheap' seems to apply both to the harvest of 1569 and to the winter of 1569–70.

Date	Text
Summer 1575 (p. 140; fols 24v., 30r.)	Item the yer of God M vᶜ sexte xv yeris on the Nyn Virgines day the prasyn and the margat was haldin and begwn at the Kenmor at the end of Lochthay and ther was na margat nor fayr haldin at Inchadin quhar it was wynt tilbe haldin. All this doin be Collyn Campbell of Glenwrquhay. [...] Item the feyr of bayr and malt that yer fyv merk and the maill tre pund.
Winter 1575–76 (p. 140; fol. 27r.)	Item the xxiij da of Merche the yer abowin vryttin I began til saw in the Borllin of Fortyrgill. Ane rych[t] ewyl Merche and ane evil December Januar and Februar bayth snaw and frost weyth and hayll and vyttellis rych[t] deyr al that wyntyr and Lentren quartyr.
Summer 1576 (p. 141; fol. 30v.)	The quhilk symer was rych[t] gud vodyr [...] Item al Junii and Julii and Awgust rych[t] ewyl vodyr mekill ran and veyth quhill September and than rych[t] fayr vodyr quhill the xvj da of September eftyr that rych[t] ewyl vodyr na ayts sorne in Fortyrgill the xxiij da of September bot rych[t] lytill and namly in Ballenecragge. Item al October evil vodyr mekil corne onsorne and onled.
Winter 1576–77 (p. 141; fol. 31r.)	Ewil haryst ewil vintyr ewil Merche contynual weyth and na ayts sawyn in Merche. The xxij da of Merche I began til saw ayts.
Summer 1577 (pp. 141–2; fol. 31r.)	That Apryll rych[t] ewill vodyr and the May mekill weyth and ran and Junii rycht evyl weyth and vynd and the bayr seyd rych[t] layth in al plasis quhil eftyr Sanc Colmis day.

Date	Translation
Summer 1575	On the feast of the Nine Virgin Saints [15 July] 1575,[87] the fixing of prices[88] and the market were held and begun at Kenmore at the end of Loch Tay, and there was no market nor fair held at Inchadney where it had habitually been held.[89] All this was done by Colin Campbell of Glenorchy. [...] The fiar of bere and malt that year was 5 merks, and oatmeal £3.
Winter 1575–76	On 23 March that year, I began to sow in the Borllin of Fortingall. A really harsh March, and a harsh December, January and February, with snow and frost, rain and hail, and foodstuffs really dear all that winter and Lent quarter.
Summer 1576	That summer there was really good weather. [...] All June, July and August there was really harsh weather, with much rain and wet until September; then there was really fine weather until 16 September. After that, really harsh weather. No oats had been harvested in Fortingall by 23 September, except for a really small quantity, mainly in Balnacraig.[90] All October, harsh weather; much corn not harvested nor carted away.
Winter 1576–77	Poor harvest,[91] harsh winter, harsh March, continual rain, and no oats sown in March. On 22 March I began to sow oats.
Summer 1577	That April, really harsh weather. In May, much wet and rain. In June, heavy rain and wind. The bere seed grew really weakly in all places until after St Columba's day [9 June].

87 The Feast of the Nine Virgin Saints ('S[anc]ta[rum] nove[m] v[ir]gi[num]') was on 15 July: *Breviarii Aberdonensis ad per celebris ecclesie Scotorum usum*, 2 vols (Edinburgh: W. Chepman, 1509–10), Calendar, *sub* 15 July. I am grateful to Professor Alasdair A. MacDonald for this reference.

88 This translation of 'prasyn' is tentative, as *DOST* has only this source for the word, but it does seem probable.

89 'Inchadney' was the name for the parish later known as Kenmore. The old church, which had a holy well that was a pilgrimage site, was located in what is now Inchadney Park, to the north-east of Taymouth Castle: William A. Gillies, *In Famed Breadalbane: The Story of the Antiquities, Lands, and People of a Highland District* (Perth, 1938), pp. 56–7. The fair's new location was thus only about 2km further up the River Tay, but the chronicler seems to have disliked the change.

90 Balnacraig is about 1km to the east of Fortingall.

91 Evidently the harvest of 1576, on which the chronicler has already commented at length.

5

Stock, Fermes, Mails and Duties in a Midlothian Barony 1587–89

Norah Carlin

Sir James Forrester II, baron of Corstorphine, died intestate on 4 June 1589, killed in a brawl or ambush. On 12 August 1589 nine men were accused in the Justiciary Court of being accessories to his slaughter, but the case was adjourned.[1] Mr Samuel Cockburn of Temple, though not named in the case, applied to the Dalkeith Presbytery on 15 March 1590 to be received as a penitent, 'together with his servants that were participant of the Laird of Corstorphine's slaughter'.[2] He later told them that he had received a royal pardon, and 'the party was almost satisfied' – probably a reference to compensating Sir James's heir.[3] Forrester's estate of Clerkington was adjacent to Cockburn's barony of Temple, and although local issues may have been involved, it is more than likely that the main conflict between the two lairds was political. Forrester had helped Mary Queen of Scots escape from Lochleven Castle and fought for her at Langside, while Cockburn was a supporter of the king's party.[4] Where and why the killing took place remains a mystery. Forrester's principal legacy to historians is not in the field of political history, however: it is the testament dative drawn up for the Edinburgh Commissary Court under the supervision of his sister Isobel, wife of James Baillie younger of Carfin, who was appointed his sole executrix.[5]

1   NRS, JC2/2, 12 August 1589.
2   NRS, CH2/424/1, p. 209.
3   Ibid., p. 233.
4   *Register of the Privy Seal of Scotland*, ed. M. Livingstone *et al.* (8 vols, Edinburgh, 1908–), vol. 6, nos. 294, 327, 334, 342.
5   NRS, CC8/8/20, fols 515–35.

The heir to Sir James's heritable estate – land, houses, and their appurtenances – was his younger brother Henry, since the deceased and his wife Jean Lauder had no surviving children. Heritable properties were not subject to testamentary disposition in Scotland, and the heir's share in the moveable goods – referred to as the 'heirship' – was also excluded from testaments. A testament dative was therefore a balance sheet of the deceased person's remaining assets and liabilities, including debts owing to and owed by them. Sir James's inventory includes an impressive array of household goods, plate, clothing and jewellery with a total value of £666 13s. 4d. (1,000 merks).[6]

Of particular interest to agricultural historians is the list of his stock on the mains or home farms – working animals, herds and flocks, crops in store and the expected return of grain growing in the fields – together with the stock held by five tenants in steelbow, a form of tenure including animals or seed corn or both whose exact equivalent was to be returned to the landlord at the end of the term. An added bonus in this testament is the listing, among the debts owing to the deceased, of arrears of rent in kind and in money due from all Forrester's estates for the last year and a half. These appear to be owing from almost every holding on the barony's estates, the greatest amount of detail being given for Corstorphine, the largest and most important estate. Since the amounts due in grain for the whole year (Martinmas 1587–88) are exactly twice those for the half year to Whitsunday 1589, it can be assumed that they represent the full amount due per annum. Sir James's testament therefore gives us much information that would normally be found in a rental rather than a testament. The predominance of grain rents in Corstorphine gives us an especially interesting picture of agricultural activity there, while the different arrangements on the other estates in Midlothian and beyond offer suggestive contrasts.

* * *

The estate of Corstorphine, from which the Forresters' barony took its title, had been in the family's possession since 1376.[7] The village at its centre (now a suburb of Edinburgh) lay about four miles west of the city, near the junction of the main roads into Edinburgh from Stirling and Glasgow. The family's castle at Corstorphine appears, disproportionately large in size, on the map of the Lothians made in the 1590s by Timothy Pont, which shows the castle and village lying between two equal expanses of

6   Margaret H. B. Sanderson, *Scottish Rural Society in the Sixteenth Century* (Edinburgh, 1982), p. 174.
7   Elizabeth Ewan, 'Forrester Family (*per.* c.1360–c.1450)', *Oxford Dictionary of National Biography* (online edition, 2004).

water.[8] Gogar Loch lay to the west, while on the east was Corstorphine Loch, over which supplies had been brought by boat to the castle in the middle ages. These details were copied into many other maps over the following century, but on Adair's manuscript map of 1682 both lochs are shown as boggy ground, the eastern one about half the size of the other.[9] Both would be thoroughly drained in the eighteenth century. The village may once have been situated on a narrow neck of dry land, but the estate also included a mains farm and extensive agricultural lands lying around the village, sweeping down from Corstorphine Hill, which reaches 161 feet at its summit and is rough and rocky to the north and east, but slopes more gently westwards towards East and West Craigs. South of the castle were low-lying fields and meadow land, and beyond these the farm of Broomhouse, the 'plewlands' feued to Sir James Forrester by the commendator of Holyrood Abbey in 1560.[10] Corstorphine's pattern of settlement, a nucleated village set in a ring of dispersed farms or 'farmtouns' (see Map 5.1), was common in Scotland.[11] The pattern of a few large and many smaller holdings was probably not, therefore, the result of deliberate consolidation, as it often was in early modern England. All but one of the farms around Corstorphine named in Sir James Forrester's testament were still cultivated in the 1950s. Although all have now disappeared into suburban housing developments, those around Samuel Cockburn's Temple are still in existence.

The Forresters' other core property, Clerkington, had also been in their possession since before 1400. It lay south-west of Temple in the valley of the South Esk, where mineral extraction – lime burning and coal mining – were to become regular supplements to arable and pasture farming by the 1620s. The Forresters kept a household and a mains or

---

8   T. Pont, *A new description of the Shyres Lothian and Linlitquo* (Amsterdam, 1630), at maps.nls.uk/counties/rec/203.

9   NLS, Adv. MS 70.2.11 (Adair 9), at maps.nls.uk/view/00001013.

10   NRS, E14/1/227. The meadow ground appears on Adair, as above. See also Sanderson, *Scottish Rural Society*, p. 129; Marguerite Wood (ed.), *The Book of Records of the Ancient Privileges of the Canongate* (Edinburgh: SRS, 1955), pp. 19, 42. For the identification of the Plewlands with Broomhouse see A. S. Cowper, *Historic Corstorphine and Roundabout: Part Two, West of Edinburgh Toun* (published privately, 1992), pp. 52–3. The four little volumes of Miss Cowper's work are a treasure-chest of information about Corstorphine's history. Though presented entirely without scholarly apparatus and in fairly random order, it is usually possible to identify the likely sources of specific information.

11   The 1539–40 rental of the lands of the order of St John in Scotland shows a similar settlement pattern in several of their baronies. Ian B. Cowan, P. H. R. Mackay and Alan Macquarrie (eds), *The Knights of St John of Jerusalem in Scotland* (Edinburgh: SHS, 1983), pp. 1–13.

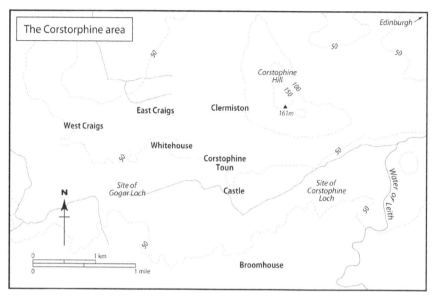

MAP 5.1. The Corstorphine area.

demesne farm at Clerkington. The farms of Friarton and Braidwood nearby, together with the pastures of Fairliehope near Carlops and a waulk mill for fulling cloth at Clerkington, were also included in this property. The family maintained a third residence at Inch House in Nether Liberton on the south side of Edinburgh. Named by the familiar Gaelic word for island, this medieval tower house – much extended by later owners – still stands on land occasionally cut off by the floodwaters of the slow-running Braid Burn. The surrounding estate evidently included productive arable land, however, capable of growing wheat as well as bere (the tough, four- to six-row barley grown all over Scotland at the time). Other properties listed in the testament were Longniddry in East Lothian, Ochtertyre and Chalmerston near Stirling, and Bedlormie near Blackridge in West Lothian.

The laird's income from his estates came in three forms. The most important of these consisted of 'fermes', or rents in grain, whose total value of £3,034 4s. 7d. accounted for 89 per cent of the total due. Money rents, or 'mails', were the main contribution from Clerkington and the outlying properties in Stirlingshire and West Lothian. A third form of income, which was due only from those estates where the laird kept a household, was called 'duties' here ('kanes' or 'cain' elsewhere in Scotland), and consisted mainly of a large supply of poultry. At Corstorphine and Liberton, 'loads of coals' were also due. These were levied on estates which did not produce any minerals, and were evidently carrying services.[12]

* * *

The testament offers a snapshot of the landlord's 'stock' – the farm animals that he owned, his stored wool and grain, his grain still standing in the fields, and finally his share of the animals and grain worked by the tenants of the steelbow holdings.

In addition to the oxen and horses set aside for the heirship, Sir James Forrester owned six work horses and one mare with a foal, located at the mains of Corstorphine, and thirty-two draught oxen at Corstorphine and Clerkington. How many oxen were in each place is not stated in the testament, but thirty-two would constitute at least four teams available for the communal activity of ploughing.[13] Other stock on the laird's demesne lands consisted of 24 cows and a bull at Braidwood, 100 lambs at Friarton, 373 sheep and 30 lambs at Fairliehope, and 8 goats at Clerkington.[14]

Twenty-four stones (336 lbs) of wool were currently in store at Clerkington, and an equal amount at Corstorphine. Eight bolls of bere were stored in the barn and barnyard at Clerkington. Twelve bolls of oats were in the barn at Corstorphine, together with eight threaves of wheat (estimated to contain four bolls of grain), and the two stacks standing in the nether yard there were estimated to contain sixteen bolls of wheat and sixteen bolls of bere respectively. A smaller stack expected to yield six bolls of wheat remained in the upper yard, and twenty bolls of oats had been 'given to make meal'.[15] One and a half arks (kists or chests) of meal containing forty bolls were stored in the castle of Corstorphine.

Hay growing on the meadows of the two mains farms was valued at £266 13s. 4d., half each at Corstorphine and Clerkington. As the fuel of horse transport, hay would be a valuable commodity near a city such as Edinburgh. Eighty bolls of oats sown in the fields at Clerkington and

---

12 The lands at Clerkington were explicitly granted *cum carbonibus* (with coals) in a charter of 1618: *RMS*, vol. 7, no. 1883. An incident recorded among the witchcraft accusations at Corstorphine sixty years later involved two Corstorphine men going with pack horses to fetch coals from 'the Coolehill', perhaps the one in Leith, who had refused one of the accused a ride into town. NRS, CH2/124/1, fols 28–9.

13 Sanderson, *Scottish Rural Society*, p. 170.

14 Livestock were normally counted by the long hundred of six score, but the testament avoided this possibly confusing system by omitting any mention of hundreds. Its 373 sheep, for instance, were recorded as 18 score thirteen.

15 The boll (= 4 firlots = 16 pecks) was the standard measure of grain in Scotland. It was six times the volume of an English bushel, being the equivalent of 48 gallons or 212.3 litres, and would weigh around 140 lbs (10 stones). A threave of unthreshed grain was equal to two stooks, each consisting of ten or twelve sheaves.

Braidwood were expected to yield 'to the third corn', producing 240 bolls for harvesting, while 16 bolls of bere and 5 of peas were expected to yield 'to the fourth corn'. Smaller amounts of bere and peas had also been sown on demesne land at Corstorphine and Clerkington, together with three bolls of wheat, which were also expected to give a fourfold yield. These grain yield estimates are around the normal expectation in sixteenth-century England and Scotland, low compared with later improved farming but showing that wheat and bere were comparatively high-yielding grains that required only one fourth of the crop to be retained for seed, as well as fetching higher prices on the market than the ubiquitous but lower-yielding oats.

Unfortunately, we do not know the location or acreage of the mains farms on which these crops were grown, nor whether they were cultivated on the infield-outfield system common in lowland Scotland at the time. The quantities of peas are too small to be part of an overall system of crop rotation, but they may have had a restorative role on intensely cultivated infield. Only one area of rigs (the Scottish open field system) can be identified: 'Corstorphine Rigs' are named in many medieval charters as the southern boundary of the Southfield of Cammo, and can still be seen (as 'Corstorphin Rigg') on John Laurie's map of 1763.[16] This area lay north of the village, west of the crest of modern Drum Brae North.

Of the five steelbow tenancies, two were situated in Corstorphine: Corstorphine Hill and West Craigs (see map). The others were at Clerkington, Longniddry and Bedlormie. Draught animals were included in the stock of these only at West Craigs and Longniddry, six oxen at each. The tenant at Corstorphine Hill owned his own ten oxen at the time of his death in 1594,[17] while the one at Clerkington may have had access to the laird's oxen mentioned above. Bedlormie, owing the laird no grain, seems to have been valued mainly as a cattle pasture. The other livestock held in steelbow amounted to 120 ewes on Corstorphine Hill, 4 one-year-old stirks (the Scots word included both bullocks and heifers) at Clerkington itself and 12 at Fairliehope, while Bedlormie had 30 cows with fifteen stirks. The grain included in steelbow stock consisted mainly of oats (20 bolls at Corstorphine Hill, 16 at West Craigs, and 12 at Longniddry) along with smaller quantities of wheat (6 bolls at Corstorphine Hill, 5 at West Craigs, and 8 at Longniddry) and bere (5 bolls at West Craigs, 8 at Longniddry). No grain was held in steelbow at Clerkington or Bedlormie.

* * *

16 John Laurie, *A Plan of the County of Mid-lothian* (1763), at maps.nls.uk/view/74400228.

17 NRS, CC8/8/28, fols 624–5. Nine are included in the testament, but the best beast would be omitted as part of the heirship.

The rents owing to Sir James Forrester were a substantial component of his assets at the time of his death. All three kinds – fermes, mails and duties – are recorded as owing from Corstorphine, fermes and duties from Nether Liberton, and fermes alone from Longniddry. The total fermes calculated below are based on the amount and valuation of grain rents given in the testament for 'the crop and year of god 1588', namely what had been due at Martinmas term (11 November) that year.[18] We have no explanation as to why these fermes had not been paid, and we do not know how much of the grain owing was still in stack, in store after threshing, already consumed, or sold by the tenants. In listing also what was due in grain for the first half of 1589, the testament was dealing in an accounting fiction, for no one could have delivered by Whitsunday (18 May 1589) crops that were still ripening in the fields. Every holding owing fermes for the year ending at Martinmas 1588 is listed as owing half that amount at Whitsunday 1589. By the time this testament was registered on 17 November, the harvest would be over and the market price known.

Eleven holdings at Corstorphine owed fermes in both wheat and bere, some with other grains also; all together these amounted to four-fifths of the value of fermes owing at Corstorphine. They included four large farms to the north and west of the village (Corstorphine Hill, Clermiston, Whitehouse and East Craigs)[19] together with Broomhouse to the south, and land held in Corstorphine by 'the goodwife of Barnton' who evidently lived north of the hill. One of these wheat-producing holdings was held jointly by five tenants (all replaced by new names in 1589), and another by a man and woman who may have been man and wife or mother and son, since married women at that time did not change their surname. Twenty-two further holdings at Corstorphine owed fermes in bere only, thirteen of them in amounts of less than five bolls, and only two owing more than ten. The acreage held is stated in only a few cases, all of them between one and six acres, but there seems to be no consistency in the amount of the ferme per acre.[20]

---

18 Documents concerning Nether Liberton in 1613–15 require fermes in victual (grains and meal) to be delivered between Yule and Candlemas (2 February), duties in hens between Candlemas and Fastingseven (Shrove Tuesday), and coal and capons between Fastingseven and Easter: NRS, GD122/2/66, GD122/2/351. It is not clear whether this would be the general practice, or a part of a strategy of spreading receipts out over the year.

19 West Craigs, though mentioned in the steelbow category, is missing from the list of payments owing. It is not clear whether this is an error, a sign that the rents from that farm had been paid, or the inclusion of William Cleghorne's tenancy there with his neighbouring farm of Whitehouse because the latter was where he lived.

20 NRS, CC8/8/20, fol. 520.

The total value of the twenty-two lesser fermes was £396 3s. 2d. – less than a fifth of the total for the group of eleven, as shown in Table 5.1. All the values in money are given as 'the price owerheid' (average). All the measures, except for amounts ending in a precise fraction of a firlot or a peck, are described as 'cheretit', a word derived from 'charity' and meaning heaped. This could add up to one-eighth extra to each boll.[21]

TABLE 5.1. Corstorphine fermes including wheat

Place	Tenant(s)	Wheat (bolls)	Bere (bolls)	Other (bolls)	Value (£.s.d.)
Broomhouse	John Aikman	50	50	44 of meal	498.13.4
Whitehouse	William Cleghorne	21	19		160.9.4
Clermiston	David Stevenson	20.25	24	10 of meal	207.10.0
Corstorphine Hill	Andrew Greg	17.75	41.5	2 of oats	264.0.10
East Craigs	James Cleghorn	16	16		128.0.0
Corstorphine	Goodwife of Barnton	72.75	27	16 of meal	322.10.0
"	Patrick Williamson + four others	21	19.5		160.9.7
"	David Crawford & Barbara Thomson	20	15		120.0.0
"	Martin Bathgate	10.25	10.25		84.0.0
"	Alexander Rankin	15.25	6		75.8.4
"	James Young	4	4		28.4.2
TOTAL					2,049.4.7

Source: NRS, CC8/8/20/515–35.

21 R. D. Connor and A. D. C. Simpson, *Weights and Measures in Scotland: A European Perspective*, ed. A. D. Morrison-Low (East Linton, 2004), pp. 207–17. By coincidence, adding one-eighth to the boll of 212.3 litres gives just under 240 litres, the capacity of a standard wheelie bin used for rubbish disposal in the UK and elsewhere – a useful aid to visualisation.

Substantial quantities of wheat and bere were also due from Nether Liberton. Four tenancies there owed 16 bolls each of wheat and bere, and later documents confirm that this was the amount owed for the standard 'room' of four oxgates (52 acres) there.[22] The remaining two tenancies in 1589 each owed half this amount, and the total fermes of Nether Liberton were valued at £672. The six holdings at Longniddry owed less uniform amounts of wheat and bere, with a total value of £313. These may have been intended for direct delivery to the Edinburgh markets rather than bypassing the city on their way to Corstorphine.

Only five individual tenants in Corstorphine are said to owe mails, or money rents, for their holdings. One was a smith, William Wilkie, who held only one acre and four falls (1.025 acres) of land, paying £3 1s. 6d. per annum – a rate of £3 per acre. James Cleghorn, who owed substantial fermes in grain for East Craigs (see Table 5.1), also owed £3 1s. 6d. 'for the rest [arrears] of his mail'. James Young owed £1 5s. 'for his mail of the meadow by the Brewstars Tryst', a location otherwise unknown. James Murray owed £6 13s. 4d. for his 'croft mail', and Robert Lauristane £2 for a holding whose nature is not stated. The tenants of Corstorphine as a body also owed £24 for their 'toun annuellis', presumably a customary payment to the laird. All this amounts to very little (£41 6s. 4d.) compared with the money value of the Corstorphine fermes, though it is possible that some of the mails for the year had already been collected.

Duties in poultry and loads of coal (carrying services) are not mentioned in the testament for the year ending at Martinmas 1588, but are listed in detail for the half year to Whitsunday 1589. At Corstorphine sixteen tenants owed a total of 44 capons, 27 hens, 3 chickens, 3 'poultry fowl' and 3 'bibbel fowl'. (These last may be turkey cocks, known locally in modern times as bubbly jocks.) The total value of all this poultry was £25 16s. 8d.; and twenty-four loads of coal were also due, at 3s. 4d. each. Three of the six tenants at Nether Liberton owed poultry duties for the half year of 6 capons, 6 hens and 6 loads of coal; while two owed half these amounts, corresponding to the size of their fermes (above). No duties were charged at Longniddry, presumably because it was too far from any of the Forresters' residences for such deliveries to be practical.

* * *

The pattern of payments was different at Forrester's fourth estate, Clerkington. Thirteen of his twenty-seven tenants there owed some deliveries of poultry to the laird's household, worth a total of £6 6s. 10d., but no fermes of grain were due from the tenants there. Instead, the tenants all paid money mails, in a pattern of husbandlands of uniform value.

22 NRS, GD122/2/66, GD122/2/349. The term chalder (= 16 bolls) is used in these documents though never in the testament.

According to a report given to Charles I's teind commissioners in 1627, Clerkington's tenant land 'of auld in the time of Sir James Forrester' consisted of sixteen husbandlands held 'in stock', paying 10 merks (£6 13s. 4d.) each. These were said in 1627 to be worth up to 80 merks each *communibus annis* (in average years), their value recently increased by the extraction of coal and lime. It was also reported to the commissioners that part of the mains farm had been let out 'in stock' for the previous twelve years for 600 merks (£400) per annum.[23] According to the testament, three of Sir James Forrester's tenants in Clerkington in 1588–89 each owed £13 6s. 8d. (20 merks) per annum for their mails, one owed £6 13s. 4d. (10 merks), and thirteen others £3 6s. 8d. (5 merks) each for their 'half lands'. Furthermore, one tenant owed £14 and another £6; if this was the result of transferring one merk's worth from a 10-merk to a 20-merk holding, the sixteen husbandlands are all accounted for. The eight remaining tenants, including the miller, owed smaller sums for their houses and yards. All these mails amounted to £105 11s. 1d. per annum, a substantial sum but still only a fraction of the value of the fermes due at Corstorphine.

The smaller outlying estates also owed mainly money. At Ochtertyre near Stirling, David Ramsay owed £40 in mails on behalf of himself and the other tenants, while the tenants of nearby Chalmerston owed £5 6s. 8d. and four bolls of oats, and those of 'Baderstoin' (not resembling the name of any known Forrester property but perhaps to be identified with Bedlormie) owed £40. In none of these three cases are the tenants' names or holdings listed, and this absence may mean that these lands were held collectively – a common arrangement in sixteenth-century Scotland – but there is no positive evidence for this.

* * *

The various grain prices in the testament deserve further attention. In the listing of fermes owed at Corstorphine for both 1588 and 1589, the price of wheat is calculated at £4 per boll, and that of bere at £3 6s. 8d. per boll. The inclusion of arrears of grain owed in a few cases from earlier years shows that these were not fixed prices, but corresponded to changes in price on the Edinburgh market at the time. The bere owed from the crop of 1586 by the heirs and widow of Alexander Ramsay, Forrester's recently deceased baron baillie, is valued at £4 10s. per boll 'owerheid' (on average). This higher price corresponds to the graph produced by Gibson and Smout based on wheat prices at Edinburgh in those years, rising in 1586–87 and falling back in 1588–89.[24] The years 1586 and 1587

---

23 *Reports on the State of Certain Parishes in Scotland, made to His Majesty's Commissioners for Plantation of Kirks 1627*, ed. Alexander Macdonald (Edinburgh: Maitland Club, 1835), p. 97.

24 NRS, CC8/8/20, fol. 519; A. J. S. Gibson and T. C. Smout, *Prices, Food and Wages*

saw high grain prices in England too.[25] Meanwhile, £4 per boll is the price of bere charged against two Corstorphine farmers for their arrears from 1587.[26] All the fermes in wheat and bere due from Nether Liberton and Longniddry for the year 1588 are valued at an average price of £4 per boll for both grains, however. One debt claimed at Nether Liberton was more longstanding: Alexander Wardlaw of Kilbaberton, a laird himself with an estate south-west of Edinburgh, had apparently refused to recognise his liability for fermes of 16 bolls of bere per annum for the past 32 years, and the total of 512 bolls outstanding is valued in the testament at an average price per boll of 40s.[27] This may not be a mathematically sophisticated calculation of inflation in the second half of the sixteenth century (which in Scotland was aggravated by repeated debasement of the currency) but it shows at least an awareness of what is known to historians as the price revolution.[28]

The idea that landowners were the chief sufferers from the price revolution, because their income from land was fixed by custom, was popular with economic historians in the early twentieth century. Many studies since then have shown, however, that landlords in some regions of England succeeded in improving their returns from land using a variety of strategies, such as moving away from customary to market-based forms of tenure, charging high entry fines when holdings changed hands, or merging small holdings into commercially more viable larger ones. Profit-orientated yeomen farmers shared in the benefits of these changes, while the number of landless and near-landless rural labourers grew.[29] Whether Scottish landlords pursued similar strategies and achieved similar results is still a matter for investigation.[30] Produce rents, such as those that Forrester received from his grain-growing estates, were a

---

in Scotland 1550–1780 (Cambridge, 1995), p. 17. Gibson and Smout number the 'crop year' by the calendar year following each harvest (during which prices were recorded or fixed by various bodies), while in the testament the 'crop and year of god' means the calendar year of the Martinmas term at which these rents were due.

25 R. W. Hoyle, 'Shrewsbury, Dearth, and Extreme Weather at the End of the Sixteenth Century', *AgHR*, 68:1 (2020), 22–36.

26 NRS, CC8/8/20, fol. 525.

27 NRS, CC8/8/20, fol. 534.

28 Gibson and Smout, *Prices, Food and Wages*, pp. 5–7, 163. The price of wheat bread at Edinburgh is said to have risen by 1586 to 'three or four times' its level in 1550: ibid., p. 163.

29 The literature on this subject is substantial, and continues to be discussed. See especially R. H. Tawney, *The Agrarian Problem in the Sixteenth Century* (London, 1912); Eric Kerridge, *Agrarian Problems in the Sixteenth Century and After* (London, 1969); Jane Whittle (ed.), *Landlords and Tenants in Britain 1440–1660: Tawney's 'Agrarian Problem' Revisited* (Woodbridge, 2013).

30 Julian Goodare, 'In Search of the Scottish Agrarian Problem', in Whittle (ed.), *Landlords and Tenants*, pp. 100–16.

traditional hedge against inflation, widespread in the east of Scotland at this time though the trend in some parts of the west seems to have been in the reverse direction, towards money rents, while in the Highlands cattle rents were preferred.[31]

Grain rents would deliver the profits of inflation to the landlord rather than the tenant, but this may not have meant impoverishment for the tenantry, especially as far as the larger farmers were concerned. It is not known what proportion of the crop it was normal for the laird to appropriate, and being expressed as a fixed volume it was at least nominally a higher share in years of poor harvests. If Christopher Smout's traditional proverb about oats, 'ane to graw, ane to gnaw, and ane to pay the laird withaw', reflects common practice, the peasants would have to hold back half of what they retained, to be sown the following year.[32] If the grain were fourfold-yielding bere or wheat, the laird could take up to half the crop with the same effect on the peasant's share. On the other hand, if the laird took only one third of these crops, the peasant would retain a significantly larger proportion. We do not know the answer to this question, but perhaps a little more can be known about some of the tenants on Sir James Forrester's estates.

* * *

Testaments have been found for four of the tenants named in Forrester's own testament, or their next successors, who died between 1592 and 1602. All the inventories include stock and grain in the hands of the deceased at the time of their death. Grain growing in the fields is also listed in some, as it is in Forrester's own testament. None of these four tenants seems to have been suffering from hardship, as each testament ends with a positive remainder, and the two which are 'testamentary', i.e. last wills made by the deceased before they died, include legacies in money to family members and others. This positive picture is probably to be expected, as people with fewer assets or none would not usually be the subjects of testaments, unless they were heavily in debt. It is unfortunately difficult to derive from any of these testaments an answer to the question posed

---

31 Keith M. Brown, *Noble Society in Scotland: Wealth, Family and Culture from Reformation to Revolution* (Edinburgh, 2000), pp. 40–1; Sanderson, *Scottish Rural Society*, pp. 28–9. A reverse trend seems to have been adopted by the post-1606 secular lordship of Holyroodhouse: the ploughlands at Broomhouse had been feued to Sir James Forrester in 1560 for £20 per annum, but in tax rolls of 1625 and 1630 the laird of Corstorphine is said to owe eight chalders (128 bolls) of victual (mixed grains) for his lands 'within the territory of Saughton', which may or may not be the same lands. As grain prices fell in the first quarter of the seventeenth century, this was much less beneficial to Holyrood.

32 T. C. Smout, *A History of the Scottish People 1560–1830* (London, 1969), pp. 119–20.

above as to what proportion of the crop would be taken by the laird, but they offer a perspective from the farmer's point of view.

James Burrell, described as 'fermoriar in Corstorphine', died in February 1588, though his testament was not registered until January 1592. His inventory included one horse, 2 cows, 2½ bolls of wheat, 3 bolls of oats and 4 firlots of peas, and 40 merks of 'reddie money' in his wife's hands. He owed a servant boy, John Walter, £1 4s. for his fee. Debts owed to the deceased exceeded those owed by him, and the remainder of his estate before the court fee was deducted amounted to £147 17s. 4d. In his will, made on 9 September 1587, he left a number of legacies in money to family members. The ferme he was said in the laird's testament to have owed for 1588 was 6 bolls 1½ pecks of bere.[33]

John Greg, Andrew Greg's successor on Corstorphine Hill farm, owned at the time of his death in September 1594 (apart from the best beast, reserved to the heirship) nine oxen, one bullock, three cows with calves, a grey horse and a mare, and forty sheep 'young and auld'. His testament dative, registered in December 1595, also lists the quantities of grain growing in the fields – presumably the crop of 1594, not yet harvested at the time of his death. The expected yields from these at the usual threefold and fourfold rates were 90 bolls of oats, 28 bolls each of wheat and bere, and 5 bolls of peas. He is said to have died owing Henry Forrester, Sir James's brother and successor, for his 1588 fermes 10 bolls of bere, 9 bolls of wheat and 24 bolls of meal. In Forrester's testament his predecessor Andrew Greg was said to have owed 17 bolls of wheat, 20 bolls of bere, 41 bolls 2 pecks of meal, and 2 bolls of oats for 1588; presumably John had already paid part of this annual amount before his death. There were no debts owing to John Greg at his death, and after those owed by him were deducted, the remainder of his estate amounted to £820.[34]

John Aikman, Sir James Forrester's tenant at Broomhouse, died in May 1594, and his testament testamentary was registered in February 1597. The inventory of his possessions at the time of his death includes 4 bullocks, 4 horses, 2 mares, 46 ewes, 26 lambs, 7 other sheep, and 14 'hoggs' (young sheep over a year old). The expected yield of his crops growing in the fields was 68 bolls of wheat, 156 bolls of oats, 28 bolls of peas and 20 bolls of bere. He also had in store 15 bolls of wheat, 11 of bere and 13 of oats. Before his death John Aikman had also contracted to pay to Robert Brown in neighbouring Saughtonhall 20 bolls each of wheat and bere, along with 40 ewes and lambs and 6 horses or mares. The circumstances in which this obligation was undertaken are unknown, but the deceased had wished it to take priority over all others. Despite these heavy burdens, the remainder of Aikman's estate came to

33 NRS, CC8/8/23, fols 458–60.
34 NRS, CC8/8/28, fols 624–5.

£220, and he left legacies to family members and others amounting to £148 13s. 4d., as well as the fees owed to five servants, £4 each to two men and a woman, £2 and £2 10s. respectively to two (presumably younger) males. Though managing to achieve a surplus, John Aikman was hardly enriching himself or his heirs.[35]

James Wardlaw, who appears as a tenant at Nether Liberton in 1589, died in May 1602. His testament lists as livestock 1 'foal mare', 4 draught oxen, 2 old oxen, 6 young bullocks, 1 cow, 6 sheep and 5 lambs. Sown on his land were 5 bolls of wheat, 3 bolls of peas, and 12 bolls of oats, and he also had in his possession 7 fleeces, worth £7. One £4 debt was owing to him, but the debts he owed to others came to a total of £221 11s. These debts included 8 bolls of wheat and 8 of bere (yet to be harvested) due to Jean Lauder, the dowager Lady Corstorphine, compared with 8 of wheat and 12 of bere in 1589. The 6 capons, 6 hens and 6 loads of coal he also owed to the lady were duties that had not changed. The deceased also owed £4 13s. 4d. in feu mail to Lord Newbattle (Mark Ker, soon to become first Earl of Lothian), but whether this feu was also located at Liberton was not stated in the testament. He also held 4 acres, presumably as a subtenant, from Andrew Simpson, for which 10 bolls of bere were due. He owed half a year's fees to two men and one woman servant, as well as a customary payment in bere to his hind or ploughman. With a remainder of £504 5s., he was not badly off by any means.[36]

* * *

The 1590s were a decade of poor and bad harvests, but food prices stabilised after 1600 and the agrarian economy slowly recovered. A rental of Corstorphine survives from 1631, but is difficult to compare directly with the material above. The effects of a further debasement of the Scottish coinage in 1601 and a reform of weights and measures in 1618 would make complicated calculations necessary. The most striking feature of the rental, however, is that, with one exception, the surnames of the tenants of the large farms surrounding the village in 1589 had changed, and some of these farms had been divided into two or more separate tenancies. There were no more Gregs at Corstorphine Hill, nor Aikmans at Broomhouse, though these surnames were still to be found among the smaller tenants. There was still a Cleghorn at West Craigs, and another held part of Whitehouse, while East Craigs was divided between a Cleghorn and a Stevenson. The Listons farming Corstorphine Hill and part of Whitehouse, and the Walker in the other part of Whitehouse, would seem to be new arrivals at Corstorphine, at least at farmer status.[37]

35 NRS, CC8/8/29, fols 82–5.
36 NRS, CC8/8/36, fols 624–6.
37 For tenants of these farms in 1588, see Table 5.1 above.

A detailed matching of the smaller tenants' names would perhaps reveal more continuity, but as their holdings are not named or located, it would be impossible to tell how much chopping and changing there had been at that level.[38] Meanwhile, at Nether Liberton in 1613–15, six tenancies had become five. The largest now consisted of six oxgates (312 acres), the others being two four-oxgate 'rooms' and two 'half rooms' of two oxgates each.[39]

These observations, limited though they are, have a bearing on the important question of security of tenure. There has been much discussion of R. H. Tawney's thesis that England's agrarian problem in the sixteenth century was related to the insecurity of copyhold tenure and the readiness of landlords to change these to fixed-term leasehold. Julian Goodare has recently suggested that although the tenure of Scottish 'rentallers' was previously as secure as the English copyhold, it was subject to successful challenges by litigious landlords in the early seventeenth century.[40]

Though there seems to be no direct evidence for pressure of this kind in Corstorphine itself, it was far otherwise with the properties that passed to Sir James's widow Jean Lauder as liferent. In 1594 her third husband, John Lindsay of Balcarres, Lord Menmuir – a Senator of the College of Justice and a leading politician – issued a warning of removal to the tenants of Clerkington and Longniddry, together with those of Upper Barnton, West Craigs, and Forresters' Niddry near Winchburgh, which she also held in liferent. This warning required each 'pretendit tennent and occupyar', with their family and servants, to 'flitt and remove thame selffis' by Whit Sunday coming, leaving their land, dwellings and all pertaining to them 'void and redd, and to suffer our tennentis and servandis in our name to enter thairto, and peaceably occupie, labour and manure the samyn as the lyferent of my spous at my pleasour'. If they refused to move, 'they salbe reputit violent possessouris' as ordained by the 1555 statute concerning removals. The notice was duly delivered to all the places named, being affixed to the gate of any addressee who could not be found at home, and read outside the local parish church before Sunday service. The outcome is not known, as there seem to be no further documents relating to Clerkington or the other properties, except for West Craigs (above), which was still held by the Cleghorn family in 1631.[41]

38 NRS, GD150/3208/1.
39 NRS, GD122/2/349, where the ninth room, being a subject of dispute, is omitted.
40 Goodare, 'In Search of the Scottish Agrarian Problem', pp. 105–6.
41 NRS, GD3/2/13/12. The 1555 statute 'anent the warning of tennentis' is *Acts of the Parliaments of Scotland*, vol. II (Edinburgh, 1814), p. 494, c. 12 (RPS, A1555/6/13). As the top part of Menmuir's warning is badly damaged, it is not clear how he had acquired his 'gude rycht to input and output' these tenants. His marriage to Jean Lauder may have been sufficient, but the word 'forfytt' is just visible. Jean's second husband, John Campbell of Cawdor, had

The case of Nether Liberton was more complex. In April 1612 a similar precept of removal was issued to the tenants there by Henry Lauder, bailie of Dunbar, as assignee of Jean Lauder's liferent there. He claimed that she, with the consent of her fourth husband Robert Gray of Crainslie and others, had conveyed these rights to him directly, but also that he had received them by a royal grant of their escheat. The tenants resisted, and were summoned before the privy council.[42] On 18 August 1613, however, the lands and barony of Nether Liberton were conveyed by Sir James's heir Henry Forrester and his son George to Alexander Gibson, then one of the clerks of session (later known as Lord Durie of the College of Justice). Gibson in turn conveyed the property to James Winram, along with the lands of Over Liberton which he had also purchased recently, and the whole was erected into a new barony of Liberton.[43]

The further complication that led to years of legal wrangling before a settlement was reached was the fact that George and Henry Forrester had guaranteed Gibson the lands of Nether Liberton – and Gibson had guaranteed them to Winram – 'frie of all takis and rychtis in the persones of the tennentis present possessouris thairof and to mak the tennentis removabill thairfra'; yet one tenant, James Liberton, was found to be in possession of a tack of his four oxgates for a term of nineteen years following the death of Dame Jean, who was still very much alive though she must now have been in her seventies. The Forresters pledged themselves to obtain James Liberton's renunciation of the tack, and although there is no record of their ever having succeeded in this, the surname Liberton no longer appears in two later rentals.[44] The other tenants of Nether Liberton kept their rooms, and in December 1615 they bound themselves to pay their fermes and dues to Gibson, who was to deliver them to Henry Lauder for the rest of Jean's lifetime.[45]

Though limited to these Forrester properties, this surely constitutes evidence that there were indeed litigious landlords in Scotland more than willing, with the help of top lawyers, to challenge their tenants' rights. It also suggests that they did so partly out of fear for their own security

---

been assassinated in the course of an internal Campbell feud in 1592. In 1595, when she returned to Menmuir after a period of separation, she promised not to consort with the king's rebels in future: Lord Lindsay, *Lives of the Lindsays* (3 vols, 2nd edn, London, 1858), vol. 1, pp. 377–8.

42 NRS, GD122/2/342, 343, 345. The case does not appear in the privy council's register, and it may be that the charge was withdrawn or a settlement reached before the property was sold on.

43 NRS, GD122/2/344, 348; *RMS*, vol. 7, nos. 739, 1260. Henry Lauder's relationship to Jean is not known, but it seems likely that he was, like her, a Lauder of the Bass.

44 NRS, GD6/1676, undated.

45 NRS, GD122/2/351, 352. Jean was still alive in 1618 but died before 21 January 1621: NRS, TE5/158.

in properties they had acquired by assignation or purchase rather than hereditary succession. They may have been willing to come to terms with tenants when they would not profit by evicting them; but the instability of the larger farm tenancies at Corstorphine and the engrossing of smaller rooms into a larger holding at Nether Liberton suggest that they could exercise this power when they chose. Overall, however, this local research would seem to confirm Michael Lynch's generalisation, 'The Jacobean economic miracle which brought prosperity to the landed classes was paid for by their tenants.'[46]

46   Michael Lynch, *Scotland: A New History*, 2nd edn (London, 1992), p. 183.

6

The Roots of Improvement: Early Seventeenth-Century Agriculture on the Mains of Dundas, Linlithgowshire

Alan R. MacDonald

Sir Walter Dundas of that ilk (1562–1636) was a politically prominent laird who represented Linlithgowshire numerous times in parliament, served as its sheriff and was convener of the county's commissioners of the peace.[1] He was also a diligent manager of his estates. His surviving estate records, while sometimes frustratingly fragmentary, contain a wealth of material that sheds light on how agriculture was overseen on a lowland Scottish estate in the early seventeenth century.

Dundas's lands, spread across five neighbouring parishes (Abercorn, Dalmeny, Linlithgow, Livingston and Kirkliston), included some of the best arable land in Scotland. Previous research has shown that, by the middle of the seventeenth century, the mains of Dundas (the farmland directly worked for the laird) was intensively cultivated, with an unusually high proportion of wheat grown alongside oats and bere, as well as significant quantities of legumes, the nitrogen-fixing properties of which permitted even more intensive cultivation. That intensity is demonstrated by the fact that around 85 per cent of the mains was under cultivation every year. Only a relatively small proportion of that land (c.30 per cent) was designated as outfield, and even that was relatively intensively cultivated with more than half of it under crops, compared to the norm of around one-third.[2] The estate has been the subject of detailed

---

1   Margaret D. Young (ed.), *The Parliaments of Scotland: Burgh and Shire Commissioners* (2 vols, Edinburgh, 1992–93), vol. 1, p. 217.
2   Ian Whyte, 'Infield-Outfield Farming on a Seventeenth-Century Scottish Estate', *Journal of Historical Geography*, 5:4 (1979), 391–401, at pp. 393, 395, 397, 399–400. Whyte also shows that, over time, outfield had been brought

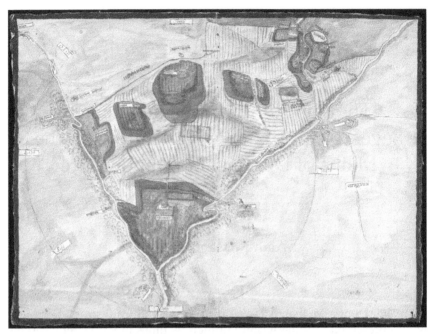

FIGURE 6.1. Detailed plan of Arniston, Midlothian, 1586. This estate plan shows
the typical agricultural landscape of Lothian at the end of the sixteenth
century. There are the residences of lairds and larger tenants, mills, open
fields of cultivation ridges (rigs), some enclosures, woodland and pasture.
Source: Crown copyright. National Records of Scotland, RHP82800.

research, largely focused on the period from the middle of the seventeenth century onwards, so an examination of earlier records has the
potential to provide further insights into a period of Scottish agricultural
history that remains largely unexplored.

* * *

This study is based on a number of surviving estate records which
suggest that, by the early seventeenth century, cultivation on the mains
of Dundas was already a highly-organised operation. Its detailed records
comprehend a whole range of activities including the sowing, harvesting,
storage and disbursement of crops, as well as expenditure on labour,
infrastructure and equipment. While there are few long sequences of
any particular type of record, those that are preserved give a strong

under cultivation and improved to such an extent that some of it was reclas-
sified as infield, a process that was still ongoing during the seventeenth
century; Ian D. Whyte, 'George Dundas of Dundas: The Context of an Early
Eighteenth-Century Scottish Improving Landowner', *SHR*, 60:1 (1981), 1–13;
R. A. Dodgshon, *Land and Society in Early Scotland* (Oxford, 1981), p. 231.

impression of systematic record-keeping.[3] The extent to which this was typical for its time has yet to be clearly established, although there is no particular reason to suppose that Dundas was unique.[4]

Many of the surviving volumes have the appearance of personal notebooks, the far from neat and regular entries suggesting that they may have been written out of doors without the benefit of a desk. Their unusual shape (*c.*30cm x *c.*5cm) indicates that they were designed for slipping down the side of the laird's riding boot as he did the rounds of his estates.[5] There are accounts of waged work, which covers a whole range of tasks, including quarrying and carrying stone in wheelbarrows, building walls, transporting coal and lime, as well as general labour. The accounts also record the sale of cereals, receipt of rents, interest paid on loans, and the purchase of personal and household items.[6] There are lists of tenants and their holdings, detailing the quantities and types of cereals that were sown, where and on which dates.[7] There are assessments of acreages, with individual holdings divided into how much consisted of infield (always described as 'muckit', i.e. manured, land) and how much was outfield. These assessments specified how much of each crop was to be sown, suggesting a predetermined allocation (akin to the practice of 'souming' by which livestock numbers were apportioned), rather than

---

3   The Dundas of Dundas papers are split between the National Library of Scotland, Adv. MS 80, and the National Records of Scotland, GD75. An account book covering 1621–23 (NLS, Adv. MS 80.3.11, fol. 13v) contains a cross-reference to the now lost 'ferme buik'. Not only does this demonstrate the existence of records that no longer survive, it also provides further evidence of meticulous record-keeping: 'vide the ferme buik in anno 1621 yeir [*sic*] markit –◊|◊–'.

4   Few single-estate or regional case studies have been carried out, and almost all focus on the period from *c.*1650 onwards: Whyte, 'Infield-Outfield Farming'; Ian D. Whyte, 'Agriculture in Aberdeenshire in the Seventeenth and Early Eighteenth Centuries: Continuity and Change', in David Stevenson (ed.), *From Lairds to Louns: Country and Burgh Life in Aberdeen 1600–1800* (Aberdeen, 1986), pp. 10–31; Mary Young, 'Rural Society in Scotland from the Restoration to the Union: Challenge and Response in the Carse of Gowrie, 1660–1707' (PhD thesis, University of Dundee, 2004). For comments on record-keeping see also Ian Whyte, 'Poverty or Prosperity? Rural Society in Lowland Scotland in the Late Sixteenth and Early Seventeenth Centuries', *Scottish Economic and Social History*, 18:1 (1998), 19–32, at pp. 19, 23–4.

5   The personal tone is clear from entries such as that which records £20 being given 'to my wyf to send for the 4 gallonis quhyte wyne' (NLS, Adv. MS 80.3.10, fol. 3v). I am grateful to Diane Janes of Duns for her insightful suggestion to explain the peculiar shape of the account books.

6   For example, NLS, Adv. MS 80.3.10 includes weekly records of payments to estate workers 1615–23.

7   NRS, GD75/462, Rental of Crop 1611; NLS, Adv. MS 80.3.13, covering the period 1636–40.

being a record of what was sown in any given year.[8] Other evidence suggests that such predetermined allocations could also help to simplify calculation of what was due from each tenant in rent and teind, the tenth part of all agricultural produce that was notionally intended for paying the clergy's stipends. While teind would have varied from year to year depending on the quality of the harvest, it could provide a handy indication of what was the norm, while still presumably allowing scope for flexibility.[9]

With regard to the harvest, there are similarly detailed records noting how much of each crop was harvested, on what days and by whom, either to ensure that labour services were fulfilled or that each worker received the correct payment according to the number of sheaves they had harvested.[10] Since these recorded only the work carried out on the mains farm, they reveal only a small part of the vast efforts involved in bringing in each year's crops. Harvest was an intensive period, involving seasonal migrant labour as well as those who lived permanently on the estate.[11] Yet the Dundas papers give the impression that many of those who worked on the estate at other times of the year were allowed time off to bring in their own crops. In 1621, for example, the laird's accounts recorded a set of weekly payments to estate workers on 15 September, followed by the statement that 'thay left aff work & ged to the harvest labour'. The very next entry is dated 20 October and records two payments to men who had just 'enterit to thair work efter harvest'.[12] Similarly, estate workers might also be released at seed-time, with one waged man noted as being given a week's leave 'to saw his beir seid' in May 1617.[13]

All of that harvest labour was, of course, carried out by the hands of women and men using sickles to cut the stalks, tying up the sheaves and arranging them into stooks of usually twelve sheaves. The sheaves were then transported for storage and stacked in circular ricks, which were thatched to keep out the rain. This practice endured well into the era of 'improvement' when a prominent Scottish writer on agriculture remarked on how 'absurd' it was that the English stored threshed

8   NLS, Adv. MS, 80.4.1, covering the period from the late sixteenth century to the early eighteenth century.

9   NLS, Adv. MS, 80.1.1, fols 33–4, a letter from Dundas's son-in-law to Dundas, written in September 1608, outlining different ways of reckoning teind: as a proportion of the rent or as a proportion of what was customarily sown.

10 NLS, Adv. MS 80.3.12, a record of the harvest from 1631. For labour services, see M. H. B. Sanderson, *Scottish Rural Society in the Sixteenth Century* (Edinburgh, 1982), pp. 21, 30, 45, although it seems that by 1600 most labour services had been commuted into money payments.

11 Young, 'Rural Society', pp. 148 (noting a tenant's obligation to provide two 'hooks', that is two people to work with sickles, during the harvest), 169–70.

12 NLS, Adv. MS 80.3.10, fol. 42r.

13 NLS, Adv. MS 80.3.10, fol. 20v.

grain in 'enormous barns' rather than on the straw, where it 'keeps infinitely better in the open', although this was in fact a common practice south of the border too.[14] Threshing before storage may not have become widespread in Scotland until the process was mechanised in the late eighteenth century.[15] Harvest was such a busy time in Linlithgowshire that, not only was all other routine manual labour on the estate suspended, it even affected the courts of the church. Every year, the presbytery of Linlithgow formally suspended its meetings for up to seven weeks to accommodate the harvest.[16] So many people were engaged in the harvest that it would have been inappropriate to distract them from that essential activity to summon them before the presbytery, and probably futile even to try. Moreover, since ministers were expected to have a glebe (land that they might cultivate themselves), they too may have been directly involved in the harvest. Not only do the Linlithgow presbytery records provide evidence of the duration of the harvest, they also indicate how it shifted in time from year to year. Between 1611 and 1624, the harvest vacation began as early as 12 August (in 1612), and as late as 21 September (in 1614).[17]

Once the harvest was over, the estate carefully monitored the stored crops. One of the earliest detailed agricultural records from the Dundas papers relates to the crop of 1604. It contained twenty-two separate entries listing disbursements of wheat, bere, oats and peas, with each of the cereal crops categorised in two different grades of quality: good corn and horse corn (for oats), good wheat and grey wheat, good bere and light bere.[18] The record noted whether the oats had come from outfield or infield, although no such distinction was made for the wheat, bere and peas, which were all grown on manured infield land.[19] It also recorded

14 For a general account of agricultural labour and harvesting in particular, see Alexander Fenton, 'Farm Workers before and after the Agricultural Improvement Period', in Mark A. Mulhern, John Beech and Elaine Thompson (eds), *The Working Life of the Scots* (Scottish Life and Society: A Compendium of Scottish Ethnology, vol. 7; Edinburgh, 2008), pp. 87–106, at pp. 87–9. One of the main seasonal jobs on a mains farm was 'constant threshing in the wintertime'. For details of how these stacks were constructed and grain stored, see John Shaw, 'Agricultural Buildings 2: Storing and Processing Crops', in Geoffrey Stell, John Shaw and Susan Storrier (eds), *Scotland's Buildings* (Scottish Life and Society: A Compendium of Scottish Ethnology, vol. 3; Edinburgh, 2003), pp. 438–64, at pp. 438–9.

15 See Whyte, 'Infield-Outfield Farming', p. 394; Fenton, 'Farm Workers', pp. 91, 94; Shaw, 'Agricultural Buildings', pp. 438–40. Threshing was one of the first major agricultural jobs to be mechanised.

16 NRS, Presbytery of Linlithgow, CH2/242/1–2. For the 1611 suspension (28 August to 2 October), see CH2/242/1, fols 11–13.

17 NRS, CH2/242/1 (1610–19), fols 31–3, 102–3; CH2/242/2 (1618–24).

18 NLS, Adv. MS 80.3.8.

19 T. C. Smout, *A History of the Scottish People 1560–1830* (London, 1969),

oats and bere being taken from the stored crops to be used for seed. After every entry, the 'stock' (what remained after the noted quantity had been removed) was stated, indicating that one of the purposes of the record was to keep a tally of how much remained in store. This would have provided the basis upon which the manager of the farm could judge how much of the remaining crop he could afford to disburse and for what purposes. It would also have allowed him to identify whether there would be a surplus from the previous year's harvest; any surplus could be sold, generating cash income for the estate.[20] Once sheaves had been removed from the stack and threshed, a record was also kept of the distribution of straw to the various byres and stables, as bedding for the horses and winter fodder for the oxen.[21]

When it came to accounting for the stored crops, they were reckoned and recorded as if they had been threshed, even though they were stored on the straw. The calculation was based on the system of 'proof sheaves', a method of reckoning volume that involved taking a selection of sheaves from a stack, threshing them, measuring the resulting volume of cereal, then extrapolating. Thereafter, the amount disbursed and the amount remaining were calculated on the basis of the number of sheaves in the stack, rather than an actual measurement of the volume of threshed grains. In each of the two surviving records, the assessment of the quantities in each of the stacks was carried out by a single person, Gavin Dundas in 1604/05 and Mark Love in 1615/16[22] – another indicator of careful oversight, as these men appear to have been successive managers of the mains farm. Mark Love's name appears repeatedly in the account books, in records of payments for all sorts of important tasks including the purchase of livestock.[23]

The notes of stored crops also show that each stack consisted of the harvest from a single field. Not only did it make practical sense to bring in all of the sheaves from one place and stack them together, it was also necessary for the proof-sheaf system, given the inevitable variations between the quality and yield of the crops from different fields. Moreover it enabled the farm manager to keep track of where the different qualities of cereal were to be found, which was especially important when it came to selecting the best seed. The selection of seed also provides an instructive insight into one aspect of the system of teinding, by which ministers' stipends were paid through the collection

---

pp. 118–20; Ian Whyte, *Agriculture and Society in Seventeenth-Century Scotland* (Edinburgh, 1979), pp. 60–79.

20 Young, 'Rural Society', p. 203.

21 NLS, Adv. MS 80.3.13 (1636–40).

22 NLS, Adv. MS 80.3.8 (from 1604/05); and NRS, GD75/475 (from 1615/16).

23 NLS, Adv. MS 80.3.10, fols 5v, 6r; 80.3.11, fols 4v, 5v, 6r.

of what was effectively a tax of one-tenth of each year's harvest.[24] In two entries relating to the selection of oats for seed early in 1605, the seeds are recorded as having been taken from the teind of two named pieces of land, while there is also evidence of teind wheat being used for seed in the later 1630s.[25] While the original purpose of teinds was to support the clergy, it was rare in this period for teinds to go directly to ministers. A complex system of setting teinds in tack had grown up since their establishment in the twelfth century.[26] The teinds from which these seed oats were taken in 1605 were drawn from lands in the parishes of Kirkliston and Dalmeny, and the laird of Dundas was able to dispose of these teinds because he held them in tack. He had the right to uplift the Kirkliston teinds in return for an annual payment to the archbishops of St Andrews, who were the 'titulars' of those teinds (i.e. they held the legal title to them). In the case of Dalmeny, Dundas held a tack from the Hamiltons of Priestfield, who were themselves tacksmen of those teinds, meaning that Dundas held a sub-tack. The titular of the teinds of Dalmeny was Alexander, Lord Home, Commendator of Jedburgh, by dint of his possession of the lands and revenues of the former Augustinian abbey of Jedburgh to which Dalmeny's teinds had been appropriated in the late twelfth century.[27] Setting teinds in tack allowed titulars to obtain a fixed annual sum which was less than the average value of the teind, but they were relieved of the cost and effort of uplifting the crops from what might be quite distant parishes. It must also have provided an opportunity for the tacksman to profit, by raising more than the annual tack duty through uplifting the teind. However, Dundas's sub-tack of the Kirkliston teinds suggests that obtaining a local supply of high-quality seed might have been as significant a motive as immediate financial profit. Since responsibility for paying the stipend of the minister of Dalmeny remained with the titular, Dundas was at liberty to use the teinds to the best advantage – as seed on his own mains farm.

* * *

24 NLS, Adv. MS 80.3.8.
25 NLS, Adv. MS 80.3.8, fol. 2r; Adv. MS 80.3.13, fol. 7r.
26 Tack = lease. For details of the complexity of the system of stipend payments from the lands of the laird of Dundas, see NLS, Adv. MS 80.2.1, a volume of receipts relating to stipend payments to ministers of the various parishes in which Dundas held lands.
27 I. B. Cowan, *The Parishes of Medieval Scotland* (Edinburgh: SRS, 1967), p. 121; D. E. R. Watt and N. F. Shead (eds), *The Heads of Religious Houses in Scotland from Twelfth to Sixteenth Centuries* (Edinburgh: SRS, 2001), pp. 44, 121. Alexander became Earl of Home in 1605 and the lands of Jedburgh Abbey and Coldingham Priory were converted to a temporal lordship for him in 1606.

The keen interest of Sir Walter Dundas in the careful organisation and recording of the agricultural activities on his lands reveals a laird for whom the productivity of his estate was a clear priority. Indeed it would not be stretching a point to suggest that it was his primary concern as a landowner. Yet neither would it be safe to conclude that this level of oversight was new just because no similar records survive from an earlier period. However, the surviving account books show that his concern in this regard went considerably further than merely maintaining diligent oversight of what may have been time-honoured practices, for they reveal that the stewardship of his estate extended to what could reasonably be described as innovation, perhaps even 'improvement'.

The most significant measure he undertook in terms of boosting yields was the application of lime to enhance the uptake of nutrients by growing crops. In January 1616, the accounts record a payment for transporting 32 chalders and 12 bolls of lime, and a note that some of it had already been 'layd upone the ... land'. This was a huge quantity, amounting to at least 80 tons.[28] Yet there is no particular reason to believe that this was the first time that liming had been carried out on the estate, for there are entries in the accounts for 1613 (the earliest that survive) recording the purchase of four loads of lime.[29] Unfortunately, the purpose to which the earlier purchase of lime was put is not noted, so it may have been intended for making mortar rather than as a soil improver, given the building works being undertaken by Dundas at the time. While the payments for lime in 1613 included both 'pryce and careage', those in 1616 were only for carriage, suggesting that the limestone came from Dundas's own lands and that the large-scale lime production attested from the mid-1620s represented an expansion of an earlier enterprise, which had involved either the laird processing his own lime or using a neighbour's kiln for the purpose.[30] Whatever was the case before the mid-1620s, from that point onwards, Dundas embarked

28 NLS, Adv. MS 80.3.10, fol. 13r. Since this lime was laid on a 'meadow' it may suggest that it was used to improve pasture as well as arable land (see Whyte, *Agriculture and Society*, p. 201, which expresses uncertainty over this). It is hard to establish how much lime was in a chalder. However, a conservative calculation, based on the minimum of 32 imperial bushels suggested for a chalder of lime or coal in the *OED*, suggests this was nearly 80 tons. It could even have been up to twice that, based on the *OED*'s maximum estimate of 64 bushels to a chalder: see 'chalder, n.1', *OED Online*, June 2018, Oxford University Press, http://www.oed.com/view/Entry/30277?isAdvanced=false &result=1&rskey=MOUgoq& (accessed 16 August 2018).

29 NRS, GD75/242, fols 2r, 3r, 4v.

30 NRS, GD75/242, fol. 3r; NLS, Adv. MS 80.3.10, fol. 13r; Whyte, 'Infield-Outfield Farming', p. 400, dates the introduction of liming at Dundas to the mid-1620s, apparently on the basis of the surviving lime accounts, NLS, Adv. MS 80.3.41–45, covering the period 1625–53.

on the production of lime, using his own coal and limestone, on what can only be called an industrial scale. A dedicated set of accounts covering the period 1625 to 1653 records the production of significant quantities of lime from multiple kilns, both for use on his own lands and to be 'sauld to the countrie', generating thousands of pounds in income.[31]

These findings add some useful new data to what is already known of the apparent boom in the use of lime to improve yields in the early seventeenth century.[32] A series of parochial reports on agricultural output was carried out in 1627, apparently in relation to the crown's attempts to reform the process by which ministers' stipends were paid through the teind system. Although none is preserved from West Lothian, those from Midlothian and East Lothian do survive and they reveal that liming was being carried out extensively there by both heritors and tenants. They also show that the practice had been ongoing for considerably longer than the 'several years' that has been previously suggested.[33] Where liming was practised, the reports detail both current yields and what they were 'of auld', with some specifying how long ago that was. In some instances it was twenty years previously and in others as much as forty, placing the beginnings of the extensive use of liming in this part of Scotland as far back as the 1580s.[34] Since the earliest surviving accounts from Dundas indicate the acquisition of substantial quantities of lime in 1613, and given that other landowners in the Lothians had already been using it for some years by then, it could very well be that Dundas too had been applying it to his lands from the first decade of the seventeenth century or even before.

Lime and, of course, manuring were not the only means available for improving the soil and increasing yields. The record of crops stored from the harvest of 1604 includes numerous references to peas, which comprised five of the twenty-three stacks (the others being nine of oats, six of bere and three of wheat).[35] Just over ten years later, the ratios were similar, with seven stacks of peas, twelve of oats, eight of bere and three of wheat.[36] Beans were also grown on the mains of Dundas, although apparently in smaller quantities than peas, with an account of the harvest for 1617 recording about half as many beans as peas (161 thraves of the

31 NLS, Adv. MS 80.3.41–45; the quotation comes from vol. 42, fol. 42r; his own coal mines are mentioned in 1615: NLS, Adv. MS 80.3.10, fol. 8r.
32 Whyte, *Agriculture and Society*, pp. 201–2.
33 For this suggestion see Whyte, *Agriculture and Society*, p. 201.
34 A. McGrigor (ed.), *Reports on the State of Certain Parishes in Scotland made to his Majesty's Commissioners for Plantation of Kirks* (Edinburgh: Maitland Club, 1835), pp. 46, 47 (forty years), 77, 107 (twenty years); see Whyte, 'Poverty or Prosperity?', pp. 28–9.
35 NLS, Adv. MS 80.3.8, fols 1–3.
36 NRS, GD75/475.

former compared to 334 of the latter).[37] The cultivation of legumes was not a recent innovation, for an act of parliament of 1426 had sought to encourage it and they were widely grown, at least in the south and east of Scotland, by the middle of the sixteenth century. The quantities apparently grown at Dundas are, however, striking.[38] While Whyte's suggestion that the unreliability and low yield of legumes meant that they were grown 'as much for their effects on the crop which followed … as for their own direct value' may be true, the volumes of stored peas recorded in 1604/05 and 1615/16, and of harvested peas and beans in 1617, are significant.[39] The estimated yield of 1604 amounted to almost 3 chalders and for 1615 it was more than 4.[40] While this was a considerably lower volume than the stored cereals (there were over 7 chalders of wheat in store in 1604/05), it would certainly have provided a substantial source of relatively high-protein food, either in the form of pease porridge or pease bread.[41] Moreover, a record of arrears of teind from *c.*1612 also suggests that legumes comprised a substantial proportion of what was grown by the tenantry, as the number of sheaves of peas and beans due was often as many as, or even more than, the number of sheaves of bere or wheat.[42]

All of this suggests that legumes must have formed a substantial proportion of what was grown in West Lothian by the beginning of the seventeenth century and were already part of an established four-break system of rotation a century before Lord Belhaven described it in his *The Countrey-Man's Rudiments of Advice to the Farmers in East Lothian*, published in 1699.[43] The 'intensification of cultivation by the gradual elimination of outfield' and an increased production of legumes and wheat on the mains of Dundas have been attributed to 'the introduction of liming in the mid 1620s'.[44] Yet since we now know that liming was being undertaken by no later than 1616, and that both wheat and legumes comprised a significant proportion of what was grown by no later than 1604, it seems reasonable

37 NLS, Adv. MS 80.3.9, fol. 18v; Adv. MS 80.3.13, Accounts of Straw and Cereals, 1636–40, fol. 7r; NRS, GD75/692, Charge against the tenants of the mains of Kirkliston etc, *c.*1612. Thrave = 24 sheaves.

38 Dodgshon, *Land and Society*, pp. 157–9; Whyte, *Agriculture and Society*, pp. 63–6.

39 Whyte, *Agriculture and Society*, p. 65.

40 NLS, Adv. MS 80.3.8 (which may be incomplete given that the record appears to break off in the middle of an entry on fol. 3v); NRS, GD75/475.

41 A. Gibson and T. C. Smout, 'Scottish Food and Scottish History, 1500–1800', in R. A. Houston and I. D. Whyte (eds), *Scottish Society 1500–1800* (Cambridge, 1989), pp. 59–84, at p. 66.

42 NRS, GD75/692.

43 Dodgshon, *Land and Society*, pp. 230–1; Whyte, 'Infield-Outfield Farming', p. 400.

44 Whyte, 'Infield-Outfield Farming', p. 400.

to suggest that at least some of the changes previously attributed to the second quarter of the seventeenth century must date from no later than the years immediately after 1600.

Through production on their mains farms combined with the rents in kind received from tenants, heritors inevitably acquired more cereals every year than were required for their households. The result was, as Sir Walter Dundas's account books show, that selling surplus cereals was an important source of cash. Situated close to the biggest market for cereals in the country, he was ideally positioned to take advantage of the demand for bere and wheat generated by the need to supply the population of Edinburgh with ale and bread. There are numerous references to sales of both to the capital's baxters (bakers) and maltmen, who supplied the burgh's brewers, while Dundas also sold smaller quantities locally. Cereals from Dundas may also have found their way into the coastal trade or the export market, via Edinburgh merchants.[45]

There is even some evidence that Dundas's tenants were able to market their own surplus cereals. In one record of the sale of nearly £200 worth of wheat to an Edinburgh baxter in May 1615, some of it was recorded as having come from two named individuals, almost certainly tenants.[46] Cereals derived from rents were always recorded in the estate accounts either as the 'ferme' of a named individual, if they derived from a single-tenant holding, or as having come from a specific part of the estate, if they came from a multiple tenancy. Neither of those things is mentioned in this particular entry, suggesting that Dundas was selling the produce on for them.[47] His accounts also record a number of tenants paying cash in lieu of their teind, and the most likely means for them to have raised that cash would have been by selling their own surplus cereals directly to local customers.[48]

Both Dodgshon and Whyte argued that only landlords are likely to have profited from the grain trade until the early eighteenth century, and Dodgshon even suggested that increasing yields may have led to an 'exploitive' process by which landlords profited at their tenants' expense, and that 'the lot of the average tenant may have worsened' as a result.[49] Even without the evidence presented here indicating that tenants marketed their own surpluses, directly or indirectly, there are problems

45 NLS, Adv. MS 80.3.10, fol. 2v (almost £200 for 22 bolls of wheat sold to an Edinburgh baxter), fol. 5v (over £1,200 for 185 bolls of bere sold in Musselburgh); NRS, GD75/242, fol. 6v (bere sold to a maltman).

46 NLS, Adv. MS 80.3.10, fol. 2v.

47 NLS, Adv. MS 80.3.10, fol. 3v, a reference to the sale of bere from a tenant's 'ferme'; Adv. MS 80.3.8, recording stored crops by type, or place of origin.

48 NLS, Adv. MS 80.3.11, fols 3–5.

49 Dodgshon, *Land and Society*, pp. 245–9 (quotations at pp. 248–9); Whyte, 'Poverty or Prosperity?', p. 27.

with this. Rents were not fixed in perpetuity; they were paid either as a proportion of the annual yield or as a set amount specified in a tenant's fixed-term tack. This means that when output rose due to increased yields, extension of the ground under cultivation or both, the surplus could not have been wholly absorbed by exploitative rent increases, as Whyte has acknowledged in more recent work.[50] To be sure, rent might rise at the expiry of one tack and the setting of another, but this must have followed negotiation between tenant and landlord to arrive at a mutually agreeable amount.[51] The parish reports from the later 1620s contain extensive evidence of the level of rents paid, consisting either of specified amounts of cereals or money, or a proportion of the annual crop, usually one-third. Where quantities are given for both rent and teind, the rent is always less than one-third of what remained after teind had been paid.[52] Thus, although landlords' rental income undoubtedly grew, the tenants also experienced an increase in what remained after teinds were uplifted and rents were paid. Suggestions that tenants were excluded from the commercial opportunities provided through surpluses can perhaps be reconciled with the evidence presented here by acknowledging that Dodgshon and Whyte were thinking about the sorts of large-scale transactions in which only landlords were capable of engaging. Yet there were smaller-scale opportunities for tenants to sell their surpluses locally, or to convert them into cash by using their landlords as intermediaries. Landlords had means of transport, and connections with Edinburgh's baxters, maltmen and merchants. In this way, both tenants and landlords might benefit from increased production.

When considered together, the cultivation of significant quantities of legumes, the introduction of extensive liming, as well as the large-scale production and sale of lime, and the marketing of surplus cereals all suggest that Dundas was an 'improving' landlord, self-consciously seeking to maximise the estate's ability to generate revenue and devoting significant capital investment to that task. The laird's account books indicate a period of intensive work on enhancing infrastructure, beginning in the autumn of 1615 with the construction of a new barn, which was being used to store cereals by the early 1620s and continued to serve that purpose into the 1650s.[53] This may even point to the beginnings of a shift

50 See Whyte, 'Poverty or Prosperity?', pp. 22–3, where increased rents and the various reasons posited for them are discussed, and p. 28, where he posits that 'For the Lothians at least ... tenants as well as proprietors' may have benefited from increased productivity.
51 Whyte, *Agriculture and Society*, p. 158.
52 *Reports on the State of Certain Parishes, passim*. On some lands in the parish of Cockpen, for example, the teind was 6 firlots, indicating an anticipated yield of 15 bolls (60 firlots), leaving 13½ bolls from which only 4 were taken in rent (p. 47). For an example of the rent being 'the thrid scheiff', see p. 51.
53 For the construction, see NLS, Adv. MS 80.3.10, fols 8–10; Adv. MS 80.3.11,

towards storing harvested cereals indoors (possibly threshed and placed in sacks) rather than on the straw in stacks.

Between 1617 and 1623 Dundas undertook further improvements, in the form of an extensive scheme of enclosure, with thousands of pounds being paid to quarriers, barrowmen, masons and dykers.[54] In its early stages, the work seems to have been confined to enhancing the laird's house and its immediate surroundings, for it was initially recorded as 'the gairden work'.[55] Without a clear idea of exactly what and where each piece of walling referred to in the accounts was, it is hard to get a good picture of how many enclosures were created in this first phase, how extensive they were, or where they lay in relation to each other. However, a decisive departure occurred in the spring of 1620, when the accounts record the following: 'Remember that upoune Fryday the 24 merche preceiding, David Craufurd, Jame Donald and David Or enterit at x houris to the park dyk bigging'.[56] The tone of this entry suggests that Dundas was conscious that something of significance was happening here, that it was the point at which the building of enclosures moved from embellishing the immediate surroundings of the house to enhancing the economic performance of the estate. This enclosure was complete before the summer of 1621, when the laird bought in five oxen from Auchtermuchty in Fife 'for the park'.[57] It could be that it was initially intended solely for keeping the draught animals for the mains, although the plan may have been for their manure to enrich the soil in preparation for cultivation. Wheat was certainly being cultivated by the later 1630s in what was referred to in 1637 as the 'North Park'.[58] The qualifying adjective strongly suggests the existence of further enclosures by that time (other 'parks'), at least some of which must have been constructed in the early 1620s. In 1622 there is a reference to another enclosure called 'the haning', and the dykers were certainly paid for numerous extensive portions of walling after the completion of the 'park dyke' in 1621, including dykes around 'the bog', perhaps for pasture or the production of hay for winter

---

fols 11r, 12r, refers to oats taken 'out of the barne' for seed; NRS, GD75/476, Account of Victual Sold out of the Barn of Dundas, 1653.

54 NLS, Adv. MS 80.3.10, fols 18–47; Adv. MS 80.3.11, fols 9–16. See also NRS, GD75/242, fol. 6r–v, which records payments to dykers as early as 1613, although the poor state of the manuscript makes it hard to tell how much activity there was at that time. For more on dykes see Briony Kincaid, 'The Use of Dykes in Scottish Farming 1500–1700', Chapter 2 above in the present volume.

55 NLS, Adv. MS 80.3.10, fols 21v–24v.

56 NLS, Adv. MS 80.3.10, fol. 36v. Whyte, 'Infield-Outfield Farming', p. 394, notes the existence of this enclosed field of 13 acres by 1637 but does not establish the date of its construction.

57 NLS, Adv. MS 80.3.11, fol. 4v.

58 NLS, Adv. MS 80.3.13, fol. 7r.

fodder.[59] Although records of weekly payments to the dykers include details of how much work they had carried out, it is not easy to establish what the total extent of walling was, partly because they were paid by the 'rood of work', an area of 36 square ells, or nearly 32 square metres.[60] Still, while a number of caveats must be entered, an estimate of how much dyke-building went on in the early 1620s on the Dundas estate may be attempted from these notes of payments in the laird's accounts.[61] In total, just over 139 roods of work were recorded. While there is no record of how high the dykes were, other contemporary sources suggest that the norm was 1½ or 2 ells (1.41 or 1.88m). The approximate length of dyke constructed must therefore have been at least 2.76km but it may have been as much as 3.14km.[62]

As with liming, the evidence for the construction of these enclosures can be set alongside that found in the parish reports of the later 1620s. Whyte suggested that the origins of arable enclosures are to be found in the 1640s and 1650s, although he acknowledged their presence 'as early as the 1620s' on the basis of these reports, for they mention enclosure in two parishes, Cockpen and Cranston in Midlothian.[63] Yet there may have been more, for the reports were primarily concerned with the productivity of the parishes and its effect on rents and teinds. They had little to say about mains farms where experiments with enclosure were most likely to have been undertaken (as at Dundas), but also enclosures were incidental to the purpose of these reports – they were not required to explain why yields had increased, only whether they had or not.[64] As a result, and as with the later Statistical Accounts, the level of detail varies considerably. Some provided very full returns, while those who drew up the report

---

59 See NLS, Adv. MS 80.3.10, fol. 44v; Adv. MS 80.3.11, fols 9v, 10v, 11r–v, 12–15. See Whyte, *Agriculture and Society*, pp. 122–3, which suggests that 'more poorly drained land' was used for hay. 'Haining' = a piece of ground enclosed by a fence, hedge or wall.

60 R. D. Connor and A. D. C. Simpson, *Weights and Measures in Scotland: A European Perspective*, ed. A. D. Morrison-Low (Edinburgh, 2004), p. 87; DOST, Rud(e) etc., 8c, http://dsl.ac.uk/entry/dost/rude_n_1.

61 These caveats are: that the records of payments to dykers for completed work contained in Adv. MS 80.3.10–11 from 1620–23 record all the dyke-building that was carried out in that period; and that the surviving laird's accounts end in 1623 but there is no reason to suppose that dyke-building ceased then.

62 There were 5,004 square ells, an ell being 37 inches (0.94m). Heights of dykes are mentioned in the following sources: NRS, GD45/18/1621 (dated 1694, which mentions both heights); NRS, GD109/3260 (dated 1682, which stipulates a dyke 'six quarters' high, i.e. 1½ ells).

63 *Reports on the State of Certain Parishes*, pp. 48, 52; Whyte, *Agriculture and Society*, p. 126.

64 *Reports on the State of Certain Parishes*, p. 97, showing that, for the mains of Clerkington, less information is provided because it was worked by its heritor.

from one parish were admonished for refusing to state current values, 'alleging it was not pertinent to them to tray the rents of gentlemen'.[65] The evidence for liming and enclosure contained within these reports should not, therefore, be regarded as exhaustive.

If enclosures were indeed more widespread than was previously assumed, this raises questions about a key source used by historians to trace their development, early maps. John Adair's maps from the late seventeenth century and General Roy's military survey of *c*.1750 have been used to show how enclosure was widespread but limited in its extent before 1700 and quite extensive by the middle of the eighteenth century.[66] We know that Sir Walter Dundas was enclosing ground in the early 1620s, yet these enclosures are not shown in Adair's map of Linlithgowshire, which depicts only the policies around the house itself, well planted with trees.[67] Roy's military survey of the 1750s does show the north park as well as a number of other enclosures beyond the immediate surroundings of the house, at least some of which may also have been there since the 1620s.[68] So while Adair did not fail to record agricultural enclosures altogether, as his maps of the Carse of Gowrie and East Lothian demonstrate, he clearly missed some.[69] Roy may well provide a reasonably good impression of the extent of enclosure by *c*.1750, but Adair cannot be said to provide a reliable guide to the extent of enclosures by the 1680s, far less any idea of the period before that decade.

The progress of enclosure has been characterised by Whyte as a three-stage process. The first focused upon enhancing the immediate environs of the house; the second involved enclosure of mains farms, which 'began in the middle of the seventeenth century'; and, in the third, enclosure spread across the whole estate.[70] At Dundas, Whyte's stage two was already underway in 1620. While that may have been unusual for its time (and the coming of stage three took a good deal longer), without further research to establish how extensive enclosure was in the first few decades of the seventeenth century, it would be rash to assume that Dundas was engaged in an isolated venture.

*   *   *

65 *Reports on the State of Certain Parishes*, p. 93.
66 Whyte, *Agriculture and Society*, pp. 131–2.
67 NLS, John Adair, 'Mappe of Wast Lothian commonly called Linlithgowshire', Adv. MS 70.2.11 (Adair 8).
68 *Military Survey of Scotland*, 1747–55, Section 7, Sheet 4 (https://maps.nls.uk/geo/roy/#zoom=7&lat=56.8860&lon=-4.0709&layers=roy-lowlands).
69 NLS, John Adair, 'The Mappe of Straithern, Stormont, & Cars of Gourie with the rivers Tay and Ern', 1683, Adv. MS 70.2.11 (Adair 2); 'East Lothian', 1682, Adv. MS 70.2.11 (Adair 10); Young, 'Rural Society', pp. 234–6.
70 Whyte, *Agriculture and Society*, pp. 130–1.

In 1994, Tom Devine opened his landmark work *The Transformation of Rural Scotland* with an overview of 'The Old Order'.[71] He started by noting how recent decades had seen the former portrayal of Scotland before the parliamentary union of 1707 as 'a society of feud, poverty, economic backwardness and religious intolerance' give way to 'a more sympathetic and positive' view. Giving due recognition to the work of Whyte and Dodgshon, among others, he noted that scholars now recognised that the 'crucial shift in élite priorities', by which 'the lairds started to become less concerned with military power ... and more interested in the profit and economy of their estates', had happened in the later seventeenth century. Elite architecture had undergone a transformation by which 'the castle and the tower were giving way to the country house' and lairds had become more concerned with 'purchases of clothing, furniture and paintings and increased spending on building and travel'.[72] These changes thus provided the crucial context in which to understand the background to the era of 'improvement'. To Devine, they showed that the major developments in Scottish agriculture which occurred during the eighteenth century had deeper roots and that the origins of that transformation were to be sought in the period between 1660 and 1700.

Until the 1990s, these supposed changes in the outlook of the nobility after 1660 both helped to explain why landlords began to manage their estates for profit at that time and why their predecessors had not. Since then, however, there has been a profound reappraisal of the Scottish aristocracy before the Restoration. In particular, the works of Keith Brown and Charles McKean have shown that, far from being rough, ignorant men who lived in grim fortresses and were inclined to resort to the bloodfeud to resolve their disputes, the nobility of early seventeenth-century Scotland were educated, even well-read, and with a European outlook that included a concern for comfortable living and ostentatious display through symbolic use of military imagery in both portraiture and architecture.[73] They have demonstrated that the priorities of Scotland's nobility had undergone the very transformation described by Devine at least half a century earlier than he had suggested. Thus it is no longer possible to characterise early seventeenth-century Scotland as a country hampered by a primitive, warlike nobility and 'the belated penetration of

---

71   T. M. Devine, *The Transformation of Rural Scotland: Social Change and the Agrarian Economy 1660–1815* (Edinburgh, 1994), ch. 1.

72   Devine, *Transformation of Rural Scotland*, pp. 1–2.

73   Keith M. Brown, *Noble Society in Scotland: Wealth, Family and Culture, from Reformation to Revolution* (Edinburgh, 2000), esp. chs 3, 8; Charles A. McKean, *The Scottish Chateau: The Country House of Renaissance Scotland* (Stroud, 2004), esp. chs 1, 3. See also Aonghus MacKechnie, '"For Friendship and Conversation": Martial Scotland's Domestic Castles', *Architectural Heritage*, 26:1 (2015), 5–24; Duncan MacMillan, *Scottish Art 1460–2000* (Edinburgh, 2000), ch. 3.

Renaissance ideas of art and architecture'.[74] By the beginning of the seventeenth century, the Scottish aristocracy had already made the cultural transition once attributed to the Restoration period, a transition that has been cited as a necessary precondition for agricultural innovation and commercially-orientated estate management. If we can no longer accept the former characterisation of the Scottish nobility before the Restoration, we must therefore reconsider how we characterise their approach to managing their estates, for the key argument for their failure to innovate was that their military bent acted as a brake on such activities by giving priority to maximising the number of tenants they could call out in time of war over the generation of profit.

Sir Walter Dundas of that ilk perfectly fits Devine's characterisation of the pioneering improving laird of the *later* seventeenth century: he was university-educated, he engaged in conspicuous consumption, the adornment of his house and its policies, the education of his sons, service to the crown as a magistrate, and the enhancement of the productivity and profitability of his lands.[75] Indeed, these other aspects of the life of Sir Walter Dundas are worthy of detailed study in their own right, for his papers provide ample evidence of significant attention to all of those things, but few if any references to warfare or its trappings. By 1998, Ian Whyte was already pondering the likelihood of earlier and more widespread innovation in estate management than he had previously acknowledged. He therefore urged 'further investigation … at the level of the individual estate or locality'.[76] This case study suggests that Whyte's suspicions were well-founded, for Sir Walter Dundas of that ilk provides clear evidence that at least one middle-sized proprietor was indeed focusing his efforts on the embellishment and commercial reorientation of his estate. If the innovations that can be seen on the mains of Dundas are found to have been present more widely, it may be time for another reassessment of the story of the origins of 'improvement' in Scottish agriculture. The turbulent middle decades of the seventeenth century may come to be seen as an interruption, rather than a watershed.

74 Whyte, *Agriculture and Society*, p. 115.
75 For example: NRS, GD75/288 records thousands of pounds spent on clothing between 1608 and 1622; GD75/462 notes payments to masons for fifty-seven weeks of high-quality work probably on a new domestic range at Dundas; NLS, Adv. MS 80.3.10 records the purchase of books of Latin and French poetry (fols 4v, 5r); Adv. MS 80.3.11 has references to a painter (fol. 7r) and to embellishing the laird's coat of arms (fol. 5v), which can still be seen on the walls of Dundas Castle.
76 Whyte, 'Poverty or Prosperity?', p. 29.

7

'God Knowis my Sleipis ar Short and Unsound': Andro Smyth's Collection of Rent, Tax, Teind and Tolls in Shetland, c.1640[1]

Brian Smith

The social and judicial world weighed on his breast like a nightmare.
— Honoré de Balzac, *Le Colonel Chabert* (1832), ch. 2

Over a quarter of a century ago, Roy Campbell issued a plea that historians of Scotland should pay less attention to the Highlands. He said that a certain 'crucial matter' – 'the relations of landowner and tenant in the Lowlands in the [nineteenth] century' – should instead take centre stage.[2]

Here I utter a parallel request: that Scottish historians should pay more attention to the Northern Isles of Scotland than they have been in the habit of doing. There is, for instance, not a single reference to Shetland or Orkney in Tom Devine's *The Scottish Nation 1700–2000* (2000). The reason for this neglect must be a view by historians, but not archaeologists or sociologists, that the affairs of the small-scale northern societies are insignificant. It would be a difficult argument to sustain.

Sometimes the historians blunder about in the history of the north. The late Rosalind Mitchison, writing in 1983, summarised what she thought happened in Orkney and Shetland in the first half of the seventeenth century. Bishop James Law, she said,

> enabled James [VI] to create an alternative administration in the Northern Isles, and so to bring down [James's] cousin [Patrick Stewart,] the earl of Orkney, who was imprisoned and eventually executed …
> [This new R]oyal control involved an attack on the local culture. The

1 I am very grateful to John Ballantyne for assistance.
2 R. H. Campbell, 'Too Much on the Highlands? A Plea for Change', *JSHS*, 36 (1994), 58–76, at p. 58.

separate laws of the Northern Isles were declared invalid and Scots law was to take over. This gave the opportunity for a Scottish landowning class to enter the Norse society.[3]

It's a dramatic account. I hope to show, by looking closely at an episode around 1640, that it is over-simple and wrong.

* * *

Bishop Law moved from Orkney to Glasgow in 1615. He was succeeded in the north by George Graham, who had been bishop of Dunblane since 1603. Graham had become foster-parent to two lads from Scone, Patrik Smyth and Andro Smyth, sons of a Perthshire laird, and he took them to Orkney. Patrik married the bishop's daughter and became a prominent Orkney laird; Andro, my key figure, made a career with his neat, fluent handwriting, and married a daughter of Harie Aitken, the commissary, another key figure in the new establishment in the islands.[4]

In the 1620s Andro became a collector of rent and revenue in Shetland for Sir John Buchanan, who had a lease from the crown.[5] The Smyths lived in a circle of important people, with the bishop predominant. There is no evidence, however, that they had strong views, or any views, about episcopacy; they were lukewarm Laodiceans. When Bishop Graham came to grief, in the climactic year 1638, it doesn't seem to have affected them.[6] A month later Andro and Patrik got their own five-year lease ('tack' as it was called) of Shetland, from the Covenanter-supporting Sir William Dick, for 16,500 merks per annum.[7]

Andro thus spent much time in Shetland, from 1638 until 1642, collecting rents, tax and teinds from those liable, that is, from nearly every household in the islands, and acting as sheriff there. His records of his transactions, ignored by historians until recently, have survived. By studying them we can determine whether Andro Smyth and his brother were rapacious tax-collectors, out of sympathy with and unpopular among the Shetlanders, and judge if Mitchison's account of the political economy of Shetland in the first half of the seventeenth century is right.

3   Rosalind Mitchison, *Lordship to Patronage: Scotland 1603–1745* (London, 1983), p. 17.

4   Obligation by George Graham, 1 October 1604, NRS, GD190/3/138/3; Rev. J. B. Craven, *History of the Church in Orkney 1558–1662: Bishops Bothwell, Law, and Grahame* (Kirkwall, 1907), pp. 119–23; John A. Inglis, 'The Last Episcopal Minister of Moneydie', *SHR*, 13 (1916), 229–43, at pp. 229–30.

5   John H. Ballantyne (ed.), *Shetland Documents 1612–1637* (Lerwick, 2016), pp. 191, 199, etc. His account book containing 'The recept of the wodmell [of Shetland] crope 1625 in anno 1626' is in NRS, GD190/3/244.

6   Craven, *History of the Church in Orkney*, pp. 176–94.

7   Rehearsed in registered discharge by William Dick, 29 March 1647, NRS, GD190/3/232/18.

Shetlanders paid the rent of crown lands, tax (called scat) from all ancient settlements, and cornteind from most townships in the islands, to the crown or its tacksmen. The kingslands comprised only about 10 per cent of the whole; not many of them were feued. None of the payments was made in grain or fish, the main products of Shetland; even cornteind had been paid in butter and oil for at least seventy years. Instead sheep provided wool for payments in wadmal, coarse cloth; cows gave rise to payments of butter; and fish to oil. It looks as if women were the main producers. The amounts paid, and the denominations used in payment,[8] were traditional, rather than any sort of new imposition by Andro: the structure of the payments seems to have derived from a reorganisation of fiscal affairs in Shetland in around 1300.[9]

The cloth, butter and oil were a nightmare to collect and dispose of. We have letters by Andro from the summer of 1640, where he deals with some of the problems. Based in Scalloway Castle, which was semi-ruinous, he decided to house the 'packs' of wadmal in a warehouse at Laxfirth, on the east coast of Shetland, 'for fear of rottenis', rats infesting the castle. Meanwhile he was waiting for a ship to come to take the packs of cloth to Norway, and terrified that if it was late he would miss the opportunity to sell them there. That is what had happened the year previously, with the result that he now had two cargoes of the bulky material.[10]

Three weeks later he was even more frantic. He had been travelling around the Mainland of Shetland, demanding that the payers come with their wadmal at once. He didn't, and couldn't, collect it; he 'advertised' for it. He had discovered that there was no room at Laxfirth, because the previous year's consignment was still languishing there, taking up all the room, and he directed the payers to come to Scalloway Castle instead. 'I have stayit heir to resave it this 5 dayis', he said, 'and none come as yit, bot word that some is weaving and most part unwalkit as yit. I know not what to do thairintill for I expect the same hourlie and can nocht remove fra this till it be ressavit.'[11]

The problems didn't end there; they were just beginning. In 1642 a ship-load of Andro's wadmal actually arrived in Norway. Soon afterwards James Dischington, a merchant in Bergen, sent a letter to Andro.[12] He wasn't reassuring. 'Trewlie, Sir', he said,

---

8 For all the lands and payments see a rental of Shetland of c.1622x1625, written by Andro Smyth, in Ballantyne (ed.), *Shetland Documents 1612–1637*, appendix 1.

9 Brian Smith, 'Hákon Magnusson's Root-and-Branch Reform of Public Institutions in Shetland c.1300', in Steinar Imsen (ed.), *Taxes, Tributes and Tributary Lands in the Making of the Scandinavian Realm in the Middle Ages* (Trondheim, 2011), pp. 103–14.

10 Andro Smyth to Patrik Smyth, 2 July 1640, NRS, GD190/3/234/4.

11 Andro Smyth to Patrik Smyth, 21 July 1640, NRS, GD190/3/234/5.

12 NRS, GD190/3/234/9.

in tymis bypast [Shetland wadmal] haithe bein ane verrie good comodittie heir, bot nu within sum few yeirs the Norland bours [Norse peasants] quho usethe to by it complaineth mikill of the onsufficientie therof, how it haithe bein befor; and schawethe it is neather so thicht or suo long by sex or 7 els as it ussethe to be, quhairby they ar peis and peis, and nu at the last quhollilly comid out of use therof.

Instead they were buying 'sum cours sort of Duche clothe, quhilk they sey is moer comodious for them, and nu for the present trewlie will not speir at aney tym for [the Shetland version]'. It was a disaster for collectors of crown rent and tax in Shetland, and may have been the end of the crown payment in that form.

Butter was bulky as well. Once again, the payers had to be cajoled to bring it. There is some evidence, indeed, that the Shetlanders resented payment in butter and oil more than any other – no doubt because of the labour involved, and the necessity of providing containers for it. 'As for butter', Andro mused vaguely in July 1640, 'I think we sall get very litle, for ought I can perceave'.[13] Then the oily material had to be transferred from the kegs in which the Shetlanders presented it, and packed in hundreds of 'trees', barrels, for transport to market. Some of it went to Hamburg, or even to Gothenburg, perhaps for making soap, carried by German merchants who, as we will see, were the main actors in the Shetland fish trade.[14] The rest went to merchants in Leith. Sir William Dick himself seems to have been partial to large consignments of it.[15]

At the same time, or on separate vessels, Smyth sent south dozens of barrels of fish oil,[16] filled up from large numbers of small 'cans' brought to Scalloway by payers. With that product there was a different problem. 'I fear we sall get too much oyll', Andro wrote in September 1640. 'What difficultie and trouble we have for housing to it I can hardlie expres.'[17]

The preparation of all these cargoes took time, and required help from Shetlanders, especially since some at least of the containers might be attacked by gnawing dogs or rats, or spirited away by Shetlanders under cloud of night. And there might even be disaster after it left Shetland. 'We look for a bark shortlie to transport the butter and oyll', Andro wrote to his brother, 'for it is all in many hazards of ill weather and evill hands'.[18]

* * *

13 Andro Smyth to Patrik Smyth, 21 July 1640, NRS, GD190/3/234/5.
14 Memorandum by Andro Smyth, 1641, NRS, GD190/3/235/2.
15 'Item, sent south to Sir William Dick the second year [of the tack] with George Sheills, skipper, 152½ barell butter': NRS, GD190/3/241/1, fol. 3r.
16 For instance, 'sent south with [Hutcheoun Polsone] … to Mareoun Sandilands, 63 barells oyll': NRS, GD190/3/241/1, fol. 3v.
17 Andro Smyth to Patrik Smyth, 22 September 1640, NRS, GD190/3/234/8.
18 Andro Smyth to Patrik Smyth, 22 September 1640, NRS, GD190/3/234/8.

The Shetlanders had other payments to make, which will be addressed below, but as far as the wadmal, butter or oil were concerned, there were several reasons why they might not have been paid at the appointed time. If land in Shetland was 'ley' (untenanted), no collector could demand rent, tax or teind from it. When Andro in due course formulated his 'exoneratioun', his account of the five years of the tack, he listed all the land that was ley during each year.[19] It should be kept in mind that in 1634 and 1635, not too many years before the Smyth tack began, there had been severe famine in Shetland.[20] Michael Flinn and his colleagues in their synoptic work *Scottish Population History*, in 1977,[21] and Geoffrey Parker, in his *Europe in Crisis* (1979),[22] speak about it as a classic example of the social and demographic havoc that such an episode could cause. But the interesting thing about Shetland in 1638, three years later, is that there were a mere fourteen parcels of ley land in the islands. That incidence actually decreased during the period of the Smyths' tack. It looks as if the famine of the mid-1630s was less calamitous than the contemporary observers and the modern historians claimed. The contrast with the 1690s, and the whole period up to 1720, is stark: there were hundreds of ley parcels in Shetland by then, the result of famine, disease and war.[23]

That is not to say that Andro Smyth had things all his own way when it came to payments. Quite the reverse. His papers are full of lists of 'rests', instances of deliberate non-payment by Shetlanders in every parish. Smyth made allowances for 'depauperat' tenants, men and women who, it was clear to both sides, could not pay, and were not worth pursuing. But the numbers who wouldn't pay were far more numerous. That was inevitable, given Smyth's solitary situation in Shetland. If he had servants with him we don't know their names. We have seen how he 'advertised' for the payers to come forward, and how he waited in Scalloway, sometimes fruitlessly, for them to arrive. But he didn't have the time or personnel to hunt the defaulters out, lurking as they were in hundreds of townships throughout the islands. 'This busines is nocht for me alone', he said ruefully to his brother. 'It wold requyre better headis and mo handis, for the countrey layis voyd' – by which he meant sparsely populated – 'and can nocht be rune throw suddenly.'[24] '[W]hat difficultie is to travell in this countrie this tyme of yeir I have fund it since I cam', he wrote

19 NRS, GD190/3/241/1, fol. 3r.
20 Ballantyne (ed.), *Shetland Documents 1612–1637*, pp. 524–5, 551–4, 563–5.
21 Michael Flinn (ed.), *Scottish Population History from the 17th Century to the 1930s* (Cambridge, 1977), p. 130.
22 Geoffrey Parker, *Europe in Crisis 1598–1648* (1979; London, 2001), p. 11.
23 Cf. Rental of Shetland, 1716, NRS, RH9/15/176.
24 Andro Smyth to Patrik Smyth, 21 July 1640, NRS, GD190/3/234/5.

elsewhere, 'both for want of horssis and boatis, the people being fra home at thair fischingis.'[25]

Andro blamed his predecessor, William Dick's factor, for the Shetlanders' evasions. James Scott, he said, had 'bred thir people in such custome to do what they lyk and when they please'.[26] But he didn't stir himself very much to galvanise them. Although he was the sheriff of the islands, and might have proceeded against the debtors in his court, he doesn't seem to have had the time or energy to do so. 'Thir tymes', he wrote, 'makis many of this people to cair litle for a chairge of horning, and I am loth to caus denunce whill [i.e. until] it pleas God that we heir of sum guid setlings.'[27]

* * *

I've dealt with payments made in produce; but there were other exactions, demanded in money. As elsewhere in Scotland, tenants on the estate had to pay girsums, what lawyers described as 'anticipation' of rent, a fine before entering a property. Andro did this work in the winter of 1639, in October and November. On 7 November, for instance, he arrived at Hillswick, in the parish of Northmavine, to distribute leases to tenants for the five years of his tack. He dealt with twenty-five bigger or smaller parcels of land, and collected about £300 Scots in that parish.[28]

It is interesting to note that there were fewer 'rests' of girsums than rests of wadmal, butter and oil. Part of that must be because Andro attended in person, to collect the payment in advance. There is no doubt, however, that the Shetlanders had access to more hard cash than might have been expected. At the end of 1639 Andro took the cash that he had collected in Shetland to Orkney. It included 'ane harne pok' – a hemp bag – of English money, containing £634 2s. and 185 dollars. In another pok there were 436 Dutch stivers, and no fewer than 1,581 double stivers.[29] The source of most of this money was the Dutch fishing fleet, which since the late sixteenth century had called at Shetland every summer, and bought vast numbers of knitted stockings from Shetland women. In later years it was suggested that this huge work by the women was enough to pay the rent of the whole islands, and it was without doubt a major contribution to it in 1639, unacknowledged though it has been by historians.[30]

25 Andro Smyth to Patrik Smyth, 27 July 1640, NRS, GD190/3/234/6.
26 Andro Smyth to Patrik Smyth, 21 July 1640, NRS, GD190/3/234/5.
27 Andro Smyth to Patrik Smyth, 13 August 1640, NRS, GD190/3/234/7.
28 'Compt of ressait of the gersumes of Yetland for fyve yeiris, begining at the crop 1638': NRS, GD190/3/243, no. 3, fol. 6v.
29 Note of money brought from Shetland, 1639, NRS, GD190/3/235/1.
30 Brian Smith, 'Stockings and Mittens 1580–1851', in Sarah Laurenson (ed.), *Shetland Textiles, 800 BC to the Present* (Lerwick, 2013), pp. 52–61, at p. 52.

Shetlanders paid other taxes in money to Andro. 'The [tax called] wattill', Andro said, in an *aide-mémoire* written during one of his first visits to Shetland, in the 1620s, was 'ane dewtie off auld payit be the inhabitantis f[or] the mainteinance of the schireff yeirly as he cam to do justice, [in meat] and drink for men and hors'. It had originally been levied in 'nights' of such entertainment, but in the mid-sixteenth century the payment had been commuted into stock fish, almost the only Shetland impost paid in that way. But in due course it was transformed again, this time into money: a gold angel plus an English sixpence per erstwhile night.[31] Once again, there is no evidence that the Shetlanders couldn't pay that cash, or that they preferred a payment in kind.

* * *

It wasn't the Shetlanders, however, who furnished most of the money that Andro took home from Shetland to Orkney. Most of Shetland's trade was in the hands of merchants from northern Germany, who sailed to the islands every summer, and bought cargoes of fish there. The Germans didn't pay the Shetlanders in money, like the Hollanders; they gave them food, cloth, iron, hemp and the like in exchange. Those foreigners weren't colonialists, as some scholars have erroneously argued; they were well and truly under the control of the Shetland community, with regard to the harbours where they traded, and the prices they gave for the fish.[32] Andro Smyth collected tolls and customs dues from them, mainly in money.

We have a lot of information about how these payments worked in practice, because we have Andro's customs account book for each year of his tack. In 1639, for instance, Derek Brand, a German merchant based at the island of Papa Stour, paid seven dollars, one of them a 'cross' dollar, worth £18 17s. 4d. Scots altogether. That wasn't all that he owed, however: it was 'in part of payment' of the toll. So he did what most of the Germans did, when they didn't have sufficient cash with them: he signed a bond for the remaining thirty dollars owing.[33] There is every sign that Andro trusted the merchants to pay.

Derek did, however, pay three 'lasts' of beer barrels and a barrel of beer. Those barrels were useful to Andro: he could recycle them for his

31 NRS, RH9/15/169.
32 Linda Riddell, 'Shetland's German Trade – On the Verge of Colonialism?', *Northern Scotland*, new ser., 10 (2019), 1–19, is a good critique of Natascha Mehler and Mark Gardiner, 'On the Verge of Colonialism: English and Hanseatic Trade in the North Atlantic Islands', in Peter E. Pope and Shannon Lewis-Simpson (eds), *Exploring Atlantic Transitions: Archaeologies of Transience and Permanence in New Found Lands* (Woodbridge, 2013), pp. 1–15.
33 'Compt of ressait of the custumes toll and buleoun 1639': NRS, GD190/3/243, no. 1, fol. 2r.

butter and oil. There were always complications and variations in such cases: some of the inhabitants of Papa Stour borrowed one of the barrels to put their own oil in, for submission to Andro Smyth, and another was stolen.

The final payment demanded from the Germans was the most bizarre of all. It was a gun, or guns. Derek brought one in 1639. The following year he took two, 'somewhat gilt, without caises', plus a third 'litle gun'.[34] Sometimes these firearms are described in loving detail: Derek's offerings of 1640 are said to have had 'calmes, measures, wormes [and] scrollis', terms used to describe gun-decoration. (I remember, years ago, consulting Chris Smout about these gun-tolls, as they were still called in Shetland customs accounts sixty years later. 'I have never heard the like of these payments in guns', he replied.) Hazarding a guess, because they don't reappear in Andro's papers, I wonder if they were destined for gentlemen's houses, as fowling pieces or even decorations. Certainly Earl Patrick Stewart had festooned his Orkney house with decorative guns in the early years of the century.[35]

Like everything in Andro Smyth's Shetland career, his relations with the Germans didn't always go smoothly. In July 1640 he reported that 'I have bein throw the countrey at the Dutches' – the Germans – 'and have nocht gottin fra them 80 dollours as yit of thair dewis … The Dutches have brought litle or no money with them … for sindrie I fear salbe restand over year.'[36] There were more and more rests to add to his accounts. But despite such lamentations, there always appears to have been confidence that the Germans would reappear and fulfil their obligations. After all, they were necessary for the good health of the local economy and community: they were the recipients of fish from the whole local population, they provided the Shetlanders with goods that they couldn't otherwise have acquired, and they sometimes bought butter from Andro himself and took it to market. The Germans did keep their bargains: they came back to Shetland, year after year.[37]

* * *

As a result of their tack the Smyths were admirals of Shetland, and entitled to its maritime 'accidents'. But Andro was never very sure about what those rights were. It's an area where he wasn't rapacious in the least.

---

34 NRS, GD190/3/243, no. 1, fol. 3r.

35 *The Historie and Life of King James the Sext*, ed. Thomas Thomson (Edinburgh: Bannatyne Club, 1825), p. 387.

36 Andro Smyth to Patrik Smyth, 21 July 1640, NRS, GD190/3/234/5.

37 Brian Smith, 'Shetland and Her German Merchants c.1450–1710', in Natascha Mehler, Mark Gardiner and Endre Elvestad (eds), *German Trade in the North Atlantic (c.1400–1700): Interdisciplinary Perspectives* (Stavanger, 2019), pp. 147–52.

In the summer of 1640, for instance, privateers attacked and destroyed three Dutch ships near Lerwick. 'Thair is thrie shippes of the Hollanders brunt heir', Andro wrote to his brother. 'The people', he reported,

> hes medlit with the yron work thairof, pairtlie be thameselfis and pairtlie be the Hollanderis thair gift and selling of these commodities. Thair is lying as yit in the boddome of these 3 shippis abone a hunder gunis, some mountit, some nocht. Also thair is with them 10 or 12 great ankeris.[38]

There can be no doubt what Earl Patrick Stewart would have done in such a situation: he would have claimed and salvaged everything, by force if necessary. Andro by contrast was timorous. 'The country people', he wrote to his brother,

> will nocht aknowledge any pairt thairof dew to the admirall. I will medle with nothing thairof, becaus I nather know nor can for sindrie respectis. Ye will advyse what may be done thairanent ... and I think it wer nocht amiss that thair wer some resolutioun thairof from the south country.

He needed to be certain, to know the rules, before 'meddling'.

A year later he was still seeking reassurance. He wanted his brother

> [t]o resolve, in particular be wreat, what is dew to us as admiralls of the admiralitie, of broken shippis with thair ornaments and loadinge, of wrak and waith, timber and uther guids, driven upon the land, or found upon the sea. Or of whalls driven or brought ashoir, quik or dead, if any part thairof will belong to the possessor of the ground ...[39]

Earl Patrick had ruthlessly disregarded local custom about shares of whales assumed to belong to the proprietors of land where they were driven ashore;[40] Andro seems to have been willing to consider them.

And, as I have hinted before, it looks as if he didn't have time to be a sheriff. He had been appointed by his tack by William Dick to hold sheriff and admiralty courts in Shetland. But public service and business didn't mix. The situation preyed on his mind: 'The tyme speeds; justice is not ministrat, our awin busines lyis abak', he wrote in August 1640.[41] One drawback of that for the Smyths was a lack of the fines which made such a tack worthwhile: they do not feature in Andro's accounts. When

---

38 Andro Smyth to Patrik Smyth, 2 July 1640, NRS, GD190/3/234/4

39 Memorandum by Andro Smyth, 1641, NRS, GD190/3/235/2.

40 Brian Smith, 'Pilot Whales, Udal Law and Custom in Shetland: Legal Red Herrings', *Northern Scotland*, 23 (2003), 85–97, at pp. 88–9.

41 Andro Smyth to Patrik Smyth, 13 August 1640, NRS, GD190/3/234/7.

he handed over to his successor in the tack, it turned out that the maiden, the guillotining instrument in Scalloway Castle, was in need of a new blade and weight:[42] not, I expect and hope, from overuse, but perhaps because of rust.

There are of course different ways of looking at the vigorous or sloppy administration of justice. Earl Patrick had specialised in the forceful. The contrast with the post-Patrick regimes is notable. It's worth considering the opinion of William Lithgow, a traveller who visited the Northern Isles in Patrick's time, and again during William Dick's era, a quarter of a century later. Lithgow preferred vigorous administrations. He said that the Orcadians by Dick's time only had 'a burgess-sheriff to administer justice, and he too an alien to them, and a residenter in Edinburgh': that is, Dick's son. And the Shetlanders, he went on, in his inimitable way, 'have found such a sting of deocular government within these few years, that these once happy isles … are metamorphosed in the anatomy of succourless oppression, and the felicity of the inhabitants reinvolved within the closet of a Cittadinean cluster'.[43]

Andro Smyth gave the keys of Scalloway Castle to James Mowat, a Shetlander, his successor, on 13 March 1644. James was a new broom: his first act on that very day was 'to put the witches in the severall rowmes' of the castle,[44] something that Andro hadn't got round to doing. James might almost have been reading Kirsty Larner on the subject.

'God knowis my sleipis ar short and unsound.' So Andro Smyth mused at the height of his tack of Shetland.[45] Pent-up in a dilapidated castle, scunnered by the non-appearance of the payers, and lack of accommodation for the payments, up to the oxters in preparing bulky cloth, butter and oil for export, short of everyday goods such as starch for his

---

42 NRS, GD190/3/243, no. 1, fol. 22v.
43 William Lithgow, *Travels & Voyages through Europe, Asia, and Africa, for Nineteen Years*, 12th edn (Leith, 1814), p. 400; also quoted in P. Hume Brown (ed.), *Scotland Before 1700 from Contemporary Documents* (Edinburgh, 1893), p. 302. What Lithgow seems to mean is that the new regime in Orkney and Shetland was a clique of oppressive citizens (royal officials and local landowners), and that the inhabitants' 'felicity' had suffered. They had been stung! ('Cittadinean', not in the *Oxford English Dictionary*, seems to be related to Italian *cittadinanza*, citizenry.)
44 NRS, GD190/3/243, no. 1, fol. 23r. At least one of these witches, Marion Pardoun, was executed a couple of weeks later: Gardie House Archive, GHA/bi/156. Mowat had received a tack with much the same arrangements as the Smyths in October 1642: NRS, RD1/601, fols 451–3.
45 Andro Smyth to Patrik Smyth, 21 July 1640, NRS, GD190/3/234/5.

clothes,[46] it doesn't appear that he had a good time. In 1647 he completed his accounts of the tack.[47] A year later he died.[48]

* * *

Having seen the difficulties that Andro faced in Shetland, and the compromises he had to make, we may ask: what was the experience of the Shetlanders during those five years? First, the rent and tax regime that Andro had been operating wasn't new: it was at least seventy years old, in all its aspects. In most of them it was much older. Andro hadn't come north with any surprises. He used well-certified rentals and books of rates for the tolls. There was a proposal to levy extraordinary taxation in 1640, but Andro thought better of it, anticipating resistance. He blamed his predecessor again. 'I fear we sall come sober speid of the extraordinar taxatioun', he wrote, 'for the people will stur thairwith at thir tymes, for we keip silence anent the ordinar taxatioun and sindrie uther dewis dew to us, quhilk James Scot hes put the countrey out of use of.'[49] His exactions were milder than they might have been.

Sixty years ago the late Gordon Donaldson summed up the nature of Earl Patrick Stewart's polity in Shetland, as he saw it, and, by extension, the polities of his successors. 'While it is true', he said,

> that in Earl Patrick's time the members of the Shetland middle class were, as we should say nowadays, still maintaining their standard of living, there are indications that the exactions levied on them, in one way or another, were so severe that their position was being under-mined. There was, quite apart from any exceptional or new impositions, steady pressure on them through the manifold dues known as scat, landmails, girsum, wattle and teinds.[50]

Donaldson added that this attrition, traditional or not, 'represented a steady drain of wealth from the core of native Shetland society'.

He didn't offer any evidence. In fact, his analysis seems to me to be the kind sometimes offered by senior academics perturbed about their own income tax. Without doubt the Shetlanders, not just the 'middle class', but all of them, would have preferred not to make payments of cloth and butter to Andro. But there is evidence, as we have seen, that they

---

46   He wanted 'some soap and some stuffing [i.e. stiffing, starch] for our clothes, for thair is none to be haid heir': Andro Smyth to Patrik Smyth, 21 July 1640, NRS, GD190/3/234/5.

47   NRS, GD190/3/232/18. Future research in these accounts may ascertain the scale of the arrears that Smyth failed to collect.

48   Registered testament dative and inventory of Andro Smyth, NRS, CC17/2/2, 24 March 1653.

49   Andro Smyth to Patrik Smyth, 22 September 1640, NRS, GD190/3/234/8.

50   Gordon Donaldson, *Shetland Life under Earl Patrick* (Edinburgh, 1958), p. 89.

sometimes refrained from making them, and that there wasn't much he could do about it.

Andro had to come to an understanding with the Shetlanders, and with the German merchants. There isn't much sign that any of them resented his regime. There had been manifold complaints by Shetlanders about Earl Patrick, and about his successors in the 1620s and 1630s.[51] Things were quieter in the Smyth years: as we have seen, Shetland around 1640 wasn't the famine-distressed land that some have imagined. Andro Smyth managed to sit out his five Shetland years without grave mishap. He is not a good instance of Rosalind Mitchison's rapacious Scotsmen running riot in the islands and attacking the local culture.[52] It might not be too much to say that the Shetlanders ran rings round him.

---

51   John H. Ballantyne and Brian Smith (eds), *Shetland Documents 1580–1611* (Lerwick, 1994); and Ballantyne (ed.), *Shetland Documents 1612–1637*, both *passim*.
52   Mitchison, *Lordship to Patronage*, p. 17; see above.

8

Farming in the Stirling Area 1560–1750

John G. Harrison

This chapter examines farming in the old counties of Stirling and Clackmannan with some contiguous areas of Perthshire but excluding the Highland area around Ben Lomond. It includes the carselands of the Forth Valley, the Ochils and parts of the Fintry Hills. Variations in ecology throughout this region, compounded by differences in tenure, communications, capitalisation and other human factors, contributed to a wide range of farming economies. Change accelerated in all zones in the 1750s but was certainly not new. Whilst recognising that there were many barriers to change – including climate and warfare – the emphasis here is on specific and local changes and the impediments hindering decisive transformation. We are rightly warned against using the 'argument from example' to overstate the changes before 1750.[1] So this chapter asks: 'What were the signs of change before 1750?' The answers suggest that we also need to avoid dismissing earlier changes as merely preparatory for 'real' change later.

* * *

Contemporaries divided the region into carse, dryfield and muir. The carse – below about 30m, beside the River Forth – and the dryfield (between carse and muir) were the main arable zones.[2] Above 100m or so was primarily pastoral, though arable was found to c.350m. 'The Crucks of the Forth are worth an Earldom in the North', was a 'Common saying'

---

1   T. M. Devine, *The Transformation of Rural Scotland: Social Change and the Agrarian Economy 1660–1815* (Edinburgh, 1994), p. 30.

2   *OSA*, vol. 9, pp. 343 (Gargunnock, p. 91), 572 (St Ninians, p. 387); *Register of the Privy Seal of Scotland*, vol. II (Edinburgh, 1921), no. 3584; Robert Renwick (ed.), *Extracts from the Records of the Royal Burgh of Stirling 1519–1666* (Glasgow, 1887), pp. 309–11.

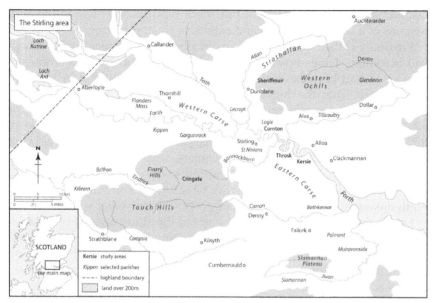

MAP 8.1. The Stirling area

in 1706, underlining the fertility of the eastern carselands.[3] But the carse clay had some sandier areas, some wet meadows and areas of raised peat bog and salt grass. West of Stirling, with higher rainfall and later harvests, very similar soils produced lower-quality grains, and there was more emphasis on dairying.[4] The dryfield soils varied from sandy to heavy clays, and were also of very variable aspect and slope. There were bogs and woodlands, and the zone was intersected by streams. Perhaps half the dryfield was pasture, rocks or braes, or covered with whins (gorse) or broom.[5] The hill pastures were also a mosaic. For example, Sheriffmuir provided common grazing for the farms of Strathallan but also peat, turf, limestone, heather and rushes for thatch, essential resources for farms on the lower ground. Above the head dykes of the muir, herds named around forty features – peat workings, lime kilns, standing stones, streams; and the head dykes were themselves being pushed up, onto former muir, before 1750. Nearby, a settlement at Glentye, at around 350m Ordnance

3   Robert Sibbald, *Sibbald's History and Description of Stirling-shire, Ancient and Modern, 1707* (Stirling, 1892), p. 36.
4   John G. Harrison and Richard Tipping, 'Early Historic Settlement on the Western Carselands of the Forth Valley: A Reappraisal', *PSAS*, 137 (2007), 461–70; Richard Tipping, 'What Did the Carse Look Like in 1314?', *History Scotland*, 14:3 (May–June 2014), 42–6; *OSA*, vol. 9, pp. 539–40 (Kippen, pp. 346–7).
5   NRS, E616/1, E646/3/13; *OSA*, vol. 9, p. 348 (Gargunnock, p. 96).

Datum, was primarily pastoral but there was documented arable and remains of a corn-drying kiln and extensive rig and furrow.[6]

Proximity to the Highlands had an obvious military impact, with reiving and blackmail. James Boswell's wife's family, tenants for generations in the Ochils, had been 'several times reduced to have nothing by plunder and robbery from the highlanders'.[7] But there were further economic connections. Many of the hundreds of horses sold yearly at Stirling's fairs were from the Highlands. Increasing flows of Highland cattle passed through on their way to southern markets. Migration, particularly of young women from the Highland fringes, was significant enough for 'Highlander' to be an insult in seventeenth-century Stirling.[8] Most of the area was within a day's ride of either Glasgow or Edinburgh. The River Forth linked Stirling, Alloa and other ports with the wider world.

Estate papers cover very limited parts of the study area. Several large estates were forfeited after the 1715 uprising, with the loss of older documents partly compensated for by detailed surveys at the moment of their demise.[9] But it was, anyway, an area dominated by properties of modest scale. In consequence, this study relies extensively on testaments, the evidence in Divisions of Commonty cases and baron court books. Particularly important are hundreds of tacks from the local Registers of Deeds. These sources cover every part of the area, though with problems of comparability across time and place. They tend to emphasise the role of tenants and feuars, the small-scale and the local, more reminiscent of the work of Whyte than of later work by Devine and Dodgshon with their emphasis on the estate and its 'bottom line'.[10] The picture these sources

6   https://canmore.org.uk/site/25280/glentye; Bill Inglis, 'James Menteith in Glentye (Sheriffmuir) c.1675–1719', *Forth Naturalist and Historian*, 27 (2004), 111–24; NRS, Dunblane Register of Testaments, 1539–1825, CC6/5/13, pp. 564–6, CC6/5/15, pp. 71–2, CC6/5/4, pp. 39–42; NRS, Register House Plans, RHP 1042; NRS, Court of Session, Vouchers, Durie Office, 1677–1810, CS25/1772/12/2/4.

7   NRS, Wright of Loss Papers, 1655–1769, RH15/115/5/2/G; David Stevenson, *The Hunt for Rob Roy: The Man and the Myths* (Edinburgh, 2004), pp. 114–15, 227; Bill Inglis, *Dunblane 1560–1919* (Stirling, 2016), p. 30.

8   Robert Renwick (ed.), *Charters and Documents Relating to the Royal Burgh of Stirling AD 1124–1705* (Glasgow, 1884), p. 148; Renwick, *Stirling Extracts*, pp. 301–4; Sibbald, *History and Description of Stirling-shire*, p. 39.

9   NRS, Forfeited Estates, Mar, 1716–21, E646/3, E616/1; Forfeited Estates, Kilsyth, 1716–19, E640/1; Forfeited Estates, Powhouse, 1717–20, E653.

10 Ian Whyte, *Agriculture and Society in Seventeenth-Century Scotland* (Edinburgh, 1979); Devine, *Transformation of Rural Scotland*; Robert Dodgshon, 'The Clearances and the Transformation of the Scottish Countryside', and T. M. Devine, 'Reappraising the Early Modern Economy 1500–1650', in T. M. Devine and Jenny Wormald (eds), *The Oxford Handbook of Modern Scottish History* (Oxford, 2014), pp. 130–58, 236–50.

paint is of gradual and incremental change, essential underpinnings of the transformation which was to follow 1750.

* * *

Agriculture needs to be set in the context of the broader economy. The valuation of Stirlingshire in 1691 was £108,457.[11] The Earl of Callendar had the greatest valuation, with £5,491 in Muiravonside and Falkirk parishes. There were six other properties over £2,000. But the county was mostly an area of small landlords, with 55 per cent of the valuation attributable to properties under £1,000.[12] The abundance of feuars around Falkirk, Slamannan, Muiravonside and Denny was a matter of contemporary comment, contrasting sharply with the larger estates in many parts of Scotland.[13] The feus of Temple Denny were created in 1565, and the feuars still acted as a group 200 years later.[14] The average property value in Slamannan in 1691 was only £58 – by far the lowest in the sheriffdom. The hearth tax records show the dearth of substantial houses in the poorer parishes compared with prosperous Bothkennar, on the carse-lands.[15] Feuars held much of the land in the uplands of Tillicoultry and Glendevon parishes even before 1500. The Foot family, resident feuars in Glenquey (Glendevon parish), built themselves a substantial house with a seventeenth-century date-stone.[16] Comparable lairds' houses survive or are documented at Auchentroig and elsewhere.[17]

Other proprietors, in the Ochils and elsewhere, had more substantial estates, with the main focus and the mansion house on the low ground. Abundant small properties brought a fairly fluid property market. Nimmo

11 All sums of money are in £ Scots unless otherwise stated.

12 SCA, Central Region Historical Photocopies, CRHP/92; Stirling County Valuation Roll, 1691 & 1831, SC4/3/1.

13 Sibbald, *History and Description of Stirling-shire*, p. 20; A. Mitchell (ed.), *Geographical Collections Relating to Scotland Made by Walter Macfarlane*, 3 vols (Edinburgh: SHS, 1906–08), vol. 1, p. 332; Devine, *Transformation of Rural Scotland*, p. 5.

14 NRS, Court of Session Acts and Decreets, 1542–1659, CS7/35, fols 116v.–119r.; SCA, Feuars of Denny v. Stirling, 1733, PD16/5/9.

15 NRS, Callendar Judicial Rental, 1717, RH11/10/1; E69/22/1; Loretta R. Timperley, *A Directory of Landownership in Scotland c.1770* (Edinburgh: SRS, 1976), pp. 335–6.

16 Norman Macdougall, *James IV* (Edinburgh, 1989), p. 160; http://www.british listedbuildings.co.uk/200344403-glenquey-house; *RMS*, vol. 7, no. 924; *RMS*, vol. 8, no. 284; *RMS*, vol. 9, no. 1444; *RMS*, vol. 11, no. 1190; NRS, CC6/5/21, pp. 120–1; CC21/5/10, pp. 53–4.

17 *Stirlingshire: An Inventory of the Ancient Monuments*, 2 vols (Edinburgh: Royal Commission on the Ancient and Historical Monuments of Scotland, 1963), vol. 2, pp. 369–70; NRS, Stirling Sheriff Court Register of Deeds, 1658–1952, SC67/49/10, p. 76; SC67/49/11, pp. 107, 115, 156.

in 1777 wrote that 'there are few estates ... which have not changed their owners in the memory of people yet alive', adding that merchants and tradesmen who purchased land 'carried into their rural possessions the same spirit ... which they had exercised in trade'.[18] Purchasers between 1660 and 1750 included lawyers, merchants, government contractors, army officers and tenants. Around 1655 Graham of Fintry feued parts of Cringate to the tenants and in 1656 he sold the superiority of his estate to the Marquess of Montrose. Nearby, in the 1710s to 1730s, the lairds of Cultenhove and Touchgorm feued the farms of Greathill and North Third to the tenants, though those feus were later reabsorbed.[19]

Villages spread rapidly after 1660. Initiated by landlords, the core of their populations were small feuars, each with just a house and plot, contributing to the relatively urbanised character of the Forth area.[20] In 1700 Stirling complained of competition from thirty-three settlements; some were tiny, but Falkirk and Alloa were clearly towns.[21] In 1683 the presbytery pressed for a new kirk at Kirkton of St Ninians on account of its prosperity. Within a kilometre or so of Kirkton were Newmarket of Bannockburn (from the 1690s) and an annual fair at Broxbrae (from 1681).[22] Testaments show rural weavers, notaries, merchants and shoemakers (who doubled as tanners) trading with local farmers and often farming themselves. These developments reduced rural dependence on remote towns. Stirling's annual fairs were increased from two to six between 1641 and 1706, extending trading into the winter months.[23] Records of drovers, and of other livestock dealers, increase steadily from about the 1670s.

There were several rural industries including coal mining, lime working and pottery. Their workers were also farmers, but their industrial work was a significant diversification. Potters are first recorded in the Throsk area in 1610, and fifteen are named in 1754.[24] In 1701 the lessee of the Polmont coal mine was required to employ only ten miners but could

---

18 William Nimmo, *A General History of Stirlingshire* (Edinburgh, 1777), pp. 486, 490.

19 John G. Smith, *Strathendrick and its Inhabitants from Early Times: An Account of the Parishes of Fintry, Balfron, Killearn, Drymen, Buchanan and Kilmaronock* (Glasgow, 1896), pp. 153, 161; NRS, General Register of Deeds, RD2/41, p. 195; NRS, Court of Session, Deeds Warrants, Mackenzie's Office CS29/15/2 (1772); Timperley, *Directory of Landownership*, p. 334.

20 Devine, 'Reappraising the Early Modern Economy', p. 247.

21 SCA, Commissioners of Supply for Stirlingshire, 1693–1740, SC1/1/A.

22 SCA, Presbytery of Stirling Minutes, CH2/722/7, p. 222; John G. Harrison, 'Clay and the Buildings of the Bannockburn Estate in 1716', *Vernacular Building*, 37 (2014), 74–86.

23 Renwick (ed.), *Charters and Documents Relating to Stirling*, pp. 144–5, 178–9.

24 John G. Harrison, 'The Pottery at Throsk, Stirlingshire *c.*1600–*c.*1800', *PSAS*, 132 (2002), 459–73.

have employed more.[25] There were also mines at Alloa, Clackmannan, Bannockburn, Auchenbowie and elsewhere. By about 1750 some farmers, citing the work and costs involved in peat cutting, had turned to buying coal instead.[26]

Improved transport helped push down coal prices. Carts had largely replaced sleds well before 1700; carters were increasingly transporting anything from parcels to bulk commodities. Cart sheds appear on some farms in the early eighteenth century. Landlords required tenants to cart coal from their mines to the harbours.[27] Testaments and witness statements reveal the displacement of oxen by horses, sequentially from the western, then the eastern carse (about the 1680s) and finally from Clackmannanshire by 1750; the discrepancy is clearly significant but the reasons, which may be complex, remain obscure.[28]

A road and bridge improvement programme from the 1660s was symptomatic of changing attitudes and had the potential to affect agriculture in many ways. In 1663 parliament allowed the landowners of Gargunnock and Kippen parishes to levy tolls to defray the costs of rebuilding a local bridge, and allowed a new fair in Kippen since the distance from markets and fairs was a serious disadvantage. In 1681, Stirling opened a new corn exchange, low on the hill where it would be accessible to road vehicles. Road works slowed between 1688 and about 1710 but the programme was re-invigorated from 1711.[29] The 1680s saw increasing numbers of sizeable grain purchases, some for the army.[30] But there were dangers. James Heigin bought 6,000 bolls of grain in 1684–85, intending it for export, but he was over-reliant on credit, was made bankrupt and had to sell his estate to one of his creditors.[31]

The century to 1750 saw many directly agricultural changes – liming, new types of livestock, new crops and rotations, enclosure and land claim, amongst others. In 1698–99 a landlord near Stirling supplied lime to his new tenant for the 'improvement' of the land, specified a rotation involving legumes, and defined what would happen if he (the landlord) decided to hedge and ditch the land in the future; Napier of Craigannat

25 NRAS, Papers of the Dukes of Hamilton and Brandon, 332/E/4/24/11.
26 NRS, CS25/1772/12/2/4, pp. 127–8; NRS, Court of Session Processes, Adams-Mackenzie Office, 1661–1836, CS229/M/3/1/A, pp. 75, 81.
27 NRS, E646/3, pp. 13–16; SC67/49/7, pp. 135–6; SC67/49/12, pp. 66 –71; NRS, Clackmannanshire Sheriff Court, Vouchers of Deeds, SC64/55/2/20, tack to Lindsay 1726; John G. Harrison, 'Improving the Roads and Bridges of the Stirling Area *c.*1660–1706', *PSAS*, 135 (2005), 287–307.
28 NRS, CS229/M/3/1; NRS, Abercairney Papers, GD24/1/319, p. 8.
29 SCA, Minutes of the Stirlingshire Justices of the Peace, 1688–1723, JP19/2/7, pp. 340–1, 363–5.
30 NRS, SC67/50/6, bundle 1682.
31 NRS, RH15/106/573/2; Register of the Great Seal, 1685–88, C2/70 (1) fol. 1r.–v.

made similar provision in 1723.[32] The idea of 'improvement' was in the air – an essential if not a sufficient condition for it being put into practice.

* * *

The specifically agricultural analysis may commence with a consideration of hill farming and herding of sheep. Problems consequent on feuing and the fragmentation of medieval estates in the uplands were exacerbated as the hills were used in ways unforeseen in vaguely-worded charters, or many people came to share assets such as peat or pasture. Disputes were already current by the early seventeenth century when detailed records begin. Most disputes were resolved by the late eighteenth century as stock-proof march dykes were built and herding regimes changed again.[33] Witnesses, whose memories stretched back to the 1640s, explained the context of disputes and change, not just in the hills but on the adjacent low ground. In 1699, John Sharp recalled that forty years or so earlier, tenants from Strathallan 'did set up Sheilds [shieling huts] … but immediately, within Twenty four hours, they were thrown down' by rivals from Tillicoultry. John Galloway preferred to lime his land rather than risk his capital with sheep on the hills. Tenants questioned the value of improvement; land 'taken in' from the Sheriffmuir with considerable effort was still 'bad and would scarcely have pastured two ewes being as bad as the muir contiguous'. Typical of the intermittency of disputes, John Ritchie recalled that (perhaps in the 1720s) when he was cutting peats in a bog claimed by Balhaldie, 'the young laird of Balhaldie came past without challenging him and gave him a snuff'.[34]

This was a period of changing types of sheep, though these were less consistent and stable than modern breeds. The forerunners of Blackface sheep, the Southland type, are usually thought to have appeared in central Scotland about the mid-eighteenth century.[35] However, John Fisher already had forty-six Southland wethers (castrated males) and forty-eight Hameland wethers in Glendevon parish in 1619. Some later

---

32 NRS, SC67/49/4, pp. 254–8; SC67/49/9, p. 215.

33 Albert Bil, *The Shieling 1600–1840: The Case of the Central Scottish Highlands* (Edinburgh, 1990), p. 71; David Cowley and John G. Harrison, *Well Shelterd & Watered: Menstrie Glen, a Farming Landscape Near Stirling* (Edinburgh: Royal Commission on the Ancient and Historical Monuments of Scotland, 2001), pp. 58–9. For more on dykes, and the march dykes legislation of the 1660s, see Briony Kincaid, 'The Use of Dykes in Scottish Farming 1500–1700', Chapter 2 above in the present volume.

34 NRS, GD24/1/319, Printed Depositions, p. 3; CS221/M/3/1, Process, pp. 230–1; CS25/1772/12/2, Process, pp. 173–80; CS25/1772/12/2, Process, pp. 125–7.

35 M. J. H. Robson, *Sheep of the Borders* (Newcastleton, 1988); M. L. Ryder, 'Sheep and the Clearances in the Scottish Highlands: A Biologist's View', *AgHR*, 16:2 (1968), 155–8.

lists also mention these types.[36] In 1699, witnesses said that the tenants on the north side of the Ochils had few or no Southland sheep, in contrast to their rivals from Tillicoultry.[37]

Hameland sheep were small, hornless and fine-wooled.[38] They were a breeding flock, providing their own replacements; some ewes were milked. But they were not thought hardy. Most of the numerous sheep on the low ground were Hameland types. Those put to the hill in summer were brought down in winter. Southland sheep or 'great sheep' are also mentioned in tacks and testaments.[39] Witnesses (mainly from Tillicoultry in the 1760s) explained that they were bought at Linton, kept for three years for wool, then sold fat. The witnesses did not suggest that they were an innovation. These sheep were wethers, so expensive replacements were required. Attempts at breeding failed at first, due to heavy losses from braxy;[40] but keepers of Hameland sheep might have hoped to increase their flocks.

Southland sheep were seamlessly replaced by Blackface sheep by the 1790s. Between 1688 and 1696 the Dinns of Cringate (St Ninians) bought large numbers of sheep at Linton, later well known as the main market for Blackface sheep. The Dinns were feuars and dealers, buying on credit, to be paid when the sheep were sold. They were still dealing in 1708.[41] Southland sheep were hardy, so were on the hills in all but the worst weather. Andrew Cairns said that 'the feuar who had more to purchase sheep put more to the hill'.[42] Deep snow could cause heavy losses; some witnesses would not risk their capital in this way. John Cairns, tenant of Backhills of Tillicoultry about 1700, confirmed awareness of the balance of cost and risk, saying that even if he could afford to stock such a large farm, he would not risk so much capital on the hills in winter.[43] A way round the capitalisation and risk issues (used by John Cairns and many others from the 1640s onward) was to lease grazing to others for payment per head (known as 'grass goods' or agistment), some for the summer, some all year round.[44] Conversely, upland farmers who owned Hameland sheep must have sent them to the low ground in winter,

---

36 NRS, CC6/5/3, p. 36; NRS, Stirling Commissary Register of Testaments, CC21/5/9, pp. 187–8.
37 NRS, GD24/1/319/C.
38 *OSA*, vol. 9, pp. 236–7 (Campsie, pp. 346–7); NRS, CS229/M/3/1, bundle A, p. 126; Whyte, *Agriculture and Society*, p. 80.
39 NRS, SC67/50/3/1666, tack to Baxter; CC6/5/13, pp. 494–5.
40 NRS, RH15/115/1/1/G, McAdam to Wright.
41 NRS, Register of Deeds, Mackenzie's Office, 1661–70, RD2/69/1377; RD4/43, p. 185; RD4/53, p. 247; RD2/69, p. 5; RD4/62, p. 88; RD4/63, p. 235; RD4/63, pp. 900–5, 915; Stirling Sheriff Court, Register of Decreets, SC67/5/3, p. 177.
42 NRS, CS229/M/3/1/A, p. 170.
43 NRS, CS229/M/3/1/E/99.
44 NRAS, 234, Atholl Papers, Box 42 I (1) 3 and Box 42 I (1) 18; NRS, Dunblane

again, for a payment. On the low ground, sheep were herded rather than roaming freely. Their diurnal movement transported nutrients from pasture to arable areas, the dung recognised as a valuable asset.[45]

The sixteenth-century steelbow system, in which stock was provided by the landlord to be returned at the end of the lease, had largely vanished by the 1660s.[46] It was seemingly replaced by the grass goods system, which gave tenants more control. One reason for the feuars' leading role might be their ability to obtain loans, secured on their properties. In 1775 a small proprietor explained that 'for want of money, my improvements have been carried on very slowly'.[47] Capitalisation was a key issue, its importance well recognised.

Seasonal stock movements had financial implications, linking the economies of upland and lowland zones, as well as allowing fuller use of the pastures. However, from the 1740s, many landlords forbade tenants to keep sheep on the low ground, claiming that they might damage newly planted hedges. Demand for more beef and for bigger sheep carcasses increased demand for hill pastures; a season's grass rent tripled, to reach 20 or 25 per cent of the value of a Hameland sheep. Hameland sheep had vanished by the 1790s, unmourned by most Improvers whose Southland flocks now dominated the hills.[48]

But the grass goods system, increasing numbers of beef cattle in the hills and use of the pastures in summer and winter by Southland sheep, increased pressure on pastures and potential for conflict. By the 1750s and 1760s, some hill pastures were described as 'oppressed'.[49] Copious remains of shieling huts, for example in Menstrie Glen, attest to widespread transhumance in the past, but, by the 1670s, active shieling survived only on the Highland margins. Pressure on the Ochil Hills pastures is

---

Commissary Court Register of Deeds, CC6/12/1, p. 161; GD24/1/319/C, David Harley.

45 Alexander Allardyce (ed.), *Scotland and Scotsmen in the Eighteenth Century, from the manuscripts of John Ramsay, Esq. of Ochtertyre*, 2 vols (Edinburgh, 1888), vol. 2, pp. 250–1; Robert Shiel, 'Science and Practice: The Ecology of Manure in Historical Perspective', in Richard Jones (ed.), *Manure Matters: Historical, Archaeological and Ethnographic Perspectives* (Farnham, 2012), pp. 13–23, at pp. 13–14.

46 Margaret H. B. Sanderson, *Scottish Rural Society in the Sixteenth Century* (Edinburgh, 1982), p. 22; *The Exchequer Rolls of Scotland*, ed. J. Stuart *et al.*, 23 vols (Edinburgh, 1878–), vol. 12, p. 73; NRS, Graham, Dukes of Montrose, tacks, GD220/6/1897/4; SC67/49/7, p. 198.

47 Andrew Wight, *Present State of Husbandry in Scotland: Extracted from Reports made to the Commissioners of the Annexed Estates*, 4 vols (Edinburgh, 1778), vol. 2, p. 117.

48 NRS, CS229/M/3/1/D, John Cairns; Glasgow City Archives, Keir and Cadder Papers, T-SK9/7/13–15, 18; Allardyce (ed.), *Scotland and Scotsmen*, vol. 2, pp. 250–1.

49 NRS, CS25/1772/12/2/4, pp. 157–60.

demonstrated by conflict between two rival communities seeking hill pasture. Occupants of Strathallan, to the north of the Ochils, and of Tillicoultry, to the south, had probably pastured the high hills earlier, removing stock from arable areas by using the summer pastures in the hills. The two groups were already in conflict by 1610. Later tradition claimed that the Strathallan tenants suffered heavy losses in the wars of the 1640s, their reduced flocks no longer requiring the hill pasture. By the 1670s they attempted to reassert their rights to summer pasture, building shieling huts as a legal ploy (also used elsewhere) knowing that they would be quickly pulled down by their rivals. This strategy was abandoned from 1674 when the laird gave a lease to two Highlanders, specifically charged with defending the disputed areas; a new settlement was established on Strathallan's southern march. But, about 1699, the legal dispute was resolved in favour of the Tillicoultry people, who built a new settlement on their side of the march.[50]

Such settlements, with the tenants charged with guarding the marches, became widespread. From the 1670s, the Touchadam estate (St Ninians) built a shepherd's hut on its march with Cringate, where the feuars, the Dinns, were posing a challenge, which increased as the Touchadam tenants increased their own stock and took in more grass goods.[51] Nearby, Leckie built a shelter in the hills on land disputed with Touch, Boquhan, Cringate and others (St Ninians and Gargunnock).[52] Reflecting those tensions, by 1610 a settlement existed at Shelloch (Kippen) paying a substantial *c.*500kg cheese for rent, clearly only a small part of total yield; that settlement was later abandoned, probably when, by 1730, the contentious march was defined by a stone dyke.[53]

In 1660 most herds were children and youths, taking family flocks on a diurnal route to common grazing, as vividly described by James Finlayson, who had been a child herd on the Sheriffmuir in the 1650s and 1660s. John Paterson said 'the sheep belonging to the best herd were best off', meaning that they beat rivals in accessing disputed areas.[54] In Gargunnock in the 1690s and 1710s there were frequent complaints of damage by flocks going to the muir through unenclosed land.[55] Walled

---

50 Cowley and Harrison, *Well Shelterd & Watered*, pp. 30–1; Bil, *The Shieling*, ch. 6; Inglis, *Dunblane*, p. 30; NRS, GD24/1/319, Declarations of Witnesses; CS229/M/3/1.
51 SCA, Murray of Polmaise, Barony Court Minutes, 1657–74, TD79/30/1; Smith, *Strathendrick*, pp. 153, 161; NRS, CC21/5/2, p. 248; CC21/5, p. 130; RD2/41, p. 195.
52 NRS, Court of Session, Processes, Shield Office, 1669–1866, CS238/M/6/55; RHP82763.
53 NRS, CC21/5/2, pp. 181–4; CC21/5/2, pp. 400–1; GD220/6/1599/5.
54 NRS, CS25/1772/12/2/4 /244–5; CS238/M/6/55.
55 NRS, Court Book of Leckie and Culbeg, 1687–1724, GD1/132/1, pp. 15, 20, 22, 34.

loans (tracks) to deal with such problems were appearing by the 1660s and widespread by 1730.[56] Increasingly, common herds watched the stock of a whole community.[57] These systems, with many variations, were eventually replaced by professional herds keeping unitary commercial flocks on the hills – a great and unexplored social change. Meanwhile, loans and joint flocks facilitated diurnal movements and so maintained the flow of nutrients to the arable provided by Hameland flocks.

* * *

Liming for fertiliser has attracted much attention as a seventeenth-century technological innovation.[58] There are no unequivocal records of agricultural liming in the region prior to a 1641 tack at Gartclush (St Ninians). This was followed by a flurry of such tacks, in the 1640s and 1650s, in Slamannan, St Ninians, Falkirk, Denny, Logie and elsewhere, perhaps reflecting increased survival of written tacks rather than innovation. One tack in 1655 listed eight potential sources of lime across the adjacent parishes, strongly suggestive of supply difficulties.[59] The case for innovation is stronger in western Stirlingshire where, in the 1660s–1690s, tenants were to lime only with the landlord's permission or where landlords would pay for the lime if the results were unsatisfactory.[60] In some western areas, the lime was from small deposits of 'cornstone', low-quality stone with a high sand content.[61] In central and eastern Stirlingshire the deposits were of better-quality carboniferous limestone, though the geology often made extraction difficult. These deposits were

56 Jean Dunlop (ed.), *Court Minutes of Balgair 1706–1736* (Edinburgh: SRS, 1957), pp. 7, 10, 18, 21, 22; NRS, SC67/49/1, pp. 133–6; SC67/50/6/1681, tack to Shirray; SC67/49/9, pp. 189–91.

57 SC64/55/2, bundle 25; Allardyce, *Scotland and Scotsmen*, vol. 2, pp. 200–1.

58 For further discussion of liming, see Alan R. MacDonald, 'The Roots of Improvement: Early Seventeenth-Century Agriculture on the Mains of Dundas, Linlithgowshire', Chapter 6 above in the present volume.

59 John G. Harrison, 'Lime Supply in the Stirling Area from the 14th to the 18th Centuries', *Forth Naturalist and Historian*, 16 (1993), 82–9; John Reid, *The Place Names of Falkirk and East Stirlingshire* (Falkirk, 2009), pp. 42–3; Doreen M. Hunter (ed.), *The Court Book of the Barony and Regality of Falkirk and Callendar*, vol. 1: *1638–1656* (Edinburgh: Stair Society, 1991), p. 29; NRS, Edmondstone of Duntreath, 1288–1870, GD97/1/333, GD97/1/387; SC67/50/1, bundle 1652; SC67/50/1, bundle 1657; Stirling Commissary Court Deeds, 1600–1809, CC21/13/4, pp. 23–5; SC67/50/2, bundle 1662; CC21/13/4, pp. 54–5; SC67/50/1, bundle 1652; SC67/5/1a/209; NRS, SC67/49/1, pp. 79–81.

60 NRS, GD220/6/1895/16; GD220/6/1896/5; SC67/50/3, bundle 1671; SC67/50/7, bundle 1685; SC67/50/7, bundle 1688 (McLay, 1685); SC67/49/2, p. 106.

61 John Mitchell, 'Cornstone Burning for Fertilizer in Eighteenth Century Dunbartonshire and Stirlingshire', *Scottish Local History*, 85 (Spring 2013), 43–5.

being exploited for building by the 1570s, but lime continued to be brought in by ship from Fife, as it had been since the fourteenth century.[62] Significant workings associated with Dunfermline Abbey are recorded about 1560.[63] In 1655 a boatful of limestone was to be provided for land at Bothkennar. There are many later records of boat lime on farms close to the tidal river.[64]

Where coal and limestone were found together, the workings were sometimes integrated.[65] Despite the road improvements of the 1670s and 1680s, distance from quarries and mines remained an issue.[66] Some estates built kilns and licensed individual tenants to quarry and burn lime, but often restricting sale, perhaps trying to conserve the resource or prioritising farm work over commercial activity. Limestone is heavy but is easier to handle in its raw state than after it is burned to make lighter but caustic quicklime or slaked lime. Even into the 1770s, some farms bought limestone and burned it themselves despite the logistical problems and seeming inefficiency.[67] In spite of the impediments to heavy use, many tacks warned against over-liming.[68]

From the outset, liming was about improvement. In 1661, at Denny, lime was to be applied to land taken in from the muir for arable but which was to revert to grass after six years, for at least two years.[69] At Craigforth (St Ninians) in 1683 the rent was to increase as benefits accrued from liming the outfield.[70] From the early eighteenth century, it became more common to rule that land (sometimes explicitly former outfield) must be rested, mucked and limed after three or four successive crops.[71] In 1727, at Cornton, on land already enclosed with hedges, the landlord was to supply one boatful of limestone and the tenants another, while the tenants were to burn it themselves.[72] So, before 1750 liming was widespread but limited in scale. However, it had allowed real expansion of the arable

62   K. J. H. Mackay, 'Limestone Working: A Forgotten Stirlingshire Industry', *Forth Naturalist and Historian*, 2 (1977), 81–105; Harrison, 'Lime Supply', pp. 83–4.
63   Cosmo Innes (ed.), *Registrum de Dunfermelyn c.1124–1611* (Edinburgh: Bannatyne Club, 1842), p. 433; J. Kirk (ed.), *The Books of Assumption of the Thirds of Benefices* (Oxford, 1995), pp. 23–9.
64   NRS, SC67/50/2, bundle 1663; SC67/49/2, pp. 37–9, 101–2; SC67/49/3, pp. 40–1; SC67/49/12, pp. 80–3.
65   NRS, SC67/49/15, pp. 278–82.
66   Harrison, 'Roads and Bridges'; Reid, *Place Names of Falkirk*, pp. 42–3.
67   Paul Bishop and David Munro, 'Further Comment on OS Mapping of Limekilns in Scotland', *Sheetlines*, 101 (2014), 42–7; NRS, SC67/50/2/1665; SC67/49/16, pp. 67–9; SC67/50/8/1684 (Harrower).
68   NRS, SC67/49/2, pp. 45–7; SC67/49/11, pp. 130–1.
69   NRS, CC21/13/4, pp. 23–5.
70   NRS, SC67/50/6/1683.
71   NRS, SC67/49/9, pp. 93–4; SC67/49/8, pp. 25–8; SC67/49, pp. 18, 181–3.
72   NRS, SC67/49/12, pp. 80–3.

area, had increased productivity and had allowed experience of use to be developed.

John Ramsay of Ochtertyre thought that rates of usage of lime in Menteith had doubled between the early eighteenth century and 1760. Prior to the 1770s, clamp kilns, using a batch process, were the rule.[73] Thereafter, much lime was shipped upstream from the huge draw kilns, using a continuous process, at Charlestown. Improving roads and carts, encouraged by rising land prices and legal changes after 1745, stimulated demand.[74] Draw kilns were built on the shores of the Forth at Fallin (St Ninians) in 1767 and at Murrayshall (St Ninians) in 1785.[75] Investment in such kilns, as in transport and coal mining, was the key to increased use; but this boost, after 1760, followed a century of experience.

* * *

Clearance of raised peat bogs on the carselands provides the area's most distinctive agricultural narrative – a nationally significant example of 'improvement'.[76] Contrary to a widespread modern perception, the mosses were discontinuous; the carselands, 'in constant tillage since time immemorial', were extensively settled. Distribution of peat was related to variations in soils across the carselands.[77]

Bothkennar, entirely on the carse, produced wheat and other marketable grains in the 1290s.[78] Carse grains provided revenues for several medieval monasteries.[79] There was arable, peat clearance and substantial drains at Cornton (a significant name) in the thirteenth century.[80] Numerous

73 NRS, SC67/50/2, bundle 1662 (Squire); SC67/49/8, pp. 2–5; SC67/50/1/1658; SCA, Murray of Polmaise Papers, PD189/68/1, 12 January 1662, 29 May 1668, 21 February 1668; Wight, *Husbandry in Scotland*, p. 111.

74 Allardyce, *Scotland and Scotsmen*, vol. 2, pp. 206, 213–17, 252–4; https://canmore.org.uk/site/49496/charlestown-harbourpassim/

75 NRS, SC67/49/26, pp. 1, 6; SCA, PD189/73.

76 Susanna Wade Martins, *Farmers, Landlords and Landscapes: Rural Britain 1720–1870* (Macclesfield, 2004), pp. 52–3; Dodgshon, 'Clearances'.

77 Sibbald, *History and Description of Stirling-shire*, pp. 36, 59–60; Nimmo, *General History of Stirlingshire*, p. 489; Harrison and Tipping, 'Early Historic Settlement'; Richard Tipping, Aden Beresford, Gordon Cook, Derek Hamilton, John G. Harrison, Jason Jordan, Paul Ledger, Dmitri Mauquoy, John McArthur, Stuart Morrison, Danny Paterson, Nicola Russell and David Smith, 'Landscape Dynamics and Climate Change as Agents at the Battle of Bannockburn', in Michael Penman (ed.), *Bannockburn 1314–2014: Battle and Legacy: Proceedings of the 2014 Stirling Conference* (Donington, 2016), 111–28.

78 John Reid, 'The Carse of Stirling in the Thirteenth and Fourteenth Centuries', *Calatria*, 30 (2014), 57–74.

79 Richard Oram, 'Cambuskenneth Abbey and Its Estate: Lands, Resources and Rights', *Forth Naturalist and Historian*, 35 (2012), 99–112.

80 Alasdair Ross, 'Recreating the Bannockburn Environment and Climate', in

testaments show the eastern carse producing wheat, legumes and white (good-quality) oats in the late sixteenth century.[81]

Removing the peat created new arable on the fertile soil beneath. Clearance was an incidental result of extracting fuel for medieval salt pans along the tidal Forth. Skeoch Moss, cut for fuel for the burgh of Stirling since at least the thirteenth century, had vanished by 1700.[82] Drainage of moss surfaces to facilitate peat cutting and pasture was long-established.[83] Paring and burning, which had the primary aim of creating arable, was slow, the main input being the tenants' labour.[84] A 1678 tack at Throsk was the first of many explicitly requiring the tenant to recover arable from the moss. By the 1710s, tenants at nearby Kersie paid small rents for lots fringing the moss, which they were to clear for arable. They did so by gathering rainwater in dams on the moss surface and floating the peat off as waste into the river. This sacrificed the potential use of the peat itself, but speed, and lack of significant markets for peat, made flotation the favourite local clearance method into the nineteenth century.[85]

Flotation initially depended on the tenants' unpaid work. In 1743 a tenant at Cockspow (St Ninians) was to build himself a new house and farm steading and to remove an acre of peat every four years, or be evicted. At Throsk, in 1745, a nineteen-year lease for fifteen acres of arable was to become heritable if the tenants added an acre every six years but to be terminated if they failed to do so. Such onerous conditions, even when the rent was modest, suggest the tenants' desperation for land, presumably related to rising population; desperation is also suggested by the widespread re-appearance of entry fines (grassums) about 1700.[86] Capital investment in land claim by landlords was minimal before 1750. The most famous later example, the Blairdrummond project (from the 1760s), involved significant capital investment in a wheel to pump the water and ditches to distribute it, which greatly speeded up the peat

Penman (ed.), *Bannockburn 1314–2014*, pp. 96–110, at pp. 99–102.

81 NRS, Edinburgh Commissary Court Register of Testaments, CC8/8 *passim*.

82 Richard Oram, 'The Sea-Salt Industry in Medieval Scotland', *Studies in Medieval and Renaissance History*, 3 (2012), 209–32; SCA, PD189/68/1–4.

83 NRS, SC67/5/1a /316.

84 Sibbald, *History and Description of Stirling-shire*, pp. 59–60; NRS, CC21/13/6, p. 5.

85 NRS, SC67/49/3, p. 121; NRS, Letter re. Lord Kames (1807), GD1/1008; John G. Harrison, 'East Flanders Moss, Perthshire, a Documentary Study', *Landscape History*, 30:1 (2009), 5–19; John G. Harrison, 'East Flanders Moss: Some Historical Myths and Some Historical Evidence', *Scottish Local History*, 77 (Winter 2009), 18–24.

86 NRS, SC67/49/18, pp. 77–9; SC67/49/19, pp. 371–9; SC67/49/5, p. 214; SC67/49/5, p. 216; SC67/49/8, pp. 279–80.

clearance process. But underlying the project were the Kersie methods of flotation and cheap tenant labour.[87]

There were other forms of land claim. Land in Denny taken from the common muir and cultivated was already regarded as private property before the late sixteenth century. By 1618, four and a half oxgangs at Polmont had been enlarged by 'outriving' the muir and commonty. Such intakes, widespread elsewhere, continued in this area to 1750 and beyond, often by an intensification of settlement, apparently linked to population growth.[88] In the Carron Valley, from the 1690s, tenants of new units paid entry fines, built their own steadings and met the costs of liming.[89] At Glinns (Kippen) tiny farms were created on new intakes on marginal land at 150–200m.[90] From about 1710 feuars and tenants were involved in 'breaking' the former common muir of Muiravonside and 'taking in' the outfield to make arable.[91] At Seamore (Denny) in 1734, the tenants were to rive out any part of the land they thought fit.[92]

Even after 1700, on the favoured eastern carselands, tenancies seldom exceeded 25 acres and many were less than 4.[93] Settlement splitting was particularly common on the carse. In 1706 Easter and Wester Corsepatrick (St Ninians) were split to form a 'new mailing', while at Cornton (Logie) in the 1720s tenants of newly-split small tenancies were not to damage the growing hedges.[94] At Kersebonny (St Ninians) in the 1710s, liming, planting of trees, ditching and settlement splitting went hand in hand.[95] In 1741–42 at King's Park (Stirling) the prime tenant paid the tenants of adjacent farms to cultivate 48 acres of previously unlaboured wet carse ground, the kind of labour which many tenants were undertaking for themselves.[96]

87 Harrison, 'East Flanders Moss: Some Historical Myths'; Allardyce, *Scotland and Scotsmen*, vol. 2, pp. 206, 213–17, 252–4; Wade Martins, *Farmers, Landlords and Landscapes*, p. 12; Harrison, 'Roads and Bridges'.

88 John Reid, 'The Feudal Divisions of Denny and Dunipace, Part 2', *Calatria*, 9 (1996), 35–54; NRAS, Papers of Dukes of Hamilton and Brandon, 332/E/1/4; Cowley and Harrison, *Well Shelterd & Watered*, 15–19; Dodgshon, 'Clearances', pp. 138–9.

89 NRS, SC67/49/11, pp. 122–3; SC67/49/11, pp. 131–2.

90 NRS, SC67/49/8, pp. 279–80; SC67/49/15, pp. 518–22; SC67/49/9, pp. 161–2; SC67/49/22, p. 279; SCA, Protocol Book of David Williamson, 1622–28, B66/1/16, fol. 9r.

91 Reid, *Place Names of Falkirk*, p. 221; NRS, SC67/49/7, pp. 35–8; SC67/49/10, p. 170; SC67/49/9, pp. 15–16, 74–5; SC67/49/14, pp. 15–16; SC67/49/17, pp. 153–5; SC67/49/15, pp. 248–51.

92 NRS, SC67/49/17, pp. 211–15.

93 NRS, SC67/49/7, pp. 254–7; SC67/49/8, pp. 297–8; SC67/49/3, pp. 45–6; SC67/49/10, pp. 168–70.

94 NRS, SC67/49/7, pp. 93–5; SC67/49/12, pp. 54–5 & 80–3; SC67/49/14, pp. 123–4.

95 NRS, SC67/49/8, pp. 26–7; SC67/49/12, pp. 72–4.

96 NRS, SC67/49/16, pp. 353–5; NLS, Decreet arbitral, Erskines and Rothes, 1723,

Both land claim and improved cultivation could increase arable production but both depended on massive labour inputs. Tenants benefited from expansion of the arable area but they risked being replaced, at the end of their leases (or sooner if they failed to keep up the required pace), by better capitalised tenants, taking on larger units of land now in prime condition. Surely, only desperation could have driven tenants to accept such leases, whilst landlords were bound to gain new arable, of rising value, at minimal cost.

* * *

One familiar dynamic of 'improvement' was the consolidation of individual farms and the division of shared resources formerly held in common. However, in the Stirling area we find that many forward-looking arrangements explicitly continued to share resources, most commonly pasture, thatch, fuel, lime and woodland products (from brushwood to major timbers). All of these were ultimately – via fire or dunghill – plant nutrients, used to replace those consumed as grains, meat and dairy products.[97] The advantage of sharing was that larger units, containing all these resources, would have required more capital.

In 1721, in a process clearly indicative of 'improvement', the four ploughgates of Easterton of Balgrochan (Campsie) were said to be 'in runrig and otherwise in disorder'; the feuars agreed to divide the land into four equal parts 'for their advantage in time coming'. Though free to do as they chose, the feuars did not divide their lands by straight lines into discrete units. Each retained an interest in the Black Moss for cutting peats, whilst only the north quarter could use it for pasture. The north quarter could use parts of a meadow which lay within the middle quarters, whilst the north was relieved from pasturing cattle for the mill as it would suffer damage from the coal mine and the lime craig.[98]

The seeming confusion is most likely explained by shortage of capital and the need for ready access to specific resources, such as fuel. Most pre-1750 divisions were similarly qualified. When Westerton was split from Airthrey (Logie) in 1682 the common pasture remained undivided, some areas remained intermixed and one tenant of Westerton could continue to dig earth in an adjacent marsh for 'gooding' his land.[99] Division of runrig properties at Mugdock in 1718 and of feus at Orchyard and Balmore in 1723, both intended to facilitate enclosure and abolition of infield-outfield, left the muirs as commonties.[100] At Killearn in 1721

Ms 17603, fols 81–2.
97   Shiel, 'Science and Practice: The Ecology of Manure', pp. 13–23.
98   NRS, SC67/49/9, pp. 11–14.
99   NRS, SC67/49/9, pp. 1–5.
100 NRS, SC67/49/8, pp. 80–1; SC67/49/9, pp. 189–91.

the muir was to be divided but parts of the low ground could remain common for fuel if necessary.[101] In Slamannan in 1736, a landlord and tenant exchanged land so their holdings were distinct, but the roadsides were common for pasture, the moss was common for peat, and the byre was shared – the tenant was to rebuild its gable.[102] Most divisions were initiated by proprietors, but some were initiated by tenants, as at Caverkae (Alva) in 1703, each wanting an equal share of hill ground and other ground, their arable to be adjacent to their houses.[103]

Two near-universal clauses in pre-improvement tacks aimed to gather and conserve plant nutrients. The first required outgoing tenants to leave the last year's manure on departure; the second required the fodder to be consumed on the farm, particularly in the last year. The manure comprised 'winter fulzie' – animal dung plus domestic wastes – and 'summer tathe' – the dung of stock feeding on peripheral pastures during the day but housed or folded on potential arable or grass at night, so transporting nutrients from one area to the other.[104] Hay was widespread, but the main fodder was straw. One estimate, for a carseland farm in 1729, was that straw and chaff was worth 15 per cent of the total grains.[105] The ratio would be higher on poorer, wetter farms where crops were grown primarily as fodder. Symptomatic of the pressures are frequent complaints of stock pasturing in coppiced woodland or the feeding of whins (gorse) and broom, common invaders of the dryfield.[106] Woodland grass, rank vegetation or marshy areas were cut for hay, the mud of ponds and ditches was used as manure, all effortful methods of increasing the flow of plant nutrients.[107]

Adequate manure supplies required a balance between livestock, fodder and grains. These pressures could be eased but not obviated by seasonal stock movements, whilst liming made existing plant nutrients more readily available, increasing productivity.[108] Distinctive Scots

---

101 NRS, SC67/49/8, pp. 250–1.

102 NRS, SC67/49/15, pp. 548–62.

103 NRS, SC67/49/4, pp. 226–7.

104 NRS, SC67/49/8, pp. 80–1; SC67/50/6, tack (1683); SC67/50/7/1688, tack (1685); SC67/49/14, pp. 91–2; GD220/6/1895/16; John A. Atkinson *et al.*, 'Ben Lawers: An Archaeological Landscape in Time: Results from the Ben Lawers Historic Landscape Project 1996–2005', *Scottish Archaeological Internet Reports*, 62 (2016), 104 (DOI: 10.9750/issn.1473–803.2016.62).

105 NRS, SC67/49/12, pp. 66–7.

106 George Buchan-Hepburn, *General View of the Agriculture and Rural Economy of East Lothian* (Edinburgh, 1794), pp. 53–4; NRS, CS229/M/3/1/A, p. 67; RPS, 1458/3/2; Harrison, 'Clay and the Buildings of the Bannockburn Estate', pp. 80–2; NRS, SC64/55/1/8, tack.

107 SCA, RHP3790; NRS, CC21/13/7, pp. 18–19; *OSA*, vol. 9, p. 540 (Kippen, p. 347).

108 Robert A. Dodgshon, 'The Scottish Highlands before and after the Clearances:

systems of water meadows were deployed, including where land was being 'taken in' adjacent to the Sheriffmuir (Dunblane).[109]

Liming, fallowing and more intensive cultivation (e.g. of the outfields), together with the substantial increase in the arable area in the innumerable land claims from moss, muir and mudflats, had the potential to greatly increase arable production. Tacks requiring arable to be periodically 'rested' in pasture became commoner after 1661.[110] That, even without use of sown grass, would help with weed control. Spade agriculture, with the potential to greatly increase productivity, is mentioned as something unsurprising by witnesses as late as 1770; in Tillicoultry it was used on steep ground, difficult to plough, but it may also have been used on small, low ground holdings.[111] The smallest units can hardly have supported their own draught animals. Improver Robert Maxwell's methods for moss clearance, deployed on East Flanders Moss within the Stirling area, were explicitly directed to tenants without draught animals, who would do the work themselves with breast ploughs.[112] A Fife laird noted that he was 'leaving nothing unessayd ... to render ... the Mains ... as fruitful as a cotterman does to his single aiker of land', suggesting that human labour, attention to detail and cultivation were crucial factors in raising productivity.[113] Improved cultivation and nutrient supplies surely underlie the increased importance of white oats as compared with grey, though fiars prices for grey oats continued to be struck in Stirlingshire until 1776.[114] Beyond that, whilst there was clearly pressure to increase overall arable production, and growing of legumes and wheat continued to be important on the carselands (as noted above), the sources do not allow assessment of the balance until the advent of new crops (see below).

Even in the sixteenth century there was some specialisation. Orchards had existed on monastic lands for centuries, but new ones were created,

---

An Ecological Perspective', in Ian D. Whyte and Angus J. L. Winchester (eds), *Society, Landscape and Environment in Upland Britain* (Edinburgh, 2004), pp. 67–78; Whyte, *Agriculture and Society*, p. 57.

109 Hadrian Cook and Tom Williamson (eds), *Water Meadows: History, Ecology and Conservation* (Bollington, 2007), p. 58; NRS, CS25/1772/12/2/4, pp. 30–1, 86–92, 173–80.

110 NRS, CC21/13/4, pp. 23–5; GD220/6/1897/4; SC67/49/6, pp. 168–9; SC67/49/9, p. 151.

111 NRS, CS229/M/3/1/D, pp. 139, 185.

112 Whyte, *Agriculture and Society*, p. 72; NRS, Papers of Steel Maitland Family, 1489–1947, GD193/69/10, GD193/69/15; this method is described in Harrison, 'East Flanders Moss, Perthshire, a Documentary Study', pp. 9–10.

113 Mary Young, 'Scottish Crop Yields in the Second Half of the Seventeenth Century: Evidence from the Mains of Castle Lyon in the Carse of Gowrie', *AgHR*, 55:1 (2007), 51–74, at p. 62.

114 A. J. S. Gibson and T. C. Smout, *Prices, Food and Wages in Scotland 1550–1780* (Cambridge, 1995), p. 93.

one at Cockspow (St Ninians) by 1642 and one at Clackmannan in 1728. Orchards required sophisticated marketing, storage and transport. As valuable assets, they were often hedged.[115] Other examples of specialisation are that in 1539, the laird of Knockhill (Lecropt/Logie) gave gifts of kid meat to James V, while, in the eighteenth century, tenants of Knockhill's former lands of Fossachie (and adjacent Lipnoch) sold goat whey for visiting invalids.[116] From the later seventeenth century, several farmers in the Carron Valley area were also stock dealers growing significant areas of hay. In 1719, a tack at Gartcarron encouraged 'grassing' rather than arable. By the 1790s the valley was the site of one of the biggest water meadows in Britain.[117] As early as the 1620s, it was possible to buy hundreds of thorns for hedging; by the 1750s, nurseries supplied thousands, at specified sizes.[118] Records of new crops, on the other hand, are rare before 1750, though potatoes, rye grass and clover mixes and turnips then increase rapidly (examples are given below).

Enclosure is rightly seen as a pivotal change. But even the best land was often still in tiny, unenclosed parcels in 1750. In 1739 a lease at Queenshaugh, on the carse close to Stirling, described fourteen acres divided into six parcels, the largest a little over three acres, several including mixes of arable and grass.[119] Enclosures around mansion houses were increasing from the 1660s, often leased to commercial graziers for high rents. Though small, such enclosures continued to be created down to 1750.[120]

---

115 NRS, SC67/1/2, pp. 104–5; SC64/55/2/19; John G. Harrison, 'Gardens and Gardeners in Early-Modern Stirling', *Forth Naturalist and Historian*, 36 (2013), 103–16; *RPC*, 2nd ser., vol. 7, pp. 265–7.

116 Cowley and Harrison, *Well Shelterd & Watered*, p. 27; Athol L. Murray (ed.), 'Accounts of the King's Pursemaster, 1539–40', *Miscellany of the Scottish History Society*, vol. 10 (Edinburgh: SHS, 1965), pp. 11–51, at pp. 38, 39, 44.

117 NRS, SC67/49/11, pp. 121, 131; SC67/49/9, p. 10; SC67/49/10, pp. 19–21; SC67/49/8, p. 211; SC67/49/11, p. 66; John Mitchell, 'Wet Meadows in Lowland West Central Scotland: An Almost Forgotten Botanical Habitat', *Botanical Journal of Scotland*, 49:2 (1996), 341–5; *OSA*, vol. 9, p. 331 (Fintry, p. 372); Cook and Williamson (eds), *Water Meadows*, p. 58; T. C. Smout, *Nature Contested: Environmental History in Scotland and Northern England since 1600* (Edinburgh, 2000), pp. 96–7.

118 SCA, Accounts of Spittal's Hospital, SB6/1a, discharge, 1622–23; Cowley and Harrison, *Well Shelterd & Watered*, pp. 56–7; Wight, *Husbandry in Scotland*, vol. 2, pp. 105, 114, 117–21; vol. 3, p. 342.

119 NRS, SC67/49/16, pp. 151–3.

120 T. R. Slater, 'The Mansion and Policy', in M. L. Parry and T. R. Slater (eds), *The Making of the Scottish Countryside* (London, 1980), pp. 223–47, at p. 230; NRS, GD220/6/1897/5; SC67/49/8, p. 201; SC67/49/16, pp. 299–303; Miles Glendinning and Susanna Wade Martins, *Buildings of the Land: Scotland's Farms 1750–2000* (Edinburgh, 2008), p. 14.

Complete enclosure of a substantial estate was an extended process, perhaps taking decades. Circumstances varied greatly but a typical sequence on low ground was to resolve boundary issues, then enclose property and farm boundaries, then individual fields.[121] Closure of minor roads, symptomatic of an early stage, was increasingly common from 1660.[122] Meanwhile, enclosed and unenclosed were intermixed. At Balgair, near Balfron, in 1693, a tack excepted a dyked enclosure of three acres recently created and use of an adjacent bog, allocated to another tenant.[123] During these intermediate, half-enclosed stages, despite the early investment, neither old nor new systems operated optimally – a good reason for caution.

Hedges, often on small properties on the stone-free carselands, are the most frequently recorded early permanent enclosures since, though paid for by landlords, tacks required the tenants to manage them. Records increase after 1700, sometimes in surprisingly high situations where, it was thought, hedges helped warm the ground.[124] Some of the documented hedges, for example at Dashers (Kippen) and Causewayhead (Logie), are shown on Roy's map. Hedges were typically planted alongside newly dug ditches, and improved drainage may have been one of the main benefits. Covered stone drains, a new technology which usually involved landlord investment, are recorded only from the early 1750s.[125] Extensive drainage, along with the biggest enclosure projects, came much later, as landlords (locally and more widely) invested more heavily in farming.[126]

* * *

By 1750, farming in the Stirling area was on the cusp of a new phase which would culminate in some dramatic projects, including the Blairdrummond Wheel and extensive estuarine land claim. William Forbes's project around Falkirk was claimed to involve the planting of 6 million thorns in 400 miles of hedges.[127] Prior to 1750 there was no such drama. But this chapter has shown that the major schemes had smaller-scale forerunners.

121 NRS, SC67/50/8/1694 (1693).
122 Harrison, 'Roads and Bridges', p. 294.
123 NRS, SC67/49/8, p. 156.
124 NRS, Letters to Erskine of Alva, 1716, GD1/44/7/5; SC67/49/12, pp. 80–3; Papers of Calders of Redford 1562–1941, GD332/48, Decreet, Muiravonside, 1707; SC67/49/18, pp. 33–5. See also *OSA*, vol. 9, p. 146 (Alva, p. 130).
125 NRS, SC67/49/13, p. 23; SC67/49/9, pp. 244–6; SC67/49/12, pp. 149–51; SC67/49/19, pp. 371–9; SC67/49/37, pp. 206–20; SC67/49/12, pp. 54–5.
126 Wade Martins, *Farmers, Landlords and Landscapes*, p. 4.
127 Harrison, 'East Flanders Moss, Perthshire, a Documentary Study', pp. 8–12; T. C. Smout and Mairi Stewart, *The Firth of Forth: An Environmental History* (Edinburgh, 2012); John Sinclair, *General Report of the Agricultural State and Political Circumstances of Scotland*, 3 vols (Edinburgh, 1814), vol. 1, p. 315.

The great water meadow of the Carron Valley, described in the 1790s, had been preceded by smaller projects for almost a century. Many of these forerunners were commissioned by small proprietors who left no consecutive documentary collections, so they are difficult to identify, describe and quantify. Nevertheless, once the evidence has been assembled, patterns begin to emerge.

Two changes getting under way in the 1750s were the adoption of new crops and of subsoil stone drains. These are both illustrated by James Wright of Loss, proprietor of a small estate in the Ochils, whose astonishingly detailed records furnish a concluding case study. In Stirlingshire, potatoes were first grown as a field crop about 1739. The second record is for a field of potatoes at Carnock (St Ninians) in 1748. Wright provides the third record, planting increasing areas from 1752 but still in rigs which he only enclosed and reformed later. The need to learn about storage and to create a market for a new product must have encouraged caution with potatoes. Wright also provides the first local records of stone subsoil drains and of sowing a rye grass and clover mix, again starting with small areas, so failure would not have been disastrous. Retention of rigs facilitated a fluid approach; when a rig of peas did not grow, he sowed barley and harvested a crop. He partly rebuilt his stone and lime house and steading. Wright deferred building march dykes until the 1760s. His approach, cautiously progressive, is only revealed by his uniquely-detailed records. He cannot have been alone in his caution nor in adopting new crops or drainage systems. Stone drains remained sparse on the dryfield in the 1770s and far from widespread in the 1790s; drainage on the carselands (where stones were unavailable) was still by reforming and straightening rigs in the 1770s.[128]

Liming, one of the most important changes, may well have preceded the 1640s when relevant documents first survive in quantity. The limits on lime's availability, transport costs, and the trouble of burning it on the farm, all constrained its use. It is little wonder that farmers in the 1670s did not, like those in the 1770s, apply 80 bolls of lime to ground which might yield 8 or 10 bolls of grain per acre per year, but only if it was also enclosed, the rigs reformed and straightened and put into a complex, arduous rotation – fallowing, sown grass, legumes and grains.[129] By the 1660s, the grass goods system and Southland sheep contributed to greater pressure on the hill pastures, symptomatic of growth in the agricultural sector generally but potentially raising the question of sustainability.

Settlement splitting now appears like a diversion from the main direction of change towards enlargement of tenancies. However, where

---

128 *OSA*, vol. 9, p. 475 (Kilsyth, p. 282); NRS, SC67/49/18, pp. 315–19; Cowley and Harrison, *Well Shelterd & Watered*, p. 25; Wight, *Husbandry in Scotland*, vol. 3, pp. 342, 344.
129 Wight, *Husbandry in Scotland*, passim.

land was to be taken in or brought into a higher state of cultivation, splitting harnessed an abundant and cheap resource – human labour – that was easily dispensed with when no longer required. Walled tracks from low ground to common grazings reduced the problems of regular stock movements in unenclosed countryside, so traditional nutrient flows could continue; they later became redundant when the farms were reorganised. Many of the settlements on estate margins were similarly short-lived, transitional arrangements. They were superseded by stone walls, legal judgments and maps – that is, by capital and new ideas. Other changes must have looked ambiguous to many. Whins and broom had once been useful as fodder, but the Improvers strove to extirpate them, to create a more homogeneous, single-purpose landscape, just as they cleared mosses by flotation.

Straightening of marches, divisions of commonties and of runrig, though spasmodic, go back to the 1650s. They thus constitute evidence at least of new thinking. But while such adjustments, often achieved via arbitration, were not expensive, they were not necessarily followed by capital investment or enclosure. At Muiravonside, division was quickly followed by reorganisation, taking in land from the muir, and new settlement, but much of the investment, as in land claim elsewhere, was in the form of tenants' labour. Tenants' unpaid labour also made a major contribution to the road improvements programme.[130]

Indeed, beyond building themselves more comfortable houses, capital investment by landlords was sparse. The lairds had 'modern' houses at Alloa and Bannockburn; but the surveys of the two estates in 1716 show that all the tenants' farms – the houses, byres, barns and sheds – were of unimproved construction with clay and turf as primary materials.[131] There is no reason to think that this was untypical; indeed, documented rebuilding even in the 1740s was often paid for by tenants. If landlords regularly paid for anything it was for a first application of lime, though even then the payment was made only if the tenant did not otherwise recover the costs during the residue of the tack.

The non-agricultural changes described earlier in this chapter, concerning land ownership, new markets, transport and rural industries, clearly had impacts on farming, even if the connection is not always so clear as the switch from peat to coal. Markets were influenced by demand for grain and beef for the army and navy. The emergence of livestock dealers, including those supplying Southland sheep, is indicative of financial plasticity, new connections between agriculture and commerce. Those Southland sheep probably passed through at least six hands and

130 Harrison, 'Roads and Bridges'.
131 Harrison, 'Roads and Bridges'; John C. Gibson, 'The Baronies and Owners of Sauchie and Bannockburn', *Transactions of the Stirling Natural History and Archaeological Society*, 56 (1934), 61–129, at pp. 127–8.

might have travelled hundreds of miles before final sale. Farmers were no longer just serving local markets, and it was only in this way that the producers could respond to the ultimate driver of change, rising population. However, other sources and methods would be required to elucidate those links.

Adoption of change was uneven across the area. Southland sheep were most important in the hills. The drier eastern carse had more sophisticated crop rotations than the western, even in the sixteenth century. Moreover, some farms or estates adopted change more quickly than others. Moss clearance, beginning at Kersie, spread only gradually, first on the eastern carse where land values were higher, and only later to the west. The impetus for liming seems to have come sometimes from landlords, sometimes from tenants. Usage always depended on local availability of lime – via road or river, from local or remote sources. The upshot was to create what may seem like a confused mosaic of change and stasis.

But the confusion was more apparent than real. The witnesses give rational reasons why some people were reluctant to invest in Southland sheep – cost, risk and the existence of a better alternative. Others were, surely, making equally rational choices: why adopt new methods if the old yielded adequate returns, at less cost and with less risk? This, implicitly, was the riposte of the tenants of the Carse of Falkirk, criticised by Wight in the 1770s for their conservative approach. Such an approach eventually became untenable, but it was not irrational at the time.[132] Many costs came early in a big project which might then take decades to mature. The tenant farmers of Stirlingshire left no eloquent statements about 'improvement'; they seem to have understood the opportunities that change might bring, but also the barriers to bringing it about.

---

132 Wight, *Husbandry in Scotland*, vol. 2, pp. 352–3.

9

What Were the Fiars Prices Used For?

T. C. Smout

The old minister had died of drink ... and his last words were, so the story went, *and what might the feare's prices be today?*
          – Lewis Grassic Gibbon, *Cloud Howe* (1933), ch. 1

Fiars prices have long been appreciated as an analytical tool by Scottish economic historians, who have used them to construct price series for grain and meal, and to enable studies in market integration.[1] But the question has seldom been asked in any depth – what were they originally for? How were the fiars used by contemporaries?

Let us first remind ourselves of what the fiars prices were. They apparently emerge in the sixteenth century. Gemmill and Mayhew's account of Scottish medieval prices makes no mention of them, but there is a passing reference in the Register of the Great Seal for 1524 to an annual price known as 'le feir' having been used in the Glasgow region for at least ten years beforehand.[2] They were intended to be a factual statement of the average market price of various grains (and of meal) within a county, since the preceding harvest. They were normally 'struck' (calculated) by a legal process before a court sitting in February. They are of uncertain origin: the word 'fiar' is accepted to be allied to 'forum', and to mean

---

1 Rosalind Mitchison, 'The Movements of Scottish Corn Prices in the Seventeenth and Eighteenth Centuries', *EcHR*, 2nd ser., 18 (1965), 278–91; M. W. Flinn (ed.), *Scottish Population History from the Seventeenth Century to the 1930s* (Cambridge, 1977); A. J. S. Gibson and T. C. Smout, *Prices, Food and Wages in Scotland 1550–1780* (Cambridge, 1995), 66–129; A. J. S. Gibson and T. C. Smout, 'Regional Prices and Market Regions: The Evolution of the Early Scottish Grain Market', *EcHR*, 2nd ser., 48 (1995), 258–82.

2 Elizabeth Gemmill and Nicholas Mayhew, *Changing Values in Medieval Scotland: A Study of Prices, Money and Weights and Measures* (Cambridge, 1995); *RMS*, vol. 3, no. 271.

'market', so 'fiars price' means 'market price'.[3] Their main legal basis was custom and practice; neither the Scottish parliament, nor, after 1707, the British parliament, ever legislated to make fiars mandatory. However, the fiars acquired a firm institutional basis through becoming attached to various other administrative and commercial procedures. This chapter will investigate those procedures.

Sixteenth-century sources refer to fiars being struck by Commissary Courts, but later the surviving fiars seem invariably to have been drawn up in the Sheriff Courts. For a time in the seventeenth century, Commissary and Sheriff fiars seem sometimes to have been in existence together. Although there are no surviving examples of rival lists, in a case involving the parish of Edrom in Berwickshire in 1696 the Commissary fiars were preferred over the Sheriff fiars because the dispute involved the sale of teinds.[4] The earliest extant fiars series is one for Fife, for the period 1556–86, followed by a gap until 1619. More series follow the reform of the teinds in the 1630s, but only after 1708 do they become general for Scottish lowland counties.[5]

In the eighteenth century, after the Union, fiars were regulated by an Act of Sederunt of the Court of Session of 1723 proposing (but not insisting upon) the use before the Sheriff of a jury of fifteen men, of whom eight should be heritors, whose duty was to report the market price.[6] Under the superior court's direct authority, a Court of Teinds replaced the Commissary Courts in dealing with stipend augmentations and disputes, and nothing more is heard of Commissary fiars thereafter.

In 1771 the Court of Session upheld and even commended the Sheriff of Haddington in his alternative method of striking the fiars. Instead of summoning a jury, he summoned between sixty and eighty 'buyers and sellers' of grain, examined them upon oath as to the actual prices at which they had bought and sold, and calculated an average price from this data. He also added 2½ per cent to the prices, on the understanding that grain was usually sold wholesale on six months' credit and that the initial prices gathered in evidence were ready-money prices. The court opined that the Haddington fiars were generally recognised as 'more accurate

---

3   *The Compact Scottish National Dictionary*, ed. William Grant and David D. Murison (2 vols, Aberdeen, 1986), vol. 1, p. 271; *DOST*, s.v. feir, n.; *Scottish National Dictionary* (online at www.dsl.ac.uk), s.v. fiar, n[2].

4   John Connell, *A Treatise on the Law of Scotland respecting Tithes and the Stipends of the Parochial Clergy*, 2nd edn (2 vols, Edinburgh, 1830), vol. 1, p. 431; George Paterson, *Historical Account of Fiars in Scotland* (Edinburgh, 1852), p. 7.

5   The most comprehensive collection is in Gibson and Smout, *Prices, Food and Wages*, pp. 82–129, but there is significant additional material in NRS, CS96/1/111/1–7.

6   Court of Session, *Acts of Sederunt of the Lords of Council and Session* (Edinburgh, 1811), p. 278.

SHERIFF FIARS.

ABERDEEN.

CROPS.	WHEAT.		BEAR.		OATS.		MEAL.		PEASE or BEANS.	
	s.	d.	s.	d.	s.	d.	s.	d.	s.	d.
1 Crop 1756	21	—	16	8	13	4	15	—	15	—
2 57	18	4	15	—	10	6	13	8	14	2
3 58	14	—	10	—	8	$10\frac{8}{12}$	8	4	10	—
4 59	12	—	9	6	6	4	7	4	7	4
5 1760	12	6	8	6	7	—	7	$9\frac{4}{12}$	8	4
6 61	13	4	9	6	7	6	8	$10\frac{8}{12}$	8	4
7 62	17	—	15	—	13	4	15	4	13	4
8 63	14	—	13	4	10	4	10	8	13	4
9 64	16	8	14	—	11	8	13	4	13	4
10 65	18	—	16	8	13	4	15	10	13	4
11 66	20	—	18	4	13	4	15	2	14	2
12 67	20	—	15	—	11	8	13	—	13	4
13 68	17	—	11	8	9	8	11	3	13	4
14 69	15	—	12	6	6	8	11	8	13	4
15 1770	17	6	14	—	12	—	14	4	13	4
16 71	21	—	15	6	14	—	16	—	14	—
17 72	21	8	18	6	14	6	16	8	14	6
18 73	21	—	16	—	15	—	15	6	14	6
19 74	20	3	17	6	15	—	16	8	16	—
20 75	16	6	15	6	12	6	14	—	15	—
21 1776	16	—	10	6	10	—	10	4	10	—
Total	362	9	293	2	236	$6\frac{8}{12}$	270	9	268	—
General Average.	17	$3\frac{1}{12}$	13	$11\frac{6}{12}$	11	$9\frac{2}{12}$	12	$10\frac{8}{12}$	12	$9\frac{1}{12}$
Av. of first 7 years.	15	$5\frac{5}{12}$	12	$0\frac{3}{12}$	9	$6\frac{8}{12}$	10	$10\frac{10}{12}$	10	$11\frac{3}{12}$
Av. of next 7 years.	17	$2\frac{10}{12}$	14	6	10	$11\frac{4}{12}$	12	$11\frac{10}{12}$	13	$5\frac{4}{12}$
Av. of last 7 years.	19	$1\frac{6}{12}$	15	$4\frac{3}{12}$	13	$3\frac{5}{12}$	14	$9\frac{5}{12}$	13	$10\frac{10}{12}$
Av. of the 7 cheapest	14	$1\frac{5}{12}$	10	$5\frac{1}{12}$	8	$6\frac{4}{12}$	9	$2\frac{5}{12}$	10	$1\frac{1}{12}$
Av. of the 7 middling	17	$10\frac{3}{12}$	14	8	11	$2\frac{3}{12}$	13	$6\frac{10}{12}$	13	$11\frac{3}{12}$
Av. of the 7 highest.	19	$10\frac{2}{12}$	16	$9\frac{5}{12}$	14	$0\frac{10}{12}$	15	$10\frac{6}{12}$	14	$3\frac{1}{12}$

3 E

FIGURE 9.1. This table is an example of how fiars prices were presented in the eighteenth century. Prices were set each year, in shillings and pence per boll – a measure of dry capacity, equivalent to about 140 litres. There were prices for wheat, bere, oats, oatmeal, and peas and beans (these last two being priced together). Alexander Bald's book, published in 1780, listed the fiars prices in each county for each year from 1756 to 1776 inclusive. This page shows the fiars prices of Aberdeenshire.

Source: Alexander Bald, *The Farmer and Corn-Dealer's Assistant … To which are added, tables of all the fiars in Scotland for twenty-one years from 1756 …* (Edinburgh, 1780), p. 393. Image reproduced by the kind permission of the National Library of Scotland.

than those of any other county in Scotland', noting that contracts were even made in other counties with reference to the Haddington fiars.[7]

A case of 1760 sheds further light on the relationship between these procedures and economic interests. A group of feuars in Kincardineshire held lands from the burgh of Aberdeen, paying feu duties that consisted of a set quantity of grain, to be converted into money at the fiars prices. In 1760 they raised a suspension of their payment before the Court of Session, claiming that the fiars prices had been set 'extravagantly high', and that 'the majority of the jury were composed of farmers, millers, or maltmen, who might have an interest to raise the price of the commodity in which they dealt'. They cited the Act of Sederunt of 1723, which, they claimed, required a majority of the jury to be landed men. However, the defence claimed that 'this branch of the act, as to the majority being heritors, is gone into disuse, or rather never was in use in many counties'. The court ruled against the feuars, possibly indicating their concurrence with the defence, though they may also have been swayed by the defence's alternative argument that the feuars' proper remedy was to sue the sheriff rather than to challenge the burgh's demand for payment.[8]

As we shall see, fiars got a new lease of life in the nineteenth century, when their accuracy also became the subject of various investigations. The business of striking the fiars was not finally abolished until 1973. There is no close parallel to the fiars in England nor (apparently) in any of Scotland's Continental neighbours. Many pre-modern countries and towns had assizes to regulate the price of grain, as Scotland also did, but no others seem to have had a mechanism systematically to *report* the price, at least not before the nineteenth century.

* * *

The Court of Session in 1723 was clear on the fiars' basic purpose: to 'liquidate' (i.e. to convert) the average price of different kinds of grains into their money equivalents, for 'all legal purposes in which such calculations may be required'.[9] So what legal purposes were these?

Apparently, one of the earliest uses of the fiars drawn up by the Commissary Courts was to facilitate rental payments to the proprietors of church lands (clerical or lay) in money rather than in kind, perhaps because many churches had land remote from storage barns. Similarly, they were used to facilitate the conversion of teinds to cash, where this

---

7 William Maxwell Morison, *The Decisions of the Court of Session, from its First Institution to the Present Time, Digested under Proper Heads, in the Form of a Dictionary* (42 vols bound in 21 (citations to these 21), Edinburgh, 1801–11), vol. 11, pp. 4420–4; cf. Gibson and Smout, *Prices, Food and Wages*, pp. 72–3.

8 Morison, *Decisions*, vol. 11, pp. 4415–16.

9 Court of Session, *Acts of Sederunt*, p. 278.

was required by the holders of teinds, especially prior to 1633.[10] Later, the most conspicuous purpose of the fiars prices, at least from the 1630s, was to put a money value on feu duties and other obligations reckoned in kind that were owed to the crown. Receiving rents in kind rather than cash was probably always expensive and inconvenient for the crown. The Exchequer compiled its own fiars from returns from the sheriffs, making assumptions of its own about those counties (mainly in the Highlands) that did not strike fiars, and giving a handsome discount to payees. These Exchequer fiars exist as a complete series from 1708, but were in existence certainly from 1634.[11]

Other uses of the fiars were many and various. According to Lauder of Fountainhall in 1677, the main purpose of fiars (other than by the crown) was to place a money value on arrears of rents, due in kind but undelivered to lords. Burt, writing from near Inverness around 1730, similarly said that the fiars were used for everything relating to rents and bargains, and if a tenant could not meet his obligations in kind 'then that which is wanting may be converted into money'.[12] The Baron Court Book of Urie in May 1617 provides an example of how this worked. James Mancur was pursued for the monetary value of three bolls of meal for the past crop of 1615 'conform to the feir of the zeir': but he was also expected to pay in kind at the next meeting of the court what he owed of the current crop of 1616.[13] It was clearly unreasonable to expect tenants to pay all their arrears of rent in kind, especially after a bad harvest. Arrears of teinds, similarly, were valued in money by means of the fiars.[14] However, a Court of Session decision of 1682 ruled that tenants had to pay arrears 'at the neighbouring prices, though exceeding the fiars'. The only exception was if they had formerly offered to deliver their victual at the time and the landlord had not taken up the offer; then 'they were only liable for the fiars'.[15]

10 David Littlejohn, 'Some General Observations on Aberdeenshire Fiars Courts and Prices', *Miscellany of the New Spalding Club*, vol. 2 (Aberdeen: New Spalding Club, 1906), pp. 3–4.

11 M. P. Brown, *Supplement to the Dictionary of the Decisions of the Court of Session*, vol. 3 (Edinburgh, 1826), Decisions of the Lords of Council and Session as reported by Sir John Lauder of Fountainhall, p. 133; Nenion Elliot, *The Position of the Fiars Prices* (Edinburgh, 1879), p. 5; NRS, E20/34 lists Exchequer fiars for crops 1634–48.

12 Brown, *Supplement*, p. 132; *Burt's Letters from the North of Scotland*, ed. C. W. J. Withers (Edinburgh, 1998), pp. 215–16.

13 *Court Book of the Barony of Urie in Kincardineshire 1604–1747*, ed. D. G. Barron (Edinburgh: SHS, 1892), pp. 22–3.

14 William Forbes, *A Treatise of Church-Lands and Tithes* (Edinburgh, 1705), pp. 356, 442.

15 Morison, *Decisions*, vol. 11, p. 4413.

Other examples of how the fiars were used include calculating the money value of debts in kind left after death or in bankruptcy proceedings, by an act of 1621, and fixing the price to be paid for corn by government soldiers as enforced by Commissioners of Supply in the shires, by an act of 1681.[16] The Mar and Kellie papers contain a table of the fiars prices in different places between 1756 and 1776, used to regulate the opening and shutting of ports to facilitate the Corn Laws.[17] The fiars were used to pay a woman's annuity in 1686. She was a liferenter (presumably the widow of a previous laird), and she wanted to be paid in money, not at the fiars prices, but at the higher prices for which the laird had actually sold grain that year. The Court of Session declared, however, that she was entitled only to the fiars price: after all, they asked, what if the laird had sold at a *lower* price than the fiars?[18] In 1734, though, the court decided a similar case differently: 'the current prices must be the rule', and the fiars should be used only when there was no evidence of current prices.[19] In 1704 a heritor was sued by the widow of the minister of Cluny in Perthshire for arrears of her husband's stipend as valued by the fiars.[20]

A Stirlingshire legal case of 1697 raised issues of local price variation that were debated at length before the Court of Session. A preferential creditor could obtain possession of a debtor's whole estate, and then use the proceeds to repay other creditors. If this involved the preferential creditor selling victual, 'at what rate they were to count, whether for the highest prices any neighbours in that country [i.e. county] got for their victual, or at the Sheriff's fiars, or at the price they sold the victual at themselves?' The other creditors alleged that 'the fiars ought not to be the rule here; because they are made for the common victual of the shire; whereas this lying in Bothkennar, or the Carse of Stirling, is better than in the rest of the shire'. The court ruled that if the other creditors could show that the preferential creditor had received a higher price then they could claim that, but otherwise they should 'accept of the fiars'.[21]

In 1712 the brewers of Edinburgh raised a process before the Court of Session alleging that the Sheriff Court of Edinburgh had set the fiars too high, and without calling witnesses to an inquest. Fountainhall noted the brewers' claim that they 'had a special interest, for they had bought many gentlemen's victual without any other price but the fiars'. So the brewers were acting as a guild, limiting competition through cooperative purchasing.[22]

16 RPS, 1621/6/19, 1681/7/23.
17 NRS, GD124/18/81.
18 Morison, *Decisions*, vol. 11, p. 4413.
19 Morison, *Decisions*, vol. 11, p. 4415.
20 Elliot, *Position of the Fiars Prices*, p. 7; NRS, GD124/6/156.
21 Morison, *Decisions*, vol. 11, pp. 4414–15.
22 Morison, *Decisions*, vol. 9, p. 7463.

Lord Bankton in 1752 regarded the fiars, not as something used routinely in any specific annual procedure, but as a means of resolving disputes over occasional late payments in grain: 'where a party liable in a quantity of grain or victual fails in delivering or tendering it in due time'. He summarised the procedure for striking fiars as it had been laid down in 1723 (mentioned above), and added that the party injured by late payment had the option either 'to content himself with the fiar-prices, which are commonly struck of the middle kind, neither at the highest or lowest rates', or to 'insist for the highest prices, which he will be found entitled to, unless the defenders had a probable ground for their deficiency'.[23]

One interesting case was also one of the earliest involving fiars of which we have record. In 1574, a case came before the Aberdeen Sheriff Court in which one farmer sued another for theft of a yoke of oxen two years before, demanding not only the return of the animals but the price of six firlots of meal for each of the past two years, as ascertained by the fiars, as the value of the work which they would have performed.[24] This illustrates a society preferring to value things in kind rather than cash. At the time one might point to the exceptional levels of monetary devaluation in sixteenth-century Scotland as the root cause, but it was to be a persistent characteristic of Scottish life, as we shall see.

Further early material comes from the Chronicle of Fortingall, a local chronicle from Highland Perthshire. This mentions fiars of meal and bere for 1560, fiars of meal for 1563, fiars of bere for 1569, fiars of meal for 1570, and fiars of bere and malt for 1575. The summer of 1563, in particular, was 'rycht deyr viz. the boll of maill v merk and the feyr of meill in mony partis iiii merk and the lady of Straythort tuk v merk for the boll of maill for the feyr'.[25] The phrase 'in mony partis' indicates that there was no single uniform valuation for the whole of Perthshire. The lady of Strathord (in Lowland Perthshire) was Janet Ruthven, daughter of William, 2nd Lord Ruthven, and wife of John Crichton of Strathord. She was evidently selling oatmeal at a high price of which the chronicler disapproved, but why this was a 'fiar' price does not appear.

* * *

23 Andrew McDouall, Lord Bankton, *An Institute of the Laws of Scotland* (3 vols, Edinburgh, 1751–53; repr. Edinburgh: Stair Society, 1993–95), vol. 2, pp. 557–8.

24 Littlejohn, 'Some General Observations', pp. 3–4.

25 'The Chronicle of Fortirgall', *The Black Book of Taymouth*, ed. Cosmo Innes (Edinburgh: Bannatyne Club, 1855), pp. 129, 131–2, 136, 140 (quotation at pp. 131–2). For more on this episode see Julian Goodare, 'Weather and Farming through the Eyes of a Sixteenth-Century Highland Peasant', Chapter 4 above in the present volume.

What about fiars and the payment of teinds? Before the act of 1633, teinds were frequently paid in kind as well as being reckoned in kind, but this could be an inconvenience to the farmer, who might have to wait until the holder of the teind had uplifted his share of the crop from the harvest field.[26] Where barns were far off, this might also be an inconvenience to the teind holder, if he had obtained right to the teind from a distant church. There was therefore an incentive to both parties to pay teinds in money according to the fiars. In 1633, the College of Glasgow had accepted cash in lieu of teind grain from a farm at Govan for the past thirty or forty years, but now wanted to claim the teind bolls in grain again – a wish contested by the farmer.[27] After the important act of that year, which reformed the system by valuing teinds at one-fifth of rents, and obliged all titulars or tacksmen to sell to heritors at nine years' purchase, teinding in kind gradually fell into disuse.

Given all these many and various uses to which fiars were put, one might expect to find that good use had been made of them to facilitate two other important changes impelling Scotland towards a fully monetised modern world. The first would have been to allow the calculation of payment in money of ministers' stipends that were reckoned in grain or meal, the second similarly to facilitate payment in money of agricultural rents that were also reckoned in grain or meal. Rentals reckoned in kind might not always mean rents paid in kind, if the value of the grain calculated by the fiars was in practice paid in money, as a halfway-house to fully monetised rentals.

It therefore comes as a surprise to find before 1800 relatively few unequivocal examples of the fiars being used to calculate payment of ministers' stipends, and none in estate papers of fiars being used to convert rents in kind to rents in cash. It is of course always difficult to prove a negative, and, as we shall see, there is every reason to think that the second was not in fact unusual.

To take the stipends first, the legislation of 1633 fixed the minimum stipend at 800 merks Scots or 8 chalders of victual. A firlot was roughly a sack; there were 4 firlots to a boll and 16 bolls to a chalder, so 512 sacks would make up the minimum stipend if paid in kind. Today we can calculate this as equivalent to the contents of a little over 140 standard-size Edinburgh wheelie bins.[28] It was common in the seventeenth and eighteenth centuries for some ministers to be paid in cash,

---

26 Littlejohn, 'Some General Observations', pp. 3–4. Teinds were also due on other produce, such as fish, wool and young animals. However, these teinds, sometimes known as 'lesser teinds', had no connection with fiars prices.

27 A. A. Cormack, *Teinds and Agriculture: An Historical Survey* (Oxford, 1930), pp. 121–2.

28 I owe the idea of measuring in wheelie bins to Norah Carlin's paper at the conference that preceded this volume.

some in kind, but most in a mixture of both. To be paid entirely in kind might seem an inconvenience, as it would imply storage enough to keep the grain as well as willingness for the minister to enter the market to sell what his household could not eat. Yet one can see in the former Church of Scotland manse in Anstruther, which was built in the 1590s, and also in the so-called Prior's Lodging in Pittenweem, probably dating from the early sixteenth century, how the ground floor might be wholly taken up with vaulted storage. As late as 1783 it was the law that a manse should include a barn, stable and byre, and in 1806 we hear of a new manse at Culsalmond in Aberdeenshire with a barn 42½ feet by 12 feet and a grain loft 13½ feet by 12 feet.[29] It was said that, after the Union when the Court of Teinds was established, most ministers preferred to be paid in kind anyway, no doubt because this gave some security in times of grain shortage like the previous decade, when a fixed money income might not have enough purchasing power.[30]

There is a snapshot of ministers insisting on cash payments in the 1630s, both using and abusing the fiars. Robert Baillie, minister of Kilwinning, lamented the moral shortcomings of his fellow-ministers in January 1637, and had this to say about their grasping approach to their stipends:

> Allace! We make our self more and more unsavorie daylie; when we have gottin our augmentationes, we are so severe in exacting, that we are a common talking. The 34 year of God wes a sore year to our labourers; bot the 35 yeir wes the worst that in this last age wes seen. The Commissar feirs wes ten pound for meill and bear; bot sundrie of our brethren are charging, to the shame of us all, for twelve and above.[31]

This indicates that ministers were not necessarily bound to the fiars (Commissary fiars are specified), but could demand higher rates of conversion.

The 'Old Statistical Account' of the 1790s gives extensive details of the value of stipends, usually again reckoned in both cash and kind, but the information seldom extends to how they were actually paid. The possibility to be considered is that at least some stipends were reckoned in kind, but paid in cash according to the fiars. A handful of examples indicate that this could have been the case even before the Union: Jedburgh in 1668, Inveresk in 1699 and Mertoun in Berwickshire

---

29 John Erskine, *Principles of the Laws of Scotland*, 6th edn (Edinburgh, 1783), bk 1, p. 52; *Farmers' Magazine*, vol. 7 (Edinburgh, 1806), p. 488.

30 Connell, *Treatise*, vol. 1, p. 422 – though on p. 371 the same authority said of a case in 1698 that 'at this period and for a long time afterwards, a victual stipend was not thought more valuable than one in money'.

31 Baillie to William Spang, 29 January 1637, Robert Baillie, *Letters and Journals 1637–1662*, ed. David Laing (2 vols, Edinburgh: Bannatyne Club, 1841–42), vol. 1, p. 5.

in 1705.[32] A search of the *OSA* volumes for Fife, Lothian, Lanarkshire and Renfrewshire revealed only six unequivocal instances of the use of the fiars in this way: in Inveresk (again), in Rutherglen, and in four parishes (Cadder, East Kilbride, East Monkland and Renfrew) where the College of Glasgow was titular of the teinds.[33]

William Forbes cited a case in 1699 (a year of famine) where a minister successfully insisted upon being paid the actual market price received by the debtor, and not the lower fiars price, for the value of the stipend bolls that he was owed; but this was balanced by another case in 1705 where the minister was made to accept the fiars for payment of a similar debt.[34] A case of 1668 determined that feuars who were obliged to pay a minister's stipend in kind were entitled to compensation in money from the teind-master, with the money equivalent being determined by the fiars.[35]

The Court of Teinds in 1708, in adjudicating disputes and awarding augmentations, used, instead of the fiars, its own conversion rate of 100 merks Scots per chalder of victual, which seems to have been the market price at the time. The rate later became £100 Scots per chalder, which, said John Connell (writing in 1830), 'continued to be the Court conversion until very lately, although the market price of victual became much higher'.[36] Connell added that the Court of Teinds had recently adopted the practice of insisting on the use of the standard Linlithgow grain measures when modifying stipends, even though the fiars prices 'generally' used local measures in those counties which had distinct measures.[37] Even assessment by the fiars could, according to the minister of Ratho, underestimate the market value of victual by 20 per cent – about twice what Gibson and Smout concluded was the average fiars' underestimation of the market price. One can understand why payment in kind remained acceptable and popular among ministers, especially in another decade of rising grain prices at the end of the century.[38] Sometimes payment was only in cash (as in Penicuik and the second charge of St Andrews), but there are far more numerous instances where at least part-payment in kind can be assumed or inferred.[39]

---

32 Connell, *Treatise*, vol. 1, p. 431.
33 *OSA*, vol. 2, p. 303 (Inveresk, p. 25); vol. 7, pp. 74–5 (Cadder, pp. 478–9), 414–15 (East Kilbride, pp. 427–8), 516 (New or East Monkland, p. 272), 869 (Renfrew, p. 174).
34 Forbes, *Treatise*, p. 427.
35 Forbes, *Treatise*, p. 488.
36 Connell, *Treatise*, vol. 1, pp. 422–3.
37 Connell, *Treatise*, vol. 1, pp. 436–7. For a list and discussion of the local measures see Gibson and Smout, *Prices, Food and Wages*, pp. 372–5.
38 *OSA*, vol. 2, pp. 418–19 (Ratho, pp. 264–5).
39 *OSA*, vol. 2, p. 372 (Penicuik, p. 423); vol. 10, p. 725 (St Andrews and St Leonard's, p. 210).

Ministers sometimes showed a lively sense of what they were owed in kind, and sharp awareness of the grain market. In the National Museum of Scotland is a square oaken box without a lid, holding 52 cubic inches, constructed by the Rev. Alexander Bryce, minister of Kirknewton in Midlothian, 1744–86, and a keen mathematician, 'for the purpose of tallying his stipend'.[40] In 1794 the minister of Kinnedar in Moray complained about the type of oats in which his stipend was paid, observing that grey horse oats were unmarketable and no longer grown in the area except by the heritor to pay the minister. He wanted white oats – but he was told that, at best, he had to accept in white oats the value of the grey oats, as the original stipulation of 1634 had been to pay in grey oats and that could not be changed.[41]

* * *

If it is hard to find documented cases of the fiars being used to pay stipends at this time, it is harder still to find such evidence for paying rents in this way, unless those rents were in arrears as already mentioned. Even the most intense scrutiny of estate papers throws up no more than sporadic and tangential references. Muir Johnstone's examination of rents in East Lothian and Lanarkshire, from 1670 and through the eighteenth century, mentions only an instance at Newhailes in 1745 when fiars were used to reckon compensation for seven deficient bolls of grain in one rent payment, and another in 1756 when five tenants of Saltoun offered to buy surplus wheat from the laird 'at the fiars of the year'. More significant is that, from the 1770s, Ramsay of Ochtertyre in Perthshire set cash rents according to the fiars for certain quantities of oatmeal so that they should 'in some measure reflect the price of oatmeal'.[42]

There was a massive switch in agricultural rentals from payment in kind to payment in money from the middle of the eighteenth century onwards. However, there is little indication in the sources normally used by historians to suggest that the fiars were used to facilitate or to cushion this transfer. Rather, a straight change to cash was apparently seen as the simplest way of increasing gross rents, incentivising tenants and ensuring future flexibility.

Yet the law of Scotland in the eighteenth century was clear that when a tenant was obliged by the terms of his lease to pay his rent in grain, he had to offer it in grain; but, if the landlord refused it, he would be entitled instead to receive the value in money *according to the fiars*. Cases involving

---

40 R. D. Connor and A. D. C. Simpson, *Weights and Measures in Scotland: A European Perspective* (Edinburgh, 2004), pp. 376–7.
41 Connell, *Treatise*, vol. 1, pp. 437–8.
42 Muir Johnstone, 'Farm Rents and Improvement: East Lothian and Lanarkshire 1670–1830', *AgHR*, 57:1 (2009), 37–57, at pp. 44–5.

the landlord receiving the value of a grain rent in money apparently occur quite often even in the later sixteenth century, via the device of the lord selling the grain back to the tenant, though it is unclear if the fiars were involved at this date. That the fiars must be involved was a principle established by a legal case in 1682.[43] Such a transaction would not appear in rentals, though it might in estate accounts. This suggests that the effective monetisation of rents might well have begun to take place much earlier than historians usually suppose.

This explains how Adam Smith in *The Wealth of Nations* (1776) could describe 'the institution of the public fiars', and then add that 'this institution rendered it sufficiently safe for the tenant, and much more convenient for the landlord, to convert as they call it, the corn rent, rather at what should happen to be the price of the fiars of each year, than at any certain fixed price'.[44] Smith's approving reference to the fiars prices, along with his statement that the price of grain was 'a more accurate statement of value than any other commodity or set of commodities', clearly contributed to the remarkable revival in the importance of fiars in the nineteenth century. This had two aspects: in the payment of rents and in the payment of stipends. By 1834 it was said that the value of property 'in rents, stipends, feu duties, out-going crops and bargains in victual', set by the fiars, far exceeded that determined in all other Scottish courts in the course of a year.[45]

Let us consider rents first. During the period 1780–1815, and especially during the Napoleonic Wars, inflation of rents was accompanied both by more moderate inflation in the price of grain and by bigger increases in output, so that both landlords and farmers (or at least those landlords and farmers in a position to supply the market) enjoyed considerable prosperity. Enclosure, the building of new farmhouses and steadings, improvements to transport, and other structural changes in the countryside were rapid.[46] With the coming of peace, agricultural price deflation set in, despite the efforts of the landed classes to keep prices high through the Corn Laws. Tenants began to have a hard time to meet their obligations, and landlords to retain their tenants.

One reaction to this, advocated in a pamphlet of 1815 that approvingly quoted Adam Smith on the benefit of the fiars, was to introduce 'corn rents'. These were rents entirely or partly reckoned in grain, but

---

43 Bankton, *Institute*, vol. 2, p. 102; Ian Whyte, *Agriculture and Society in Seventeenth-Century Scotland* (Edinburgh, 1979), p. 179.

44 Adam Smith, *The Wealth of Nations* (Everyman edition, London, 1957), vol. 1, pp. 166–7, 171.

45 *Report of the General Assembly's Committee on the Fiars*, Parliamentary Papers, 1834, vol. 49, p. 5.

46 T. M. Devine, *The Transformation of Rural Scotland: Social Change and the Agrarian Economy 1660–1815* (Edinburgh, 1994).

paid in cash according to the county fiars prices, though usually with a maximum and a minimum cut-off point and an element of fixed cash price as well.[47] Corn rents had been initiated by the Earl of Galloway on his estate in Wigtownshire in 1814, offering to all his tenants who had taken farms between 1806 and 1812 a reduction of one-third of their rent for 1814 and 1815, calculated by the wheat fiars for Midlothian and Wigtown, and fixing new rents in accordance with the price of wheat, subject to a maximum and a minimum.[48] Wigtownshire was not much of a wheat-growing area, but the Earl evidently accepted Smith's belief that the price of corn ultimately governed all other prices.

Corn rents, as defined above, were subsequently adopted much more widely in the grain-growing districts of Lothian, Fife and Angus. They were expected by some to spread even more widely. In 1817 a report on how the fiars were drawn up in Lanarkshire stated that the question was becoming of ever greater public importance, partly because the fiars will 'probably within a short period become the only standard by which land rents will be paid throughout the kingdom'. Due to volatility of grain prices, now 'no landlord is willing to rent his property out, nor any tenant to take a lease for long, unless a medium can be found other than money'.[49] These expectations proved too sanguine, but certainly in 1825 it was said that corn rents were 'becoming every day more common' and had been 'very extensively introduced in some of the best cultivated parts of Scotland'; they were long-standing practice in the Carse of Gowrie and were 'now generally adopted' in East Lothian.[50] Testifying before a parliamentary committee in 1833, Thomas Oliver, a Midlothian farmer and valuer, said that whereas fifteen years ago 'there was nothing known but fixed money rents', now 'scarcely any prudent tenant in the corn-growing districts' would take land without reference to the price of grain. On the other hand, David Low, professor of agriculture at Edinburgh University, considered that the popularity of grain rents was then falling, especially in the Border counties of Berwickshire and Roxburghshire where farmers would not offer grain rents because the bulk of their rent was paid from the profits of stock and they 'prefer a fixed claim on the part of their landlords to a fluctuating one'.[51]

---

47 [Anon.,] *Plan for Regulating the Rents of Land in Scotland with Equal Safety both to Landlord and Tenant* (Cupar, 1815), cites Smith on p. 25.

48 *Farmers' Magazine*, vol. 17 (Edinburgh, 1816), pp. 35–9.

49 *Report of a Committee of Commission of Supply for Lanarkshire … [on] the Fiars of Grain* (Edinburgh, 1817), pp. 10–11.

50 John Hugh Maclean, *Remarks on Fiars Prices and Produce Rents* (Edinburgh, 1825), pp. 1, 50.

51 *Report of the Select Committee on Agriculture with Minutes of Evidence taken before them*, Parliamentary Papers, 1833, pp. 122–4, 537.

Tentative attempts to introduce a similar system on the estates of the Duke of Norfolk, in Ireland, Worcestershire and Gloucestershire, had failed because of the 'want of an authentic standard of value' equivalent to the fiars outside Scotland.[52] As late as 1852 Neilson Hancock listed the practice of basing at least half the annual rent on grain prices as one of the advantages of Lothian husbandry not found outside Scotland.[53] But after that time the fiars apparently went into terminal decline. In the second half of the nineteenth century, as grain prices fell, they came less and less to decide the fortunes of Scottish farming compared to livestock and dairy prices, so it made no sense to stick any longer with the system of setting rents via the fiars.

* * *

There were in the nineteenth century other still more novel uses to which the fiars were put. Here it may help to begin with a review of the fiars' purposes by a Church committee in 1895. This focused on fiars' use in determining stipends (to be discussed in the next section), but also collected information, county by county, about 'other interests' served by the fiars. The committee reported:

> In every county there are peculiarities of tenure and of burdens on property which it would need much and widely-collected evidence to state exactly. On the whole, this appears to be true, that since 1831 a great change has passed over the practice in Scotland, and that very few farm-rents are now paid according to the fiars. Such rents are mentioned as existing to some little extent in Ayr, Caithness, Elgin, Fife, Haddington (six farms), Kincardine, Linlithgow, Perth, Orkney (to a greater extent), Stirling, and Wigtown. In some few counties – such as Berwick, Clackmannan (on one estate), Dumbarton, Forfar, Kinross, and Stirling – old feu-duties exist that depend on the fiars. Crown-duties, thirlage, multures, are also mentioned in parts. The chief interest, apart from ministers, is found in the valuations of crop which are made between outgoing and incoming tenants on farms. These in many parts of Scotland seem to be based on the fiars.[54]

This confirms that the 'corn rents' experiment of the early nineteenth century, in which rents had been linked to fiars, did not survive beyond that period. But it mentions various other uses of the fiars prices. Not all of these can be pursued in the present chapter; in particular, the issue of

52 *Select Committee*, p. 537; Maclean, *Remarks*, p. 49.
53 W. Neilson Hancock, *What are the Causes of the Prosperous Agriculture in the Lothians of Scotland?* (Edinburgh, 1852).
54 David Hunter, 'Report of the Committee on Fiars Prices to the General Assembly of the Church of Scotland', *Reports on the Schemes of the Church of Scotland for the Year 1895* (Edinburgh, 1895), pp. 1037–78, at p. 1061.

'valuations of crop' must be left to future research. However, something can be said on some nineteenth-century uses of fiars prices.

Thirlage to mills, by which tenants were obliged to bring their grain to be ground in the landlord's mill, was abolished in 1799. Commutation arrangements were made to compensate millers for the loss of the 'multures' that tenants had been obliged to pay to them under the thirlage system. Compensation sums were set in grain, but tenants could opt to convert this into cash – using the fiars prices. This gave rise to much business in nineteenth-century Sheriff Courts. Since commutation was optional and proceeded piecemeal, fiars prices remained significant for the remainder of the century. A few tenants continued paying multures into the early twentieth century at least.[55]

In 1803, the Parochial Schools (Scotland) Act proposed that the salaries of schoolmasters should immediately be set at between 200 and 300 merks Scots (roughly £17 and £22 sterling) a year, but that after twenty-five years the fiars should be inspected in each county to see what the average price of meal had been over that period, the Court of Exchequer charged with declaring a national average, and new salaries then set so that the teachers got the equivalent of one and a half to two chalders of meal a year. Every twenty-five years thereafter a similar revision should be made until parliament decided otherwise.[56] This was a pioneering proposal to use the fiars as a kind of retail price index to ensure that salaries kept up with the standard of living, as they had plainly not been doing in the previous century. The mechanism was invoked once, in 1828, when salaries were raised in accordance with the price of corn in the previous twenty-five years, to approximately £26 to £34 a year.[57] But when during the next quarter-century the price of grain in the fiars fell substantially, no one was prepared to force a pay cut on the teachers. A series of unopposed parliamentary acts was passed until a new and differently based act was introduced in 1861.[58]

The 1803 act was the prelude to an even more direct and long-lasting use of the fiars: to set the stipends of the clergy. This came about in 1808 and lasted (for the established Church) until 1925. In this case, the principle behind the change had evidently been considered for a long time. As early as 1789 a calculation preserved in the Mar and Kellie papers showed what it would cost in money to pay stipends, calculated at various levels of notional payment in kind, across the different counties

55 Enid Gauldie, *The Scottish Country Miller 1700–1900* (Edinburgh, 1981), pp. 57–8.
56 43 Geo. III, c. 54.
57 James Kay-Shuttleworth, *Public Education* (London, 1853), pp. 339–40. I am grateful to Robert Anderson for this reference.
58 24 and 25 Vict., c. 108.

of Scotland, using the average fiars prices of the previous twenty years.[59] In 1798 the Court of Teinds departed from its long-established practice of valuing all victual at 100 merks per chalder when awarding augmentations, and in a case relating to the parish of Lamington in Lanarkshire declared that in this 'and in any similar case' the average county fiars for the past seven years should be used.[60]

The 1808 act was more thoroughgoing. It provided that, for every stipend augmented in the future, the sum should be expressed ('modified' was the term) in grain or victual, but paid in money. This money amount was initially set according to the local county fiars price averaged over the past seven years, and thereafter varied according to the current year's fiars. Once the settlement in a given parish had been made, it could not be reviewed again for twenty years. The change was stated to be necessary because payments in kind led to disputes between ministers and heritors, and because 'trafficking in grain was not quite consistent with the dignity of the clergy'. Payments in kind continued until an augmentation was applied for, but in time virtually all the stipends came to be paid in money and set in this way.[61]

That was welcome enough during the Napoleonic inflation, but in the post-war depression of grain prices there were soon complaints when stipends were reduced. In particular there was a row in Lanarkshire in 1816 about the way in which the fiars were calculated, accompanied by suspicion that a jury dominated by heritors was biasing the calculations in their own interest.[62]

From time to time thereafter in the nineteenth century, as in the 1820s, the 1850s, and the 1870s, the ministers complained of mistreatment by the system, but it was not abandoned until 1925, when the proposed merger of the Church of Scotland with the United Free Church promoted a complete reassessment of how stipends were paid.[63]

* * *

It would be a worthwhile study in its own right to consider the varying real income of the Church of Scotland clergy in the nineteenth century in relation to that of other professions and denominations. It might also be asked why the system of using the fiars was not abolished earlier, as it had been for the teachers. Part of the answer to both questions is probably

59 NRS, GD124/9/128.
60 Connell, *Treatise*, vol. 1, p. 424.
61 48 Geo. III, c. 138.
62 *Report of a Committee ... for Lanarkshire; Some Observations on the Report of the Commissioners of Supply for Lanarkshire by a Committee of the Reverend the Presbytery of Hamilton* (1817).
63 William Buchanan, *Treatise on Teinds* (Edinburgh, 1862); Elliot, *Position of the Fiars Prices*.

that the Teind Court was relatively generous in its awards of augmentations, and abandoned the idea that the total value of the stipend should be linked to 8 chalders of victual; by the end of the nineteenth century, it could be anything between 24 and 40 chalders.[64] After the Disruption of 1843 it would presumably not have been considered acceptable that the income of the established clergy should fall below that of the Free Church ministers or other presbyterian groups upheld by the generosity of committed middle-class congregations. There must have been competition between the churches at a financial level, as in every other aspect of church life.

The Church committee that enquired into the fiars in 1895 noted that, in 1831 and 1832, a previous committee had proposed a legislative reform, 'disclaiming all desire to raise or lower the fiars' but ensuring 'that they should be struck on correct principles' – which in practice meant a detailed, uniform system of rules for determining grain prices, and a reduction in local discretion and heritors' influence. The committee thought that the proposal had been dropped because the attention of the Church was absorbed by the controversy leading to the Disruption.[65] It also believed that 'the methods in use tend in the direction of keeping the fiars low', and lamented the 'fluctuations (or rather in recent years the disastrous fall) in the fiars', due to the abolition of the Corn Laws in 1846 and 'the increase in foreign imports since 1872'. Consequently, stipends had fallen by one-third between 1873 and 1893.[66] That ministers were not totally freed even in the early twentieth century from worldly worries about the price of corn is illustrated by the anxiety of the minister in *Cloud Howe* with which this chapter began.

After 1925, fiars prices played no further part in calculating clerical incomes. Nevertheless, the fiars continued to be struck annually by Sheriff Courts, and used in a variety of traditional ways. These included the calculation of feu duties payable to the crown (as had been done since at least the seventeenth century), and the reckoning of the value of standing crops when a tenancy passed from one farmer to another. They eventually ceased to be struck in 1973 as part of the reform of feu duties, and four centuries of usage, albeit often obscure usage, came to an end.[67]

64 John M. Duncan, *The Parochial Ecclesiastical Law of Scotland* (Edinburgh, 1903), p. 326.
65 Hunter, 'Report of the Committee on Fiars Prices', pp. 1044–6.
66 Hunter, 'Report of the Committee on Fiars Prices', p. 1073.
67 Thanks to the many colleagues with whom I have discussed the fiars over the years, but especially to Thomas Green, Rab Houston and Julian Goodare who have provided new information and perspectives for this chapter.

10

Agriculture and Banking in Eighteenth-Century Scotland 1695–1750

Gains Murdoch

Despite the emergence of new economic sectors, or the marked modernisation of others throughout the eighteenth century, Scotland's economy remained overwhelmingly based upon what land and livestock could provide. The Scottish agricultural sector was fundamentally changed during this period, with a whole raft of 'improvements' taking place. These boosted the productivity and profitability of the country's soil, but could also cause severe social dislocation within rural communities. Many of these alterations would not have taken place without the establishment of a formal banking system. The chartered banks provided vital capital for landowners operating in an area of the economy, and a country, which at this time suffered from a lack of liquidity.

This chapter considers the intrinsic link between the development of Scottish banking and agricultural reform. It does so by examining some of the records of the Bank of Scotland and the Royal Bank of Scotland during the first half of the eighteenth century, particularly the court minutes for both banking houses. An analysis of these sources sheds some light on the nature of agricultural improvement during a period which has been somewhat under-examined by historians, when compared with the period after 1760 when the speed of improvement increased.

The specific questions considered include the following: What proportion of bank loans went to landowners? Were landowners based in particular regions more likely to receive credit than those from other parts of the country? To what extent was money loaned to landowners used to improve their estates? These considerations are also placed within the context of Scottish economic thought, which often prioritised the modernisation of the rural economy and felt that the emerging banking sector should be geared to serve its development.

* * *

Throughout most of the eighteenth century, Scotland's economy remained overwhelmingly based upon what land and livestock could provide in spite of the emergence of new and profitable sectors, such as the tobacco and sugar trades, as well as the modernisation of linen production and other fledgling industries. One of the most comprehensive studies of the Scottish tobacco trade has asserted that, in spite of its growth, by as late as 1760 at least 80 per cent of the country's output was still generated by agriculture.[1] In this century, Scottish farming certainly did not stand still. More and more of Scotland's arable land was enclosed, planned villages were established throughout the country and countless innovations were adopted.[2] However a historiographical consensus exists which contends that prior to the 1760s the pace of this agricultural improvement was generally slow. There is a degree of disagreement as to how slow it was; some scholars, including Philipp Rössner and T. C. Smout, have argued that Scottish farming remained stagnant at this time, while Tom Devine and Ian Adams have contended that there was growth and reform but it was uneven, varying significantly from region to region and even estate to estate.[3] Improvement was held back largely by low grain prices and limited markets for produce.[4] When prices rose during the final four decades of the eighteenth century, and urbanisation accelerated, this gave lairds and tenant farmers the necessary financial incentive to invest in modernising their practices.[5]

1   Philipp Robinson Rössner, *Scottish Trade in the Wake of Union 1700–1760: The Rise of a Warehouse Economy* (Stuttgart, 2008), p. 301.

2   Christopher Whatley, *Scottish Society 1707–1830: Beyond Jacobitism, Towards Industrialisation* (Manchester, 2000), p. 237; Malcolm Gray, 'Scottish Emigration: The Social Impact of Agrarian Change in the Rural Lowlands 1775–1875', *Perspectives in American History*, 7 (1973), 95–174, at pp. 124–6; T. C. Smout, *Exploring Environmental History: Selected Essays* (Edinburgh, 2009), p. 150.

3   Rössner, *Scottish Trade in the Wake of Union*, p. 301; T. C. Smout, 'Where Had the Scottish Economy Got to by the Third Quarter of the Eighteenth Century?', in Istvan Hont and Michael Ignatieff (eds), *Wealth and Virtue: The Shaping of Political Economy in the Scottish Enlightenment* (Cambridge, 1983), pp. 45–72, at pp. 48–9; Ian Adams, 'Economic Process and the Scottish Land Surveyor', *Imago Mundi*, 27:1 (1975), 13–18, at p. 14; T. M. Devine, *The Transformation of Rural Scotland: Social Change and the Agrarian Economy 1660–1815* (Edinburgh, 1994), p. 92.

4   Rosalind Mitchison, 'The Movements of Scottish Corn Prices in the Seventeenth and Eighteenth Centuries', *EcHR*, 2nd ser., 18 (1965), 278–91; Christopher A. Whatley, 'Custom, Commerce and Lord Meadowbank: The Management of the Meal Market in Urban Scotland *c*.1740–*c*.1820', *JSHS*, 32:1 (2012), 1–27.

5   D. G. Lockhart, 'Planned Village Development in Scotland and Ireland 1700–1850', in T. M. Devine and David Dickson (eds), *Ireland and Scotland 1600–1850: Parallels and Contrast in Economic and Social Development* (Edinburgh,

Despite the unpromising conditions for this sector's reform, the first half of this century saw an ever-growing interest in and support for agricultural improvement within Scottish society.[6] It was part of a wider effort for Scotland's economy to catch up with other more prosperous European societies, which predated the Union of the parliaments in 1707. Of course there were innumerable ideas offered to fill this perceived gap (ranging from the adoption of Dutch busses by the fishing fleet to establishing a Scottish colony in Central America), but raising crop yields and the adoption of new husbandry methods remained objectives which were far more consistently and vocally expressed. Many contemporary observers felt that the pursuit of these goals would lower the costs of countless raw materials, allowing other parts of the economy to develop and catch up with England's previous economic development.[7]

Another factor which held back agrarian improvement was a shortage of ready capital in the hands of the landowning class, even as rents were increasingly paid in cash rather than in such forms as livestock, grain or coal.[8] During the late seventeenth century it was possible for members of the landed gentry to find credit from lawyers and goldsmiths in the country's largest burghs or indeed from particular landowners known to lend money within their region including the earls of Dundonald in Ayrshire and the Steuarts of Grandtully in Perthshire.[9] Even so, as Richard Saville has noted, borrowing money was an expensive, risky, arcane and frustratingly complex process complicated by perpetual legal disputes.[10]

From the 1690s, the Scottish establishment began to confront this problem through the formation of a formal banking system. Two banks were founded at this time which would have a major impact on the future

---

1983), pp. 132–45, at p. 133; Jan De Vries, *European Urbanisation 1500–1850* (London, 1984), pp. 39–48.

6 Brian Bonnyman, *The Third Duke of Buccleuch and Adam Smith: Estate Management and Improvement in Enlightenment Scotland* (Edinburgh, 2014), p. 5; Heather Holmes, 'The Circulation of Scottish Agricultural Books during the Eighteenth Century', *AgHR*, 54:1 (2006), 45–78, at p. 57.

7 John Clerk of Penicuik, *Observations on the Present Circumstances of Scotland* (Edinburgh, 1730), pp. 207–8; Robert Maxwell of Arkland (ed.), *Select Transactions of the Honourable Society of Improvers in the Knowledge of Agriculture in Scotland* (Edinburgh, 1743), p. 1.

8 Ian Whyte, *Agriculture and Society in Seventeenth-Century Scotland* (Edinburgh, 1979), p. 86; Muir Johnstone, 'Farm Rents and Improvement: East Lothian and Lanarkshire 1670–1830', *AgHR*, 57:1 (2009), 37–57.

9 Lorna A. Ewan, 'Debt and Credit in Early Modern Scotland: The Grandtully Estates 1650–1765' (PhD thesis, University of Edinburgh, 1988), pp. 55–64; NRS, GD233/108/1/1, Inventory of Debts due to John, Earl of Dundonald (1737).

10 Richard Saville, *Bank of Scotland: A History 1695–1995* (Edinburgh, 1996), p. xxxiii.

of the country's economy, namely the Bank of Scotland and the Royal Bank of Scotland. This chapter will consider the intrinsic link between the early development of Scottish banking and attempted agricultural reform. It will do so primarily by examining the banks' court minutes and showing tables which demonstrate how many loans were approved in particular years, how many were granted to landowners in comparison to merchants, and what was the regional distribution. An analysis of these tables will reveal underlying economic trends, assess the business objectives of the bank directors and illustrate how these goals correlate with emerging and distinct views on political economy expressed by prominent members of early eighteenth-century Scottish society.

* * *

First, though, it is worthwhile to consider why these banks were established and their close links with the agricultural sector. The foundation of the Bank of Scotland, through an act of the Scottish parliament in 1695, was part of a wider drive for economic growth during a decade when some of the worst famines the country had ever seen took place.[11] This drive also led to the creation of the Company of Scotland Trading to Africa and the Indies, whose proprietors devised the disastrous Darien scheme.[12] The bank was very much designed with domestic development in mind; unlike most chartered financial institutions up to this point it had no direct connection to the state but depended on the commercial opportunities available within Scottish agriculture, trade and industry for its business.[13] There was another very significant difference between the Bank of Scotland and the Bank of England, founded in 1694. The Bank of England was viewed by many English landowners as solely concerned with supplying credit to the mercantile sector and so Tory politicians achieved statutory approval for the National Land Bank in 1696.[14] Nevertheless because members of the merchant community

---

11 Karen J. Cullen, Christopher A. Whatley and Mary Young, 'King William's Ill Years: New Evidence on the Impact of Scarcity and Harvest Failure during the Crisis of the 1690s on Tayside', *SHR*, 85:2 (2006), 250–76; Robert E. Tyson, 'The Population of Aberdeenshire 1695–1755: A New Approach', *Northern Scotland*, 6 (1985), 113–31.

12 W. Douglas Jones, '"The Bold Adventurers": A Quantitative Analysis of the Darien Subscription List (1696)', *JSHS*, 21:1 (2001), 22–42; Douglas Watt, *The Price of Scotland: Darien, Union and the Wealth of Nations* (Edinburgh, 2007), ch. 7.

13 S. G. Checkland, *Scottish Banking: A History 1695–1973* (London, 1975), p. 24.

14 Steve Pincus, *1688: The First Modern Revolution* (New Haven, 2009), p. 394; Halley Goodman, 'The Formation of the Bank of England: A Response to Changing Political and Economic Climate 1694', *Penn History Review*, 17:1 (2009), 10–30, at p. 25.

failed to subscribe, that scheme quickly collapsed.[15] This shows the early domination of the English banking system by the mercantile sector, which was not reflected within Scotland.

Scottish lairds and nobles were heavily involved in the management of the bank but also in the raising of capital.[16] While £300,000 Scots was raised from Scottish merchants, £390,000 Scots came from the country's landed gentry and aristocracy.[17] There were many prominent individuals within Scotland, including the Edinburgh solicitor John Armour and the economist John Law, who were supportive of Dr Hugh Chamberlain's 'land bank' proposal, where a bank's wealth was based on the value of the country's land rather than the specie in its vaults.[18] The Bank of Scotland was not founded on this principle but its lending practices were very sympathetic to the needs of landowners. Three different types of loans were offered. First, there were loans upon a personal bond of up to £500; for merchants, this was usually based on the value of imperishable commodities they held, but for landowners it often meant family heirlooms like silver plate. Secondly, loans of a similar value could be gained through a conjunct personal bond which involved the support of two cautioners (guarantors) known to the bank; these were used primarily, but not exclusively, by merchants. The third type of loan was based on a heritable bond; this was almost exclusively tailored for landowners. Applicants could borrow sums of up to two-thirds of the total value of their estates, the value of which was rigorously checked in the register of sasines by bank officials.[19] This ability to borrow on the value of land allowed lairds and peers to be lent much larger sums than merchants and those in other occupations. Within the agricultural sector this also made it a lot harder for tenant farmers to be lent larger sums given their comparative lack of collateral. In the first year of business (1696), three loans of £2,000 sterling or more were approved for Sir John Gibson of Pentland, John Erskine of Carriden and Peter Wedderburn of Gosford.[20] In terms of general rules for lending set out by the bank in

15 Pincus, *1688*, p. 394.
16 Saville, *Bank of Scotland*, p. 7; C. A. Malcolm, *The Bank of Scotland 1695–1945* (Edinburgh, 1948), pp. 21–3.
17 Saville, *Bank of Scotland*, p. 4. Sums of money in this chapter are given in £s sterling unless otherwise stated. The £ Scots, used in Scotland before the Union of 1707, was worth one-twelfth of the £ sterling. Some amounts continued to be stated in 'merks', worth two-thirds of a £; these have been converted to £s in the tables.
18 John Armour, *A Premonitor Warning* (Edinburgh, 1702); John Law, *Money and Trade Consider'd with a Proposal for Supplying the Nation with Money* (London, 1705), p. 35; Hugh Chamberlain, *Papers relating to a Bank of Credit upon Land Security proposed to the Parliament of Scotland* (Edinburgh, 1693).
19 Saville, *Bank of Scotland*, p. 27.
20 BOS, M (7 May 1696, 13 May 1696).

1696, interest was set at 6 per cent but with punctual payments leading to a reduction to 4 per cent.[21] Conversely a failure to pay the interest promptly left the borrower at risk of the loan being called in.

The Bank of Scotland maintained a monopoly until 1727 when the Royal Bank was founded through an act passed at Westminster. In a similar way to the 1690s, the mid-1720s marked a point when the Scottish political establishment made a number of efforts to modernise and stimulate the country's economy.[22] In the wake of two recent Jacobite revolts and violent protests against the deeply unpopular malt tax, Scottish Hanoverian politicians began to see economic growth as not just a desirable goal but also necessary to make the political union of 1707 more palatable to the Scottish public. The leader of the Whig Argyll faction (one of the two Scottish political parties loyal to the Hanoverians which survived the Union) was Archibald Campbell, Earl of Ilay and later third Duke of Argyll. As his most recent biographer Roger Emerson has made clear, Ilay possessed a keen interest in agrarian improvement but also in financial innovation.[23] Ilay had been financially involved in both the Mississippi Scheme and the South Sea Company, though these reverses did not diminish his enthusiasm for the concept of credit. In a letter from his political colleague and friend Lord Milton, dated 11 April 1724, Milton confirmed he had arranged Ilay's purchase of £1,000 worth of Bank of Scotland stock.[24] Ilay's political efforts in the mid-1720s led to the creation of the Board of Trustees (a body designed to use the surplus from the malt tax to stimulate agriculture as well as the fisheries and linen manufacturing) but also of a new bank.[25] It must be noted that Ilay wanted to use the new bank, of which he was made the first governor, to serve his own political ends. Most of the Bank of Scotland directors were members of the rival Squadrone faction and a minority had proven themselves to be supporters of the Jacobite cause during the uprising of 1715.[26] Thus the Royal Bank was formed not just to challenge this older financial institution but, in Ilay's own words, to 'demolish it'.[27] The result was the so-called 'Bank War' which was only resolved by a Court of Session

21 Ibid. (9 April, 1696).
22 Whatley, *Scottish Society*, p. 64; Christopher Whatley, *The Scots and the Union: Then and Now* (Edinburgh, 2014), pp. 394–5; John Stuart Shaw, *The Management of Scottish Society 1707–1764* (Edinburgh, 1983), p. 124; Alexander Murdoch, *The People Above: Politics and Administration in Mid-Eighteenth-Century Scotland* (Edinburgh, 1980), p. 21.
23 Roger Emerson, *An Enlightened Duke: The Life of Archibald Campbell (1682–1761), Earl of Ilay, 3rd Duke of Argyll* (Kilkerran, 2013), pp. 236–9.
24 NLS, Saltoun Papers, MS 16529, Milton to Ilay (11 April 1724).
25 Checkland, *Scottish Banking*, p. 44; Julian Hoppit, *Britain's Political Economies: Parliament and Economic Life 1660–1800* (Cambridge, 2017), p. 120.
26 Malcolm, *Bank of Scotland*, p. 227; Saville, *Bank of Scotland*, p. 91.
27 NLS, Saltoun Papers, MS 16535, Ilay to Milton (31 May 1727).

decision in July 1728.[28] The court ruled that the Royal Bank's attempt to put its rival out of business, through collecting Bank of Scotland notes and demanding immediate payment, amounted to harassment.

Despite some of the self-serving motivations behind its establishment, the Royal Bank became (during the next twenty years at least) the more expansive and innovative business. This was true not just in terms of loans but in terms of policy as well, represented best by their decision in 1728 to create the credit cash account (CCA). This practice allowed all holders of a savings account to overdraw on their own credit by up to £300 provided they had two guarantors, and was the first overdraft facility in banking history.[29] Although CCAs were particularly helpful for merchants to facilitate operational liquidity, usually through easing the quick purchase of goods, they were also useful for landowners who were short of money between the times of the year when they would receive rents. At the same time, loans based on heritable bonds remained a very prominent part of the Royal Bank's lending strategy. An especially strong connection with the upper echelons of the Scottish aristocracy is indicated by a £5,500 loan granted by the Royal Bank to Francis Scott, the second Duke of Buccleuch, as well as the bank's management of the duke's rents as part of a separate agreement.[30] Thus began a tight-knit relationship between the bank and one of the country's great families.

* * *

A helpful way to consider the strength of the connections between the agricultural sector and Scottish banks is to analyse the lending patterns of these institutions. So this chapter will now assess the previously mentioned loan tables. The process behind compiling these tables was straightforward. During this period, every new loan, based on a bond, and credit cash account was recorded in the court minutes so it was largely a question of targeting particular years and noting each one. These tables record the number of loans and credit cash accounts approved, their total value for each year as well as the amount granted to landowners and merchants. The 'other' category refers to any individuals provided with credit who were engaged in different professions, which for most of this period were those involved in the legal sector, namely judges, advocates and solicitors. There are significant variations in the number of loans provided and their total value from year to year. These can be partially explained by differences in economic conditions but also by whether either bank was at this point pursuing a policy of expansion

---

28 NLS, Saltoun Papers, MS 16538, Milton to Ilay (July 1728).
29 Kevin Dowd, *The Experience of Free Banking* (London, 1992), p. 160; Christopher Whatley, *The Industrial Revolution in Scotland* (Cambridge, 1997), p. 19.
30 RBS, Royal Bank of Scotland Court Minutes (10 March 1732, 22 March 1732).

or consolidation. Both banks constantly feared being overextended in terms of outstanding loans and occasionally suspended the approval of new loans until supplies of specie could be brought from London to Edinburgh, arranged through a negotiated paper credit exchange.[31] A more consistent feature is that in every sample year (apart from 1717 and 1737 for the Bank of Scotland) landowners received a greater number of individual loans than merchants from the two chartered institutions. In some years there are dramatic gaps between the two social groups. Heritable bonds meant that loans to landowners also tended to be higher.

These tables show that the Royal Bank was considerably more expansive in its lending practices at this time but that the relative proportions of loans to landowners and merchants are quite similar to the 'Old Bank' (the Bank of Scotland). Two major differences between the two banks are that the Royal Bank tended to approve more loans but of a lower value, and that it granted more loans to people who were not landowners or merchants. This difference can be partially explained by its loans to Whig Argyll allies who were members of the College of Justice, but the Royal Bank also lent to people involved in a wider variety of occupations including surgeons, booksellers, goldsmiths, ministers, soldiers and weavers. Credit for these people was more likely to be based on bills, which the early Royal Bank minutes note and record and the Bank of Scotland minutes do not.[32] Potentially this demonstrates a greater willingness on the part of the Royal Bank to adapt to changing economic and social conditions within eighteenth-century Scotland.

The loan tables indicate years when there were surges in lending to landowners, which could occur at times of favourable but also unfavourable conditions for Scottish farming. Christopher Whatley has asserted that in the five years or so after the Union, the agricultural sector experienced sustained growth, which was largely due to more secure links with English markets for cattle, and rising grain prices.[33] This assertion is supported in the data presented here, as bank lending to landowners reached higher levels in 1709–10 before starting to drop in 1712–14 as the price of grain stabilised.[34] A more noticeable feature is that the banks were willing to provide landowners with vital credit at times of hardship. In the late 1690s, 1722–23 and 1739–40, Scotland suffered from harvest crises; these times also saw spikes in lending to landowners, but the Royal Bank seems to have done significantly more than the Bank of Scotland in 1740.[35] In these crisis years, landowners were for the most

31   RBS, M (January 1743, April 1744 and July 1745).
32   RBS, M (1747), *passim*.
33   Whatley, *The Scots and the Union*, pp. 390–1.
34   Saville, *Bank of Scotland*, p. 81.
35   Deborah A. Symonds, 'Death, Birth and Marriage in Early Modern Scotland', in Elizabeth Foyster and Christopher A. Whatley (eds), *A History of Everyday*

part not even expected to keep up their interest repayments.[36] The banks' activities also extended to humanitarian efforts; in the autumn of 1740, both banks approved interest-free loans to burgh councils to enable them to purchase grain for their beleaguered citizens. The Bank of Scotland lent £5,000 to Edinburgh, £550 to Dunfermline and £400 to Perth, while the Royal Bank lent £2,500 to Edinburgh and also £3,000 to their counterparts in Glasgow.[37]

These tables clearly show the extent to which both these chartered banks prioritised the agricultural sector for development and support. However, there are certain limitations with regard to their value as historical sources which must be considered. Picking which sample years to assess can be a tricky process. It was important to target years of noted boom and slump for Scottish farming but also times of 'normal' lending conditions for contrast. In early eighteenth-century Scotland, 'normal years', when the country was unaffected by wars (foreign or domestic) or other forms of civil strife, are quite hard to find. The biggest single limitation of this source is that the court minutes provide no information as to what the money was actually used for. They record only the person's name, occupation, place of residence and the amount they borrowed. Here is an example of a loan based upon a heritable bond approved by the Bank of Scotland in July 1723:

> Sir Alexander Cuming of Culler having proposed to borrow one thousand pounds for which to grant an heritable bond bearing insessment on his lands of Glenbucket. Being two thousand five hundred merks of yearly rent free from all incumbrances holding of the Crown in place of the late Earl of Marr the same is granted.[38]

When landowners sought a loan based on a personal bond, information about their estate did not need to be provided, while the only other pieces of information required for a credit cash account or loan upon a conjunct personal bond were the names of the guarantors. With regard to merchants, whether they predominantly traded in a particular type of goods was not noted, nor whether or not they were engaged in overseas trade, although clues are occasionally provided, given that some

---

Life in Scotland 1600 to 1800 (Edinburgh, 2010), pp. 83–107, at p. 87; A. J. S. Gibson and T. C. Smout, *Prices, Food and Wages in Scotland 1550–1780* (Cambridge, 1995), p. 173.

36 Saville, *Bank of Scotland*, p. 117; BOS, M (31 October 1740); RBS, M (31 October 1740).

37 BOS, M (31 October 1740, 26 December 1740); RBS, M (31 October 1740, 5 December 1740).

38 BOS, M (5 July 1723).

are described as being formerly resident in foreign cities like Gothenburg, Rotterdam or Hamburg.[39]

This information alone, therefore, cannot show that any of these loans was used for the purposes of agricultural improvement. During the eighteenth century, Scottish landed proprietors had the opportunity to invest in a number of different areas, including textiles, infrastructure projects, overseas trading ventures and coal mining.[40] At the same time it is also possible that more money was going towards facilitating estate improvements than the tables imply. It was not uncommon for Scottish merchants to own land during these decades, and approximately 85 per cent of advocates and judges (who account for a large proportion of approved loans) were also landowners.[41] It is therefore possible that the money they borrowed was used to modernise their holdings, given that, as Nicholas Phillipson has noted, their station in Scottish society came 'by virtue of their estates rather than their gowns'.[42]

Many of the most prominent improvers were loaned money by both banks, including John Dalrymple, the second Earl of Stair, Thomas Hamilton, the sixth Earl of Haddington, Charles Hope, the second Earl of Hopetoun, Sir Archibald Grant of Monymusk, Sir John Clerk of Penicuik and Thomas Hope of Rankeillor.[43] It is possible to target the loans of particular borrowers and assess why these individuals chose to borrow the money. Sasine records can show correlations between individuals who received credit from either bank (usually through a heritable bond) and land purchases within a year of the loan's approval. It would, though, be incorrect to assume that agrarian reform could be financed only through large loans worth over £1,000. A clear example of how agricultural improvements could also be carried out with small

---

39 BOS, M (14 January 1724, 9 September 1732, 23 May 1743, August 1753).

40 Alastair Durie, 'Lairds, Improvement, Banking and Industry in Eighteenth Century Scotland: Capital and Development in a Backward Economy – a Case Study', in T. M. Devine (ed.), *Lairds and Improvement in the Scotland of the Enlightenment* (n.p., 1978), pp. 21–30, at p. 21; Bob Harris, 'Landowners and Urban Society in Eighteenth-Century Scotland', *SHR*, 92:2 (2013), 231–54; T. C. Smout, 'Scottish Landowners and Economic Growth 1650–1850', *Scottish Journal of Political Economy*, 11:3 (1964), 218–34.

41 Rosalind Mitchison, 'Patriotism and National Identity in Eighteenth-Century Scotland', in T. W. Moody (ed.), *Nationality and the Pursuit of National Independence* (Belfast, 1978), pp. 73–95, at p. 83.

42 N. T. Phillipson, 'Lawyers, Landowners and the Civic Leadership of Post-Union Scotland', *Juridical Review*, new ser., 21 (1976), 97–120, at p. 111.

43 Brian Bonnyman, 'Agrarian Patriotism and the Landed Interest: The Scottish "Society of Improvers in the Knowledge of Agriculture" 1723–1746', in Koen Stapelbroek and Jani Marjanen (eds), *The Rise of Economic Societies in the Eighteenth Century: Patriotic Reform in Europe and North America* (Basingstoke, 2012), pp. 26–51, at p. 30; Donald Rutherford, *In the Shadow of Adam Smith: Founders of Scottish Economics 1700–1900* (Edinburgh, 2012), p. 6.

amounts of money is shown in the estate papers of Sir Archibald Grant, the second Baronet of Monymusk. In 1735, Grant spent only £29 13s. 10d. on agricultural innovation, but this still funded thirty separate minor modernisations, including planting trees, the preparation of new ditches and dykes and the repairing of stone walls and barns.[44]

* * *

Personal correspondence and diaries can provide some insight into the motivations of landowners who borrowed money at this time. George Home of Kimmerghame's diary shows that he used the Bank of Scotland's foundation as an opportunity to consolidate existing loans.[45] Letters between Sir Gilbert Elliot of Minto and his factor reveal extensive ditch-digging and drainage work taking place on his estate within months of his receiving a £300 credit from the Royal Bank in June 1736.[46] Andrew Fletcher, Lord Milton's account book for the mid-1730s shows a rise in work on his estate during years when he took a credit cash account from the Royal Bank.[47] Milton's papers can also reveal the potential motivations of other people who desired credit because he received many such requests from individuals in his capacity as deputy governor of the Royal Bank.[48] Sir Gilbert and Lord Milton were important members of Scotland's legal establishment – a fact that further illustrates the intrinsic link between the landed and legal sectors.[49]

Beyond this relative evidence of contributions to and prioritisation of agrarian development by the two chartered banks, their natural conservatism could still hinder their efforts to stimulate Scottish farming and other economic sectors in a number of ways. In many ways their cautious lending policies are very understandable given the often turbulent economic conditions in which they operated. With the Bank of Scotland especially it is hard to imagine a financial institution which endured as many severe challenges in the first thirty-five years of its existence. Within a year of its opening, the bank had to suspend lending in the face of competition from the Company of Scotland. This was followed by one of the worst famines in Scottish history, the dramatic failure of

44 Henry Hamilton (ed.), *Selections from the Monymusk Papers 1713–1755* (Edinburgh: SHS, 1945), p. 32.
45 NRS, GD1/891, Diary of George Home of Kimmerghame (April 1696); BOS, M (7 May 1696).
46 NLS, Minto Papers, MS 11004, George Stuart to Minto (14 June and 21 June 1736); RBS, M (23 June 1736).
47 NLS, Saltoun Papers, MS 16900, Account Book of Lord Milton (1732–33).
48 NLS, Saltoun Papers, MS 16570, James Glen to Milton (24 October 1737); MS 16570, James Christie to Lord Milton (14 December 1737).
49 George McGilvary, *East India Patronage: The Scottish Elite and Politics in the Eighteenth Century* (London, 2008), p. 122.

the Darien scheme itself and the resultant loss of capital, the financial crisis of 1704 (which again caused the bank to stop lending), the uncertainty of a political union, the Jacobite uprising of 1715, and finally a new competitor established with the immediate objective of the Bank of Scotland's destruction.

One of the most obvious signs of both banks' conservatism can be shown when the regional distribution of the loans is assessed. The disproportionate number of loans provided to landowners based in the Lothians and Fife, and in southern Scotland is striking. In most years landowners in the Lothians, Fife and southern Scotland alone received the majority of the individual loans approved. In some respects this imbalance is not surprising, as the Lothians and Scotland's southernmost counties were more advanced in their agricultural development than other regions, but it is also indicative of both banks being based in Edinburgh.[50] Applicants from counties surrounding that city had an easier time securing credit than most of those from further afield (though the more developed southern counties also did well). Edinburgh's own merchants were more likely to be successful than those from elsewhere. Geographical proximity assisted lenders, partly because they were more likely to be known by bank directors. In 1743, fifteen of the twenty-two loans granted to merchants by the Bank of Scotland went to those in Edinburgh, while twenty-four of the forty-five approved by the Royal Bank went to merchants resident in the capital.[51] The bank directors were also far more likely to provide credit to those with whom they had a prior relationship, which is important given that they themselves tended to be lairds with estates in East-Central Scotland, merchants based in Edinburgh or indeed members of the capital's legal establishment in the case of the first Royal Bank directors.[52]

There were some variations between the banks on this issue. Highland landowners were generally more likely to receive credit from the Royal Bank; Ilay had financial and political prominence in Argyll, and the Bank's cashier throughout this period was John Campbell, a Highlander and illegitimate grandson of the Earl of Breadalbane.[53] Both banks discounted numerous drovers' bills to cover purchases at sheep and cattle fairs and, as an article by Douglas Watt has highlighted, Highland

---

50 G. Whittington, 'Was There a Scottish Agricultural Revolution?', *Area*, 7 (1975), 204–6; R. A. Dodgshon, 'The Removal of Runrig in Roxburghshire and Berwickshire 1680–1766', *Scottish Studies*, 16 (1970), 121–37; Ian D. Whyte, 'George Dundas of Dundas: The Context of an Early Eighteenth-Century Scottish Improving Landowner', *SHR*, 60:1 (1981), 1–13.

51 BOS, M (1743); RBS, M (1743).

52 Saville, *Bank of Scotland*, pp. 20–1; RBS, M (10 August 1727).

53 John S. Gibson, *Edinburgh in the '45: Bonnie Prince Charlie at Holyrood* (Edinburgh, 1995), p. 10.

landowners were utilising informal means of credit as early as the first decades of the seventeenth century.[54]

A branch network would have alleviated these imbalances but this was never permanently established by either bank during this period. The Bank of Scotland at least seems to have appreciated the importance of making credit available across the country from an early stage. In 1696, it began to establish agencies in Glasgow, Dundee, Montrose and Aberdeen, but in the wake of the commercial threat posed by the Company of Scotland they were soon closed down.[55] Another effort was made to open permanent branches in Glasgow, Dundee and Aberdeen in 1731 but these were all shut down within two years, partly because the directors were worried about the extent to which the branches depended on bills of exchange to function.[56] Instead both institutions had to rely on informal agents for information about lending conditions within these burghs.[57]

As banking facilities remained fixed in Edinburgh, many landowners and merchants who lived outside of East-Central Scotland grew increasingly frustrated and, by the late 1740s, some started to found their own banking houses. The Aberdeen Bank and the Glasgow Ship Bank were established in 1746 and 1749 respectively, quickly followed by another Glaswegian institution, the Arms Bank, in 1750.[58] This was a trend which carried on into the later eighteenth century, and it is worth briefly considering how some of the established issues played out during that time. By 1770, to the impotent dismay of the chartered banks' directors, there was a private bank in virtually every major Scottish burgh. The most famous provincial bank at this time was Douglas, Heron and Company, known to posterity as the Ayr Bank, the dramatic collapse of which in 1772 precipitated the worst financial crisis in eighteenth-century Scottish history and led to a far-reaching economic downturn.[59] In the aftermath of this crisis, the chartered banks re-established themselves and started to form branch networks.[60]

There was not just a regional but also a social imbalance to the banks' lending, which motivated the founders of these new financial institutions. Virtually every rank of landowner sought and obtained loans. Conversely, only a few individuals described as tenant farmers are

---

54 Douglas Watt, '"The Laberinth of thir Difficulties": The Influence of Debt on the Highland Elite c.1550–1700', *SHR*, 85:1 (2006), 28–51.

55 Saville, *Bank of Scotland*, p. 21; BOS, M (3 April 1696).

56 Neil Munro, *The History of the Royal Bank of Scotland* (Edinburgh, 1928), p. 87.

57 Ibid.

58 Charles W. Munn, *The Scottish Provincial Banking Companies 1747–1864* (Edinburgh, 1981), p. 11; Checkland, *Scottish Banking*, p. 97.

59 Henry Hamilton, *An Economic History of Scotland in the Eighteenth Century* (Oxford, 1963), pp. 324–5; Anthony Slaven, *The Development of the West of Scotland 1750–1960* (London, 1975), p. 33.

60 BOS, M (27 July 1774, 26 September 1774).

recorded within the court minutes receiving credit (none in most years). Both banks' most common customer was an individual who possessed considerable wealth in land, property, minerals and rents but who suffered from a severe cash flow problem; tenant farmers did not fit this description.[61] This was another damaging weakness which hindered their ability to finance nationwide agricultural improvement, for many of the earliest practitioners of agricultural innovations were tenants rather than landowners.[62] It was not until the late 1770s that either of the chartered banks started to lend to men described as 'tenants', 'farmers' or 'tacksmen' in significant numbers.

* * *

So where exactly can we place the chartered banks within the context of early eighteenth-century agricultural improvement? Certainly the directors of both banks prioritised the needs of the landed class; landowners were more likely to be approved credit and special loans were created to enable them to borrow more. There is some evidence (of a direct and indirect nature) which could be developed further to show links between the finance they provided and improvement. However there were certain features of their lending practices which limited the banks' ability to perform this function. Their natural, and in many ways understandable, conservatism led to many regions of Scotland and even the important middle rung of rural society not having full access to banking facilities. It must again be noted that the unfavourable economic conditions for the Scottish agricultural sector at this time meant that landowners who borrowed money to finance improvements were taking a great risk. Indeed some of the most prominent early improvers financially overextended themselves and went bankrupt.[63]

An enlightening comparison can be made with the Honourable Society of Improvers in the Knowledge of Agriculture in Scotland which was founded in July 1723. This body was the first patriotic improving society in Europe, founded eight years before the Dublin Society and thirty-one years before the English Society for the Encouragement of Arts, Manufactures and Commerce. The Honourable Society received an impressive level of support from Scotland's aristocracy and landed gentry: of the first 300 members, three were dukes (Atholl, Hamilton and Perth), two were marquesses (Lothian and Tweeddale), twenty were

---

61 Saville, *Bank of Scotland*, p. 257.
62 Alexander Allardyce (ed.), *Scotland and Scotsmen in the Eighteenth Century from the MSS of John Ramsay of Ochtertyre* (Edinburgh, 1888), p. 557; T. C. Smout and Alexander Fenton, 'Scottish Agriculture before the Improvers – an Exploration', *AgHR*, 13:2 (1965), 73–93, at pp. 89–90; David Allan, *Scotland in the Eighteenth Century: Union and Enlightenment* (Edinburgh, 2002), p. 92.
63 Bonnyman, 'Agrarian Patriotism', p. 49.

earls, twenty-two were lords and dozens more were lairds.[64] As a sign that agricultural improvement could be a unifying goal, Hanoverians and Jacobites were members of the Society and members came from every part of Scotland with the exception of the Western and Northern Isles.[65] There were certainly connections with the banks, for seventy-eight of the members received credit from either or both banks just within the sample years. Two Bank of Scotland governors (the Earl of Hopetoun and the Marquess of Tweeddale) were members, as were the Royal Bank's first governor and deputy governor, Ilay and Milton respectively. Brian Bonnyman has recently argued that this Society deserves greater scholarly attention than it has formerly received and is an early sign of a distinctly Scottish agrarian patriotism.[66]

The Society's main function was to provide advice on farming to its subscribers and hold frequent meetings during the summer months. Its leadership included lairds with practical farming experience; the president was Thomas Hope of Rankeillor and the secretary was Robert Maxwell of Arkland. However, the Society's transactions reveal that this was a body mostly made up of enthusiastic amateurs. As well as articles on practical farming matters, such as liming or fallowing, some articles taught how to catch rats or graft a rose to a whin, and therefore belong more in the realm of home economics or gardening.[67] Amongst the Society's membership there was not a single tenant farmer, and as a consequence the Honourable Society lost a precious source of knowledge and expertise on new farming techniques.[68]

For all their limitations, these bodies (the banks and the Honourable Society) provided a crucial platform for the more sustained, widespread growth and reform of the agricultural sector which was taking place by the final forty years of the eighteenth century. Without the presence of formal banking, many of the later eighteenth-century improvers would have lacked the means to carry out their reforms. The Honourable Society was a starting point for a scientific, intellectual interest in agriculture which blossomed as a key part of the Scottish Enlightenment by the 1760s and 1770s.[69] Both the banks and the Society reveal a strong

64 Maxwell (ed.), *Select Transactions*, pp. xviii–xxiii.
65 Ibid.
66 Bonnyman, 'Agrarian Patriotism'.
67 Honourable Society of Improvers in the Knowledge of Agriculture in Scotland, *A Treatise Concerning the Manner of Fallowing of Ground, Raising of Grass-seeds, and Training of Lint and Hemp* (Edinburgh, 1724); T. C. Smout, 'A New Look at the Scottish Improvers', *SHR*, 91:1 (2012), 125–49, at p. 131.
68 Maxwell (ed.), *Select Transactions*, pp. xviii–xxiii.
69 Anand Chitnis, *The Scottish Enlightenment: A Social History* (London, 1976), p. 14; William Lehmann, *Henry Home, Lord Kames and the Scottish Enlightenment: A Study in National Character and in the History of Ideas* (The

commitment within the Scottish political establishment to prioritise agricultural development.

TABLE 10.1. Bank of Scotland loans, sample years, 1696–1747

Year	Number of loans	Total amount lent	Landowners: number	Landowners: amount lent	Merchants: number	Merchants: amount lent	Other: number	Other: amount lent
1696	46	£24,400	34	£20,400	5	£2,000	7	£2,000
1699	52	£60,137	45	£57,337	2	£800	5	£2,000
1704	13	£5,550	12	£5,150	–	–	1	£400
1709	43	£21,515	32	£17,495	7	£2,500	4	£1,520
1710	67	£53,500	53	£49,380	7	1,520	7	£2,600
1712	38	£11,970	31	£9,220	5	£1,350	2	£1,400
1714	37	£11,818	31	£10,268	1	£300	5	£1,250
1717	20	£5,400	9	£2,400	8	£2,400	3	£600
1723	50	£23,120	42	£20,020	4	£1,650	4	£1,450
1724	38	£17,490	21	£9,730	12	£6,060	5	£1,700
1726	33	£10,252	23	£6,412	5	£2,450	5	£1,390
1732	34	£12,265	18	£6,570	13	£4,295	3	£1,400
1737	36	£13,370	17	£5,920	13	£6,000	6	£1,450
1739	58	£28,660	29	£15,760	23	£10,900	6	£2,000
1740	57	£22,770	30	£9,550	15	£4,900	12	£8,320
1743	63	£21,700	31	£12,550	22	£8,500	10	£650
1747	61	£35,027	34	£24,577	14	£5,800	13	£4,650
Total	746	£378,994	464	£282,739	156	£61,425	98	£34,780
Annual average	44	£22,294	27	£16,632	9	£3,613	6	£2,046

Hague, 1971), p. xviii; C. A. Bayly, *Imperial Meridian: The British Empire and the World 1780–1830* (Harlow, 1989), p. 13.

TABLE 10.2. Royal Bank of Scotland loans, sample years, 1728–47

Year	Number of loans	Total amount lent	Landowners: number	Landowners: amount lent	Merchants: number	Merchants: amount lent	Other: number	Other: amount lent
1728	82	£29,262	40	£14,676	23	£11,145	19	£3,441
1732	36	£19,125	17	£14,045	10	£2,550	9	£2,530
1737	90	£31,277	47	£18,255	25	£7,277	18	£5,745
1739	65	£22,085	39	£15,421	17	£5,100	9	£1,564
1740	59	£39,061	32	£23,806	13	£5,270	14	£9,985
1743	139	£31,664	50	£13,429	45	£10,365	44	£7,870
1747	77	£35,877	33	£20,617	24	£7,320	20	£7,940
Total	548	£208,351	258	£120,249	157	£49,027	133	£39,075
Annual average	78	£29,764	37	£17,178	22	£7,004	19	£5,582

Loans to landowners by region

- Lothians and Fife: includes East Lothian, Midlothian, West Lothian, Fife, Clackmannanshire and Kinross.
- West-Central Scotland: includes Lanarkshire, Ayrshire, Dunbartonshire and Renfrewshire.
- North East: includes Stirlingshire, Perthshire, Angus, Kincardineshire, Aberdeenshire, Banffshire and Moray.
- Southern Scotland: includes Peeblesshire, Selkirkshire, Berwickshire, Roxburghshire, Kirkcudbrightshire, Dumfriesshire and Wigtownshire.
- Highlands and Islands: Bute, Argyll, Inverness-shire, Ross and Cromarty, Sutherland, Caithness, Orkney and Shetland.

TABLE 10.3. Bank of Scotland loans to landowners by region, sample years, 1696–1747

Year	Lothians and Fife	West-Central Scotland	North East, Perthshire and Angus	Southern Scotland	Highlands and Islands
1696	16	7	4	7	–
1699	15	8	16	6	–
1704	3	2	5	2	–
1709	9	3	8	11	1
1710	20	11	9	10	3
1712	10	1	11	6	3
1714	6	6	10	8	1
1717	6	1	1	1	–
1723	13	7	15	5	2
1724	7	2	7	3	2
1726	9	3	5	6	–
1732	7	2	6	2	1
1737	8	–	6	2	1
1739	9	5	10	5	–
1740	11	2	9	5	3
1743	10	4	11	2	4
1747	14	1	9	7	3

TABLE 10.4. Royal Bank of Scotland loans to landowners by region, sample years, 1728–47

Year	Lothians and Fife	West-Central Scotland	North East, Perthshire and Angus	Southern Scotland	Highlands and Islands
1728	20	4	6	7	3
1732	8	1	2	4	2
1737	15	5	11	10	6
1739	15	4	6	7	7
1740	8	5	7	7	5
1743	19	5	17	5	4
1747	5	7	6	8	7

Capitalism's Cradle? Ideas, Policies and the Rise of the Scottish Economy in the Mercantilist Age 1600–1800

Philipp Robinson Rössner

Nowhere else in the world did the birth of capitalism come about in so curious a fashion as in Scotland. Nothing is more surprising than the suddenness of its appearance. It is as though a pistol shot had given the signal for the capitalist spirit, fully grown, to come into the land and dominate it. You cannot help thinking of the Victoria Regia, which blooms overnight.[1]

Thus noted Werner Sombart, one of Germany's most influential thinkers on capitalism at the time (alongside Max Weber), in his study on *Der Bourgeois* in 1913. Sombart's emphasis on Scotland seems striking only inasmuch as recent global histories of capitalism, industrialisation and modern economic growth have usually been written from a perspective focusing on either England (or certain regions within England) or the Netherlands as norm template proxies for 'Western Europe', when studying the so-called 'Great Divergence' and processes of global economic modernisation.[2] The small northern presbyterian nation is

---

1 Werner Sombart, *Der Bourgeois: Zur Geistesgeschichte des modernen Wirtschaftsmenschen*, new edn (Reinbek bei Hamburg, 1988). Quotation from the 1915 translation: Werner Sombart, *The Quintessence of Capitalism*, trans. M. Epstein (New York, 1915), p. 148. This book was a concise résumé of the argument of Sombart's 1.2-million-word magnum opus *Der moderne Kapitalismus*, 4th edn (3 vols, Munich and Leipzig, 1917–27), one of the most influential accounts of capitalism in the early twentieth century.

2 Daron Acemoglu and James Robinson, *Why Nations Fail: The Origins of Power, Prosperity, and Poverty* (New York, 2012); David S. Landes, *The Wealth and Poverty of Nations: Why Some Are So Rich and Some So Poor* (New York, 1998);

usually left out of the picture, including studies taking an expressly 'British' perspective. Just consider *pars pro toto* the signature and flagship project 'Cambridge Economic History of Modern Britain': even though the second edition (2004) did feature a chapter on Scotland written by Devine, the editors of the third edition (2018) decided to leave that chapter out again; the first edition had contained no such chapter, either, conceived in the usual imperial or Anglocentric epistemic perspective. Most accounts of British economic growth in historical perspective to the present day either omit or – even worse – extrapolate Scotland after 1707, often inferring Scottish gross domestic product (GDP) growth rates by using (constant) population ratios. To the present day we lack estimates for Scottish GDP after 1707 of the sort that have been produced for England since the eleventh century using various (and changing) econometric techniques.[3]

Joel Mokyr, *The Enlightened Economy: An Economic History of Britain 1700–1850* (New Haven, 2009); Larry Neal and Jeffrey G. Williamson (eds), *The Cambridge History of Capitalism* (2 vols, Cambridge, 2015); Prasannan Parthasarathi, *Why Europe Grew Rich and Asia Did Not: Global Economic Divergence 1600–1850* (Cambridge, 2011); Kenneth Pomeranz, *The Great Divergence: China, Europe, and the Making of the Modern World Economy* (Princeton, 2000); Jean-Laurent Rosenthal and Roy Bin Wong, *Before and Beyond Divergence: The Politics of Economic Change in China and Europe* (Cambridge, MA, 2018); Jan Luiten van Zanden, *The Long Road to the Industrial Revolution: The European Economy in a Global Perspective 1000–1800* (Leiden, 2009); Peer Vries, *State, Economy and the Great Divergence: Great Britain and China 1680s–1850s* (London, 2015); Roy Bin Wong, *China Transformed: Historical Change and the Limits of European Experience* (Ithaca, 1997); Kaveh Yazdani and Dilip Menon (eds), *Capitalisms: Towards a Global History* (Oxford, 2020).

3   Roderick Floud and Paul Johnson (eds), *The Cambridge Economic History of Modern Britain*, vol. 1, 2nd edn (Cambridge, 2004). Cf. Roderick Floud, Jane Humphries and Paul Johnson (eds), *The Cambridge Economic History of Modern Britain*, vol. 1, 3rd edn (Cambridge, 2018). Regarding 'British' historical GDP estimates, the literature is vast; recent overviews include: Stephen Broadberry, Bruce M. S. Campbell, Alexander Klein, Mark Overton and Bas van der Leeuwen, *British Economic Growth 1270–1870* (Cambridge, 2015); Roger Fouquet and Stephen Broadberry, 'Seven Centuries of European Economic Growth and Decline', *Journal of Economic Perspectives*, 29:4 (2015), 227–44; or, less recently, Clive H. Lee, *The British Economy since 1700: A Macroeconomic Perspective* (Cambridge, 1986). Approaches that revolutionised the study of historical national income include Nick F. R. Crafts, *British Economic Growth during the Industrial Revolution* (Oxford, 1985), revising an earlier method presented in Phyllis Deane and W. A Cole, *British Economic Growth 1688–1959: Trends and Structure*, 2nd edn (Cambridge, 1967), none of which, however, engaged with the Scottish evidence except by inference, speculation and extrapolation based, usually, on relative population size and assumptions about the relative stage of Scottish economic development.

This is a more than sad – albeit still common – omission. Sombart, dismissing Catholic Ireland ('Down to this very day there is scarcely another land which has been so little affected by the capitalist spirit'), thought that Scotland had even influenced England in the development of capitalism: 'the course of capitalist development in England was greatly influenced by the fortunes of the capitalist spirit in the Northern Kingdom'. He quoted Andrew Fletcher of Saltoun who had mused in 1698 that, 'by an unforeseen and unexpected change of the genius of this nation', all of a sudden Scotland had become totally geared towards business and succumbed to an industrial spirit.[4] Later studies, by historians such as T. M. Devine, or sociologist Gordon Marshall, who has produced what to the present day remains the only substantial study of the capitalist spirit in early modern Scotland, would have agreed – and they added more nuance to the story than Sombart (who had dealt with Scotland in a page or two, within a survey of Great Britain extending to merely four pages – still a remarkably equitable treatment given the casual treatment Scotland receives in most other 'British' surveys).[5] At the end of the seventeenth century, Scotland was amongst Europe's poorest nations, hampered by a series of crippling harvests as well as English military and economic warfare. By about 1800, however, Scotland was like Sombart's overnight-blooming water lily. After England, Scotland was Europe's most urbanised nation, and the second one to undergo an industrial revolution.[6] Industrial modernity had set in. This was perhaps the fastest such transition ever experienced in the western hemisphere before the twentieth century.

---

4   Sombart, *Quintessence of Capitalism*, p. 148.
5   Especially his business history of the Glaswegian merchant community and Scottish capitalism: T. M. Devine, *The Tobacco Lords: A Study of the Tobacco Merchants of Glasgow and Their Trading Activities c.1740–90* (Edinburgh, 1975); and updated material in T. M. Devine, 'The Golden Age of Tobacco', in T. M. Devine and Gordon Jackson (eds), *Glasgow*, vol. 1: *Beginnings to 1830* (Manchester, 1995), pp. 139–83; Gordon Marshall, *Presbyteries and Profits: Calvinism and the Development of Capitalism in Scotland 1560–1707* (Oxford, 1980).
6   Authoritative accounts include: Christopher A. Whatley, *The Industrial Revolution in Scotland* (Cambridge, 1997); T. M. Devine, 'Urbanisation', in T. M. Devine and Rosalind Mitchison (eds), *People and Society in Scotland*, vol. 1: *1760–1830* (Edinburgh, 1988), pp. 27–52; T. M. Devine, *The Scottish Nation: A Modern History*, 3rd edn (London, 2012), ch. 8; T. M. Devine, 'Scotland', in Roderick Floud and Paul A. Johnson (eds), *The Cambridge Economic History of Modern Britain*, vol. 1: *Industrialisation 1700–1860* (Cambridge, 2004), pp. 388–416; T. M. Devine, 'The Modern Economy: Scotland and the Act of Union' and 'Industrialisation', in T. M. Devine, C. H. Lee and G. C. Peden (eds), *The Transformation of Scotland: The Economy since 1700* (Edinburgh, 2005), pp. 13–33, 34–70.

This chapter will review past models of capitalism and their possible application to Scottish economic change and development during the early modern age, before tentatively outlining the contours of how a new history of capitalism and development in Scotland during the early modern and early industrial period might look. Agriculture will not be its primary focus, but there is much to be said about it, especially within a conceptual framework for the history of capitalism, in Scotland and beyond. Recent histories of capitalism seldom pay much attention to agriculture, although a focus on industrialisation when discussing capitalism is regrettably limited. Like Sombart, earlier scholars, including Eric Kerridge, Ellen Meiksins Wood and famously Robert Brenner, highlighted profit-orientated dynamics in agriculture as something that distinguished a 'capitalist' spirit or sphere from other sectors of society.[7] Fernand Braudel's separation of capitalism from market economy is timeless, tying in well with modern economic anthropological and development economists' models of dual economies.[8] The present volume, as well as earlier works by Devine and others, can show that there were elements of profit-driven capitalist farming – and thus some sources of slight economic change – in many areas of Lowland Scotland long before the Union.[9] Bringing agriculture, and indeed the whole pre-industrial history of Scotland, back into a larger story of capitalism and economic change could hardly be timelier.

* * *

Capitalism, as such, had existed long before the industrial revolution. Although capitalism has become a fashionable historiographical concept again, historians have still not agreed what they mean by it. It is common to see the onset of 'modern' capitalism in the British industrial revolution, and some would admit traces of such 'modern' capitalism in the seventeenth-century Dutch Golden Age.[10] Sombart's 'modern' capitalism, however, does not follow a timeline. It originated (in the sense

7   The literature on the history of capitalism is vast. Classic accounts on agrarian transformations, feudalism and capitalism include: Eric Kerridge, *Agrarian Problems in the Sixteenth Century and After* (London, 1969; repr. 2006); Ellen Meiksins Wood, *The Pristine Culture of Capitalism: A Historical Essay on Old Regimes and Modern States*, new edn (London, 2015); Maurice Dobb, *Studies in the Development of Capitalism* (London, 1946); T. H. Aston and C. H. E. Philpin (eds), *The Brenner Debate: Agrarian Class Structure and Economic Development in Pre-Industrial Europe* (Cambridge, 1985).

8   Fernand Braudel, *Civilization and Capitalism, 15th–18th Century*, trans. Siân Reynolds (3 vols, London, 1981–85).

9   T. M. Devine, *The Transformation of Rural Scotland: Social Change and the Agrarian Economy 1660–1815* (Edinburgh, 1994).

10   Neal and Williamson (eds), *Cambridge History of Capitalism*.

of springing up here and there) in many places, such as the medieval demesne economy, the military *condottiere* of the fourteenth century, the early modern privateers, or manufacturing businessmen. I subscribe to Sombart's view inasmuch as I do not believe that capitalism follows a timeline nor linear or end-driven development. We can find manifestations of it in many places outside England and certainly before the industrial revolution. Sombart's thesis, in this case on presbyterianism (as one of the purest and in his view most radical expressions of the Calvinist faith) and economic growth, was part of a larger argument on mentality, culture and the 'spirit' of capitalism. It has seldom been traced, let alone applied, when studying early modern Scotland.

Max Weber, in his studies of religious sociology, did not pay much attention to Scotland either. Yet Weber has inspired the only systematic historical account of religion and capitalism in early modern Scotland, from Gordon Marshall, who connects Weber's arguments on the Protestant work ethic and capitalism with the early modern Scottish presbyterian experience.[11] The capitalism narrative has also featured in Marxist accounts.[12] But most historians of Scotland have silently passed over what used to be one of the biggest debates in the social and historical sciences. The recent revival in histories of capitalism, with its US-American-centrism, its focus on business histories, as well as its resistance to considering pre-industrial Europe, means that the time is ripe to bring early modern Scotland back into the game.[13] Here this will have to be a *pars pro toto*, with a two-pronged epistemic approach, bringing Scotland and early modernity back into the history of capitalism, but also bringing a European dimension back into Scottish historical debates.

Another big topic in recent economic and world history is the Great Divergence debate, about the relative success of the economies of Western Europe and China and India.[14] Capital, geography and resource endowment, institutions, labour productivity, empire and conquest, energy, mechanisation, and agriculture's ability to support non-farmers have been quoted as factors that enabled Western Europe to break with traditional technology and efficiency paradigms, creating a radically changed and enlarged industrial world of new goods. Capitalism has

11 Marshall, *Presbyteries and Profits*.

12 E.g. Tony Dickson (ed.), *Scottish Capitalism: Class, State, and Nation from before the Union to the Present* (London, 1980); Neil Davidson, *Discovering the Scottish Revolution 1692–1746* (London, 2003).

13 Notable exceptions to the ignoring of early modern Europe are Jürgen Kocka, *Capitalism: A Short History* (Princeton, 2017); Henry Heller, *The Birth of Capitalism: A Twenty-First-Century Perspective* (London, 2011); Henry Heller, *A Marxist History of Capitalism* (London, 2018); Eric H. Mielants, *The Origins of Capitalism and the 'Rise of the West'* (Philadelphia, 2008).

14 Patrick O'Brien, *The Economies of Imperial China and Western Europe: Debating the Great Divergence* (Basingstoke, 2020).

seldom featured in the debate;[15] nor has Scotland been part of the global history and Great Divergence debates.[16]

Given the indeterminacy, controversy and occasional fuzziness in many historians' accounts of capitalism, there are certain features characteristic for its early modern manifestations which we can observe (or find at work) in Scotland since the later seventeenth century very clearly and which are as clear-cut an expression of a Weberian-Sombartian capitalist spirit as anything else. These include (yet without being exclusive): a decidedly forward-facing, future-oriented mode of thought (which comes across especially clearly in the pamphlet debates around the Darien failure and preparing for and negotiating the economic benefits and disadvantages from incorporating Union);[17] a keen and blossoming business of producing learned treatises on political economy (starting with Fletcher and many 'anonymous' pamphleteers in the 1690s, to the towering figures of the Scottish Enlightenment such as Hutcheson, Home, Hume, Smith and Steuart); a proactive state supporting private property, private enterprise, competitive markets facilitating capital accumulation through processes of market development and protectionism of key industries;[18] an urban elite tied closely to interests of state and aligned, in a form of cronyism, with the landed elite who usually also were the political elite or 'people above' (mainly hereditary peers interested in developing the Scottish economy with the aim of raising their rents on their estates; witness the Board of Trustees established in 1727 and Argathelian rule as 'king' or 'viceroy' of Scotland).[19] They all reinforce a

15 But see recently Yazdani and Menon (eds), *Capitalisms: Towards a Global History.*

16 I have tried to outline a possibility in Philipp Robinson Rössner, 'Merchants, Mercantilism, and Economic Development: The Scottish Way c.1700–1815', *Annales Mercaturae*, 1:1 (2015), 97–126.

17 Christopher A. Whatley, 'Economic Causes and Consequences of the Union of 1707: A Survey', *SHR*, 68:1 (1989), 150–81; Christopher A. Whatley, *Bought and Sold for English Gold? Explaining the Union of 1707*, 2nd edn (East Linton, 2001); Christopher A. Whatley with Derek Patrick, *The Scots and the Union* (Edinburgh, 2006). On Scottish economic thought, the best and most comprehensive survey is Donald Rutherford, *In the Shadow of Adam Smith: Founders of Scottish Economics 1700–1900* (New York, 2012). On Enlightenment figures, the literature is near endless, especially on Adam Smith, who is one of the most-studied figures in political and economic theory. One of the best and most recent accounts of David Hume is Margaret Schabas and Carl Wennerlind, *A Philosopher's Economist: Hume and the Rise of Capitalism* (Chicago, 2020).

18 On markets and parliamentary activity, see Ian D. Whyte, 'The Growth of Periodic Market Centres in Scotland 1600–1707', *Scottish Geographical Magazine*, 95 (1979), 13–26. We still lack a systematic study of Scottish industrial development and trade policy 1660–1707, but Marshall, *Presbyteries and Profits* has a useful discussion.

19 Alexander Murdoch, *The People Above: Politics and Administration in*

model and picture of both Scottish peculiarity as well as being a characteristically or archetypally modern capitalist nation.

* * *

To explain Scotland's rapid capitalist transformation one needs to engage with previous models and move beyond a narrow frame of Scottocentrism that has marked previous debates, incorporating new comparative European, even global, histories of capitalism and economic development, or, as R. A. Houston once put it, to move 'out of the laager'.[20] Previously Scottish historians emphasised the Union of 1707, the subsequent rise of Glasgow and the tobacco trades, and Scotland's incorporation into the English Atlantic Empire, as reasons for Scottish economic success.[21] This interpretation, positively emphasising the entrepreneurial drive of Scotsmen, the Scots 'becoming British' and contributing to 'forging the Nation' as well as contributing to and benefiting from the economic gains of the British Empire after 1707, is an intellectual offspring of post-1973 neoliberalism.[22] Since until 1746 perhaps as much as half the Scottish population neither regarded themselves necessarily as British, nor the Hanoverian succession as the legitimate framework of *their* state, we should not overemphasise the British dimension in early modern Scottish economic lives.[23] Well after 1707, Scots merchants continued to pay domestic rates of customs duty in French ports, whilst English traders were charged higher duties as foreigners.[24]

Adam Smith, the author of the *Wealth of Nations*, struck a similar note when casually remarking on Scottish cattle exports to England as one of the main benefits from the Union:

> Of all the commercial advantages, however, which Scotland has derived from the union with England, this rise in the price of cattle is, perhaps, the greatest. It has not only raised the value of all highland estates, but it has, perhaps, been the principal cause of the improvement of the low country.[25]

Mid-Eighteenth Century Scotland (Edinburgh, 1980); Alexander Murdoch, *Making the Union Work: Scotland 1651–1763* (London, 2020).

20 R. A. Houston, 'Eighteenth-Century Scottish Studies: Out of the Laager?', *SHR*, 73:1 (1994), 64–81.

21 E.g. Devine, 'Industrialisation', pp. 51–6.

22 Linda Colley, *Britons: Forging the Nation 1707–1837* (New Haven, 1992).

23 I am grateful to Daniel Szechi for conversations on this point. See Daniel Szechi, *1715: The Great Jacobite Rebellion* (New Haven, 2006); Daniel Szechi, *Britain's Lost Revolution? Jacobite Scotland and French Grand Strategy 1701–8* (Manchester, 2015).

24 Siobhan Talbott, *Conflict, Commerce and Franco-Scottish Relations 1560–1713* (London, 2015), pp. 136–8.

25 Adam Smith, *An Inquiry into the Nature and Causes of the Wealth of Nations*

However, few Western nations apart from Norway have ever grown rich on primary-sector exports alone, and much of the current experience of African countries suggests that the opposite is true: specialising in agriculture or raw materials means specialising in being poor.[26] Some Scottish farmers and noblemen operated large cattle parks where Highland cattle were collected before being sent to England. But cattle exports made only a small contribution to Scottish wealth and national income.[27] If Scotland had continued to focus its export portfolio on raw materials, cattle and coarse linen, it might well have taken the high road to poverty.

No nation has grown rich based exclusively on trading, either, as we know from the example of the early modern Netherlands – which appears as the early modern trading nation *par excellence*, but a nation that had also embedded the strategy of adding value to its industrial production.[28] An oft-cited model ascribes Scotland's successful transition towards capitalism since the 1740s to a commercial economy geared towards importing and re-exporting tobacco and exporting Scots linen, the rise of the Atlantic trade and the change in the Lowland towns. This explains *regional* economic change – around Glasgow and Paisley especially, where industry developed earlier – but is unlikely to explain Scottish economic development as a whole.[29] Whatley has identified Scottish industry – especially linen, but also salt and paper making, brewing and other industries – as important stimulants to growth, whilst work by Devine on agrarian transformations and transitions to a more competitive capitalist agriculture has established incontrovertible evidence of capitalist dynamics in agrarian regimes in the Lowlands, from the border and into Aberdeenshire.[30]

Since the mid-seventeenth century, such market- and profit-driven agrarian businesses, consolidations of large tenant farms based on monetary rents and increasingly shorter leases and competitive rents, became more

---

(London, 1776), Book I, ch. XI, p. 278.

26 Erik S. Reinert, *How Rich Countries Got Rich and Why Poor Countries Stay Poor* (London, 2007).

27 Alexander-John Koufopoulos, 'The Cattle Trades of Scotland 1603–1745' (unpublished PhD thesis, University of Edinburgh, 2005); A. R. B. Haldane, *The Drove Roads of Scotland* (London, 1952).

28 Jan de Vries and Ad van der Woude, *The First Modern Economy: Success, Failure, and Perseverance of the Dutch Economy 1500–1815* (Cambridge, 1997). On the politics of Dutch development, see Oscar Gelderblom (ed.), *The Political Economy of the Dutch Republic* (Farnham, 2009).

29 Anthony Slaven, *The Development of the West of Scotland 1750–1960* (London, 1976).

30 Whatley, *Industrial Revolution*; Christopher A. Whatley, *Scottish Society 1707–1830: Beyond Jacobitism, Towards Industrialisation* (Manchester, 2000); Devine, *Transformation of Rural Scotland*.

and more characteristic of an agrarian system that saw grain farming as a profit-based enterprise following market rationales moving away from earlier traditional forms of self-contained and self-serving economy. Sombart called these traditional forms 'economies of expenditure', and Marx framed them within his famous Commodity-Money-Commodity equation which preceded its reversal to Money-Commodity-Money.[31] Large estates were increasingly organised as profit-driven businesses. The rationales behind each transition on each landed estate may be different and difficult to generalise, but Devine and others have shown that agrarian improvement towards higher rent and efficiency levels was by no means driven mainly by, or a brainchild of, the Enlightenment, when 'improvement' became a buzz-word, or the imputed 'failure' of the Union to bring the anticipated economic advantages in the 1720s and 1730s, when there was another wave of agrarian improvement. Drive toward more modern profit-oriented farming was seen in many areas of Scotland long before 1700, and the same applies to economic development more generally.[32] As we shall see below, the 1670s appear as a particularly dynamic period. Any history of Scottish capitalist farming needs to move back from the focus on either the Enlightenment, or the imputed crisis of the 1720s and 1730s, as the drivers or origin of capitalist agriculture and economic change in early modern Scotland.[33]

We may also distinguish between *economic development* in agriculture and *capitalism* in agriculture. *Capitalism* in this view would be about economic organisation (for instance, entrepreneurial farms employing free labour and selling in the market), whereas *economic development* would be about growing more crops per unit of input, thus output growth in quantitative terms. One aspect of economic development here would be that higher agricultural productivity was needed to feed the growing and increasingly industrial cities.[34] Urbanisation was sluggish in Scotland before 1750, limiting the possibilities and incentives for agrarian capitalist expansion until after that date.[35] This was also one reason why, in Scotland as well as elsewhere, government planners and merchant

---

31   Sombart, *Der moderne Kapitalismus*, vol. 2, part 2, ch. 40, p. 632.

32   Ian D. Whyte, *Scotland's Society and Economy in Transition c.1500–c.1760* (Basingstoke, 1997), pp. 21–7, 149–54.

33   Brian Bonnyman, *The Third Duke of Buccleuch and Adam Smith: Estate Management and Improvement in Enlightenment Scotland* (Edinburgh, 2014), p. 5; Devine, *Transformation of Rural Scotland*.

34   For the post–1707 period, see Devine, *Scottish Nation*, p. 155.

35   Devine, 'Urbanisation', based on figures by Jan de Vries, which, however, cover only cities in excess of 10,000 inhabitants. This metric may not capture the full dynamics of urbanisation: see A. Mączak and T. C. Smout (eds), *Gründung und Bedeutung kleinerer Städte im nördlichen Europa der frühen Neuzeit* (Wiesbaden, 1991).

capitalists focused on foreign markets and manufacturing exports as the most likely sources of growth and capitalist development.

* * *

The role of the state has been emphasised by some scholars, albeit less so in the case of Scotland. The most recent study on policy and economic life in early modern Britain almost completely disregards the Scottish experience, apart from a tangential discussion based on a Westminster view on Scotland and economic planning.[36] After 1707 Westminster devoted few acts of parliament to Scottish economic matters. Instead, economic planning occurred in intermediary and subsidiary layers of state, especially the Convention of Royal Burghs, and, after 1727, the Board of Trustees for Fisheries and Manufactures. The Westminster administration does not represent the ideal focus for a Scottish study. This contrasts remarkably with the period between about 1660 and 1707, when the Scottish parliament had actively promoted domestic economy and industry, and many new markets were licensed.[37]

As well as the broader dynamics, we also need to appreciate distinct conjunctures. The Scottish parliament appears to have lost traction on the economy in the years before 1707. This became obvious after the failure of the Darien colony, but perhaps the failure occurred earlier, when it became clear that legislation would be unable to create a Scottish equivalent to the English navigation system.[38] This loss of traction seems clear in retrospect, though how far it was clear at the time is another question. Of course, parliament was only one institution and channel of state policy, and after 1707, when the Scottish independent state had vanished, and the Westminster parliament remained silent on Scottish matters, other avenues were developed.

So there is a question of what or *who* the state actually was after 1707. Institutions of the British state were often viewed with suspicion, and Jacobitism was rife until 1746. Scotland experienced 'systematic tax evasion' and was governed by aristocratic cliques.[39] Only for linen and the fisheries was there a British state policy, through the Board of Trustees for Fisheries and Manufactures established in 1727. This was

---

36 Julian Hoppit, *Britain's Political Economies: Parliament and Economic Life 1660–1800* (Cambridge, 2017).

37 Peter G. B. McNeill and Hector L. MacQueen (eds), *Atlas of Scottish History to 1707* (Edinburgh, 1996), p. 295.

38 Julian Goodare, 'Scotland's Parliament in its British Context 1603–1707', in H. T. Dickinson and Michael Lynch (eds), *The Challenge to Westminster: Sovereignty, Devolution and Independence* (East Linton, 2000), pp. 22–32.

39 Murdoch, *Making the Union Work, passim* (quotation at p. 74); Alexander Murdoch, 'Scottish Sovereignty in the Eighteenth Century', in Dickinson and Lynch (eds), *Challenge to Westminster*, pp. 42–9.

part of a larger bundle of macroeconomic reforms from 1721 to 1723, abolishing export duties on most manufactures and reducing or waiving import duties on raw materials vital for British industry, such as flax and hemp. These measures were primarily meant to serve English economic interests. Nevertheless, in combination with the post-Restoration price and customs schedule for the colonial trades, aspects of this new system boosted Scottish colonial trade after 1740.[40]

As we have seen, even before 1707 the Scottish parliament had seen phases of lively and proactive economic planning. For instance, particularly in the 1670s and 1680s, a series of acts established new weekly market centres and fairs, or privileged cloth manufactories. These acts all followed what we could call a 'mercantilist' strategy, in the sense of using state institutions to foster manufacturing and exports. The term 'mercantilist' will be discussed further below. Here we can note that the Union of 1707 brought new priorities for the state in its British framework. Until after 1746, the British state was fragile in Scotland and faced a potential threat from Jacobitism. Parts of state economic planning were therefore directed at pacifying the northern part of Great Britain, fostering political and cultural unity through economic integration. The key pillar of economic policy was the linen industry, which received the lion's share of Westminster's economic attention. But economic managers were also concerned about other matters, such as fisheries, salt and malt (distilling), as well as brewing; these were all considered staples in the average Scot's basket of consumption, and looked upon by the state, above all, from a fiscal point of view, as means to generate revenue.[41]

Marxist-inspired historians would pick up on such questions, studying the long-term history of mercantilist Scotland transcending the Union of 1707,[42] whilst other historians have confirmed the notion of Scottish 'revolutions' in government – and also by inference the economy (because the two cannot be meaningfully separated) – in 1638 and beyond.[43] Marshall's work on the Weber hypothesis on Calvinism and capitalism in Scotland stands alone in its field, proposing that from 1641 onwards the Scottish state adopted a 'more systematic industrial

40 Philipp Robinson Rössner, *Scottish Trade in the Wake of Union 1700–1760: The Rise of a Warehouse Economy* (Stuttgart, 2008).

41 William J. Ashworth, 'The Demise of Regulation and Rise of Political Economy: Taxation, Industry and Fiscal Pressure in Britain 1763–1815', in Philipp Robinson Rössner (ed.), *Economic Growth and the Origins of Modern Political Economy: Economic Reasons of State 1500–2000* (London, 2016), pp. 122–36.

42 Dickson (ed.), *Scottish Capitalism*; Davidson, *Discovering the Scottish Revolution*.

43 Julian Goodare, 'The Scottish Revolution', in Sharon Adams and Julian Goodare (eds), *Scotland in the Age of Two Revolutions* (Woodbridge, 2014), pp. 79–96; Laura Stewart and Janay Nugent, *Union and Revolution: Scotland and Beyond 1625–1745* (Edinburgh, 2021).

policy orientated towards solving the fundamental structural problems facing Scots manufacturing, namely, lack of capital, lack of high-quality domestic raw materials, lack of skilled labour, and competition from superior foreign products'.[44]

The post-1638 'revolutionary' Scottish state became increasingly proactive in fiscal and industrial policy.[45] If such external evidence as acts of parliament, company books, sederunt books from enterprises such as the Newmills manufactory established in the 1640s and re-founded in the 1680s, and related sources, can be in any way indicative of a capitalist spirit, then the Scottish state became exceedingly entrepreneurial after the Restoration.[46] Its two most important initiatives, both in 1695, were the Company of Scotland Trading to Africa and the Indies, and the Bank of Scotland.[47] The continuous activity of the Scottish parliament in the 1670s and 1680s in founding new rural market centres has been mentioned above. Overall, the Scottish state articulated a vision of positive and dynamic economic development.

A new synthesis of Scottish transitions towards capitalism may thus be in order. Much existing work is inward-looking, and even the most recent syntheses of Scotland's economic history do not advance beyond narratives of the 1980s and 1990s.[48] Yet Scotland provides an excellent case study to draw out a much larger history of early modern European capitalist development, not only because its capitalist transition was fast, but also because the quantitative sources on commerce and development are excellent. Moreover, two of the foundational analyses of capitalist modernity – Sir James Steuart's (*An*) *Inquiry into the Principles of Political Economy* (1767) and Adam Smith's similar *Inquiry into the Nature and the Causes of the Wealth of Nations* (1776) – were written by Scots during the mercantilist age. In this way, a new economic history of modern Scotland can be written from the perspective of the state, nation and mercantilism within a comparative-European framework. In many ways, the Scottish experience remained closer to the European experience than England's. It also followed a mercantilist developmental rationale in a more positive sense than is usually acknowledged. The next section will discuss this further.

* * *

44 Marshall, *Presbyteries and Profits*, p. 131.
45 Julian Goodare, *State and Society in Early Modern Scotland* (Oxford, 1999), pp. 318–22; Marshall, *Presbyteries and Profits*, pp. 130–3.
46 Marshall, *Presbyteries and Profits*, pp. 140–97.
47 For more on banking see Gains Murdoch, 'Agriculture and Banking in Eighteenth-Century Scotland 1695–1750', Chapter 10 above in the present volume.
48 E.g. Devine *et al.* (eds), *The Transformation of Scotland*.

There has been a recent upsurge in historical as well as economics literature searching for the origin of manufacturing, prosperity and nations' competitiveness in the writings of the cameralist and mercantilist genre. This was a theory, economic discourse and – since the Italian Renaissance – also a strategy, that emphasised the virtues of manufacturing and industry in making nations rich. Cameralist and mercantilist writings flourished between the fourteenth and eighteenth centuries, and, as the industrial revolution testifies, beyond. This literature also emphasised that a strong state could and should positively influence manufacturing and industry. The fact that such mercantilist strategies continued to be applied in Scotland after 1707 is one of the reasons that the road to economic obscurity was not taken.

Scottish economic actors and politicians (usually with a noble background, as well as some proactive merchants) were part of a larger pan-European mercantilist moment that swept Continental discourses and debates from the 1660s. The later seventeenth century was the age of the 'project maker'. Significant economists such as German-Austrian cameralist Johann Joachim Becher (1635–82) not only played around with natural sciences and alchemy, but also developed deep insights into the mechanisms of competitive market economies or what Joseph Schumpeter, in his assessment of eighteenth-century German cameralist economist Johann Heinrich von Justi (1717–71), pointedly called 'laissez-faire with the nonsense left out'.[49]

Cameralists such as Justi or Becher were interested in how markets worked, how prices formed and how circulation or 'revolution' of goods and money could be promoted dynamically to improve the nation's wealth. Becher travelled widely in the German and Austrian lands, and visited the Netherlands and Britain in 1678, including a trip to Scotland, perhaps at the request of Prince Rupert of the Rhine. Apart from being known for his works on chemistry and alchemy, he erected one of the largest woollen manufactories in the Austrian city of Linz (1680s), and devised an infamous project of acquiring Guiana from the Dutch to set up an East India Company for the minuscule County of Hanau, one of the third-rank smaller territories of the Holy Roman Empire.[50]

Becher's cousin Philipp Wilhelm von Hörnigk in 1684 produced *Austria Supreme if it So Wishes*, a German-language economic bestseller that continued to be read and used for teaching in the German-speaking

---

49 Joseph A. Schumpeter, *History of Economic Analysis* (New York, 1954), p. 172. On cameralism see Philipp Robinson Rössner, *Freedom and Capitalism in Early Modern Europe: Mercantilism and the Making of the Modern Economic Mind* (Cham, 2020).

50 Pamela H. Smith, *The Business of Alchemy: Science and Culture in the Holy Roman Empire* (Princeton, 2016).

lands into the 1780s.[51] This was one of the clearest formulations of the seventeenth-century economic faith known variously as 'cameralism' (a misnomer), 'mercantilism' (a misnomer) or 'Economic Reason of State' (a little known nomer): a combination of moderate economic protectionism with a lot of capitalist laissez-faire thinking, based on standard reason of state theory. In the German imperial lands the spirit of improvement that flourished during the 1660s and 1670s is known as 'Imperial Mercantilism' (*Reichsmerkantilismus*), later blending with the Age of the *Projektemacher* or project maker – with protagonists ranging from Johann Becher, whom we have encountered above, to Daniel Defoe (1660–1731) in England.[52]

It was to an extent a European moment of optimism in what turned out to be a climatic Dark Age, an age of global conflict, revolution and climate change, with the low point of the Maunder Minimum reached in the 1680s and 1690s. In the Germanies the dust had just settled on the Thirty Years' War, and out of the Baroque age of reconstruction arose major political economy treatises written by state servants in the service of often Pietist and reformed princes, such as Veit Ludwig von Seckendorff, an administrator of the princely court of Saxe-Gotha, who published in 1655 his 1,000-page work on the 'German Princely State' (*Teutsche Fürsten Staat*), which remained in use in university teaching until the end of the eighteenth century. Seckendorff in 1665 published *Additiones* in which he discussed the virtues of infant industry protection and manufacturing.[53] In Sweden, the end of the Thirty Years' War ushered in Sweden's Age of Greatness (*Stormakstiden*), lasting until 1721. Swedish alchemists and oeconomists around chancellor Axel Oxenstierna and Bengt Skytte began to develop scientific economic models based on the idea of infinite growth: if only the right strategies were chosen, Man could subdue nature and decode Mother Nature's hidden laws, achieving infinite economic growth through natural science.[54] Prussian émigré Samuel Hartlib founded in England what would turn out to be one of Europe's most exclusive and prolific communities of letters and scientists,

51 Philipp Wilhelm von Hörnigk, *Austria Supreme (if it So Wishes) (1684): 'A Strategy for European Economic Supremacy'*, trans. Keith Tribe, ed. Philipp Robinson Rössner (London, 2018), introduction.

52 Ingomar Bog, *Der Reichsmerkantilismus: Studien zur Wirtschaftspolitik des Heiligen Römischen Reiches im 17. und 18. Jahrhundert* (Stuttgart, 1959).

53 Sophus A. Reinert, 'Cameralism and Commercial Rivalry: Nationbuilding through Economic Autarky in Seckendorff's 1665 *Additiones*', *European Journal of Law and Economics*, 19 (2005), 271–86.

54 Carl Wennerlind, 'Theatrum Œconomicum: Anders Berch and the Dramatization of the Swedish Improvement Discourse', in Robert Fredona and Sophus Reinert (eds), *The Legitimacy of Power: New Perspectives on the History of Political Economy* (Basingstoke, 2018); Carl Wennerlind, 'The Political Economy of Sweden's Age of Greatness: Johan Risingh and the Hartlib Circle', in Rössner (ed.), *Economic Growth*, pp. 156–85.

the Hartlib Circle.[55] From Scotland to Scandinavia through to the German lands an understanding developed that economy and science were the keys to cornucopia, and that moderately regulated but in principle free competitive market economies were the secret of success.

All these intellectual exercises and enterprises contributed to the formation of a mercantilist entrepreneurial consciousness which influenced European economic thinking in the early Enlightenment, including writers such as Steuart and, to an extent, Smith. The foundations of this ideology of dynamism were manufacturing, for the simple reason that the value added in manufacturing is immeasurably higher than in any primary or semi-processed industry. Writers like Botero, Hörnigk, or Swedish scientist and economist Christopher Polhelm never failed to state that manufactures were a nation's gold mine. What the Spanish had with their Cerro Rico silver mine in Potosí in the New World, other European nations had in their manufactures and manufactories. All you needed, wrote Hörnigk, was *Federn und Dinte* – ink and a quill – and a dose of human reason. It was there before your eyes. Hörnigk summarised his development strategy in his 'Nine Rules of Oeconomy': essentially a mercantilist import substitution and infant industry protection model. If you kept to the Hörnigk strategy, this would yield you an additional kingdom and a 'Peruvian Potosí' – the equivalent of a silver mine.

So, whether Scotland's industrial moment and blossoming after 1670 was an expression of Calvinism and the Weberian spirit of capitalism, it was also part of a European industrial moment and positive mercantilist-cameralist economic spirit. The pamphlet literature debating the pros and cons of incorporating Union before 1707 testifies to a high degree of economic literacy amongst the Scottish elites, even though much of it was written with at least some regard to vested interests. Writers such as John Spreull adroitly juggled numbers to estimate Scotland's balance of trade.[56] These learned exercises were early examples of modern national income accounting. They failed as badly as modern financial market prognoses usually do – but at least they were failing in a modern, capitalist way.

*   *   *

We should thus recognise positive aspects of several ventures that have usually been decried as 'failures'. These include the Darien scheme, and the series of manufactories established in Lowland Scotland between 1680 and 1707. The Darien project was crushed not so much because it

55 See e.g. Carl Wennerlind, 'Money: Hartlibian Political Economy and the New Culture of Credit', in Philip J. Stern and Carl Wennerlind (eds), *Mercantilism Reimagined: Political Economy in Early Modern Britain and Its Empire* (Oxford, 2014).

56 John Spreull, *An Accompt Current Betwixt Scotland and England Balanced ...* (Edinburgh, 1705).

was set up in the wrong location by a smaller nation that competed on unequal footing with what became one of the most powerful mercantilist fiscal-military states of its age, England, nor because England failed to support the venture upon Spanish defeat. It failed not so much because of economic unprofitability or lack of entrepreneurial spirit – quite the contrary – but rather because of an unfavourable turn in global politics at a time of general climatic deterioration. On top of this, as Douglas Watt has argued, the Company of Scotland was inadequately capitalised for the Darien venture, and the directors' decision to go to Darien may have been an avoidable error.[57] However, reasons, or bundles of reasons, for 'failure' are complex and perhaps not ultimately possible to determine in terms of causality (or causal weighing of individual factors).

So, to understand the nature of the Scottish economy, the mere establishment of such a company is more important than its business failure. It reflected an active culture of capitalism in late seventeenth-century Scotland – a capitalist spirit that was alive and kicking (capitalism is not exclusively about success!). It reflected a shared culture and public discourse of optimism, openness to opportunities, within and beyond Scotland, and thus a fundamentally new and dynamic understanding of the human-economic future as a field that was open. That future was contingent upon many factors, potentially manageable and malleable, calculable – and not necessarily inscribed any more into God's book of Providence. As I have argued elsewhere, such notions of an open future were shared across early modern Europe; they represented key foundations of the making of capitalism and economic modernity.[58]

All this suggests that we should be positive about the pre-1707 Scottish economy. It *could* have turned out better than it did, and there was enough of a 'capitalist spirit' around. Manufactories, privileged or not, were the standard instrument in early capitalist Europe for handling large-scale industrial enterprise. With their rational accounting and bookkeeping to organise production, they contained almost all the necessary characteristics of modern capitalist enterprise and industry – all except the steam engine, which was introduced towards the later eighteenth century. The manufactories have often, especially in the Prussian case, been decried as unsuccessful because the surviving records sometimes suggest that they made losses in some years. Furthermore, historians, stepping into the trap of ahistoricity and teleology, have an unfortunate inclination to interpret things that do not survive as things that were wrong and doomed to fail. But economic development rarely works like this (even though both

---

57 Douglas Watt, *The Price of Scotland: Darien, Union, and the Wealth of Nations* (Edinburgh, 2007).

58 Philipp Robinson Rössner, 'Capitalism, Cameralism, and the Discovery of the Future 1300s–2000s: Europe's Road to Wealth', *History of Political Economy*, 53:2 (2021), 443–60.

Marxism and neoliberalism would often have us believe that it does). In fact, Marx himself, in *Capital* Volume 1, devoted an entire chapter to manufactories as a precursor of the factory system.[59] They represented a crucial stage – perhaps *the* crucial stage – in the development of the modern factory system.

Not all industry was, prior to industrialisation, necessarily located in the countryside or organised on the level of individual households, as a much-debated collaborative monograph by Kriedte, Medick and Schlumbohm once suggested.[60] The 'proto-industrialisation' hypothesis has, whilst making important contributions to the debate, shifted our focus on the dynamics of pre-industrial development and transitions towards capitalism in pre-modern Europe. The shift away from an urban-centred view of the development of capitalism and industry is welcome, but the link between proto-industry and industry appears less certain. There were as many regions with strong proto-industry in the sixteenth and seventeenth centuries which did not undergo an industrial revolution in the eighteenth and nineteenth centuries as there were regions where this connection can be proven to have been strong. The 'putting-out' or *Verlag* system was the older one, dating back into the middle ages, whilst the manufactory was a classic product of the early modern mercantilist age. But the mercantilist manufactory contained many elements crucial to nineteenth- and twentieth-century industrial or factory capitalism.

Werner Sombart picked up Marx's argument, developing an important insight into the close connection between state, enterprise – chiefly in the shape of manufactories – and the making of modern capitalism. Whilst Marx, in his chapter on 'primitive accumulation',[61] had focused on an emerging class struggle between agrarian entrepreneurs and a mercantilist state which facilitated processes of alienation from the land, creating the foundations of a landless proletariat and thus fuelling the process of primitive accumulation, Sombart's eye was focused on the nascent capitalist spirit, which he had perceived in the medieval feudal-manorial economy, but whose breakthrough was finally delivered by the rise of the modern territorial and later nation states since the sixteenth and seventeenth centuries. Here the demand of the state related to supplying the armed forces. By demanding industrial products on a large scale and of

---

59 Karl Marx, *Das Kapital: Kritik der politischen Ökonomie*, vol. 1: *Der Produktionsprozess des Kapitals* ([Hamburg, 1867] Berlin, 1955), ch. 12, on 'Teilung der Arbeit und Manufaktur' (Division of Labour and Manufactories); cf. Karl Marx, *Capital: A Critique of Political Economy*, trans. Ben Fowkes and David Fernbach (3 vols, Harmondsworth, 1976–81), vol. 1, ch. 14.

60 Peter Kriedte, Hans Medick and Jürgen Schlumbohm, *Industrialisation before Industrialisation: Rural Industry in the Genesis of Capitalism*, trans. Beate Schempp (Cambridge, 1981).

61 Marx, *Kapital*, vol. 1, ch. 24; Marx, *Capital*, vol. 1, ch. 26.

standardised quality, the state facilitated capitalist enterprise. Marshall, in his magisterial *Presbyteries and Profits*, counted 106 such manufactories established in Scotland between 1560 and 1707, 76 of which were founded between 1660 and 1707.[62] The Scottish manufactories after 1661 were mostly directed at producing non-essential goods, even luxuries, such as glass, paper, silk and coaches, substituting for imports. In fact, the most dangerous foreign competing products after the Union were German and Russian linens. Nevertheless, these manufactories, which we find not only in Scotland, but also in Prussia, Saxony, Austria, Denmark and Sweden (there often run by Scotsmen),[63] must not be underestimated in their long-term contribution to development, useful knowledge and rational business organisation, perhaps even mentality. In terms of labour organisation, wages, bookkeeping and regard for the future, manufactories transcended traditional frameworks of business, and many aspects of such ventures have survived into modern days.

And there was a lot of rural industry in Scotland, too. As Whatley and others have noted, about every second or third woman and man in the eighteenth-century Scottish working population would have found at least some by-employment (seasonal, part-time) in the linen industry.[64] The industrial revolution had a longer prehistory than most accounts will admit. And a lot of this 'deep history' was marked by the large workshop and centralised manufacturing businesses characteristic of Marx's age of 'primitive' or initial accumulation – early modern Europe during its 'mercantilist' phase.

In the rural market centres and fairs, the 'spirit of capitalism' is striking. For example, the 1669 'Act in favors of the laird of Carstairs for three fairs yeerlie at Carstairs' promised 'a great deall of good and proffite' from its convenient location.[65] There were nearly 500 such acts between 1660 and 1707. They indicate a changing structure of markets, money and commerce in Lowland Scottish agriculture. Ian Whyte has compiled a time series for these acts, establishing the basic pattern of such regional market establishments from the Restoration to the Union.[66] What we now need is a sense of *timing*. To what extent did these newly-licensed markets and fairs represent and follow seasonal trade cycles allowing merchants (such as cattle dealers) to move between fairs and regions in a similar way as was the case for medieval fairs (as in Flanders and Champagne, but also lower-grade regional fairs)? Nonetheless, the

---

62 Marshall, *Presbyteries and Profits*, pp. 284–319.
63 Steve Murdoch, *Network North: Scottish Kin, Commercial and Covert Associations in Northern Europe 1603–1746* (Leiden, 2006); Chris Evans and Göran Rydén, *Baltic Iron in the Atlantic World in the Eighteenth Century* (Leiden, 2007).
64 Whatley, *Industrial Revolution*.
65 RPS, 1669/10/24.
66 Whyte, 'Growth of Periodic Market Centres'.

language and sense of the above act, to ensure that 'ther would a great deall of good and proffite arise to nighbours therabout', reflects the more general spirit of this type of legislation.

This spirit extended into manufacturing. An 'Act for naturalisation of strangers' (1669) provided, amongst other things, 'for the incres and promoveing of trade and manufactories'.[67] The 1661 'Act for incourageing of shiping and navigation' was the Scottish version of the English act of 1660 that had built upon a Cromwellian initiative of 1651 to lay the foundations of the first or 'Old' colonial English and, from 1707, British mercantilist empire.[68] The 1661 act could not achieve the same results at the time, as Scotland did not yet have colonies, but it expressed the logic that would later be put into practice when Scotland joined England's empire. Further Scottish legislation directly addressed a range of other economic matters, including fishing, the promotion of manufactories, the appointment of a Council for Trade, prohibitions on exporting woollen yarn, drinking foreign beer, the settling of debts, the exportation of money, the timing of the salmon fisheries, or the method of curing and packing fish – an industry in which the Dutch had flourished during their now waning Golden Age.[69] A dark side of mercantilism was represented by the 1672 'Act for establishing correction-houses for idle beggars and vagabonds'.[70]

Devine's landmark study on agrarian change, *The Transformation of Rural Scotland*, found patches of Lowland Scotland in which a capitalist approach to agriculture had taken root in the early eighteenth century, but dated the onset of the major transformation towards improvement chiefly to the post-1760 period.[71] Scholars such as Whyte have shown that long before the Union there existed wide regions across Lowland Scotland where traditional methods of farming had given rise to more market-driven, competitive and high-powered agrarian regimes, suggesting a commercialised tenant and landowner class working together in promoting agrarian development and change, commercialisation and productivity increases.[72]

67 RPS, 1669/10/25.
68 RPS, 1661/1/341.
69 Christiaan van Bochove and Jan Luiten van Zanden, 'Two Engines of Early Modern Economic Growth? Herring Fisheries and Whaling during the Dutch Golden Age (1600–1800)', in Simonetta Cavaciocchi (ed.), *Ricchezza del mare, ricchezza dal mare: Secoli XIII–XVIII* (Florence, 2006), pp. 557–74; de Vries and van der Woude, *First Modern Economy*.
70 RPS, 1672/6/52.
71 Devine, *Transformation of Rural Scotland*, pp. 19–34.
72 Ian Whyte, 'Pre-Improvement Rural Settlement in Scotland: Progress and Prospects', *Scottish Geographical Magazine*, 114:2 (1998), 76–84; Ian Whyte, 'Poverty or Prosperity? Rural Society in Lowland Scotland in the Late Sixteenth and Early Seventeenth Centuries', *Scottish Economic and Social*

In order to demonstrate a 'capitalistic' spirit in Scottish agriculture in the 1660s or before, it suffices to show that such a spirit can be found; it does not have to have been characteristic of the country as a whole. For capitalism and the capitalist spirit in the sense of Weber, Sombart or Braudel it matters less how many people actually subscribe to capitalism, or how great a share of output or input is derived from capitalistic processes. Capitalism moves through stages; it changes shape; it is manifested in different actors, processes, technologies and social densities over time. The industrial revolution that took place in Scotland and England after 1760 was only one manifestation of capitalism.

Thus we should not dismiss the seventeenth century as a century of capitalism's absence merely on the grounds of sluggish economic performance. The 1690s to the 1730s were indeed a period of depression for the Scottish economy, but this is not evidence of a lack of entrepreneurial spirit. Rather, it is evidence of bad climate and poor harvests, destructive wars, and sluggish population growth – problems not only for Scotland but also for much of Continental Europe. Meanwhile a shift in the global political balance was occurring, with Sweden and France declining, the Netherlands stagnating as the warehouse of the world, and England ascending as the leading political and economic player of the day.

One expression of a possible connection between presbyterianism, the Kirk and economic development comes from the 1695 'Act anent Burying in Scots Linen', a revision of an earlier act from 1686, which stated its rationale as being 'for the better improvement of the manufactory of linen within the kingdom, and restraining the import of all forraign linen'.[73] Both acts were superseded in 1707 by a much briefer 'Act for burying in woollen', also with an economic rationale: 'for encouragement of the manufacture of wooll within this kingdom'.[74] The underlying

---

History, 18:1 (1998), 19–32; Brian Bonnyman, 'Agrarian Patriotism and the Landed Interest: The Scottish "Society of Improvers in the Knowledge of Agriculture" 1723–1746', in Koen Stapelbroek and Jani Marjanen (eds), *The Rise of Economic Societies in the Eighteenth Century* (Basingstoke, 2012), pp. 26–51; Bonnyman, *Buccleuch and Adam Smith*; Hugh Cheape, 'For the Betterment of Mankind: Scotland, the Enlightenment and the Agricultural Revolution', *Folk Life*, 40:1 (2001), 7–24; T. M. Devine, 'Reappraising the Early Modern Economy 1500–1650', in T. M. Devine and Jenny Wormald (eds), *The Oxford Handbook of Modern Scottish History* (Oxford, 2012), pp. 236–50; Julian Goodare, 'In Search of the Scottish Agrarian Problem', in Jane Whittle (ed.), *Landlords and Tenants in Britain 1440–1660: Tawney's 'Agrarian Problem' Revisited* (Woodbridge, 2013), pp. 100–16; Heather Holmes, 'Scottish Agricultural Writers and the Creation of Their Personal Identities between 1697 and 1790', *Folk Life*, 44:1 (2005), 87–110; T. C. Smout, 'A New Look at the Scottish Improvers', *SHR*, 91:1 (2012), 125–49.

73 RPS, 1695/5/201; cf. 1686/4/44.
74 RPS, 1706/10/461.

mercantilist rationale and capitalist spirit of this period emerges clearly. The involvement of parish elders in administering mercantilist regulation and infant industry protectionism reveals the Kirk playing its part in the game of capitalism. This reinforces Marshall's and Sombart's instincts about Scotland, presbyterianism and the rise of a capitalist spirit, perhaps even vindicating Max Weber's speculative observations on world religions and economic development as laid out in his works on *Religionssoziologie*.[75]

* * *

The tobacco trade is another success story that has often been ascribed to the workings of the free market and the making of the 'world's biggest free trade zone' by incorporating Scotland into the English colonial empire in 1707. However, much of tobacco's success can be attributed to the state as a container and facilitator of modern capitalism in Scotland.

Around 1760 Scotland handled roughly one per cent of total European trade. And yet it was, after England, Europe's second largest purveyor of American tobacco. In 1773, when the highest figure ever was recorded, 46 million pounds of American tobacco was shipped to Continental destinations from Scotland, meeting the demand of perhaps one-quarter of the north-western European population. Tobacco accounted for up to 40 per cent of Scotland's total imports and exports. Most of it, usually 90 per cent of yearly imports, was re-exported without much processing. By the 1760s, Glasgow, with its two outports Greenock and Port Glasgow, had become Britain's largest single tobacco importer.[76] A lot of this growth was, from the point of supply, founded upon slavery.[77]

This development in the service sector economy, manifested by the colonial re-export trades, was facilitated, even triggered, by the introduction of English mercantilism with the Restoration customs system.[78] It gave rise to sophisticated business methods in Glasgow, particularly the store system in the colonies[79] (as opposed to the more traditional

---

75 Most famously his article on 'The Protestant Ethic and the Spirit of Capitalism' (1904–05). See the anthology Max Weber, *Religion Und Gesellschaft: Gesammelte Aufsätze zur Religionssoziologie* (Berlin, 2006), and recent research by economists, partly rehabilitating Weber: Sascha O. Becker, Steven Pfaff and Jared Rubin, 'Causes and Consequences of the Protestant Reformation', *Explorations in Economic History*, 62 (2016), 1–25; Sascha O. Becker and Ludger Woessmann, 'Was Weber Wrong? A Human Capital Theory of Protestant Economic History', *Quarterly Journal of Economics*, 124:2 (2009), 531–96.

76 Rössner, *Scottish Trade in the Wake of Union*, statistical appendix.

77 T. M. Devine (ed.), *Recovering Scotland's Slavery Past: The Caribbean Connection* (Edinburgh, 2015).

78 Rössner, *Scottish Trade in the Wake of Union*, chs 2, 3.

79 Devine, 'Industrialisation', p. 53. Full elaboration in the classic Devine, *Tobacco Lords*; and Devine, 'Golden Age of Tobacco'.

consignment pattern) and business networks that had flourished long before 1707.[80] Geography played a part in this, with the shorter sea route between the Chesapeake and Glasgow compared to London and other English ports.[81] Starting in Virginia, it was quicker to get to Glasgow than to London. If the tobacco was re-exported to the Continent, the voyage would have been longer from Glasgow than from London. However, politics mattered; during the numerous wars with France, the route across the northern Atlantic would not have been as full of French privateers as the southerly route. The Irish Sea was likewise not the most favourable navigation route, either. Many Scottish re-exports to Continental Europe took the northern route around Cape Wrath. Glaswegian success was also dependent on business success and productivity change, for instance due to decreasing turnaround time of tobacco ships engaged in the multi-angular voyages between America, Scotland and Europe.

Without doubt an increase in routine and practice in the trades would over time have established a pool of reliable and useful business knowledge, which was important for success in the colonial trade.[82] But it is difficult to conceive of Scotland's commercial transformation between the mid-1730s and mid-1770s without the helping hand of the British state. Sometime after the Excise Crisis in 1733 the productivity and turnover record of the Clyde tobacco trade became impressive. Meanwhile, smuggling declined as Glaswegian entrepreneurs switched from evasion to cooperation. They would now derive more benefits from collaboration with the state.[83]

Once established, the system worked as follows. The English customs system was extended to Scotland after the 1707 Union.[84] Duties on tobacco increased eightfold, and duties on plantation sugar doubled. Overall, the English structure of duties imposed a much heavier *nominal* tax burden – but the system nevertheless stimulated Scotland's commercial

80   Allan I. Macinnes, 'Scottish Circumvention of the English Navigation Acts in the American Colonies 1660–1707', in Günther Lottes, Eero Medijainen and Jón Viðar Sigurðsson (eds), *Making, Using and Resisting the Law in European History* (Pisa, 2008), pp. 109–30.

81   Jacob M. Price, 'The Rise of Glasgow in the Chesapeake Tobacco Trade 1707–1775', *William and Mary Quarterly*, 11:2 (1954), 179–99; W. Iain Stevenson, 'Some Aspects of the Geography of the Clyde Tobacco Trade in the Eighteenth Century', *Scottish Geographical Magazine*, 89:1 (1973), 19–35.

82   Richard F. Dell, 'The Operational Record of the Clyde Tobacco Fleet 1747–1775', *Scottish Economic and Social History*, 2 (1982), 1–17.

83   This does not mean that they gave up smuggling totally, as the record of the Customhouse papers of any major Scottish port at the time demonstrates. Rössner, *Scottish Trade in the Wake of Union*, chs 4, 5, especially on tea smuggling.

84   See above, and most recently Christopher A. Whatley, *The Scots and the Union: Then and Now*, 2nd edn (Edinburgh, 2014).

development.[85] For a large share of import duty could be obtained as a refund ('draw-back') when colonial imports were re-exported within three years from a British port, provided that the importers, their ships and crews were British.[86] Tobacco drew back 100 per cent (after 1723), West Indian sugar between 78 and 89 per cent, American rice up to 90 per cent. These were Scotland's main re-export commodities in the eighteenth century. Tobacco was, after 1723, the only commodity that could draw back *all* import duties. In Scotland, the principle of transforming Britain into a 'warehouse' of the world eventually came across even more clearly than in England.[87] Since the 1660s, England had diversified its export portfolio, with domestic industry such as textile manufacture supplying a considerable share of total exports.[88] Its colonial re-exports (the 'Tory' political economy schedule) created some *additional* but by no means the main dynamics. In Scotland, with re-exports usually exceeding domestic exports in value terms until late in the century, overseas trade became focused on warehousing.[89]

Regardless of whether an imported cargo would be re-exported subsequently, merchants always became liable for the full amount of nominal import duty upon declaration of their cargoes. This seems to have been, at least in the Scottish case, one of the ironies built into the system. After all, if nearly 90 per cent of tobacco imports were to be re-exported, why should the state have bothered levying import duties in the first place? The answer is that most of the payments of import duty on commodities that were destined for re-export were settled using 'book money'.[90] Cash hardly ever changed hands. Rather, parts of the duties due upon import

---

85 For the remainder of this section, I follow T. M. Devine and Philipp Robinson Rössner, 'Scots in the Atlantic Economy 1600–1800', in John MacKenzie and T. M. Devine (eds), *Scotland and the British Empire* (Oxford, 2011), pp. 30–54; Philipp Robinson Rössner, 'Interloping, Economic Underdevelopment and the State in Eighteenth-Century Northern Europe: How Scotland Became a Tobacco Entrepôt', in M. A. Denzel, Jan de Vries and Philipp Robinson Rössner (eds), *Small Is Beautiful: Interlopers and Smaller Trading Nations in the Pre-Industrial Period* (Stuttgart, 2011), pp. 103–30; and Philipp Robinson Rössner, 'New Avenues of Trade: Structural Change in the European Economy and Foreign Trade as Reflected in the Changing Structure of Scotland's Commerce', *JSHS*, 31:1 (2011), 1–25.

86 Meaning that at least 75 per cent of the crew had to be of British birth.

87 Rössner, *Scottish Trade in the Wake of Union*, pp. 51–4. Most recently, Nuala Zahedieh, *The Capital and the Colonies: London and the Atlantic Economy 1660–1700* (Cambridge, 2010).

88 Ralph Davis, 'English Foreign Trade 1700–1774', *EcHR*, 2nd ser., 15 (1962), 285–303; Ralph Davis, 'English Foreign Trade 1660–1700', *EcHR*, 2nd ser., 6 (1954), 150–66.

89 Rössner, *Scottish Trade in the Wake of Union*, esp. chs 5 and 6 and appendix.

90 These working mechanisms can be seen in a manual for newly-appointed customs officers in Scotland in 1707: NRS, Instructions for the Collectors and

could be 'bonded'. A promise was made to pay a certain amount of cash at a specified later day plus interest on the principal for the time specified, and a bond was issued by the merchant upon importation of a certain cargo in lieu of paying cash. Usually the cargoes were lodged in the crown's warehouse until their destination had been decided. When re-exported, the sums stated on the bond were refunded by clearing off the debts on the bond against the draw-back or tax refund to which the cargo was nominally entitled. Cash only changed hands to clear a small remaining difference between the sums stated on the bond and the draw-back of customs duties. Since the British customs system operated a variety of discounts upon ready payment *in cash*, but draw-backs were calculated on the basis of *nominal (pre-discount) liabilities*, a difference of about 11 per cent usually remained after clearing the books. These sums represented the net fiscal income of the Treasury from the warehouse economy around Glasgow.

The rationale of this system becomes clear when we consider the nature of eighteenth-century commerce. Especially in the colonial trades, dependent upon an intrinsically linked import and re-export business, nominal import duty easily reached into several thousands of pounds sterling that were due immediately and in cash, if the discounts were to be taken. Only a small number of merchants were able to advance these sums on-the-spot and in cash. This was still the Braudelian world of a cashless and credit economy where business and trade depended upon generous and long lines of credit – from the big merchant down to the smaller artisan.[91] In the colonial trades, and given the structure of duties and the changed price structure, with colonial goods significantly decreasing in price between the 1660s and 1770s, credit arrangements became the norm. In Scotland, where revenue accounts are available for the 1707 to 1783 period, 'bonded' customs duties, i.e. those sums that were never paid in cash, represented between 50 (in the early period) and 90 per cent of total duties payable on imported tobacco (in the later period).[92] The Glaswegian trade boom was founded upon tax credit.

It has been suggested that, alongside change in agriculture and the linen sector – both of which gathered momentum after 1760 – it was the Glaswegian tobacco trades that manifestly contributed to Scottish economic development, through the regional multiplier effects. Many Glaswegian Tobacco Lords ran iron works and textile manufactures producing those goods that were sold in the plantations and that made up the outbound cargoes of ships returning to the Clyde laden with

---

other officers employed in Her Majesty's Customs etc in the north part of Great Britain (1707), CE7/11.

91 Braudel, *Civilisation and Capitalism*, vol. 3.

92 Rössner, *Scottish Trade in the Wake of Union*, appendix.

tobacco.[93] On the other hand, trade levels remained low – Scotland's per capita trade around 1755 stood at about a quarter of the English level; the tobacco trades were a regional phenomenon, and from their sheer monetary volume unlikely to have made any more than a marginal contribution to Scotland's GDP (or total economic activity). Before the industrial revolution the Scottish economy was neither export-orientated nor trade-driven.[94] But that tells us nothing (or not much) about capitalist dynamics, which are often happening at the margins (meaning they may not necessarily appear particularly large when measured against a country's total economic activity, but take place within niches, particular areas, pockets). Capitalism thus worked by combining private enterprise, the profit-motive and laissez-faire with the more rigid interventionist fetters of the nascent modern state. Patrick O'Brien's research has proven beyond doubt that it was because of, not in spite of, English mercantilism that Britannia managed to industrialise and defeat Napoleon at Waterloo.[95] Prasannan Parthasarathi has found the British customs system and interventionist state to have been responsible for making the British cotton industry – in which Scotland participated.[96] A recent study of the development of Paisley as a major location for higher-value cotton-linen mixtures has shown that 'the growth of fine weaving relied largely on English markets'.[97]

This process may in fact have corresponded to England's eighteenth-century development in the cotton sector, when Indian cotton producers were priced out of the market. Initially the import of finished coloured textiles was banned, thus repatriating the value added by colouring and printing though the relocation of the finishing processes from Asia to Britain. English and Scottish producers eventually shifted one further stage up by restricting imports to cotton yarn, adding the weaving stage to their existing portfolio. Then cotton spinning also relocated to Britain. The final stage was achieved around 1770 or 1780, when steam-powered spinning wheels, water frames and power looms were introduced. By the 1830s Indian cotton exports had vanished almost completely, while

---

93 T. M. Devine, 'The Colonial Trades and Industrial Investments in Scotland c.1700–1815', in Pieter Emmer and Femme Gaastra (eds), *The Organization of Interoceanic Trade in European Expansion 1450–1800* (Aldershot, 1996), pp. 299–312; Devine, 'The Modern Economy'.

94 Rössner, *Scottish Trade in the Wake of Union*, chs 3–5, and statistical appendix.

95 Patrick O'Brien, 'The Nature and Historical Evolution of an Exceptional Fiscal State and Its Possible Significance for the Precocious Commercialization and Industrialization of the British Economy from Cromwell to Nelson', *EcHR*, 64:2 (2011), 408–46.

96 Parthasarathi, *Why Europe Grew Rich and Asia Did Not*; Stuart M. Nisbet, 'The Making of Scotland's First Industrial Region: The Early Cotton Industry in Renfrewshire', *JSHS*, 29:1 (2009), 1–28.

97 Nisbet, 'The Making of Scotland's First Industrial Region', p. 5.

British hotspots around Manchester and Paisley had turned into one of the world's largest suppliers of finished cottons and linen-cotton mixtures.[98]

In this way, the English Restoration customs system of 1660, and the idiosyncratic context of its adaptation for Scotland after 1707, provided a powerful stimulus to Scotland's economic development. We find a proactive state in Scotland after 1707, but it ceased to work according to the pre-1707 framework. Whilst the political histories of the post-1707 'Scottish' state – a seeming paradox – have been so aptly discussed by Alexander Murdoch, Bruce Lenman and others, the history of political economy and the post-1707 interventionist Scottish state still awaits future study.[99] Clearly it was not the British state, nor was it the Westminster parliament, which steered post-1707 Scottish economic development.[100]

* * *

One last, cursory remark may be made on the intellectual history or political economy of capitalism. The two works that would prove foundational for the intellectual legitimisation of modern Western capitalism came from Scotland: Steuart's *An Inquiry into the Principles of Political Oeconomy* (1767) and Smith's *Wealth of Nations* (1776). Steuart, a Jacobite, spent much time in exile in France and the German lands. He wrote major parts of the first two volumes of his *Principles* at Tübingen in 1755–56, where he most likely read the economic works that were fashionable in his day, most notably the works of Johann Heinrich Justi (discussed above), who had just published two of his most important works: *Staatswirthschaft* (Principles of State Economics, 1755) and *Policeywirtschaft* (Principles of Police Science, 1756, meaning 'economic policy and management'). In the role that Steuart devotes to the abstract 'statesman', and the range of topics covered, he appears much more of a Continental than a British thinker, devoting a large part of his work to questions of monetary theory, akin to the monetary scenario in the Germany of his day. One expert has even called Steuart a 'crypto-cameralist'.[101]

In a similar vein, Steuart is often dubbed the 'last of the mercantilists', partly because Smith, in the *Wealth of Nations*, never mentions him

98 Dietmar Rothermund, *Europa und Asien im Zeitalter des Merkantilismus* (Darmstadt, 1978); Parthasarathi, *Why Europe Grew Rich and Asia Did Not.*
99 Murdoch, *Making the Union Work*; Bruce P. Lenman, *Enlightenment and Change: Scotland 1746–1832* (Edinburgh, 2009).
100 Hoppit, *Britain's Political Economies.*
101 Keith Tribe, 'Polizei, Staat und die Staatswissenschaften bei J. H. G. von Justi', in Heinz Rieter and Bertram Schefold (eds), *Vademecum zu einem Klassiker des Kameralismus: [Kommentarband zur Faksimile-Ausgabe der 1756 erschienenen Erstausgabe von Johann Heinrich Gottlob von Justi: Grundsätze der Policey-Wissenschaft]* (Düsseldorf, 1993), pp. 107–40.

whilst obviously devoting at least Book IV more or less entirely to the (meaningless) task of taking mercantilism down, on largely false grounds, by insinuating that mercantilists would have succumbed to the intellectual folly known as the 'Midas Fallacy', by equating gold and silver with a nation's real wealth. However, none of the advanced mercantilist thinkers of the seventeenth and eighteenth centuries ever made the scientific mistake of identifying precious metals with a nation's real wealth. Money and a positive trade balance were only *signifiers* of real wealth. The metaphor of manufactures as the 'real gold mine' (discussed above) illustrates what I would instead like to call the 'Adam Smith Fallacy' or 'Midas Fallacy-Fallacy': the deliberate misportrayal and distortion of mercantilism's main scientific hypotheses in neoliberal master narratives. From the early nineteenth century and Adam Smith's negative portrayal, to the 1990s and theories of 'mercantilism as rent-seeking society', neoliberal ideology tried, usually successfully, to misrepresent mercantilism's scientific content.[102] We should not forget, either, that the modern Adam Smith hype – a landmark and trade sign in the neoliberal economic mind – arose in the 1970s. Only then did Smith and his *Inquiry* begin to rise to fame as the intellectual foundation stone of economic modernity.

In fact, Steuart sketched (as did Smith) the basic framework of a competitive high-level market economy based on money and commerce, profit-making and freedom of trade. It has even been argued that Steuart prefigured Marx's 'primitive accumulation', the creation of a wage-dependent labour force by evicting tenants from their established moral economies and framework of small-holding, as witnessed in Scotland from the 1760s onwards in the infamous 'Highland Clearances'.[103] Steuart may even be reckoned, alongside Marx, among the forefathers of Classical Economics (Marx admired Steuart but was rather dismissive of Smith). Contrasting Smith and Steuart in the light of a longer Continental history of modern economic analysis that, since the 1600s, had provided increasing emphasis on competitive markets, the promotion of manufacturing and commerce thus represents another lacuna in the scholarly literature. To fill it will require bridging the gap between archival economic history and the history of ideas or economic thought. Scotland may once again present a good starting point for such exercises.

* * *

Some scholars have seen the origins of capitalist behaviour and mentality within agriculture and agrarian-based systems of profit and exploitation,

102 Robert B. Ekelund and Robert D. Tollison, *Mercantilism as a Rent-Seeking Society: Economic Regulation in Historical Perspective* (College State, TX, 1982).
103 Michael Perelman, *The Invention of Capitalism: Classical Political Economy and the Secret History of Primitive Accumulation* (Durham, NC, 2000).

going back in some cases to the middle ages, the fourteenth-century 'crisis of feudalism', or the sixteenth-century age of enclosure, economic expansion and rising social conflict.[104] Others such as Sombart have seen the roots of the capitalist spirit within the medieval demesne system. Fernand Braudel on the other hand identified commerce and trade, not agriculture, as 'capitalism's home ground' and saw a long prehistory of modern capitalism that went back to the medieval and early modern world economies – as there were many 'worlds', there were many world economies before globalisation. Yet other scholars would take issue with the notion that modern capitalism was to be found either within the agrarian economy or anywhere else before the onset of industrialisation and the rise of the factory age.[105]

This chapter, meanwhile, has revisited certain aspects of this story with regard to early modern Scotland. Capitalism was old, long-predating the historian's magical boundary of AD 1800. It was not specific to Europe and not specific to any sector, but could be found in manufacturing, industry, commerce or agriculture alike. Much more than a purely economic phenomenon, it was a mode of production and needs to be studied accordingly with reference to social, cultural, psychological and institutional dimensions, including religion, as well as a comparative European dimension. Moreover, the role of the state can be seen as crucial in the process of empowering capitalism.

---

104 See Kerridge, *Agrarian Problems*; and Aston and Philpin (eds), *Brenner Debate*.
105 Providing the correct reference for what constitutes the 'mainstream view' would be like seeking the proverbial needle in the haystack. Works like the introduction to Neal and Williamson (eds), *Cambridge History of Capitalism*, vol. 1, would be indicative. Most articles and books written on the history of capitalism nowadays seem to focus on nineteenth-century business history and industrialisation.

Conclusion: A Historiographical and Bibliographical Overview

R. A. Houston

This short concluding chapter reviews the recent historiography of Scottish agriculture in the early modern period. It also, and more importantly, looks forward as well as backward. It sets 'agrarian history' in a broader social and cultural context, and outlines a variety of methodologies that are relevant in this broader context, drawn from historical geography, archaeology, landscape history and legal history. The conclusion is that scholars should focus 'on people rather than places', and should 'reject the compartmentalisation of political from social and economic history'.

The phrase 'early modern' is used for all sorts of purposes, but perhaps the most important is to describe a period linking the apparently lost world of the middle ages with modern times. In England and other parts of Europe, there is an established concern for this 'age of transition', even if changes often took place only slowly. Instead of a transformation at the end of the middle ages, there were continuities, tensions and fluidity in Scotland, with the most significant breaks happening, on a one-millennium view, in the twelfth and eighteenth centuries.[1]

Decisive change did happen during the seventeenth century in some parts of Scotland, as historical geographer Ian Whyte has shown.[2] The balance between service, family labour and day labour varied by region

---

1 Chris Dalglish, 'An Age of Transition? Castles and the Scottish Highland Estate in the 16th and 17th Centuries', *Post-Medieval Archaeology*, 39:2 (2005), 243–66.

2 Ian Whyte's contribution has been enormous. Ian Whyte, *Agriculture and Society in Seventeenth Century Scotland* (Edinburgh, 1979); Ian Whyte and Kathleen Whyte, *The Changing Scottish Landscape 1500–1800* (London, 1991); Ian Whyte, 'Pre-Improvement Rural Settlement in Scotland: Progress and Prospects', *Scottish Geographical Magazine*, 114:2 (1998), 76–84.

and locality, but by the 1690s two-fifths of adult males in the Lothians and Berwickshire were farm servants. Mostly the important transitions came later, though historians remain divided on how abrupt they were; some think both landscape and society were always in the making.[3] For example, historical geographer Bob Dodgshon finds that sheep farming was introduced gradually into the Highlands, easing the introduction of changing tenures and land use well before the classic age of clearances.[4] Colin Shepherd shows that in part of the north-east Lowlands, agriculture was flexible and dynamic from the fifteenth century, supporting a large rural population in a political economy dominated by maximising retainers. In the eighteenth century, however, landowners across Scotland systematically reorganised society 'to suit a new economic ideology based upon rationalisation and capital and underpinned by Enlightenment values of "Improvements"'.[5] A total transformation of local landscapes could occur within a generation. Capturing how people came to terms with these changes is one of many tasks facing historians of agriculture *and* society between 1500 and 1800.

Along with historical geography, archaeology has been one of the most important contributors to this undertaking. Among others, the Ben Lawers project, a mainly archaeological study of human interactions with upland landscape on the north side of Loch Tay, demonstrates that the post-medieval landscape contains a text showing us the dynamics and tensions inherent in the social changes wrought by commercialisation.[6] As Matthew Johnson puts it: 'archaeologists are in a uniquely suitable position to insist that change in the countryside was cultural and social as well as economic'.[7] The legacy of the practices and experiences of farming

3   Robert A. Dodgshon, *Land and Society in Early Scotland* (Oxford, 1981); Robert A. Dodgshon, *No Stone Unturned: A History of Farming, Landscape and Environment in the Scottish Highlands and Islands* (Edinburgh, 2015), p. 118; T. M. Devine, *The Transformation of Rural Scotland: Social Change and the Agrarian Economy 1660–1815* (Edinburgh, 1994).

4   Robert A. Dodgshon, 'Livestock Production in the Scottish Highlands before and after the Clearances', *Rural History*, 9:1 (1998), 19–42.

5   Colin Shepherd, 'Agrarian and Settlement Characterisation in Post-Medieval Strathbogie, Aberdeenshire 1600–1760', *Rural History*, 22:1 (2011), 1–30, at p. 27; Colin Shepherd, 'Changing Tenurial Forms and Service Renders in the North East of Scotland between the Fifteenth and the Eighteenth Centuries: Evidence of Social Development, Capitalised Agrarianism and Ideological Change', *Rural History*, 26:1 (2015), 35–69.

6   John A. Atkinson, 'Settlement Form and Evolution in the Central Highlands of Scotland, ca. 1100–1900', *International Journal of Historical Archaeology*, 14:3 (2010), 316–34.

7   M. H. Johnson, 'An Archaeology of Medieval to Early Modern in Northern England', in Catherine Brooks, Robin Daniels and Anthony Harding (eds), *Past, Present and Future: The Archaeology of Northern England* (Durham, 2002), p. 204.

is in important ways a material one reflected in the landscape rather than in the documentary record, much of which is concerned with estate administration. As well as the physical landscape, which geomorphology can help to reveal, depictions of it in estate plans and other maps offer a way of reading changing land use and humanity's impact upon it.[8] Scholars steeped in archaeological and historical geographical methodologies have brought much to the study of early modern environments, rural and urban alike.[9]

Archaeological cultures represent societies, but it is undeniably easier to infuse them with economic and social significance by drawing, where possible, on a documentary record. The combination allows material objects in a landscape to acquire agency, meaning and depth, bringing out relationships and associations based on the age, sex and social status of the people who used artefacts and inhabited space, in ways that shaped their identity. Thus tea-drinking wares, common in early Georgian Edinburgh, did not become normal in parts of the Highlands until early Victorian times.[10] This was the result, not only of regional differences in wealth, but also of the conscious selection and adaptation of cultural forms. A comparable example is the changing balance of language use between English, Scots and Gaelic in different regions and social classes.[11] Change in the countryside was cultural and social as well as economic. This is where folkloric and literary evidence such as ballads and chapbooks helps us to appreciate the diversity and potential richness of the rural world, bringing out the lived experience of ordinary people.[12]

8 G. Whittington and A. J. S. Gibson, *The Military Survey of Scotland 1747–1755: A Critique* (Norwich, 1986); Rosemary Gibson, *The Scottish Countryside: Its Changing Face 1700–2000* (Edinburgh, 2007).

9 Ronan Toolis and Diana Sproat, 'The Transformation of an Early Post-Medieval Town into a Major Modern City: Excavation and Survey of the Waverley Vaults, New Street, Edinburgh, Scotland', *Post-Medieval Archaeology*, 41:1 (2007), 155–79; John G. Harrison, 'East Flanders Moss, Perthshire: A Documentary Study', *Landscape History*, 30:1 (2008), 5–19; Geoffrey Stell and Robin Tait, 'Framework and Form: Burgage Plots, Street Lines and Domestic Architecture in Early Urban Scotland', *Urban History*, 43:1 (2016), 2–27.

10 Atkinson, 'Settlement Form', p. 332.

11 Charles W. J. Withers, *Gaelic Scotland: The Transformation of a Culture Region* (London, 1988); Wilson MacLeod, *Divided Gaels: Gaelic Cultural Identities in Scotland and Ireland c.1200–c.1650* (Oxford, 2004).

12 Alexander Fenton, 'Material Culture as an Aid to Local History Studies in Scotland', *Journal of the Folklore Institute*, 2:3 (1965), 326–39; J. Morris, 'The Scottish Fair as Seen in Eighteenth- and Nineteenth-Century Sources', *Scottish Studies*, 33 (1999), 89–109; Kevin J. Grant, '"And in Every Hamlet a Poet": Gaelic Oral Tradition and Postmedieval Archaeology in Scotland', *Historical Archaeology*, 48:1 (2014), 30–45; Adam Fox, 'The Emergence of the Scottish Broadside Ballad in the Late Seventeenth and Early Eighteenth Centuries', *JSHS*, 31:2 (2011), 169–94.

That means how they perceived the rights and wrongs of surplus-extraction, working, customs, nature, senses of place and boundary, relations within the family and between it and its neighbours, and so on. Travellers' accounts will also be useful here.[13]

Archaeologists analyse artefacts and landscape as a way of finding out about people. The English legal historian F. W. Maitland possessed a keen sense of place – of landscape as narrative – and a concern with 'that marvellous palimpsest ... the testimony of our fields and walls and hedges' which could be unravelled chronologically. He inspired important mid-twentieth-century English historians, like W. G. Hoskins and M. W. Beresford.[14] Hoskins wrote of 'trying to enter into the minds of the first men to break into a virgin landscape' by picking away 'the cultural humus of sixty generations'.[15] Hoskins's methods – getting the landscape to speak to him – were central to the emergence of English local history in the 1940s and 1950s, and to its subsequent influence on the 'new social history' from the 1960s onwards.[16] Landscape history remains more central in Scotland and Wales than in England, not least because issues of post-medieval land use are an important part of contemporary attitudes towards landscape and society, and thus to modern political identities and social priorities.[17] This relevance also helps to explain the

13 Margaret M. McKay (ed.), *Rev. Dr John Walker's Report on the Hebrides of 1764 and 1771* (Edinburgh, 1980); D. M. Henderson and J. H. Dickson (eds), *A Naturalist in the Highlands: James Robertson, His Life and Travels in Scotland 1767–1771* (Edinburgh, 1994); Norman Scarfe (ed.), *To the Highlands in 1786: The Inquisitive Journey of a Young French Aristocrat* (Woodbridge, 2001).

14 F. W. Maitland, *Domesday Book and Beyond: Three Essays in the Early History of England* (Cambridge, 1897), pp. 15–16; Colin Shepherd, 'Medieval Fields in North-East Scotland', *Landscape History*, 29:1 (2007), 47–74, at p. 47; W. G. Hoskins, *The Making of the English Landscape* (London, 1955); W. G. Hoskins, *Local History in England* (London, 1959), p. 38; W. G. Hoskins, *Fieldwork in Local History* (London, 1969), pp. 17, 117; M. W. Beresford, *History on the Ground: Six Studies in Maps and Landscapes* (London, 1957); M. W. Beresford, *Time and Place: An Inaugural Lecture* (Leeds, 1961), pp. 21–2; Matthew Johnson, *Ideas of Landscape* (Oxford, 2007), pp. 54–8.

15 Hoskins, *Making*, pp. 18, 235. See also the parallel influence of geographers like H. C. Darby, *The Draining of the Fens* (Cambridge, 1940); H. C. Darby, 'On the Relations of Geography and History', *Transactions and Papers (Institute of British Geographers)*, 19 (1953), 1–11.

16 C. P. Lewis, 'The Great Awakening of English Local History 1918–1939', in Christopher Dyer, Andrew Hopper, Evelyn Lord and Nigel Tringham (eds), *New Directions in Local History since Hoskins* (Hatfield, 2011), pp. 29–53, at pp. 47–8; David Matless, 'Doing the English Village 1945–90: An Essay in Imaginative Geography', in Paul J. Cloke *et al.* (eds), *Writing the Rural: Five Cultural Geographies* (London, 1994), pp. 7–88.

17 Chris Dalglish, 'For the Community: Scottish Historical Archaeology and the Politics of Land Reform', *International Journal of Historical Archaeology*, 14:3

apparently greater democratisation of serious historical publishing in Scotland, beyond the rather small circle of academic authors.

To landscape history we can add studies informed by the law and using legal sources, which have been inspired, consciously or otherwise, by Maitland's premise that 'Law was the point where life and logic met'. Maitland sought to unravel medieval society by understanding how people gained access to land, studying 'the interdependences of law and economic fact'.[18] Examples of this approach in Scotland include Hector MacQueen, a lawyer by training, and Bob Dodgshon.[19] The latter used Maitland's idea of a shift 'from the vague to the definite' when it came to understanding the development of landholding.[20] Open fields were 'not incompatible with a very perfect individualism, a very complete denial that the village community had any proprietary rights whatever'.[21] Looking at Scottish 'runrig', Dodgshon argued that communalism's significance for landownership had been overstated; Maitland had described community as a 'slippery' and 'nebulous' legal concept, a product of what the historiographer Donald R. Kelley terms 'the enthusiasms of Celticists'.[22]

One reason why Dodgshon manages to transcend the apparently arcane and parochial approaches that still form a part of Scottish agrarian history is his recognition that detail makes little sense in isolation. Some hypothesis about patterns is needed, about the structure of ideas and the relationships within society. Dodgshon uses a number of disciplines to do this, including anthropology, but an obvious alternative framework for agrarian structures and change is Marx's. Many years ago, Eric Hobsbawm took the example of Scotland to show that there were viable alternative paths to modernisation, with different institutions, resources and environments leading to different patterns of sustained development.[23] This aside, the influence of Marxism on early modern Scottish

---

(2010), 374–97; T. C. Smout, *Nature Contested: Environmental History in Scotland and Northern England since 1600* (Edinburgh, 2000).

18 F. W. Maitland, 'Introduction', in F. W. Maitland (ed.), *Year Books of Edward II*, vol. 1 (London, 1903), p. xxxiii.

19 Hector L. MacQueen, *Common Law and Feudal Society in Medieval Scotland* (Edinburgh, 1993).

20 *The Collected Papers of Frederic William Maitland*, ed. H. A. L. Fisher, 3 vols (Cambridge, 1911), vol. 2, p. 363.

21 Maitland, *Collected Papers*, vol. 1, p. 361, quoted in R. A. Dodgshon, 'Runrig and the Communal Origins of Property in Land', *Juridical Review*, 50 (1975), 189–208, at p. 191.

22 F. W. Maitland, *Township and Borough* (Cambridge, 1898), p. 84; Donald R. Kelley, *Fortunes of History: Historical Inquiry from Herder to Huizinga* (New Haven, 2003), p. 239.

23 Eric J. Hobsbawm, 'Capitalisme et agriculture: les réformateurs écossais au XVIIIe siècle', *Annales ESC*, 33:3 (1978), 580–601.

historiography has remained muted, as has that of other mainstream movements of the twentieth century, such as the *Annales*. This makes Scotland unusual because most European countries got one or the other, if rarely both.[24] Perhaps the most obvious influence of Marxism is indirect, in the search for traces of popular protest and the making of a working class as an engine of social conflict and change, which so concerned English historians like Edward Thompson:[25] what Chris Whatley termed rather less heroically 'the stragglers on Scotland's march' of progress.[26]

In the case of the *Annales* it is the interdisciplinary element that has stuck (*les sciences de l'homme*), of which *la géographie humaine* or historical geography is prominent. *Annales* history was better suited to 'immobile' pre-1789 French and other continental communities, whereas British historians sought out paradigm-shifting changes in ideas, economics and social relationships. Perhaps the best example of *histoire serielle*, because of the long-run aggregate series of economic and demographic data the authors used, is the study of wages and prices.[27] And some of the more recent developments such as climatic and environmental history are *Annaliste* in spirit. Indeed, ecological and environmental approaches together have added a great deal to understanding the rural world of Scotland.[28]

From R. H. Tawney in the 1910s and 1920s until the 1980s, much of the history of early modern English society and economy was an analysis of tenures in the style of Maitland.[29] Landholding was simpler in Scotland

---

24 Dalglish, 'An Age of Transition?', uses the Marxist idea of contradiction as a theoretical framework. But, as Neil Davidson notes, 'Marx and Engels wrote little about North Britain': Neil Davidson, 'Marx and Engels on the Scottish Highlands', *Science & Society*, 65:3 (2001), 286–326, at p. 286. There are, of course, left-leaning accounts of social change, of which the most notable is James Hunter, *The Making of the Crofting Community* (Edinburgh, 1976). On Marx and early modern history in general see David Rollison, 'Marxism', in Garthine Walker (ed.), *Writing Early Modern History* (London, 2005), pp. 2–24.

25 E. P. Thompson, *The Making of the English Working Class* (1963; rev. edn Harmondsworth, 1980).

26 Christopher A. Whatley, 'Royal Day, People's Day: The Monarch's Birthday in Scotland c.1660–1800', in Roger Mason and Norman Macdougall (eds), *People and Power in Scotland: Essays in Honour of T. C. Smout* (Edinburgh, 1992), pp. 170–84, at p. 184. T. C. Smout's path-breaking *A History of the Scottish People 1560–1830* (London, 1969) is itself an example of history from below.

27 A. J. S. Gibson and T. C. Smout, *Prices, Food and Wages in Scotland 1550–1780* (Cambridge, 1995).

28 Andrew Fleming, 'Human Ecology and the Early History of St Kilda, Scotland', *Journal of Historical Geography*, 25:2 (1999), 183–200; Fiona Watson, 'Environmental History', *SHR*, 82:2 (2003), 285–94; Richard D. Oram, 'Waste Management and Peri-Urban Agriculture in the Early Modern Scottish Burgh', *AgHR*, 59:1 (2011), 1–17.

29 R. H. Tawney, *The Agrarian Problem in the Sixteenth Century* (London, 1912);

because land was either owned or rented; Scotland had no copyhold and only a small number of landowners, even after the feuing of church and crown lands in the sixteenth century. Thus most early modern studies are of whether farmers had written leases and, if so, their length; whether tenancies were single or joint has also attracted attention, the former seen as more 'modern' than the latter. In economic terms, there is little to choose between a system of rent-paying tenants and peasant proprietorship, since in either case the farmer retains the marginal return on extra inputs. Where tenant security is limited, however, forms and levels of surplus extraction can be altered more easily to suit the landowner. The factors behind change in both farming methods and farm organisation will also be different, driven initially more by the owners rather than occupiers of land.

The power of landowners helps to explain why Scotland's early modern revolutions were religious in origin and constitutional rather than sociopolitical in nature. Civil society in Scotland was more independent of the state than it was on the continent. Thus concentration on landowners as agents of change, a criticism often directed at Scottish agrarian history, is justified to an extent – and its most abundant and tractable sources are estate records. In the classic age of the agricultural revolution after 1760, however, clergy and more successful tenant farmers were important innovators in their own right.[30] And there are other sources such as testaments, which allow historians to emulate their English counterparts in studying not only agriculture, but also family relationships and material culture.[31]

Margaret Sanderson has used testaments to particularly good effect. She is unusual among social historians in providing not only richly detailed mosaic accounts of individual lives, giving ordinary people faces and

---

Margaret Spufford, *Contrasting Communities: English Villagers in the Sixteenth and Seventeenth Centuries* (Cambridge, 1974); Jane Whittle (ed.), *Landlords and Tenants in Britain 1440–1660: Tawney's 'Agrarian Problem' Revisited* (Woodbridge, 2013).

30 T. C. Smout, 'A New Look at the Scottish Improvers', *SHR*, 91:1 (2012), 125–49. The link with Enlightenment ideas of improvability has since been explored in studies which nuance the intentions of landowners: Roger L. Emerson, *An Enlightened Duke: The Life of Archibald Campbell (1682–1761), Earl of Ilay, 3rd Duke of Argyll* (Kilkerran, 2013); Fredrik A. Jonsson, *Enlightenment's Frontier: The Scottish Highlands and the Origins of Environmentalism* (London, 2013); Brian Bonnyman, *The Third Duke of Buccleuch and Adam Smith: Estate Management and Improvement in Enlightenment Scotland* (Edinburgh, 2014).

31 Mark Overton, *Agricultural Revolution in England: The Transformation of the Agrarian Economy 1500–1850* (Cambridge, 1996); Bill Inglis, 'Scottish Testamentary Inventories: A Neglected Source for the Study of Scottish Agriculture – Illustrated by the Case of Dunblane', *Scottish Archives*, 10 (2004), 55–68.

voices, but also aggregate studies which open up the broader experience of different occupations and orders. Her article on late sixteenth- and early seventeenth-century cottars is especially valuable, showing their considerable variety of circumstances, among much else. While contextualising, she makes important points about general issues.[32] Fundamental questions that are well-mapped for England nevertheless remain only partially answered for Scotland, including the fate of different groups in rural society against a backdrop of price inflation and population rise followed by stagnation, 1550–1750.[33] How much surplus was extracted from peasants, in what forms, and how the level changed over time remain unclear – as does the impact of local and national taxation on the standard of living.[34] Hopefully work on teinds prices will broaden our understanding. Questions about the emergence of capitalism in agriculture and its transformation to a system of landed properties, entrepreneurial farming and salaried farm workers remain unresolved. There have been few studies of farm servants, despite the much greater importance of service into the twentieth century in Scotland than in southern England and parts of Scandinavia. Sources that cover internal migration would provide a helpful starting point for research, as they have in early modern England.[35]

The other challenge is to analyse how social and economic relations actually worked day-to-day. A century ago, Isabel Grant offered a model exploration of the economic, social and governmental ties between tenants and sub-tenants – a nexus often hidden from historians – using the account book of William Mackintosh of Balnespick, tacksman of

32 Margaret H. B. Sanderson, *Mary Stewart's People: Life in Mary Stewart's Scotland* (Edinburgh, 1987); Margaret H. B. Sanderson, *A Kindly Place? Living in Sixteenth-Century Scotland* (East Linton, 2002); Margaret H. B. Sanderson, 'Lives of the Scottish Cottars 1585–1620: The Evidence of Their Testaments', *Review of Scottish Culture*, 20 (2008), 15–26.

33 Ian D. Whyte, 'Scottish Population and Social Structure in the Seventeenth and Eighteenth Centuries: New Sources and Perspectives', *Archives*, 20:1 (1993), 30–41; Ian Whyte, 'Poverty or Prosperity? Rural Society in Lowland Scotland in the Late Sixteenth and Early Seventeenth Centuries', *Scottish Economic and Social History*, 18:1 (1998), 19–32; Douglas Watt, '"The Laberinth of Thir Difficulties": The Influence of Debt on the Highland Elite, c.1550–1700', *SHR*, 85:1 (2006), 28–51; S. Nenadic, *Lairds and Luxury: The Highland Gentry in Eighteenth-Century Scotland* (Edinburgh, 2007); Amy Blakeway, 'The Sixteenth-Century Price Rise: New Evidence from Scotland 1500–85', *EcHR*, 68:1 (2015), 167–90. Where conducted, studies of rural demography remain basic, partly thanks to the deficiencies of Scottish parish registers.

34 Muir Johnstone, 'Farm Rents and Improvement: East Lothian and Lanarkshire 1670–1830', *AgHR*, 57:1 (2009), 37–57.

35 Ann Kussmaul, *Servants in Husbandry in Early Modern England* (Cambridge, 1981); Ian D. Whyte, *Migration and Society in Britain 1550–1830* (Basingstoke, 2000).

Dunachton on Speyside. For example, 60 per cent of Mackintosh's transactions in grain were with his sub-tenants (with their families, 220 souls
in all), receipts from whom paid the rent for his whole farm and left him
with land that he effectively got for free; he also received labour services.
Yet as tacksman he provided a valuable service for his people by acting as
an employer and agricultural organiser, a borrower and lender of money
(including *ad hominem* gifts to the poor), and finally as an executor,
trustee and arbitrator in a rural world where people used embedded
forums more than formal law courts to resolve disputes. Within the
wider community he helped lend authority to the birlaymen and the kirk
session while acting as collector of taxes and payer of land-tax, minister's
and schoolmaster's stipend, and assessed poor relief. Mackintosh was
part of a complex web of social, economic and governmental relationships, which lay at the heart of day-to-day rural life.[36]

Everyday life at Dunachton is at least partly the story of grass-roots
or micro-politics. Where the English described themselves in legal and
institutional language, Scots spoke of their society in terms of covenants
and 'kindness' (a natural relationship), which were not part of the law.
The personal bonds upon which Scottish social relationships were based
have been best explained by the political historian Jenny Wormald and
further explicated by historians of religion and politics, such as Margo
Todd.[37] Both are excellent examples of the productive rapprochement
between political and social history, which has taken place across British
historiography since the 1980s.

Social and political historians alike often focus on conflict, but cooperation is also worth exploring, as Wormald showed. We can look at the
everyday bonds of society using sources as diverse as the sponsors
chosen for a child's baptism (something that the much-maligned Scottish
parish registers often specify) and the records of debt and credit.[38] It is this
texture of life – analysing the place of processes rather than outcomes –
which promises the most exciting way forward for agrarian historians,
both of an economic and social bent. That would include non-monetary
exchanges (gifts as well as barter), the social dimensions of marketing
agricultural produce, and the ways that social obligations and reciproc-
ities were reinforced or threatened by the changing nature of tenancies,
forms and levels of rent, agricultural productivity, and marketing.[39]

---

36 I. F. Grant, *Every-Day Life on an Old Highland Farm 1769–1782* (London, 1924).
37 Jenny Wormald, *Lords and Men in Scotland: Bonds of Manrent 1442–1603*
     (Edinburgh, 1985); Margo Todd, *The Culture of Protestantism in Early Modern
     Scotland* (New Haven, 2002).
38 Cathryn Spence, *Women, Credit and Debt in Early Modern Scotland* (Manchester,
     2016).
39 Mary Young, 'Scottish Crop Yields in the Second Half of the Seventeenth

The emergence of landscape and agricultural history discussed earlier created a distinctively local and regional set of studies in England. One outcome was the multi-volume *Agrarian History of England and Wales*, first envisaged during the 1950s, but not completed until 2000.[40] It lacks cohesiveness and fails to provide a long-term picture of agrarian changes, so it may be a good thing that there is no Scottish equivalent. There were superficial pioneering analyses by Franklin, Handley and Symon in the 1950s, and the differently focused multi-volume 'Scottish Life and Society: A Compendium of Scottish Ethnology', to which Alexander Fenton was so important and which has added hugely to our understandings of folk and their ways of doing and speaking.[41] Scottish society is not so amenable to an *AHEW* treatment because its regions in early modern times were distinctive less for farming practices (most agriculture was mixed) than for possessing a strong sense of regional identity, shared dialect and customs, styles of building and features of material culture. Scottish regions and localities were distinctive, as Fenton recognised, because of the *people* within them.[42]

People and power cannot be detached from each other. Historians used to conceive of the early modern northern Highlands as undynamic and subsistence-oriented, but the region was integrated into a mercantile framework with the North Sea and Baltic. At times, there was surplus grain to trade. But how was this possible when the famines of the 1690s were most devastating in the north and north-east and against a backdrop of 'frequent low-order crises that afflicted communities on a regular, even routine, basis, leaving them without sufficient meal'?[43] Inequality and want are choices made with the rules we create to structure economic and social relationships. Economic patterns have a political basis. Studies of

Century: Evidence from the Mains of Castle Lyon in the Carse of Gowrie', *AgHR*, 55:1 (2007), 51–74.

40 Joan Thirsk *et al.* (eds), *The Agrarian History of England and Wales*, 8 vols (Cambridge, 1967–2000).

41 T. B. Franklin, *A History of Scottish Farming* (London, 1952); J. E. Handley, *Scottish Farming in the Eighteenth Century* (London, 1953); J. A. Symon, *Scottish Farming, Past and Present* (Edinburgh, 1959). The series 'Scottish Life and Society: A Compendium of Scottish Ethnology' was published in fourteen volumes between 2000 and 2013, general editor Margaret A. Mackay. The most important volume for agriculture is Alexander Fenton and Kenneth Veitch (eds), *Farming and the Land* (Scottish Life and Society: A Compendium of Scottish Ethnology, vol. 2; Edinburgh, 2011), and there is relevant material in several other volumes.

42 Alexander Fenton, *Scottish Country Life* (Edinburgh, 1976); Alexander Fenton, *Country Life in Scotland: Our Rural Past* (Edinburgh, 1987).

43 Robert A. Dodgshon, 'Coping with Risk: Subsistence Crises in the Scottish Highlands and Islands 1600–1800', *Rural History*, 15:1 (2004), 1–25, at p. 1; Karen J. Cullen, *Famine in Scotland: The 'Ill Years' of the 1690s* (Edinburgh, 2010).

poverty tend to be about provision and its politics rather than the poor themselves (perhaps because Scottish economic history itself was seen as a function of public policy until the 1960s and 1970s) though this is changing. Famine, for example, is not just a demographic and economic event, but also a social one, and giving money to help those in need can be an exercise in power as well as humanity.[44] The effects of the poor law not only on the poor, but also on social relations, the labour market, migration and decision-making in agriculture more generally are worth further investigation.

So where are we now? For more than half a century, Christopher Smout has done much to open up agriculture, economy and society in early modern Scotland. He came out of an economic and social history background before taking an environmental turn – just as economic history imploded across Britain. His words about Scottish history as a whole could be applied to agrarian history in particular: 'we are doing well, we could do better and there is much to be done'.[45] Among other things, he points out that Scottish urban history has been persistently more attractive to scholars than rural. Yet agrarian change had important implications for urban growth, because towns grew on the back of immigration. Especially in the central Lowlands, towns pulled people from the land and so prompted new farming methods by encouraging farmers to make do with fewer workers. Rural industrial development was also important. English regions industrialised and de-industrialised over the early modern period, but in Scotland the pattern was simpler, again with the main changes during the eighteenth century.[46] In some parts of Scotland such as the north-east and west-central Lowlands there was extensive proto-industry, which enhanced household income by creating employment for women and children.[47] Rural artisans became more specialist, often working in the planned villages that were a distinctive feature of eighteenth-century Scotland and another example of its extensive social and economic engineering by landowners.[48]

44 Rosalind Mitchison, *The Old Poor Law in Scotland: The Experience of Poverty 1574–1845* (Edinburgh, 2000).

45 T. C. Smout, 'Scottish History in the Universities since the 1950s', *History Scotland*, 7:5 (May 2007), 45–50, at p. 50; Smout, *Nature Contested*; T. C. Smout, Alan R. MacDonald and Fiona Watson, *A History of the Native Woodlands of Scotland 1500–1920* (Edinburgh, 2005); T. C. Smout, *Exploring Environmental History: Selected Essays* (Edinburgh, 2009).

46 Ann Kussmaul, *A General View of the Rural Economy of England 1538–1840* (Cambridge, 1989).

47 A. J. S. Gibson, '"Proletarianization"? The Transition to Full-Time Labour on a Scottish Estate 1723–1787', *Continuity and Change*, 5:3 (1990), 357–89; Gilbert Schrank, 'Crossroad of the North: Proto-Industrialization in the Orkney Islands 1730–1840', *Journal of European Economic History*, 21:2 (1992), 365–88.

48 Craig Young, 'Rural Independent Artisan Production in the East-Central

In short, Scottish agrarian history has flourished and will continue to do so, where the focus is on people rather than places, where scholars are alert to cross-cultural encounters, where they identify their subject as part of European or global history, where they adopt interdisciplinary perspectives, and where they reject the compartmentalisation of political from social and economic history.

Lowlands of Scotland *c.*1600–*c.*1850', *Scottish Economic and Social History*, 16:1 (1996), 17–37.

INDEX

Boydell Studies in Rural History

The Real Agricultural Revolution:
The Transformation of English Farming, 1939–1985
Paul Brassley, David Harvey, Matt Lobley and Michael Winter

Agricultural Knowledge Networks in Rural Europe, 1700–2000
Edited by Yves Segers and Leen Van Molle

Landless Households in Rural Europe, 1600–1900
Edited by Christine Fertig, Richard Paping and Henry French

Printed and bound by CPI Group (UK) Ltd, Croydon, CR0 4YY

23/04/2025

14661041-0004